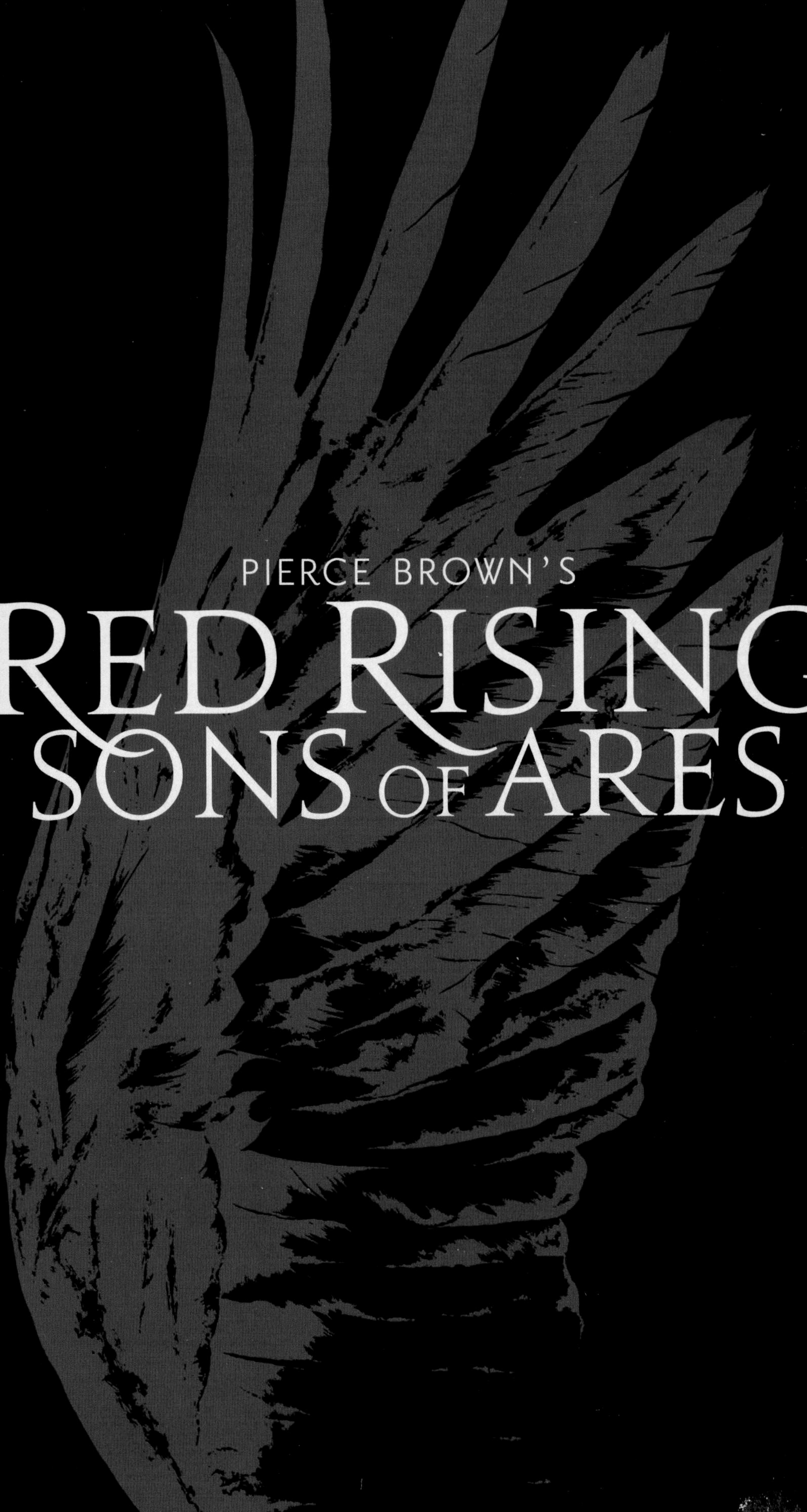

PIERCE BROWN'S

RED RISING™
SONS OF ARES

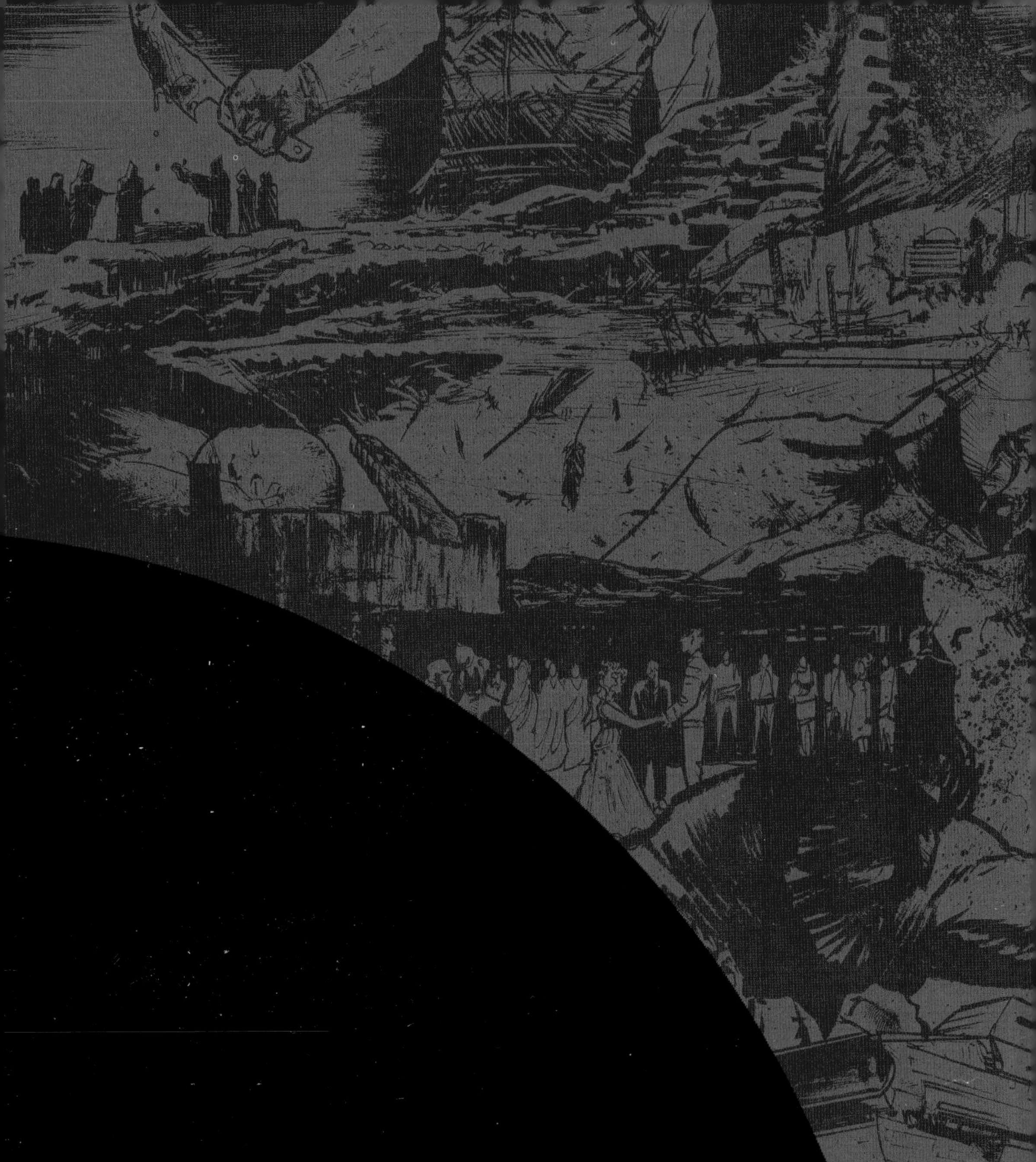

DYNAMITE®

Nick Barrucci, CEO / Publisher
Juan Collado, President / COO

Joe Rybandt, Executive Editor
Matt Idelson, Senior Editor
Anthony Marques, Associate Editor
Kevin Ketner, Assistant Editor

Jason Ullmeyer, Art Director
Geoff Harkins, Senior Graphic Designer
Cathleen Heard, Graphic Designer
Alexis Persson, Production Artist
Chris Caniano, Digital Associate
Rachel Kilbury, Digital Multimedia Associate

Brandon Dante Primavera, V.P. of IT and Operations
Rich Young, Director of Business Development

Alan Payne, V.P. of Sales and Marketing
Janie Mackenzie, Marketing Coordinator
[redacted]

SIGNED EDITION ISBN13: 978-1-5241-0520-4 First Printing 10 9 8 7 6 5 4 3 2 1
STANDARD EDITION ISBN13: 978-1-5241-0492-4

Online at **www.DYNAMITE.com** | On Facebook **/Dynamitecomics**
On Instagram **/Dynamitecomics** | On Tumblr **dynamitecomics.tumblr.com**
On Twitter **@dynamitecomics** | On YouTube **/Dynamitecomics**

PIERCE BROWN'S RED RISING™: SONS OF ARES, VOLUME 1. First printing. Collection contains material orginally published in magazine form as Pierce Brow's Red Rising™: Son of Ares issues 1-6. Published by Dynamite Entertainment, 113 Gaither Dr., STE 205, Mt. Laurel, NJ 08054 and 121 W. 27th St., STE801, New York, NY 10001.

For information regarding press, media rights, foreign rights, licensing, promotions, and adver- [redacted]

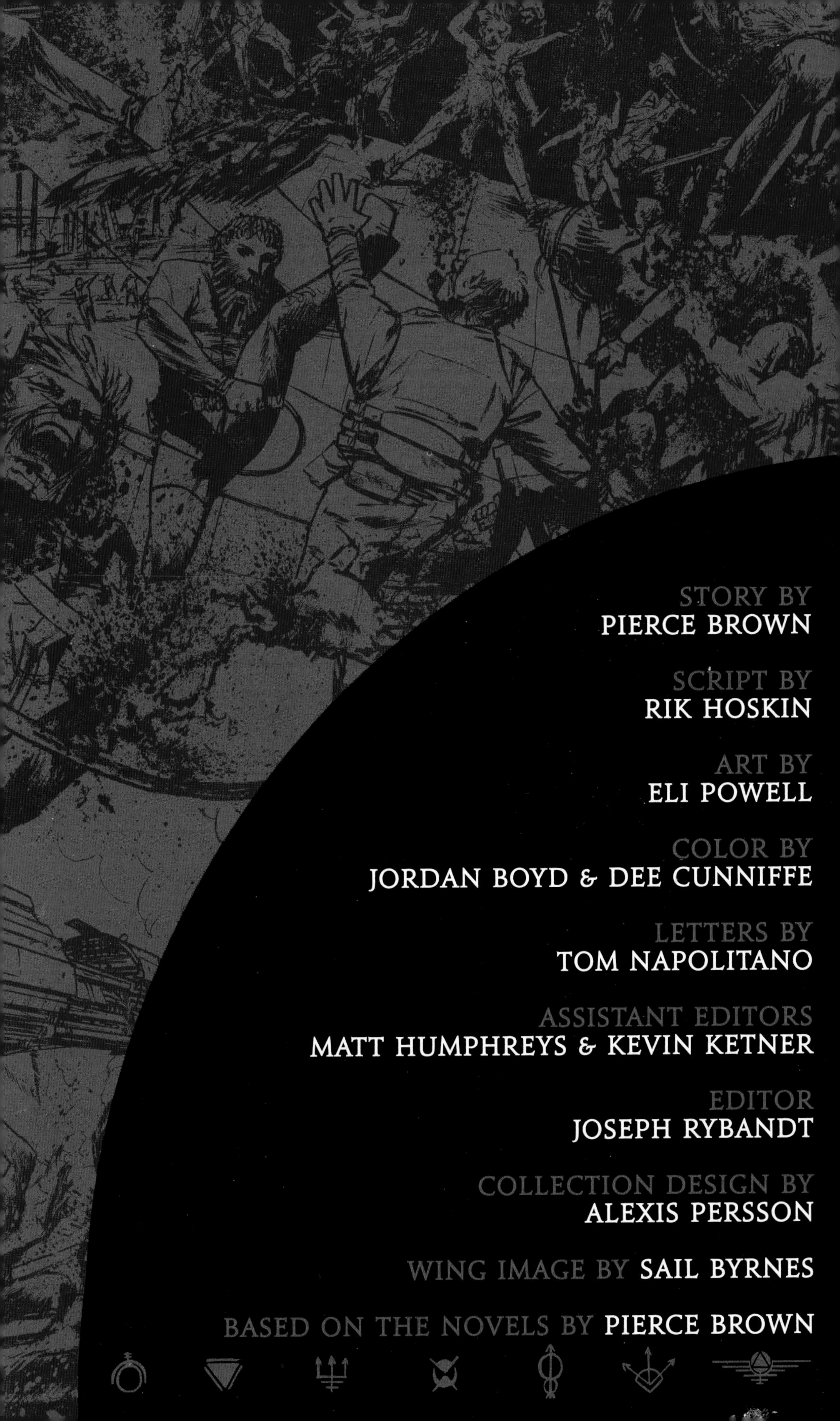

STORY BY
PIERCE BROWN

SCRIPT BY
RIK HOSKIN

ART BY
ELI POWELL

COLOR BY
JORDAN BOYD & DEE CUNNIFFE

LETTERS BY
TOM NAPOLITANO

ASSISTANT EDITORS
MATT HUMPHREYS & KEVIN KETNER

EDITOR
JOSEPH RYBANDT

COLLECTION DESIGN BY
ALEXIS PERSSON

WING IMAGE BY SAIL BYRNES

BASED ON THE NOVELS BY PIERCE BROWN

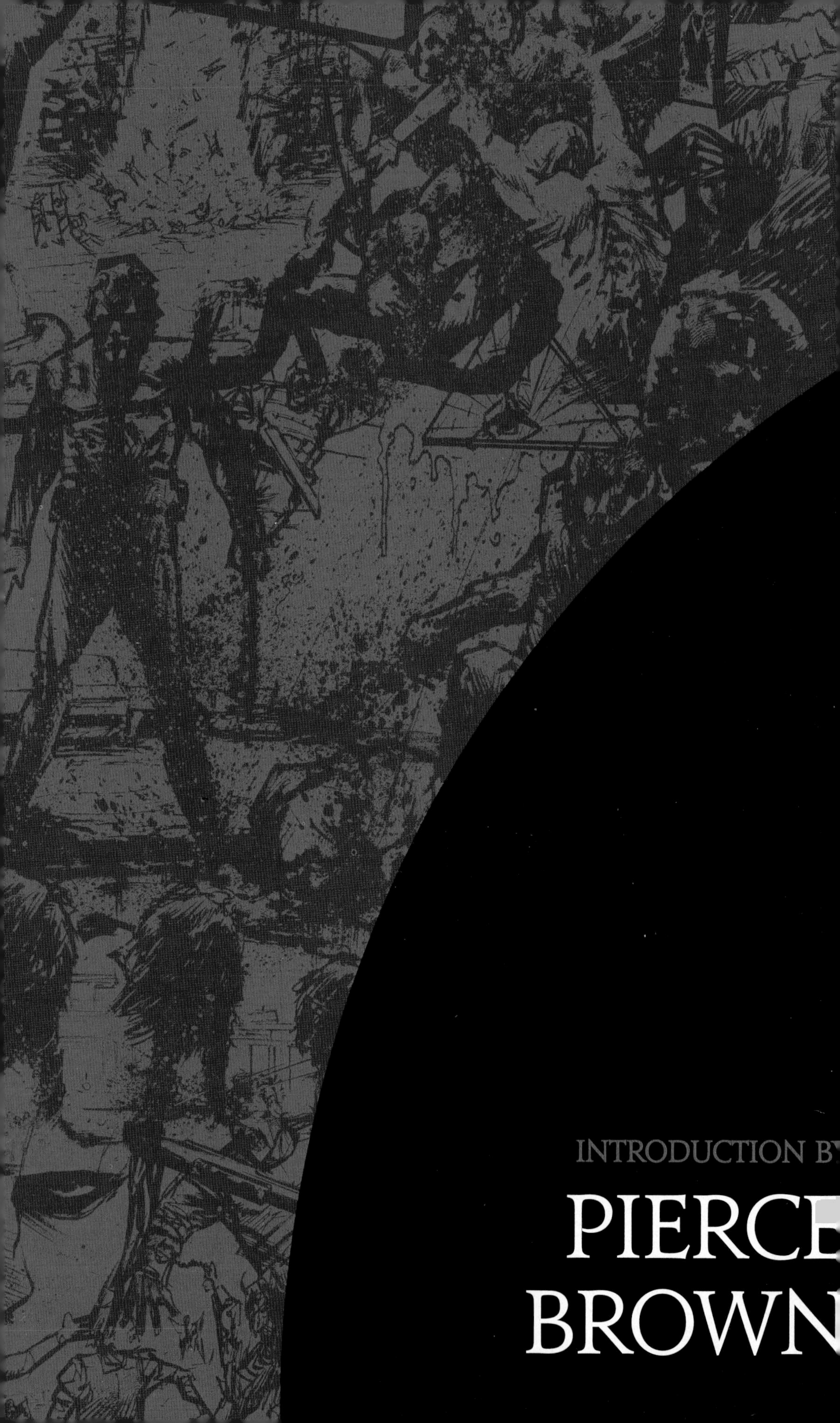

INTRODUCTION BY

PIERCE
BROWN

REVOLUTION. UPHEAVAL.
THAT IS THE STORY OF THE RED RISING.

Each generation has their version. One witnessed the rebirth of that Athenian experiment, democracy, in a far-flung colony of the British Empire. Another watched in horror as a no-name Austrian rose from a beer-hall lectern to the heights of German power. Another saw international communism creep across the globe before collapsing in on itself. And our own has seen the Arab Spring upturn tyrants, Wall Street upturn Main Street, and a shifting of financial power from West to East.

In writing the Red Rising novels, I wanted to hold a grim mirror up to our reality and show revolution on a cosmic scale through the eyes of a young man, Darrow of Lykos.

A slave to a corrupt interplanetary regime, Darrow rises from the dirt of his birth to be the sword of his people. But Darrow's story, which is many books and many coffee pots now in the telling, did not begin with him. It began before he was ever born.

In telling Darrow's story it became more and more apparent that I would be doing a disservice to the overall tale if I didn't trace it back to its roots. Combine that with an entirely vain wish to see razors, pulseFists, Golds, and torchShips in all their illustrated glory, and you see why I jumped at the chance to have the world of Red Rising continue in comics under the stewardship of Rik Hoskin's pen and Eli Powell's art.

If you were a political science major like I was, or if you're a student of history or simply paying attention (as all good stewards of democracy ought), you might have noticed that Hollywood got it wrong. Rebellions don't happen in a flash. Revolutions aren't overnight spectacles instigated because of some onerous tax or mishandled execution. No, rebellions are slow. Glacially slow, and often generations in the making. But nearly all can be traced to one seismic moment. One catalyst that ignites that slow burn of discontent into a raging madhouse wildfire that brings regimes to their knees.

The Sons of Ares is about that catalyst. How simmering discontent can spread, intensify, then erupt—not by accident, but through the careful shepherding of a single man and his lieutenants.

Fitchner au Barca is rustic castoff in the upper echelons of his caste-based society. Fitchner's life is not pleasant, but it is privileged compared to those of the masses beneath him. He's blind to their plight because of his own troubles. And only when he falls in love with a woman beneath his station does he begin to see the cracks and cruelty in the world around him. When that cruelty touches him, he faces a choice: suffer it, or become a terrorist and break an empire.

I can't wait for you to see what choice he makes.

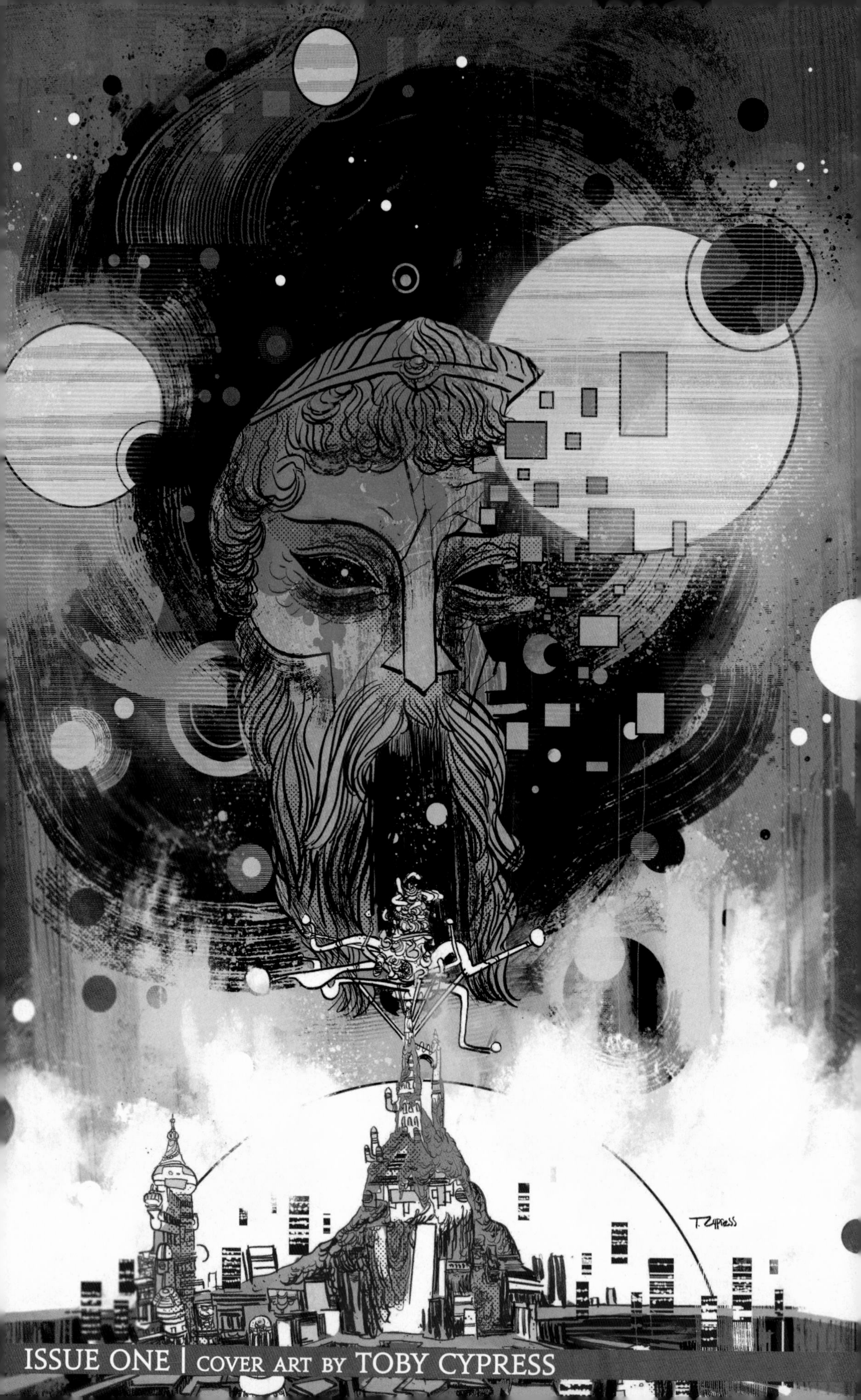
T. CYPRESS

ISSUE ONE | COVER ART BY TOBY CYPRESS

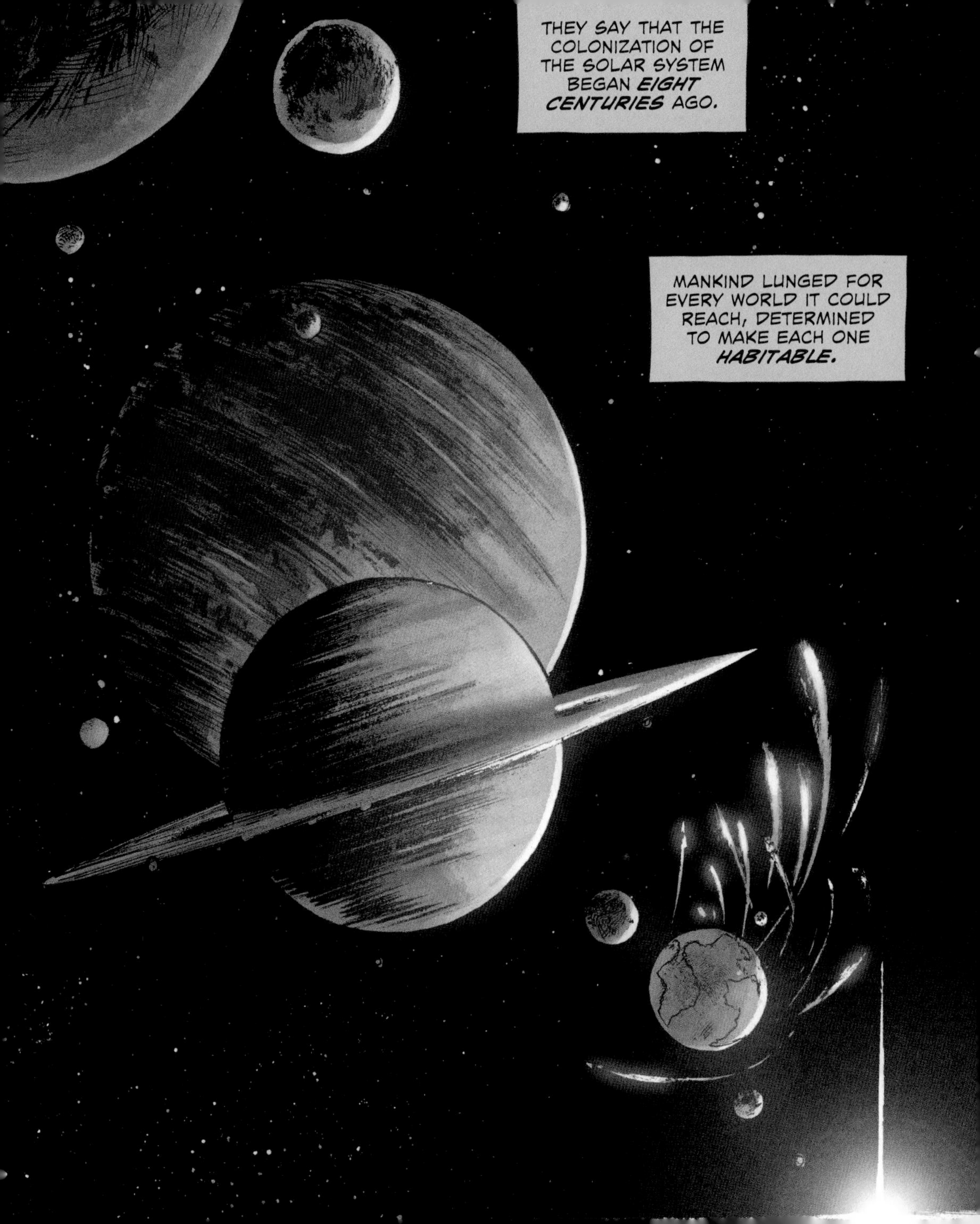
THEY SAY THAT THE COLONIZATION OF THE SOLAR SYSTEM BEGAN *EIGHT CENTURIES* AGO.
MANKIND LUNGED FOR EVERY WORLD IT COULD REACH, DETERMINED TO MAKE EACH ONE *HABITABLE.*

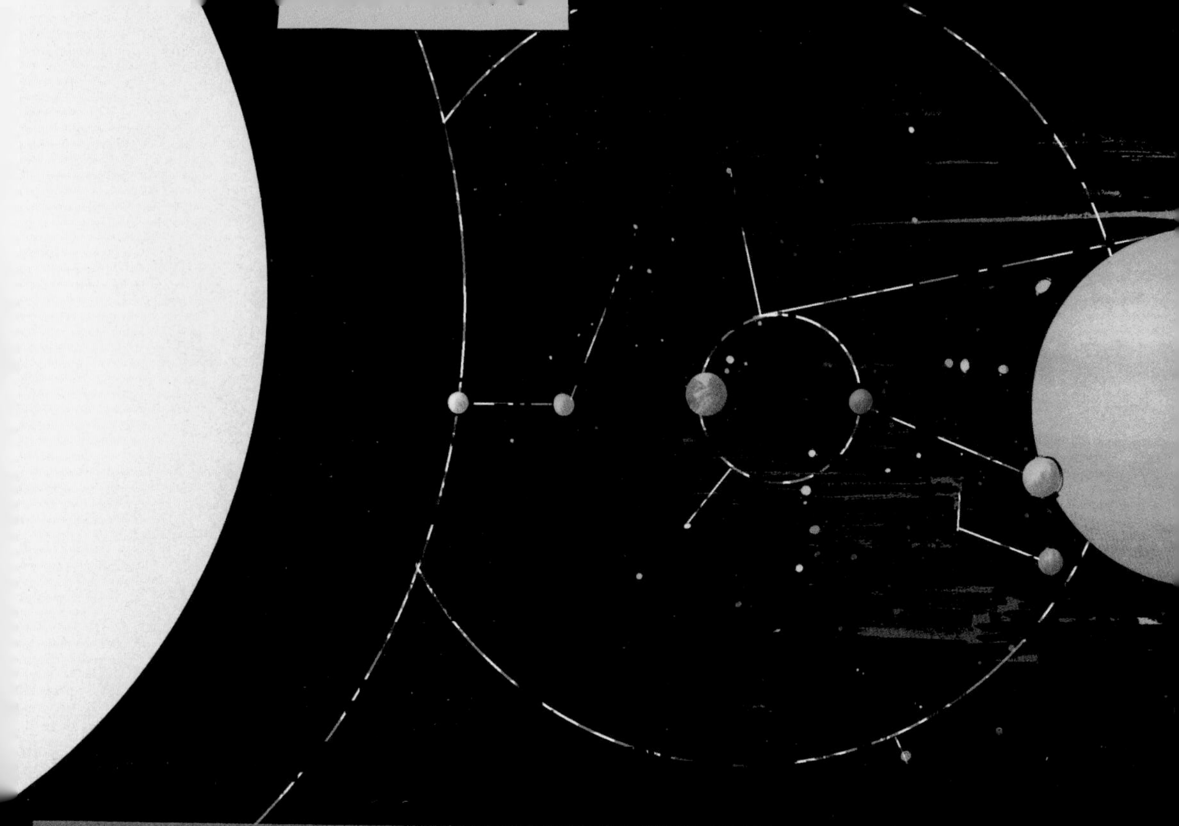

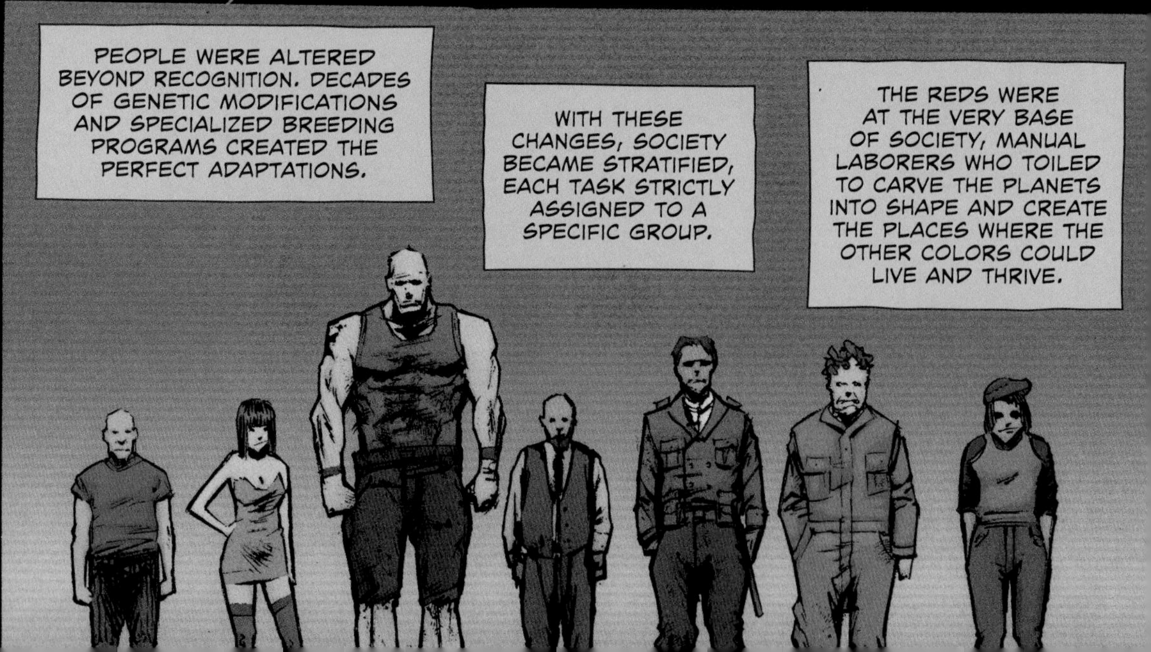
PEOPLE WERE ALTERED BEYOND RECOGNITION. DECADES OF GENETIC MODIFICATIONS AND SPECIALIZED BREEDING PROGRAMS CREATED THE PERFECT ADAPTATIONS.
WITH THESE CHANGES, SOCIETY BECAME STRATIFIED, EACH TASK STRICTLY ASSIGNED TO A SPECIFIC GROUP.
THE REDS WERE AT THE VERY BASE OF SOCIETY, MANUAL LABORERS WHO TOILED TO CARVE THE PLANETS INTO SHAPE AND CREATE THE PLACES WHERE THE OTHER COLORS COULD LIVE AND THRIVE.

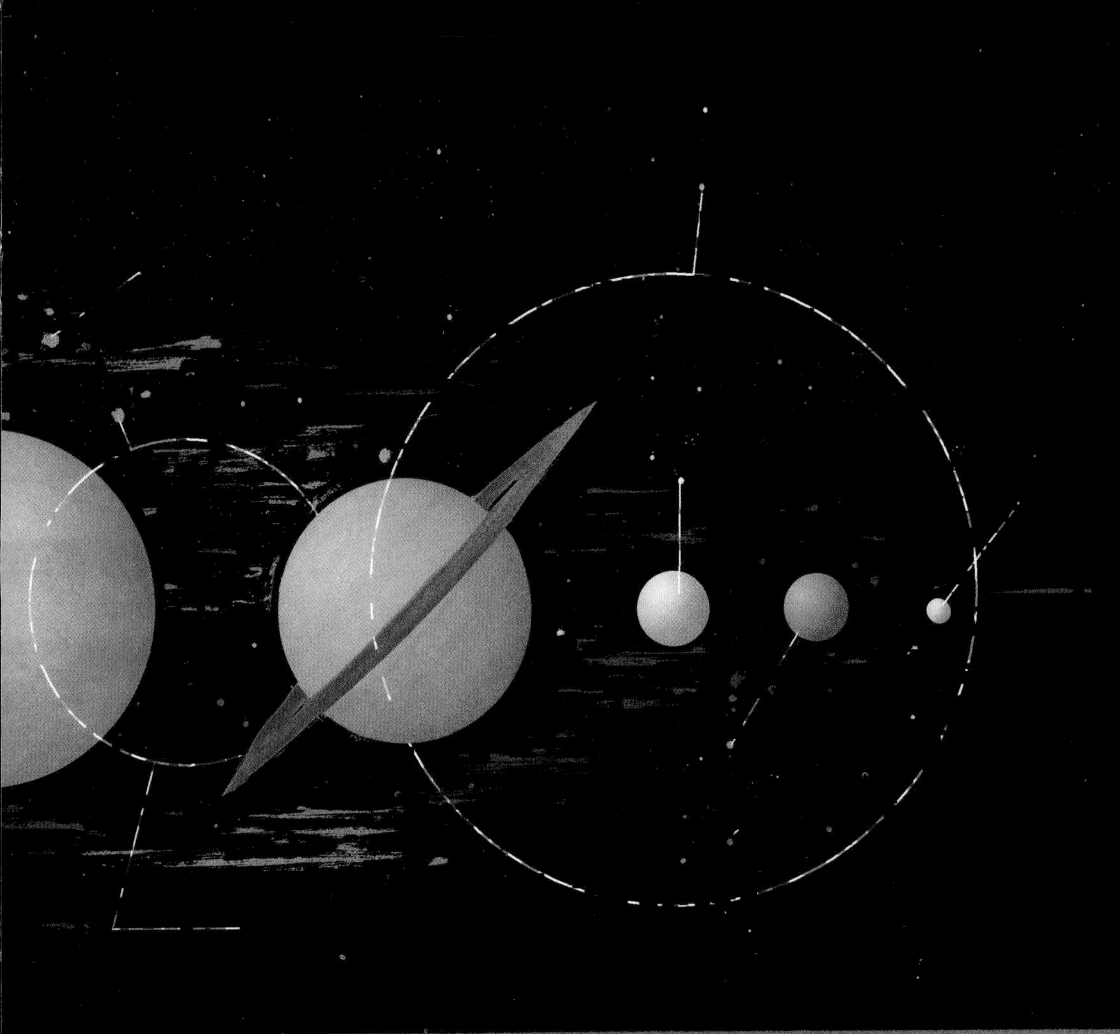

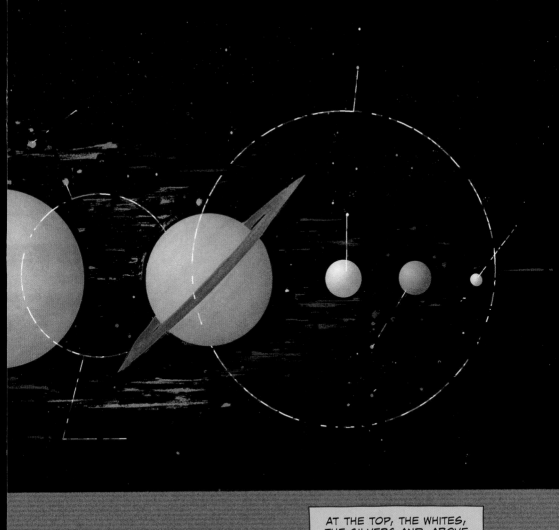

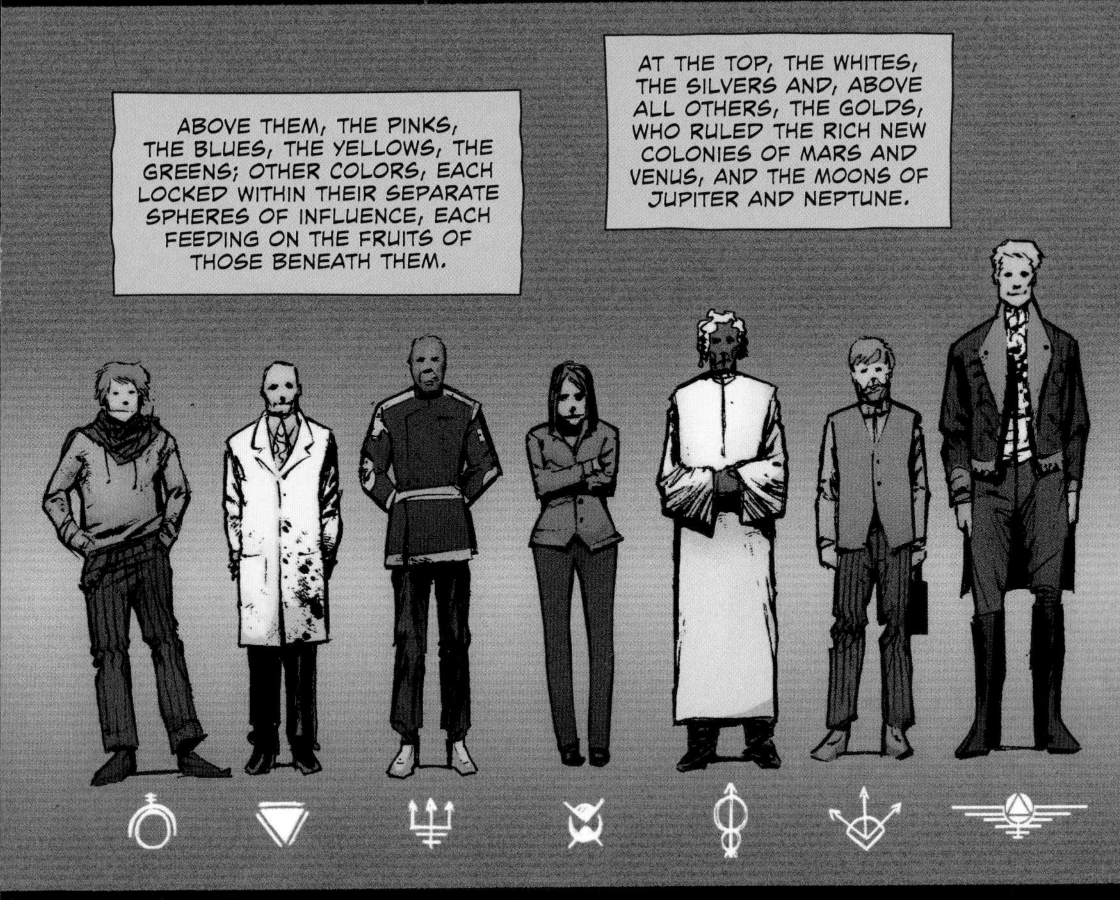
ABOVE THEM, THE PINKS, THE BLUES, THE YELLOWS, THE GREENS; OTHER COLORS, EACH LOCKED WITHIN THEIR SEPARATE SPHERES OF INFLUENCE, EACH FEEDING ON THE FRUITS OF THOSE BENEATH THEM.
AT THE TOP, THE WHITES, THE SILVERS AND, ABOVE ALL OTHERS, THE GOLDS, WHO RULED THE RICH NEW COLONIES OF MARS AND VENUS, AND THE MOONS OF JUPITER AND NEPTUNE.

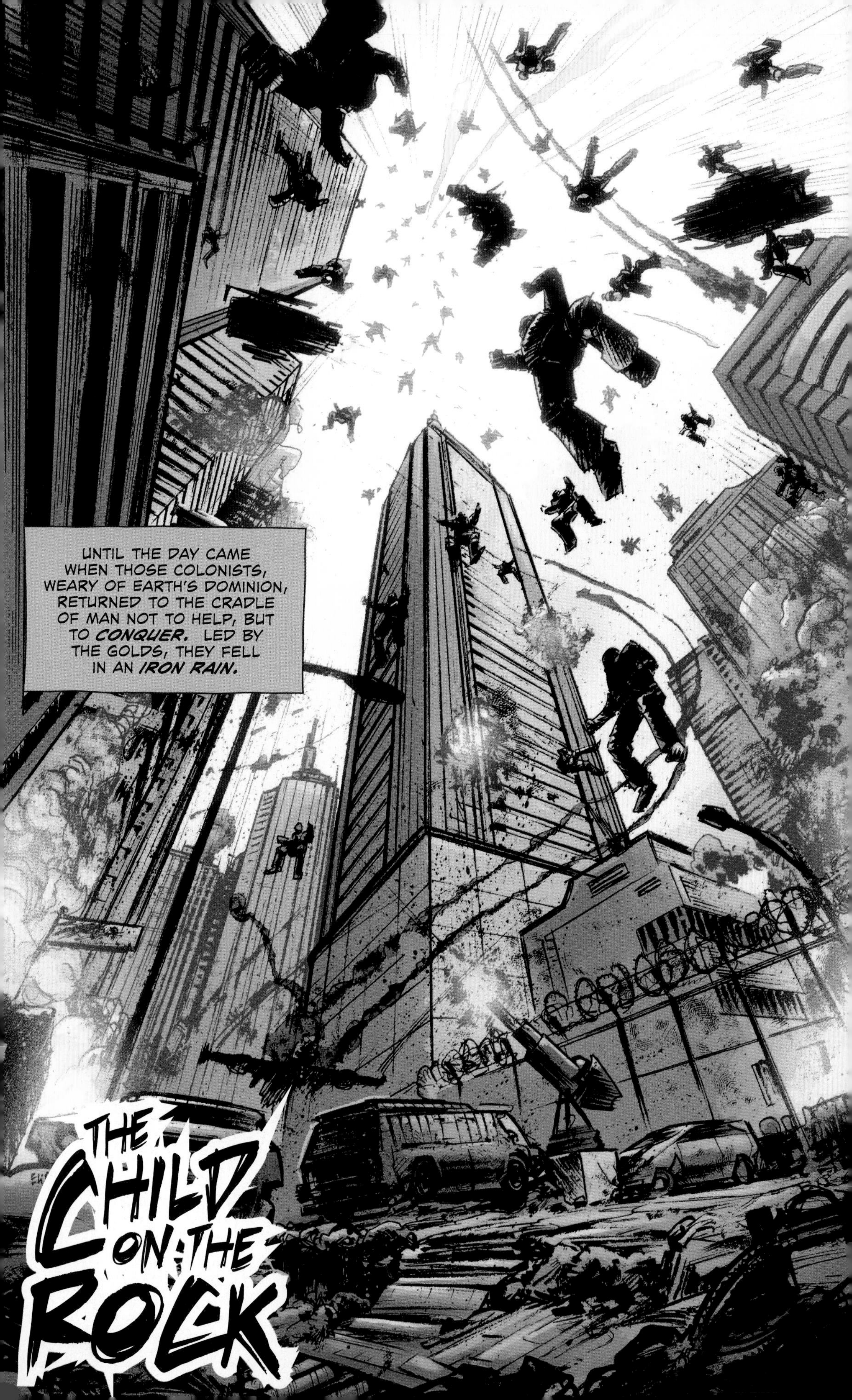
UNTIL THE DAY CAME WHEN THOSE COLONISTS, WEARY OF EARTH'S DOMINION, RETURNED TO THE CRADLE OF MAN NOT TO HELP, BUT TO *CONQUER.* LED BY THE GOLDS, THEY FELL IN AN *IRON RAIN.*
THE CHILD ON THE ROCK

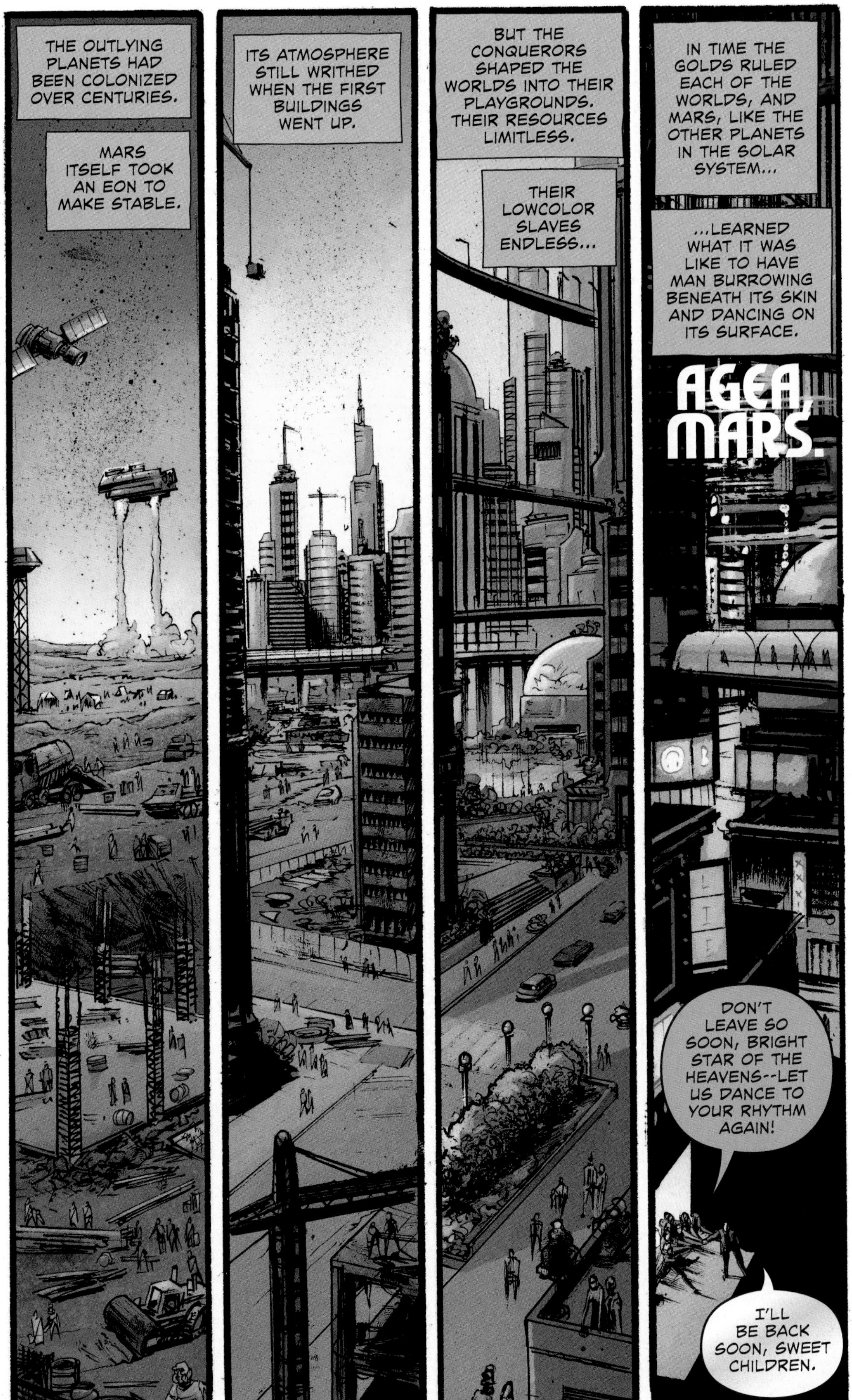
THE OUTLYING PLANETS HAD BEEN COLONIZED OVER CENTURIES.
MARS ITSELF TOOK AN EON TO MAKE STABLE.
ITS ATMOSPHERE STILL WRITHED WHEN THE FIRST BUILDINGS WENT UP.
BUT THE CONQUERORS SHAPED THE WORLDS INTO THEIR PLAYGROUNDS. THEIR RESOURCES LIMITLESS.
THEIR LOWCOLOR SLAVES ENDLESS...
IN TIME THE GOLDS RULED EACH OF THE WORLDS, AND MARS, LIKE THE OTHER PLANETS IN THE SOLAR SYSTEM...
...LEARNED WHAT IT WAS LIKE TO HAVE MAN BURROWING BENEATH ITS SKIN AND DANCING ON ITS SURFACE.
AGEA, MARS.
DON'T LEAVE SO SOON, BRIGHT STAR OF THE HEAVENS--LET US DANCE TO YOUR RHYTHM AGAIN!
I'LL BE BACK SOON, SWEET CHILDREN.

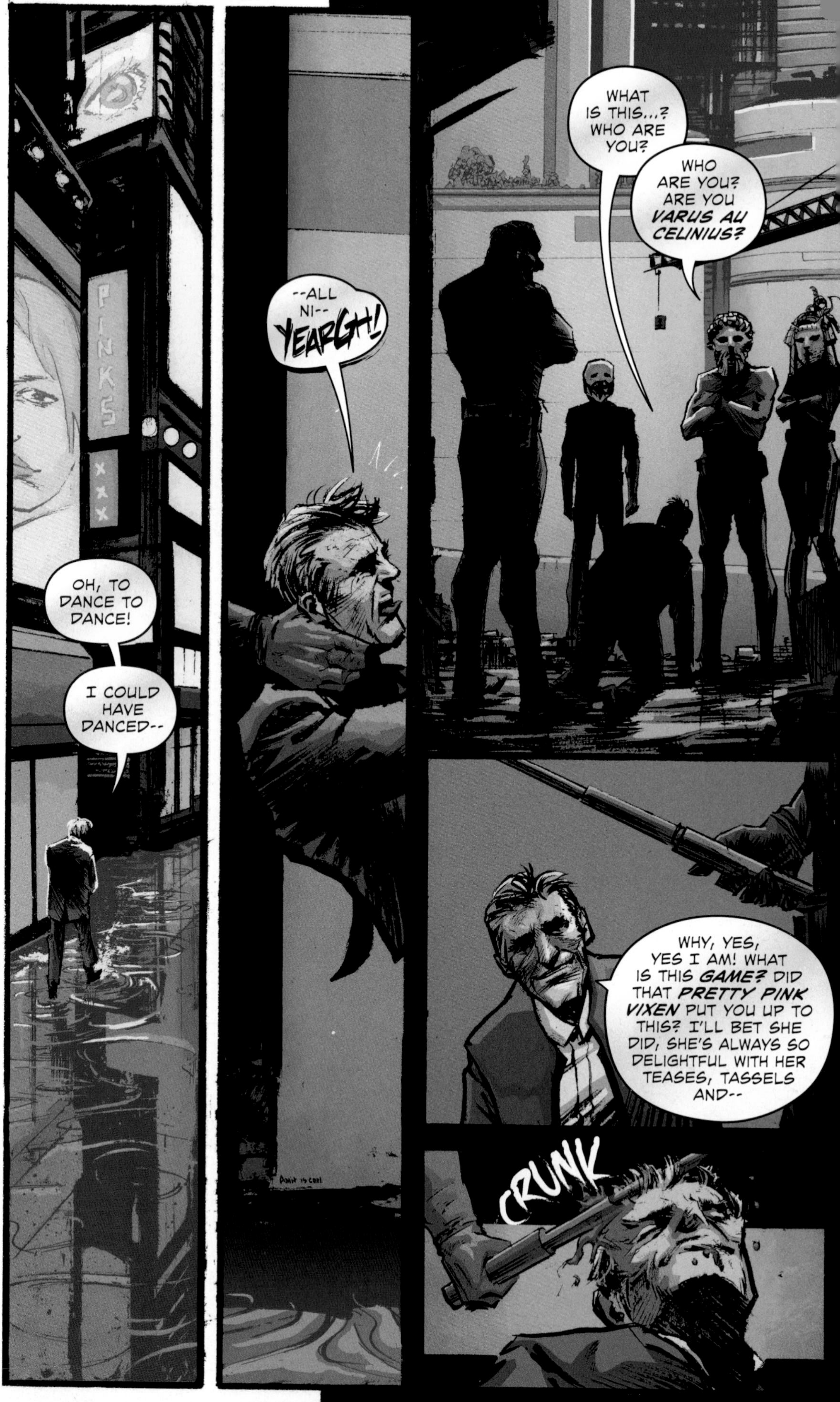
PINKS
XXX
OH, TO DANCE TO DANCE!
I COULD HAVE DANCED--
--ALL NI-- YEARGH!
WHAT IS THIS...? WHO ARE YOU?
WHO ARE YOU? ARE YOU VARUS AU CELINIUS?
WHY, YES, YES I AM! WHAT IS THIS GAME? DID THAT PRETTY PINK VIXEN PUT YOU UP TO THIS? I'LL BET SHE DID, SHE'S ALWAYS SO DELIGHTFUL WITH HER TEASES, TASSELS AND--
CRUNK

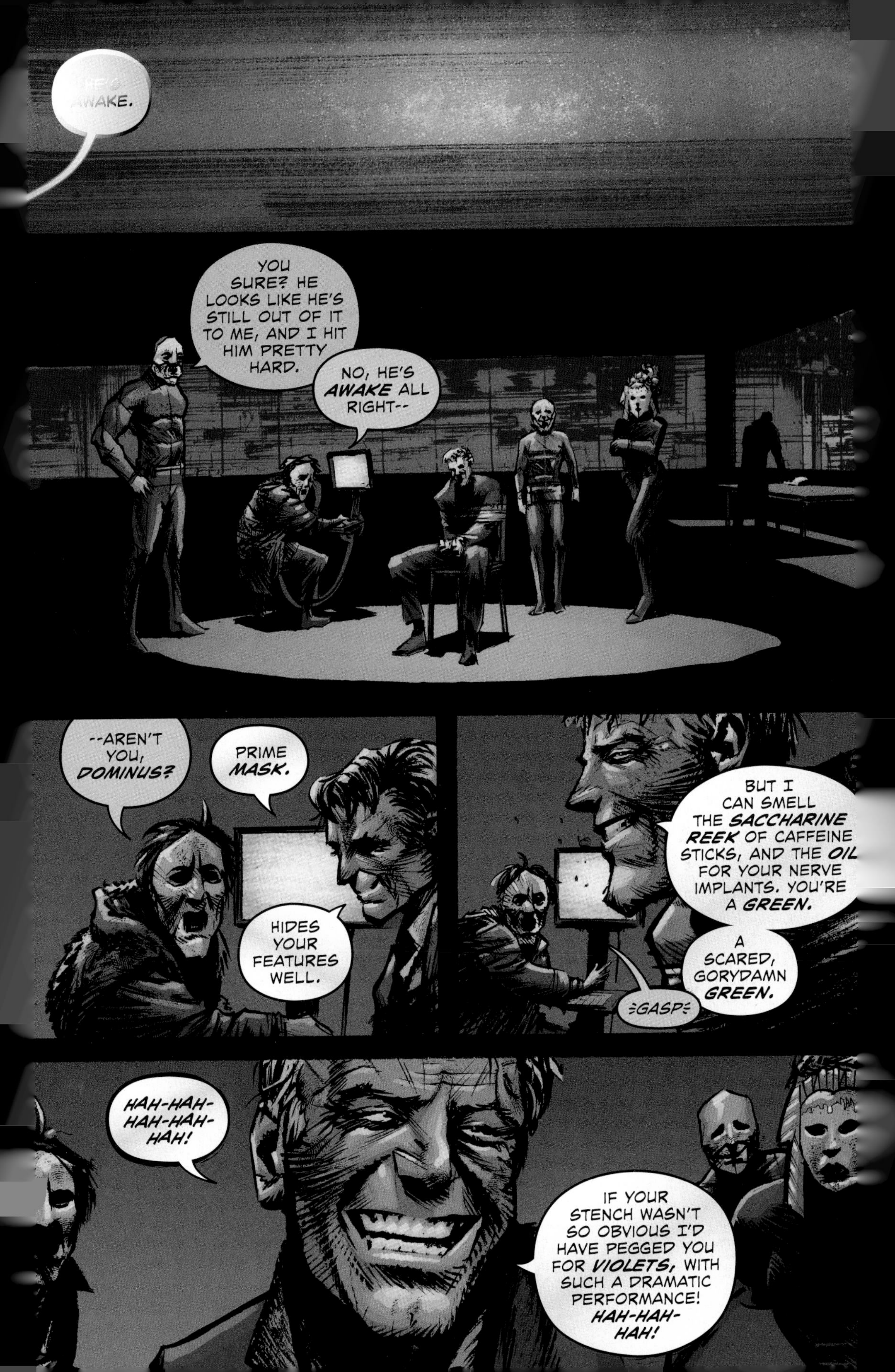
HE'S AWAKE.
YOU SURE? HE LOOKS LIKE HE'S STILL OUT OF IT TO ME, AND I HIT HIM PRETTY HARD.
NO, HE'S AWAKE ALL RIGHT--
--AREN'T YOU, DOMINUS?
PRIME MASK.
HIDES YOUR FEATURES WELL.
BUT I CAN SMELL THE SACCHARINE REEK OF CAFFEINE STICKS, AND THE OIL FOR YOUR NERVE IMPLANTS. YOU'RE A GREEN.
A SCARED, GORYDAMN GREEN.
GASP
HAH-HAH-HAH-HAH-HAH!
IF YOUR STENCH WASN'T SO OBVIOUS I'D HAVE PEGGED YOU FOR VIOLETS, WITH SUCH A DRAMATIC PERFORMANCE! HAH-HAH-HAH!

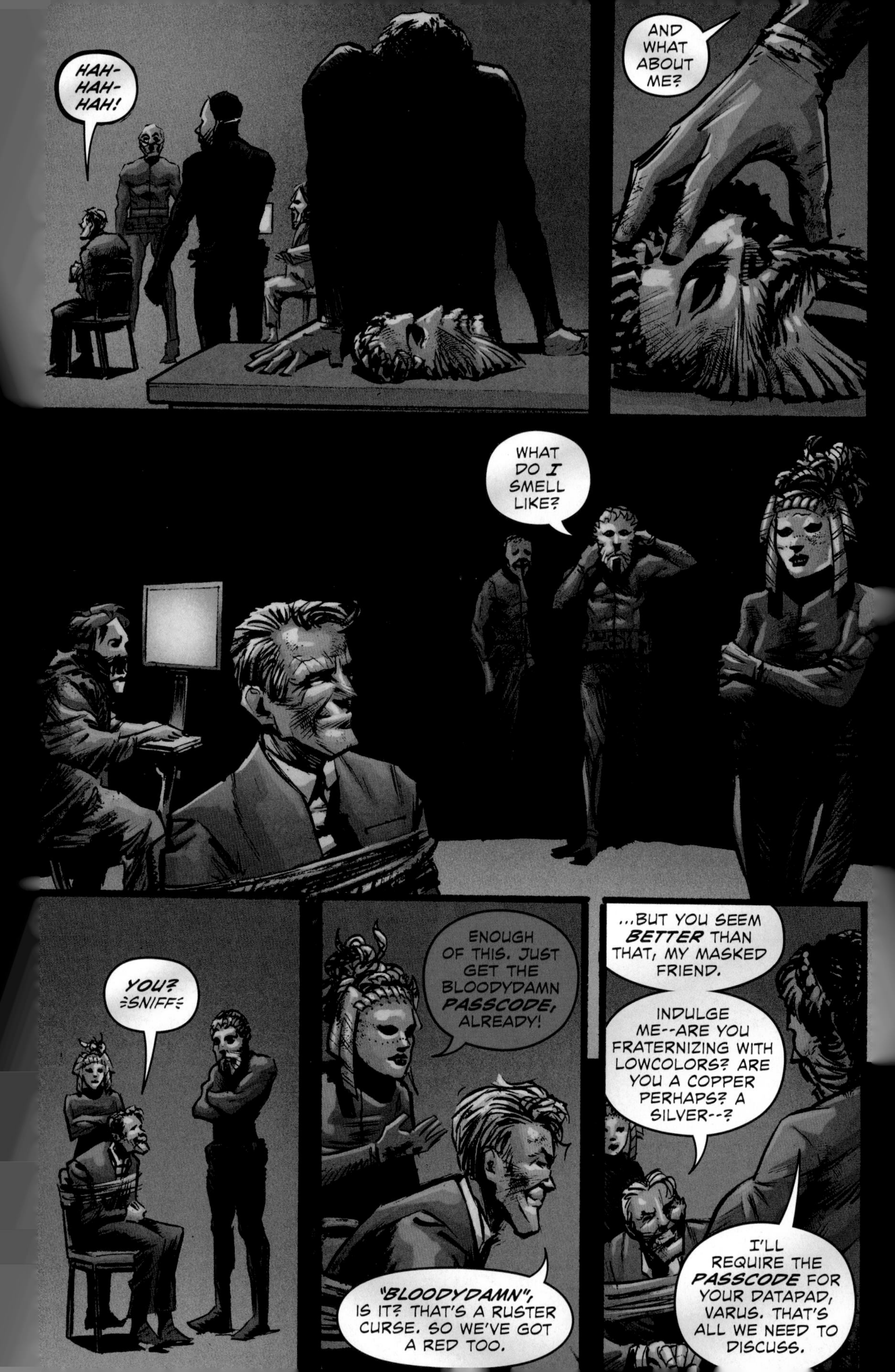
HAH-
HAH-
HAH!
AND WHAT ABOUT ME?
WHAT DO *I* SMELL LIKE?
YOU? ≶SNIFF≶
ENOUGH OF THIS. JUST GET THE BLOODYDAMN *PASSCODE,* ALREADY!
"BLOODYDAMN", IS IT? THAT'S A RUSTER CURSE. SO WE'VE GOT A RED TOO.
...BUT YOU SEEM *BETTER* THAN THAT, MY MASKED FRIEND.
INDULGE ME--ARE YOU FRATERNIZING WITH LOWCOLORS? ARE YOU A COPPER PERHAPS? A SILVER--?
I'LL REQUIRE THE *PASSCODE* FOR YOUR DATAPAD, VARUS. THAT'S ALL WE NEED TO DISCUSS.

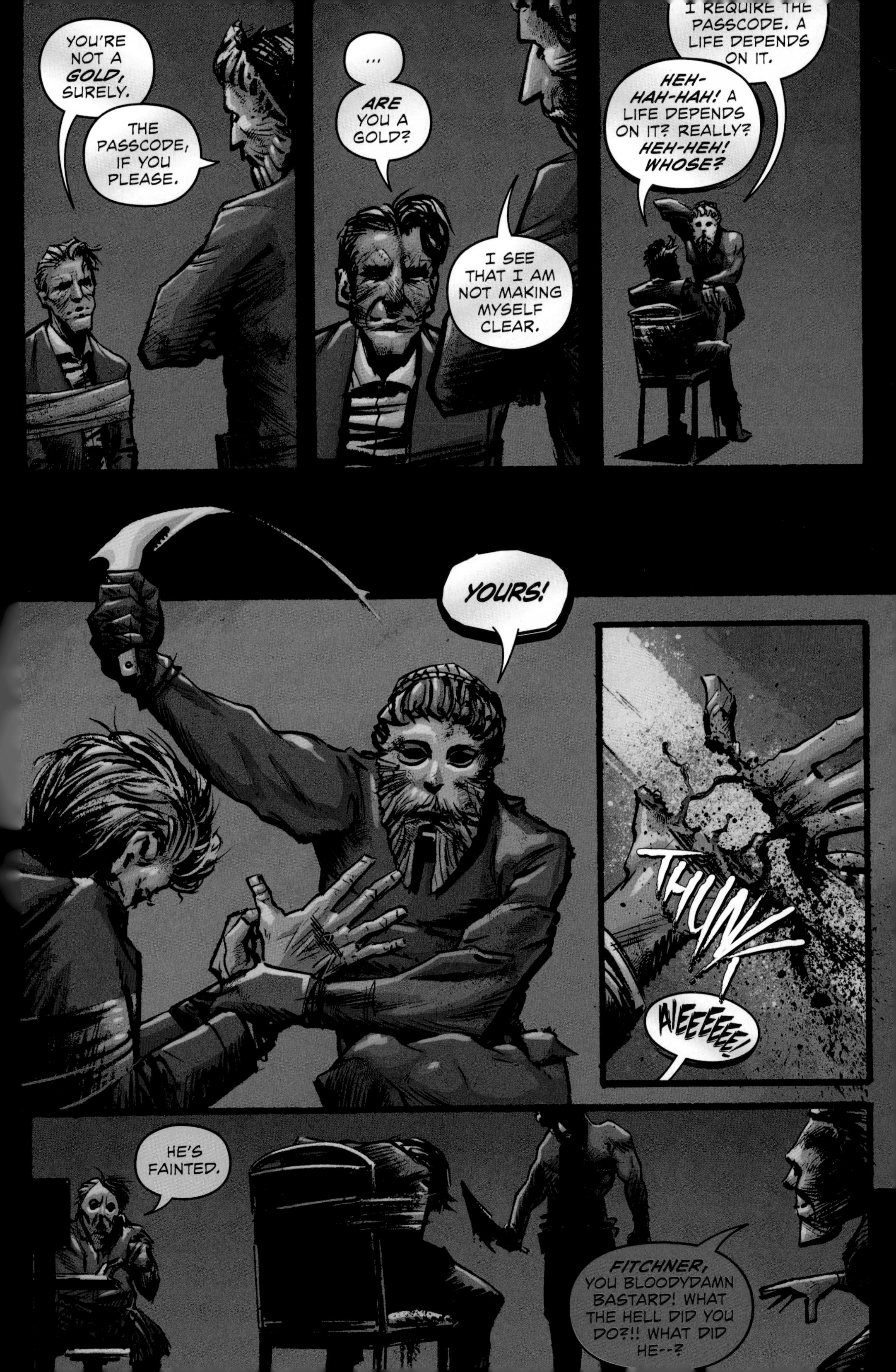
YOU'RE NOT A GOLD, SURELY.
THE PASSCODE, IF YOU PLEASE.
...
ARE YOU A GOLD?
I SEE THAT I AM NOT MAKING MYSELF CLEAR.
I REQUIRE THE PASSCODE. A LIFE DEPENDS ON IT.
HEH-HAH-HAH! A LIFE DEPENDS ON IT? REALLY? HEH-HEH! WHOSE?
YOURS!
THUNK!
AIEEEEEE!
HE'S FAINTED.
FITCHNER, YOU BLOODYDAMN BASTARD! WHAT THE HELL DID YOU DO?!! WHAT DID HE--?

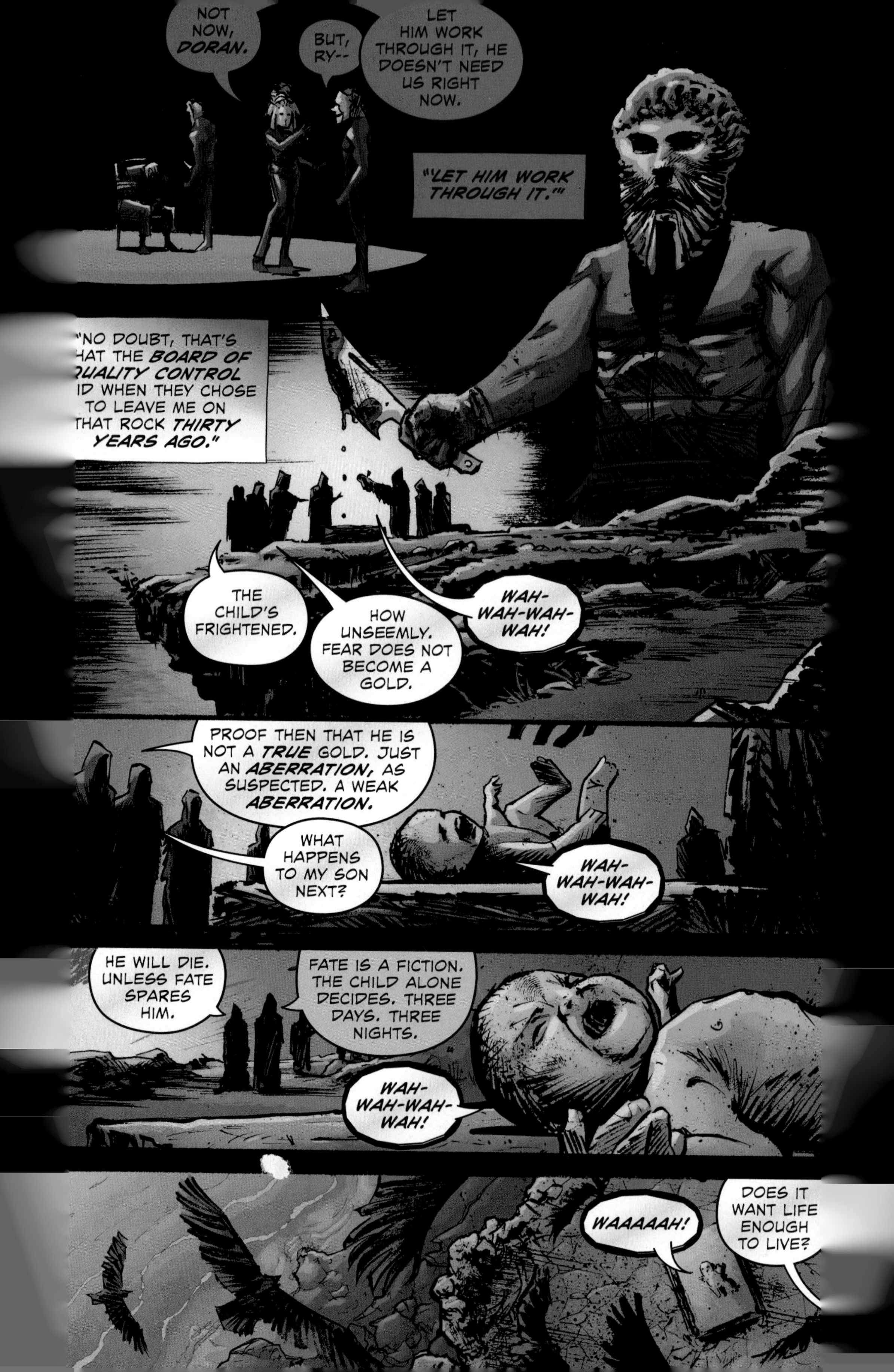
NOT NOW, DORAN.
BUT, RY--
LET HIM WORK THROUGH IT, HE DOESN'T NEED US RIGHT NOW.
"LET HIM WORK THROUGH IT."
"NO DOUBT, THAT'S HAT THE BOARD OF UALITY CONTROL ID WHEN THEY CHOSE TO LEAVE ME ON THAT ROCK THIRTY YEARS AGO."
THE CHILD'S FRIGHTENED.
HOW UNSEEMLY. FEAR DOES NOT BECOME A GOLD.
WAH-WAH-WAH-WAH!
PROOF THEN THAT HE IS NOT A TRUE GOLD. JUST AN ABERRATION, AS SUSPECTED. A WEAK ABERRATION.
WHAT HAPPENS TO MY SON NEXT?
WAH-WAH-WAH-WAH!
HE WILL DIE. UNLESS FATE SPARES HIM.
FATE IS A FICTION. THE CHILD ALONE DECIDES. THREE DAYS. THREE NIGHTS.
WAH-WAH-WAH-WAH!
WAAAAAH!
DOES IT WANT LIFE ENOUGH TO LIVE?

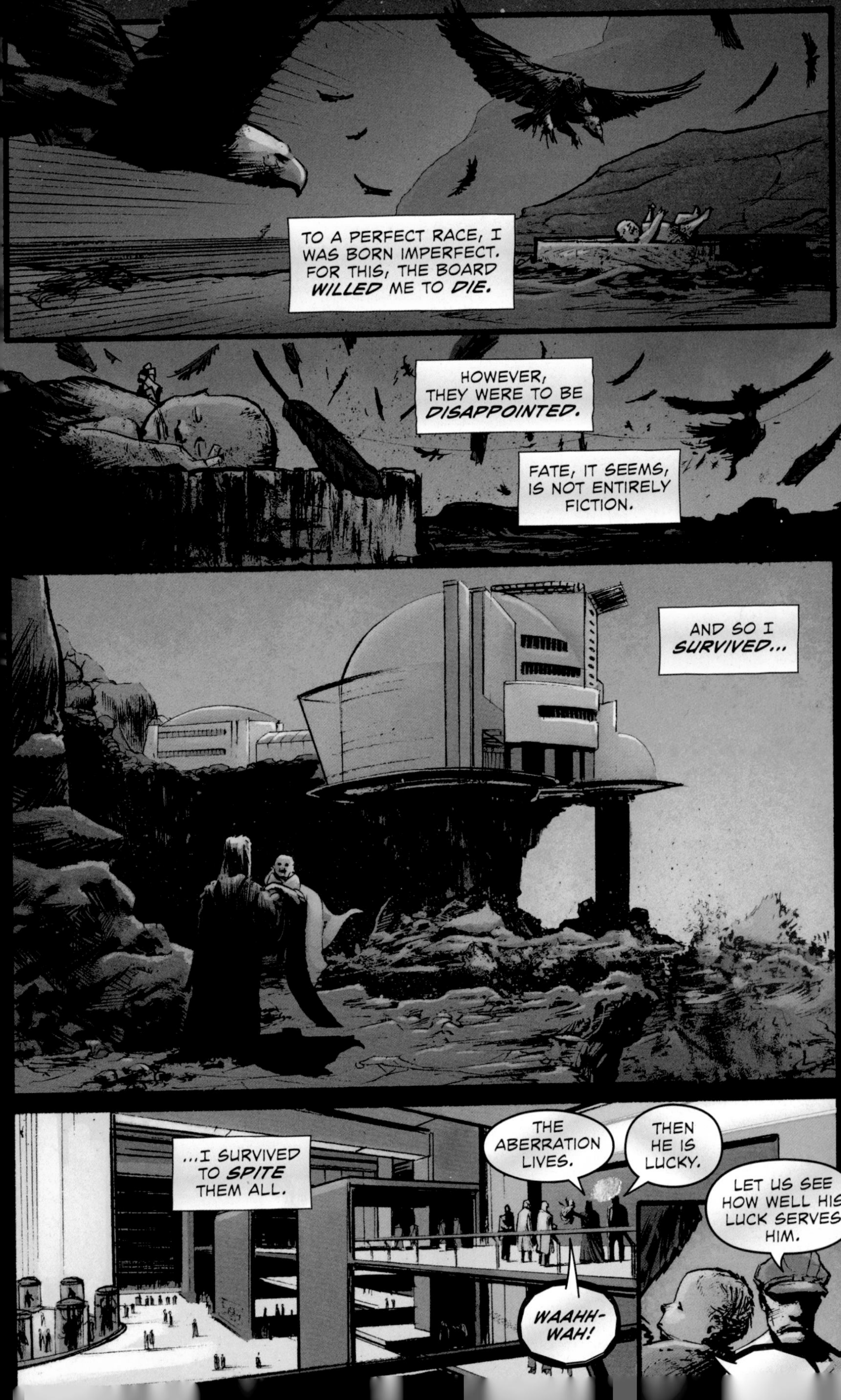
TO A PERFECT RACE, I WAS BORN IMPERFECT. FOR THIS, THE BOARD WILLED ME TO DIE.
HOWEVER, THEY WERE TO BE DISAPPOINTED.
FATE, IT SEEMS, IS NOT ENTIRELY FICTION.
AND SO I SURVIVED...
...I SURVIVED TO SPITE THEM ALL.
THE ABERRATION LIVES.
THEN HE IS LUCKY.
WAAHH-WAH!
LET US SEE HOW WELL HIS LUCK SERVES HIM.

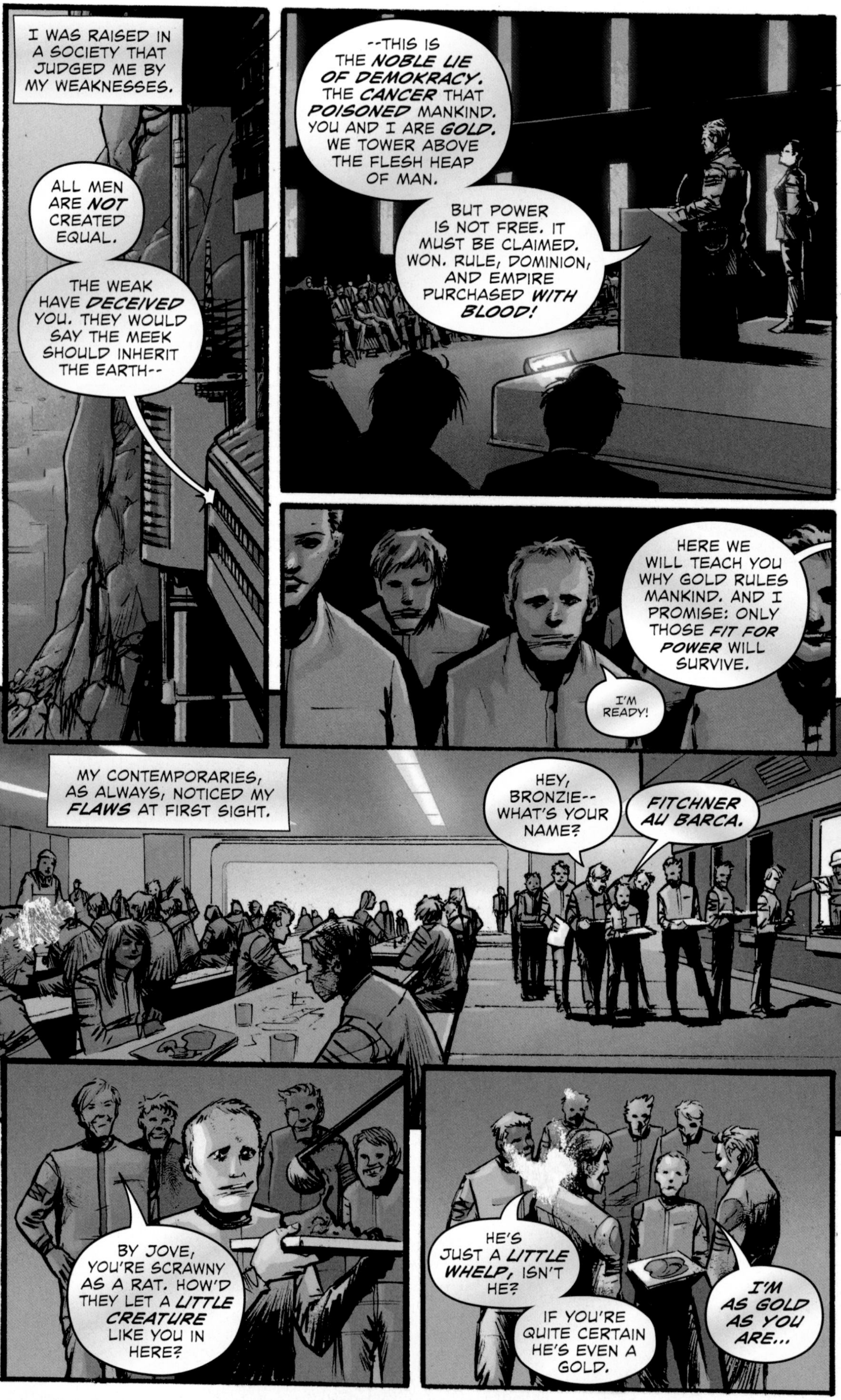
I WAS RAISED IN A SOCIETY THAT JUDGED ME BY MY WEAKNESSES.
ALL MEN ARE NOT CREATED EQUAL.
THE WEAK HAVE DECEIVED YOU. THEY WOULD SAY THE MEEK SHOULD INHERIT THE EARTH--
--THIS IS THE NOBLE LIE OF DEMOKRACY. THE CANCER THAT POISONED MANKIND. YOU AND I ARE GOLD. WE TOWER ABOVE THE FLESH HEAP OF MAN.
BUT POWER IS NOT FREE. IT MUST BE CLAIMED. WON. RULE, DOMINION, AND EMPIRE PURCHASED WITH BLOOD!
HERE WE WILL TEACH YOU WHY GOLD RULES MANKIND. AND I PROMISE: ONLY THOSE FIT FOR POWER WILL SURVIVE.
I'M READY!
MY CONTEMPORARIES, AS ALWAYS, NOTICED MY FLAWS AT FIRST SIGHT.
HEY, BRONZIE-- WHAT'S YOUR NAME?
FITCHNER AU BARCA.
BY JOVE, YOU'RE SCRAWNY AS A RAT. HOW'D THEY LET A LITTLE CREATURE LIKE YOU IN HERE?
HE'S JUST A LITTLE WHELP, ISN'T HE?
IF YOU'RE QUITE CERTAIN HE'S EVEN A GOLD.
I'M AS GOLD AS YOU ARE...

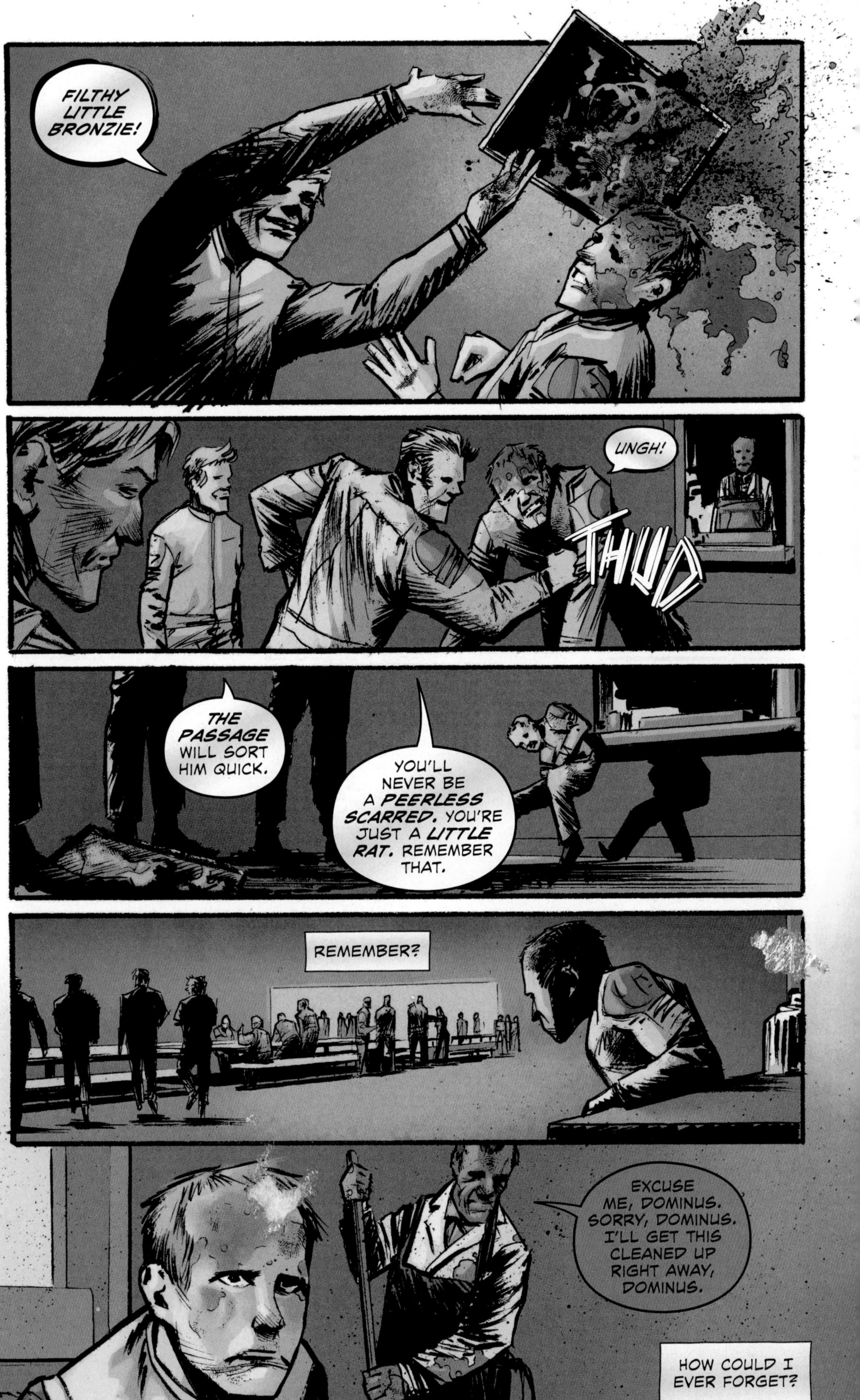
FILTHY LITTLE BRONZIE!
UNGH!
THUD
THE PASSAGE WILL SORT HIM QUICK.
YOU'LL NEVER BE A PEERLESS SCARRED. YOU'RE JUST A LITTLE RAT. REMEMBER THAT.
REMEMBER?
EXCUSE ME, DOMINUS. SORRY, DOMINUS. I'LL GET THIS CLEANED UP RIGHT AWAY, DOMINUS.
HOW COULD I EVER FORGET?

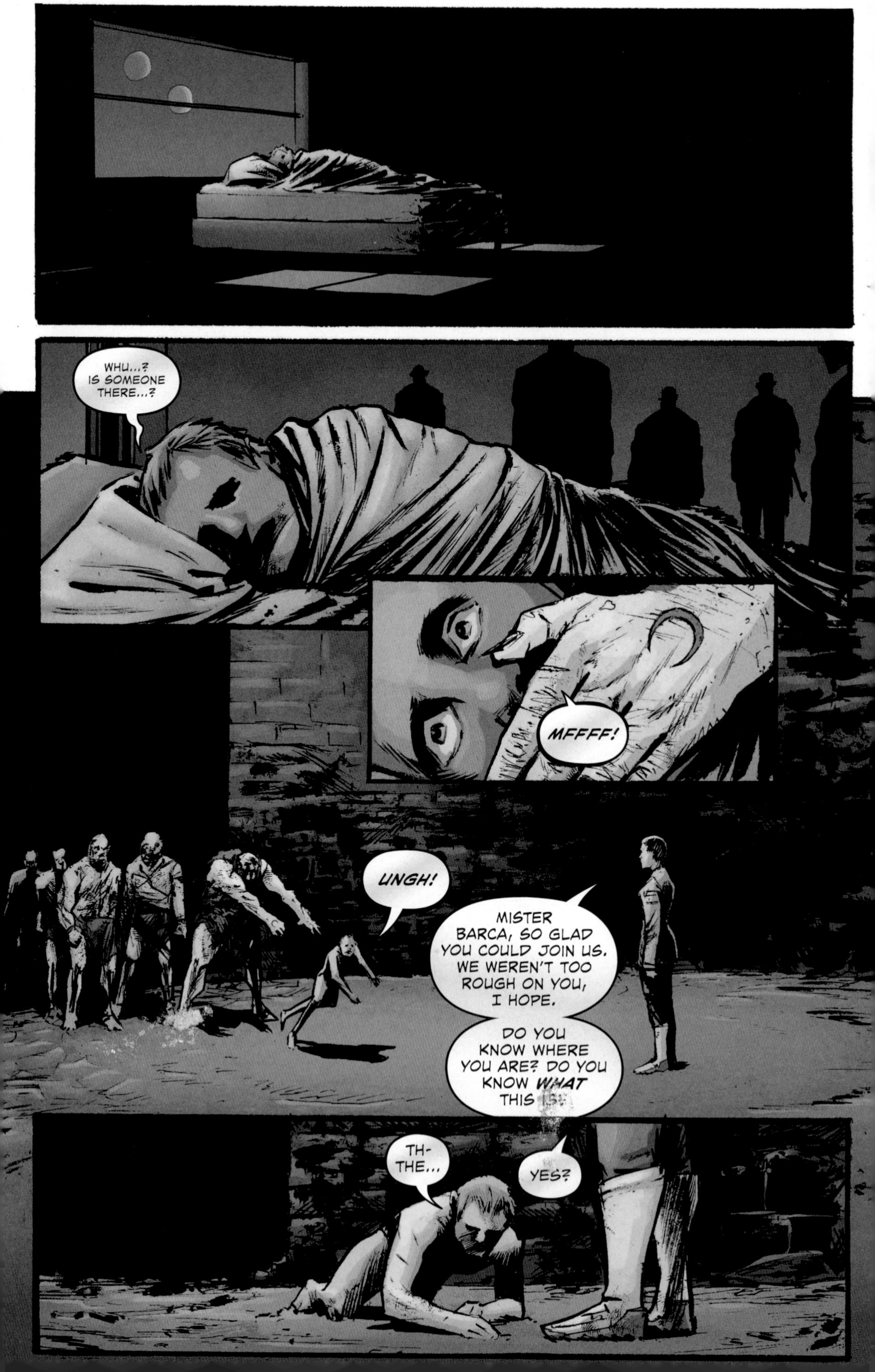
WHU...? IS SOMEONE THERE...?
MFFFF!
UNGH!
MISTER BARCA, SO GLAD YOU COULD JOIN US. WE WEREN'T TOO ROUGH ON YOU, I HOPE.
DO YOU KNOW WHERE YOU ARE? DO YOU KNOW *WHAT* THIS IS?
TH- THE...
YES?

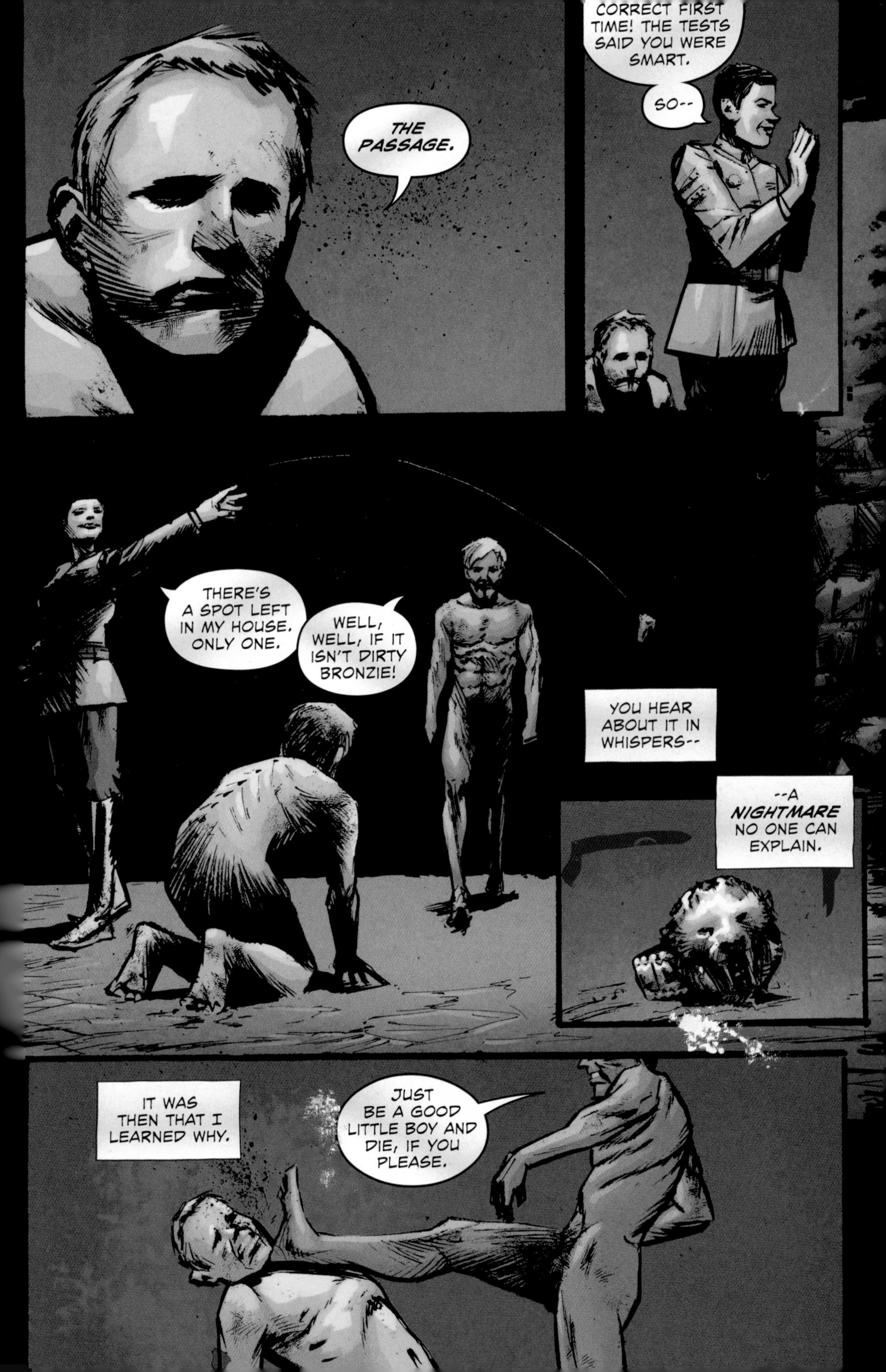
THE PASSAGE.
CORRECT FIRST TIME! THE TESTS SAID YOU WERE SMART.
SO--
THERE'S A SPOT LEFT IN MY HOUSE. ONLY ONE.
WELL, WELL, IF IT ISN'T DIRTY BRONZIE!
YOU HEAR ABOUT IT IN WHISPERS--
--A NIGHTMARE NO ONE CAN EXPLAIN.
IT WAS THEN THAT I LEARNED WHY.
JUST BE A GOOD LITTLE BOY AND DIE, IF YOU PLEASE.

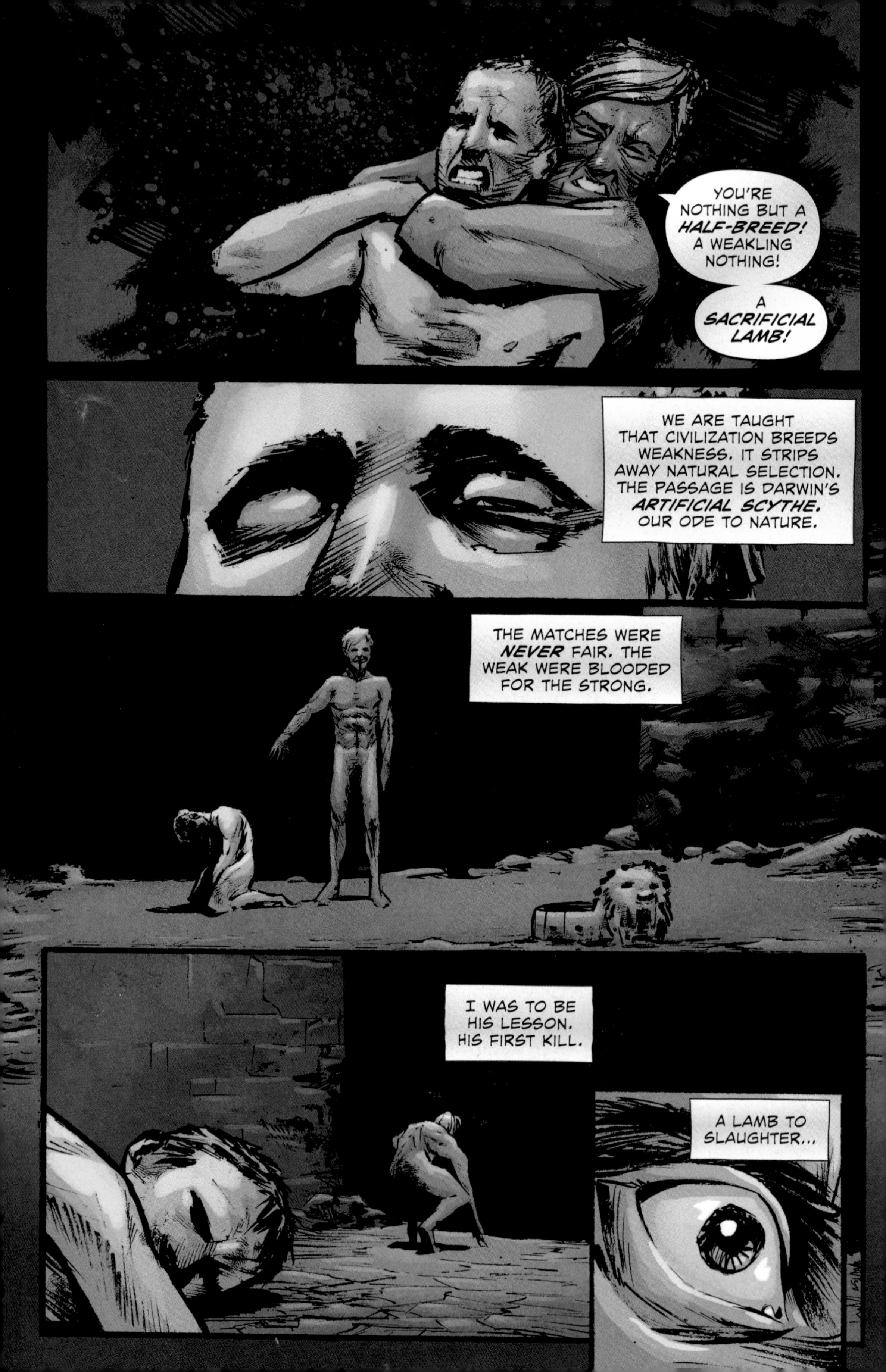
YOU'RE NOTHING BUT A *HALF-BREED!* A WEAKLING NOTHING!
A *SACRIFICIAL LAMB!*
WE ARE TAUGHT THAT CIVILIZATION BREEDS WEAKNESS. IT STRIPS AWAY NATURAL SELECTION. THE PASSAGE IS DARWIN'S *ARTIFICIAL SCYTHE.* OUR ODE TO NATURE.
THE MATCHES WERE *NEVER* FAIR. THE WEAK WERE BLOODED FOR THE STRONG.
I WAS TO BE HIS LESSON. HIS FIRST KILL.
A LAMB TO SLAUGHTER...

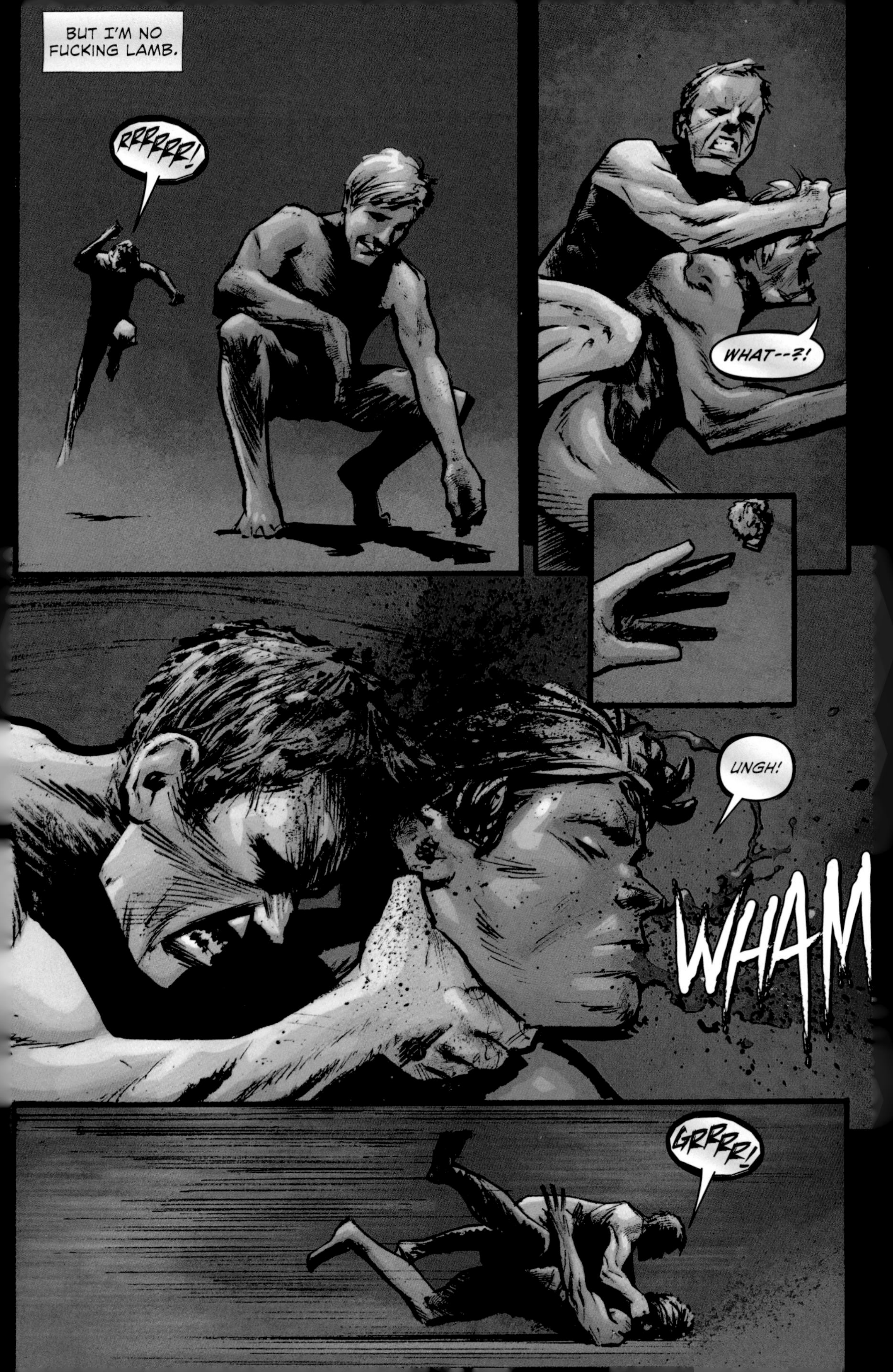
BUT I'M NO FUCKING LAMB.
RRRRRR!
WHAT--?!
UNGH!
WHAM
GRRRR!

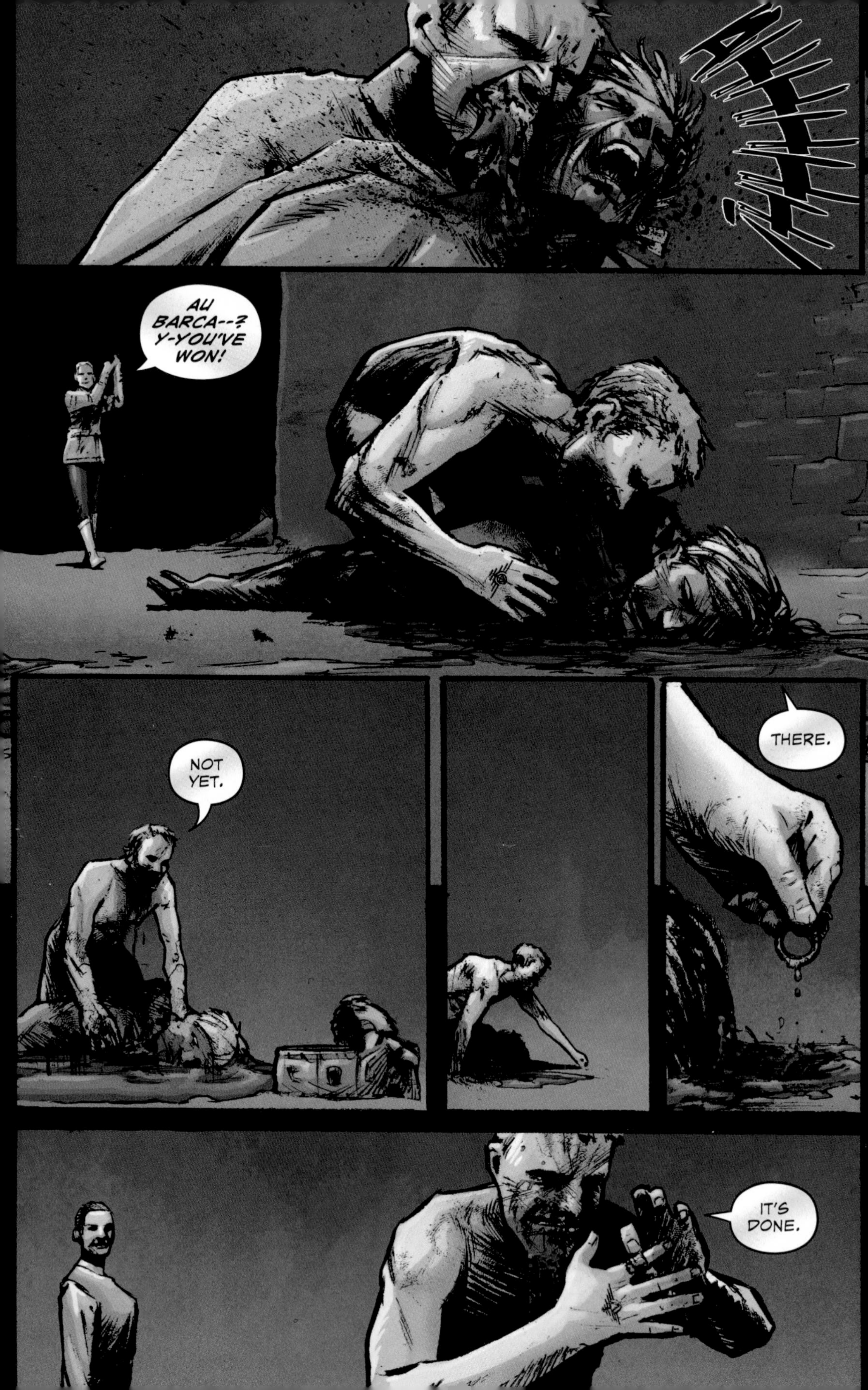
AAAAHHH!
AU BARCA--? Y-YOU'VE WON!
NOT YET.
THERE.
IT'S DONE.

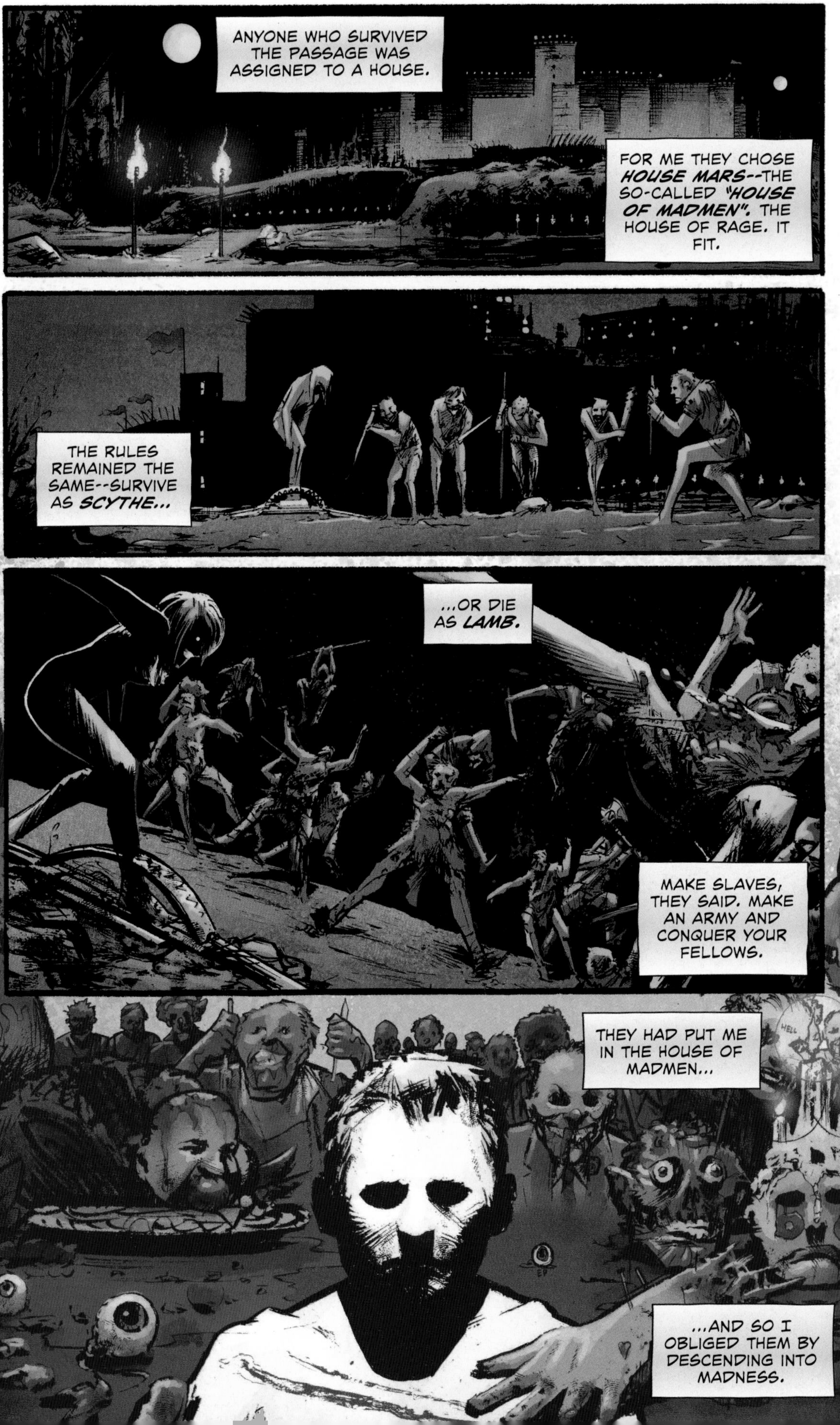
ANYONE WHO SURVIVED THE PASSAGE WAS ASSIGNED TO A HOUSE.
FOR ME THEY CHOSE HOUSE MARS--THE SO-CALLED "HOUSE OF MADMEN". THE HOUSE OF RAGE. IT FIT.
THE RULES REMAINED THE SAME--SURVIVE AS SCYTHE...
...OR DIE AS LAMB.
MAKE SLAVES, THEY SAID. MAKE AN ARMY AND CONQUER YOUR FELLOWS.
THEY HAD PUT ME IN THE HOUSE OF MADMEN...
...AND SO I OBLIGED THEM BY DESCENDING INTO MADNESS.

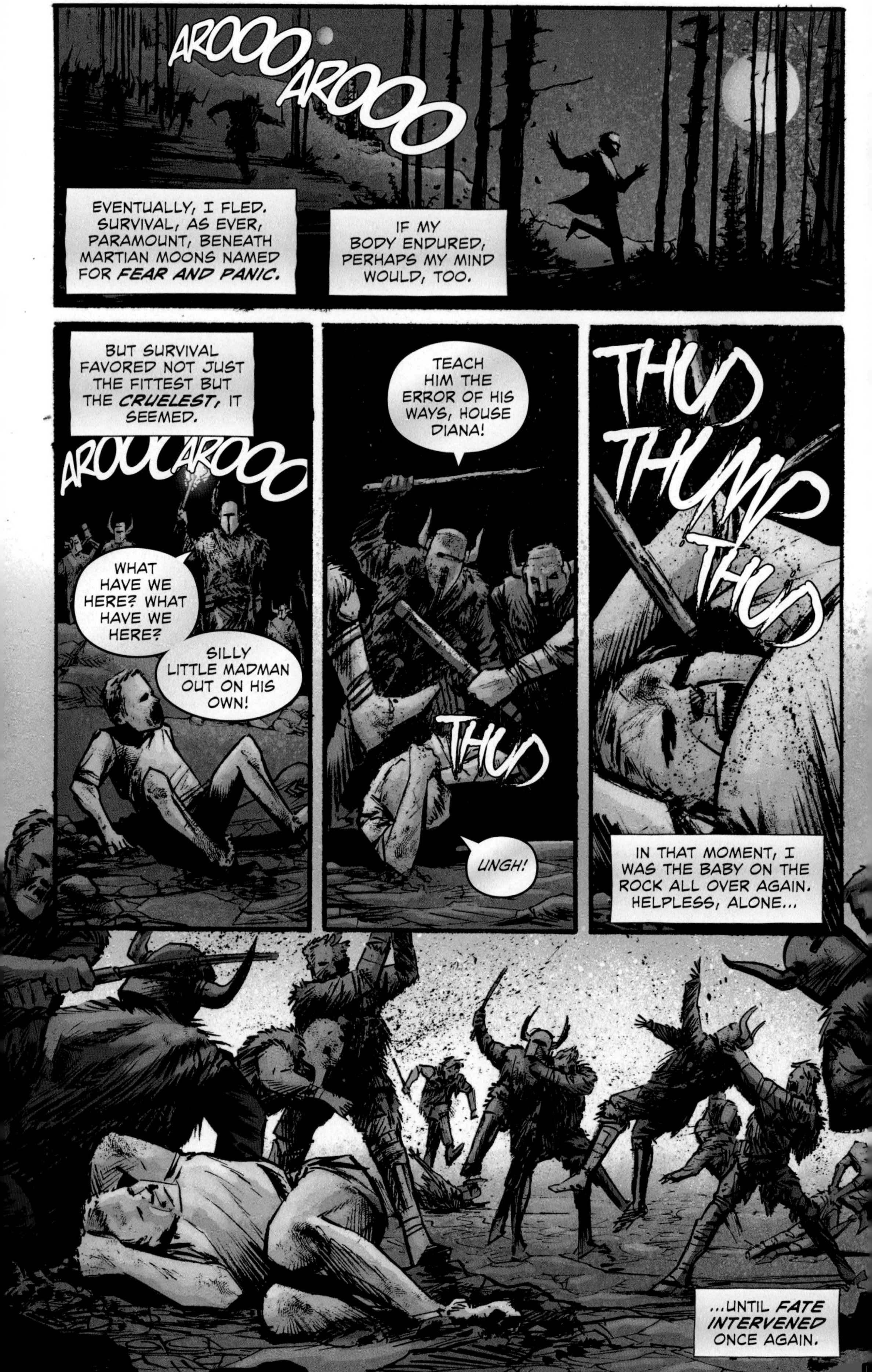
AROOO AROOO
EVENTUALLY, I FLED. SURVIVAL, AS EVER, PARAMOUNT, BENEATH MARTIAN MOONS NAMED FOR *FEAR AND PANIC.*
IF MY BODY ENDURED, PERHAPS MY MIND WOULD, TOO.
BUT SURVIVAL FAVORED NOT JUST THE FITTEST BUT THE *CRUELEST,* IT SEEMED.
AROOO AROOO
WHAT HAVE WE HERE? WHAT HAVE WE HERE?
SILLY LITTLE MADMAN OUT ON HIS OWN!
TEACH HIM THE ERROR OF HIS WAYS, HOUSE DIANA!
THUD
UNGH!
THUD THUMP THUD
IN THAT MOMENT, I WAS THE BABY ON THE ROCK ALL OVER AGAIN. HELPLESS, ALONE...
...UNTIL *FATE INTERVENED* ONCE AGAIN.

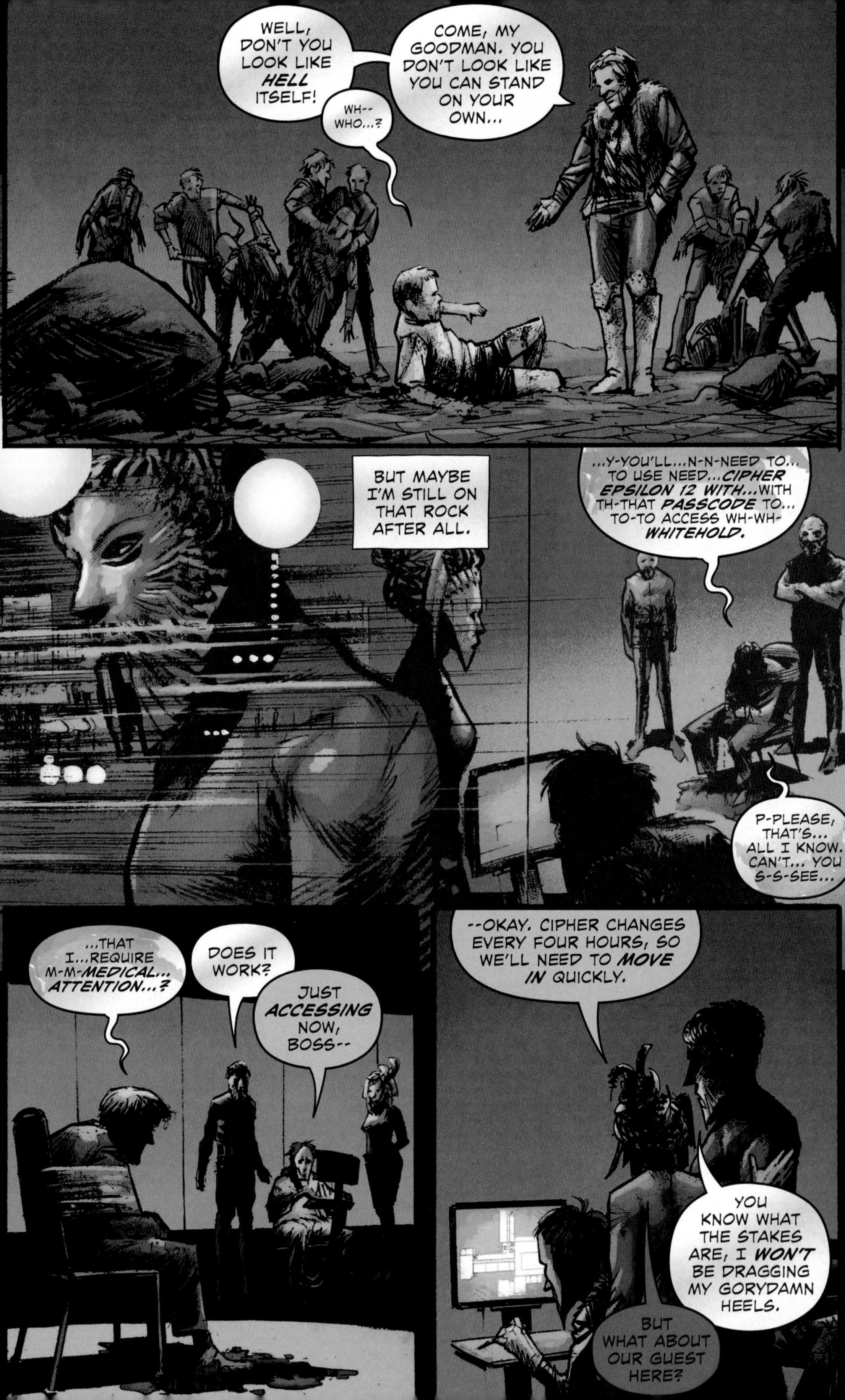
WELL, DON'T YOU LOOK LIKE HELL ITSELF!
COME, MY GOODMAN. YOU DON'T LOOK LIKE YOU CAN STAND ON YOUR OWN...
WH-- WHO...?
BUT MAYBE I'M STILL ON THAT ROCK AFTER ALL.
...Y-YOU'LL...N-N-NEED TO... TO USE NEED...CIPHER EPSILON 12 WITH...WITH TH-THAT PASSCODE TO... TO-TO ACCESS WH-WH-WHITEHOLD.
P-PLEASE, THAT'S... ALL I KNOW. CAN'T... YOU S-S-SEE...
...THAT I...REQUIRE M-M-MEDICAL... ATTENTION...?
DOES IT WORK?
JUST ACCESSING NOW, BOSS--
--OKAY. CIPHER CHANGES EVERY FOUR HOURS, SO WE'LL NEED TO MOVE IN QUICKLY.
YOU KNOW WHAT THE STAKES ARE, I WON'T BE DRAGGING MY GORYDAMN HEELS.
BUT WHAT ABOUT OUR GUEST HERE?

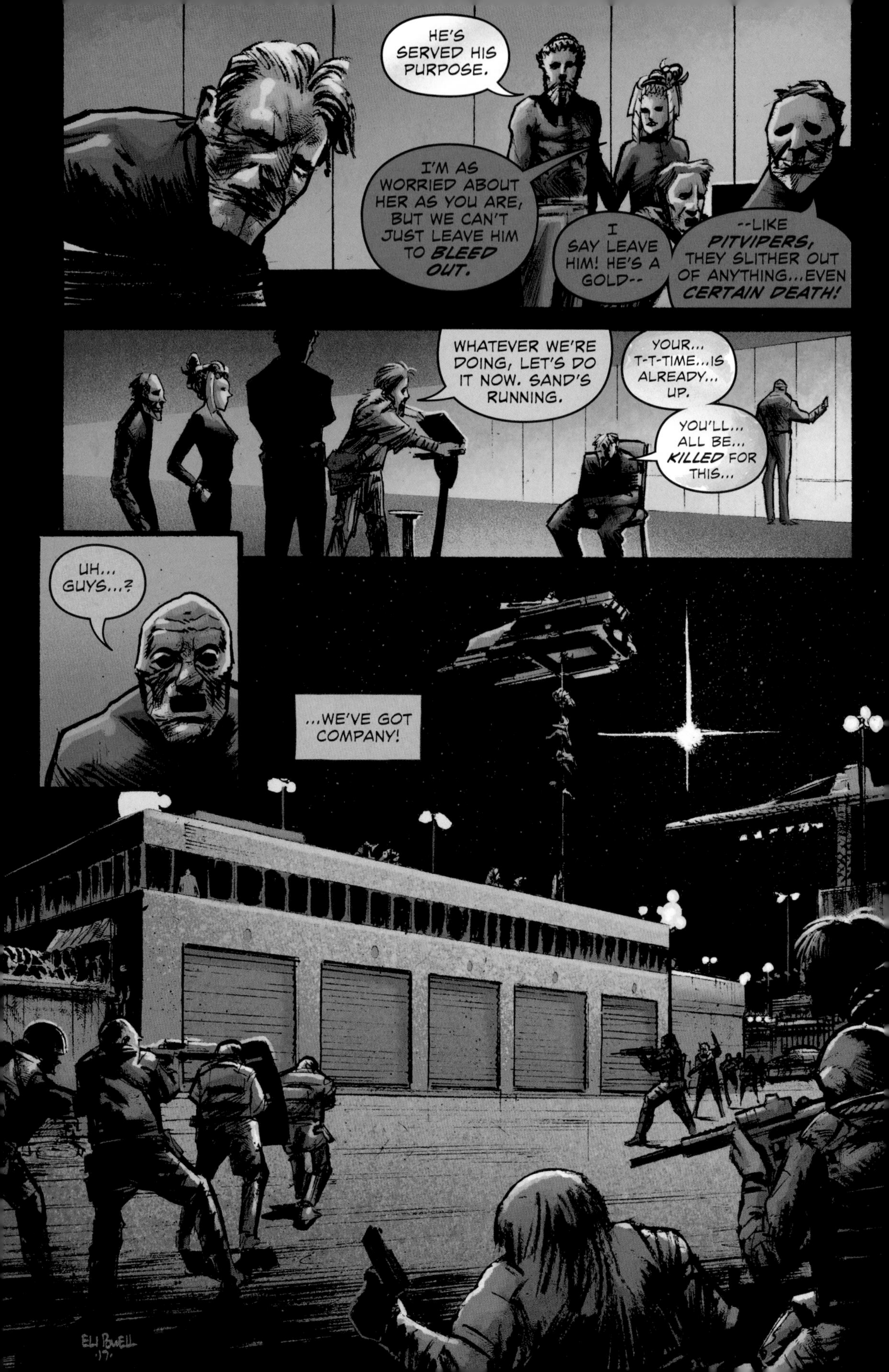
HE'S SERVED HIS PURPOSE.
I'M AS WORRIED ABOUT HER AS YOU ARE, BUT WE CAN'T JUST LEAVE HIM TO BLEED OUT.
I SAY LEAVE HIM! HE'S A GOLD--
--LIKE PITVIPERS, THEY SLITHER OUT OF ANYTHING...EVEN CERTAIN DEATH!
WHATEVER WE'RE DOING, LET'S DO IT NOW. SAND'S RUNNING.
YOUR... T-T-TIME...IS ALREADY... UP.
YOU'LL... ALL BE... KILLED FOR THIS...
UH... GUYS...?
...WE'VE GOT COMPANY!
ELI POWELL '17

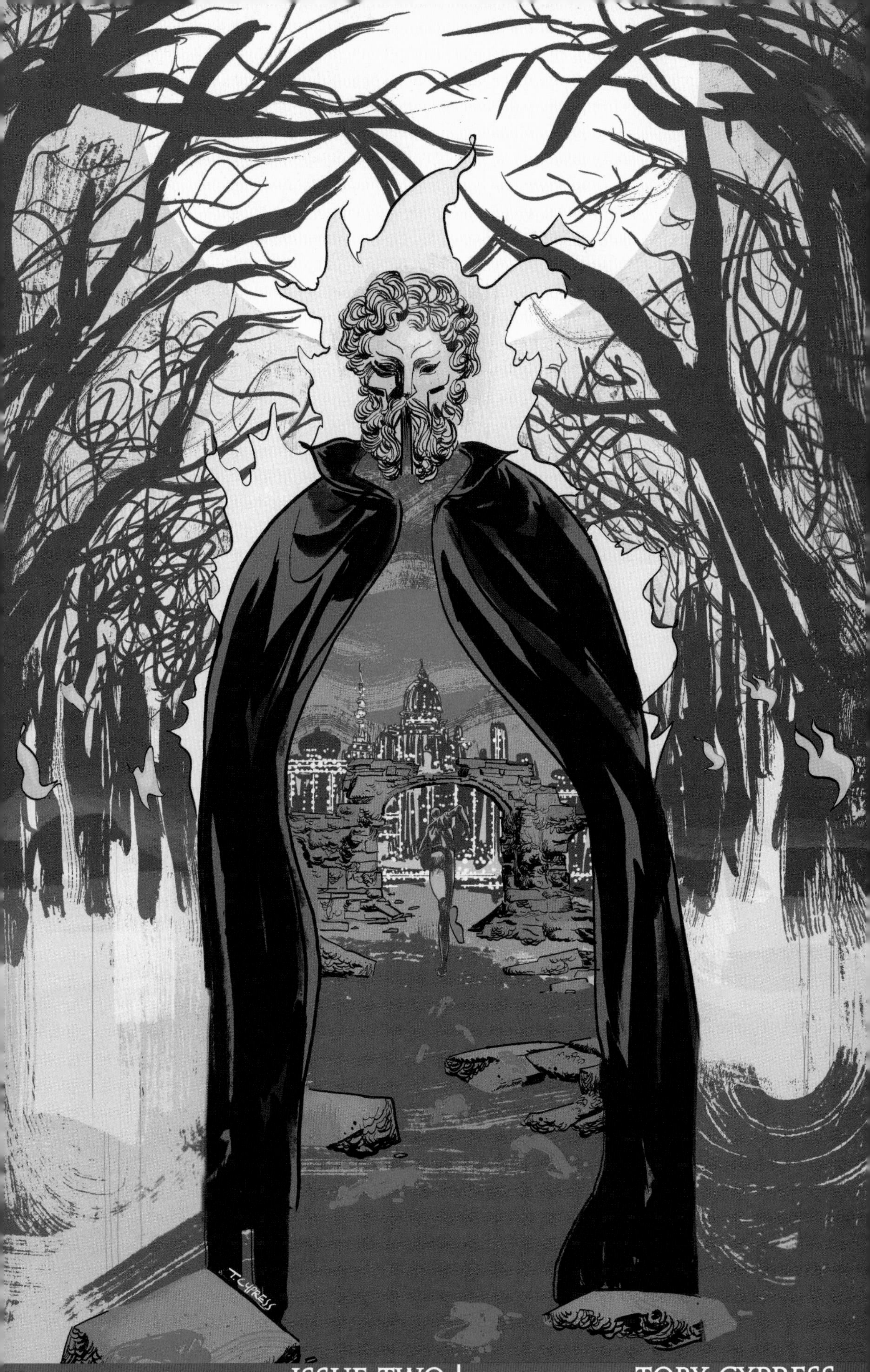
T. CYPRESS

ISSUE TWO | COVER ART BY TOBY CYPRESS

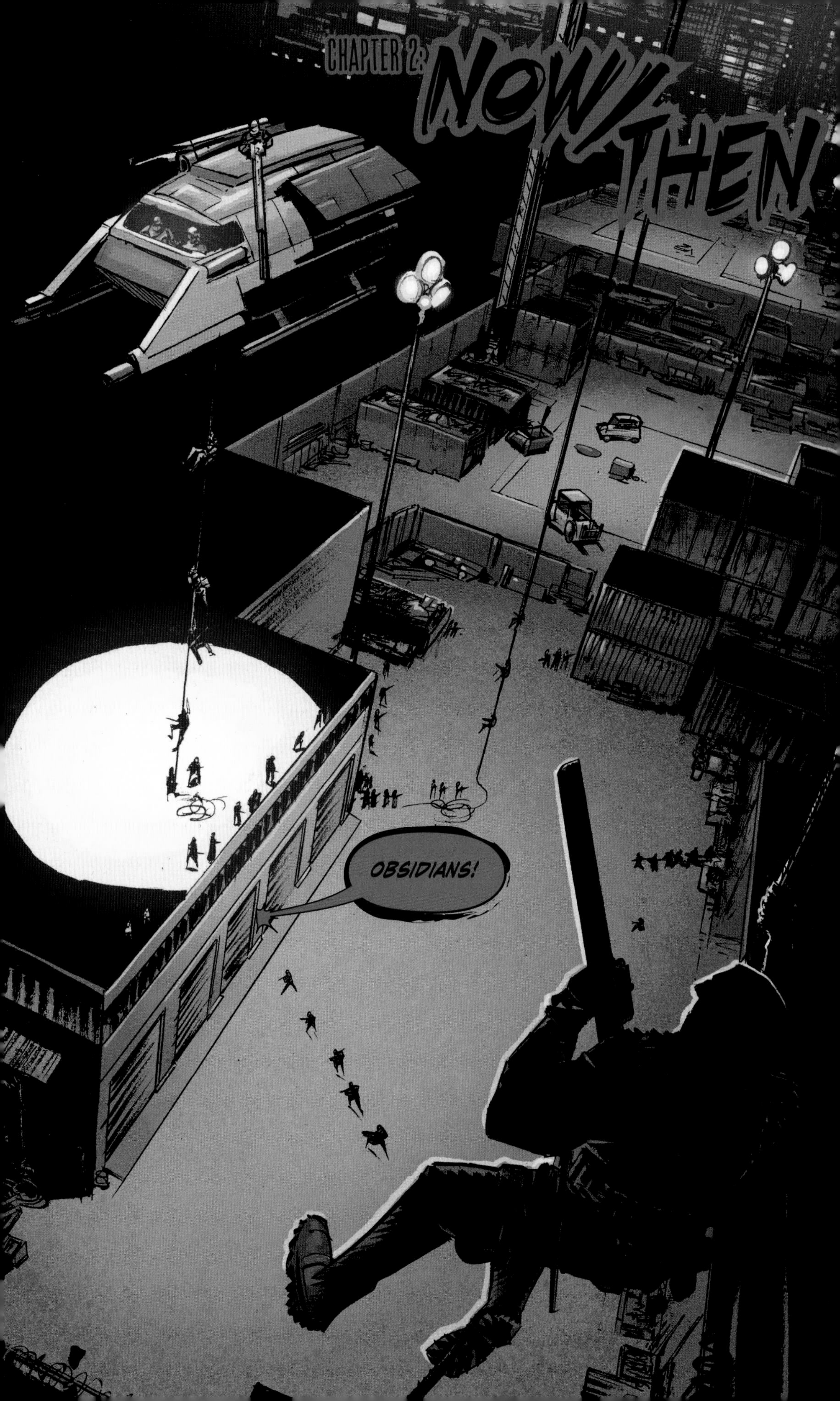
CHAPTER 2: NOW/THEN
OBSIDIANS!

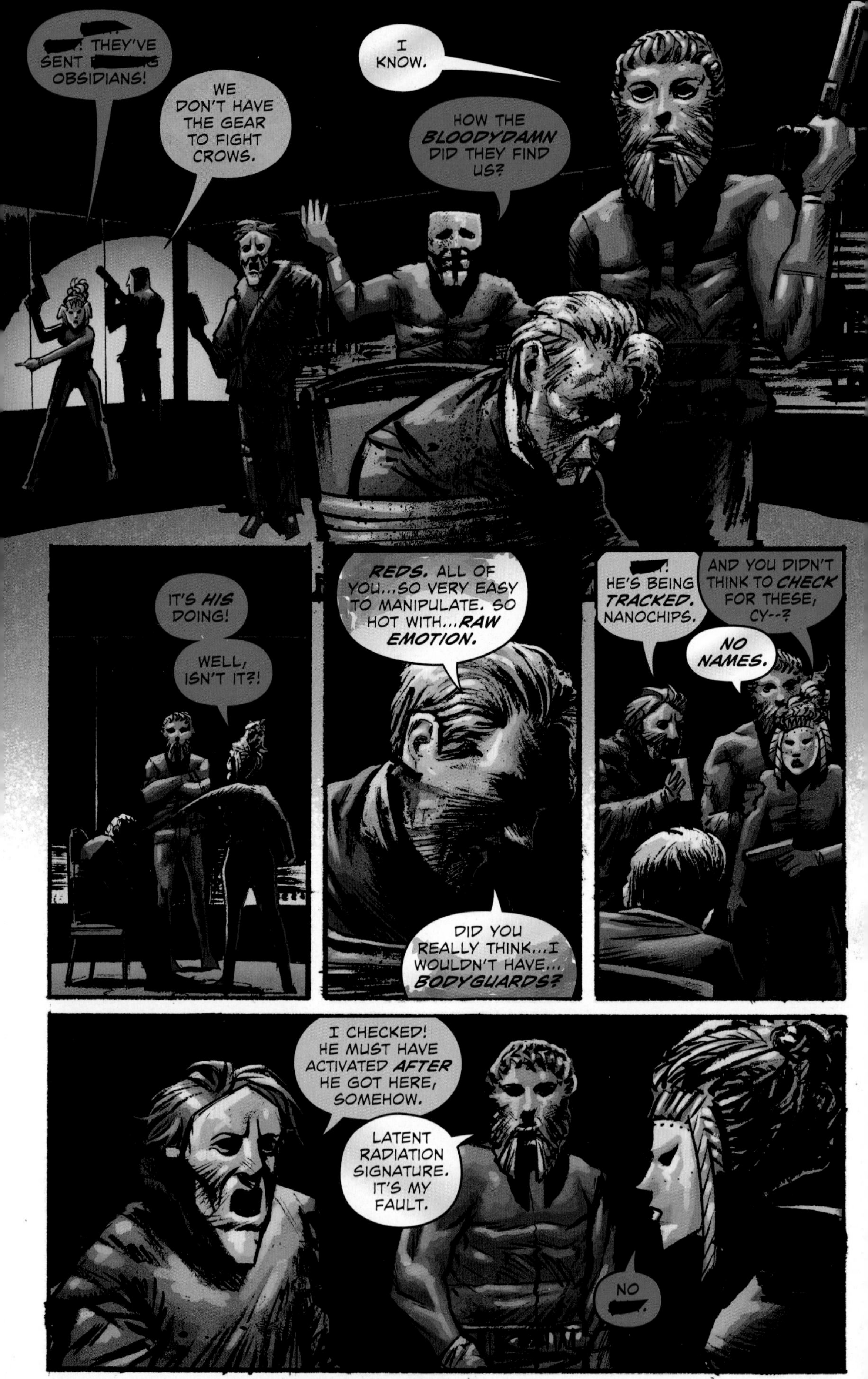
[redacted]! THEY'VE SENT [redacted] OBSIDIANS!
WE DON'T HAVE THE GEAR TO FIGHT CROWS.
I KNOW.
HOW THE *BLOODYDAMN* DID THEY FIND US?
IT'S *HIS* DOING!
WELL, ISN'T IT?!
REDS. ALL OF YOU...SO VERY EASY TO MANIPULATE. SO HOT WITH...*RAW EMOTION.*
DID YOU REALLY THINK...I WOULDN'T HAVE... *BODYGUARDS?*
[redacted]! HE'S BEING *TRACKED.* NANOCHIPS.
AND YOU DIDN'T THINK TO *CHECK* FOR THESE, CY--?
NO NAMES.
I CHECKED! HE MUST HAVE ACTIVATED *AFTER* HE GOT HERE, SOMEHOW.
LATENT RADIATION SIGNATURE. IT'S MY FAULT.
NO [redacted].

THEY'RE COMING.

WILL YOUR PISTOL EVEN PENETRATE THEIR ARMOR?!

NO.

CHIEF, IF YOU GOT A PLAN, *TIME TO SPILL.*

MIGHT I SUGGEST YOU *RELEASE ME AND SURRENDER?* I WOULD WAGER IT IS YOUR BEST HOPE OF SURVIVAL. MY BODYGUARDS CAN BE RATHER, SHALL WE SAY...

LISTEN TO HIM. IT'S NOT TOO LATE. FITCHNER...

BLAM

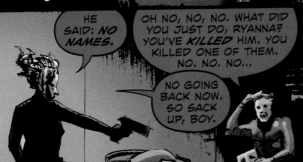

HE SAID: *NO NAMES.*

OH NO, NO, NO. WHAT DID YOU JUST DO, RYANNA? YOU'VE *KILLED* HIM. YOU KILLED ONE OF THEM. NO, NO, NO...

NO GOING BACK NOW. SO SACK UP, BOY.

DO YOU HAVE A PLAN?

RUN.

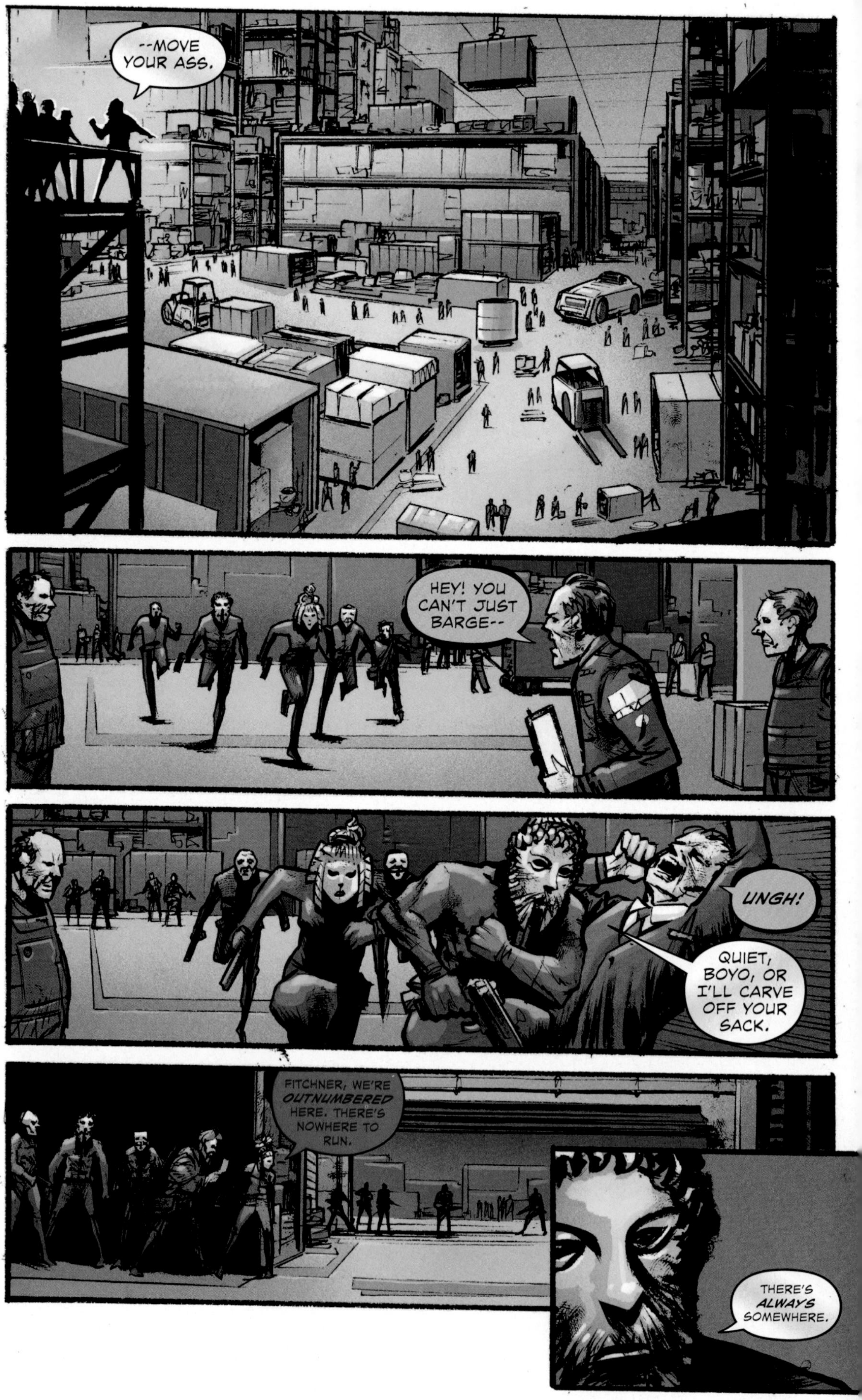
--MOVE YOUR ASS.
HEY! YOU CAN'T JUST BARGE--
UNGH!
QUIET, BOYO, OR I'LL CARVE OFF YOUR SACK.
FITCHNER, WE'RE OUTNUMBERED HERE. THERE'S NOWHERE TO RUN.
THERE'S ALWAYS SOMEWHERE.

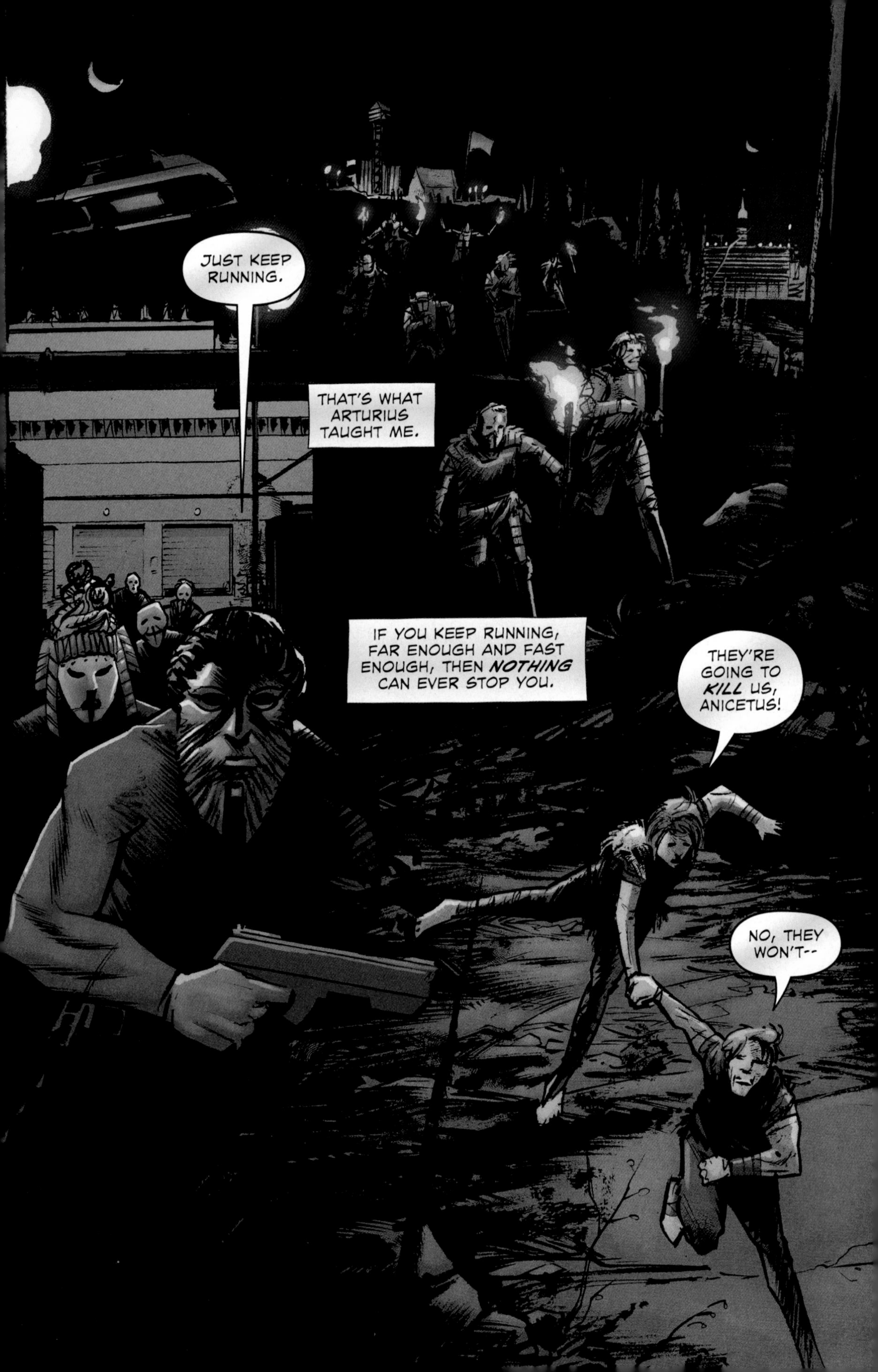
JUST KEEP RUNNING.
THAT'S WHAT ARTURIUS TAUGHT ME.
IF YOU KEEP RUNNING, FAR ENOUGH AND FAST ENOUGH, THEN NOTHING CAN EVER STOP YOU.
THEY'RE GOING TO KILL US, ANICETUS!
NO, THEY WON'T--

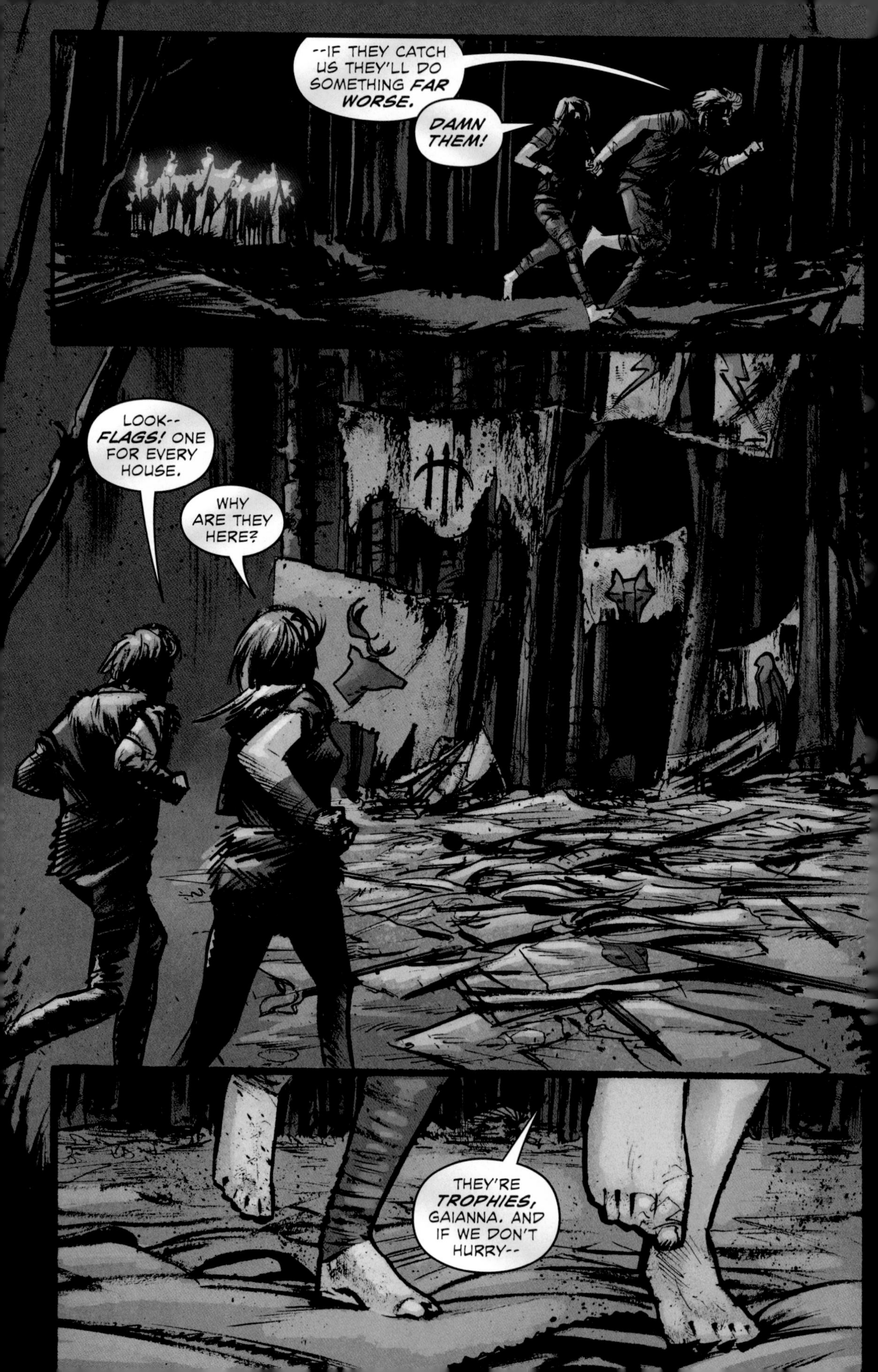
--IF THEY CATCH US THEY'LL DO SOMETHING FAR WORSE.
DAMN THEM!
LOOK-- FLAGS! ONE FOR EVERY HOUSE.
WHY ARE THEY HERE?
THEY'RE TROPHIES, GAIANNA. AND IF WE DON'T HURRY--

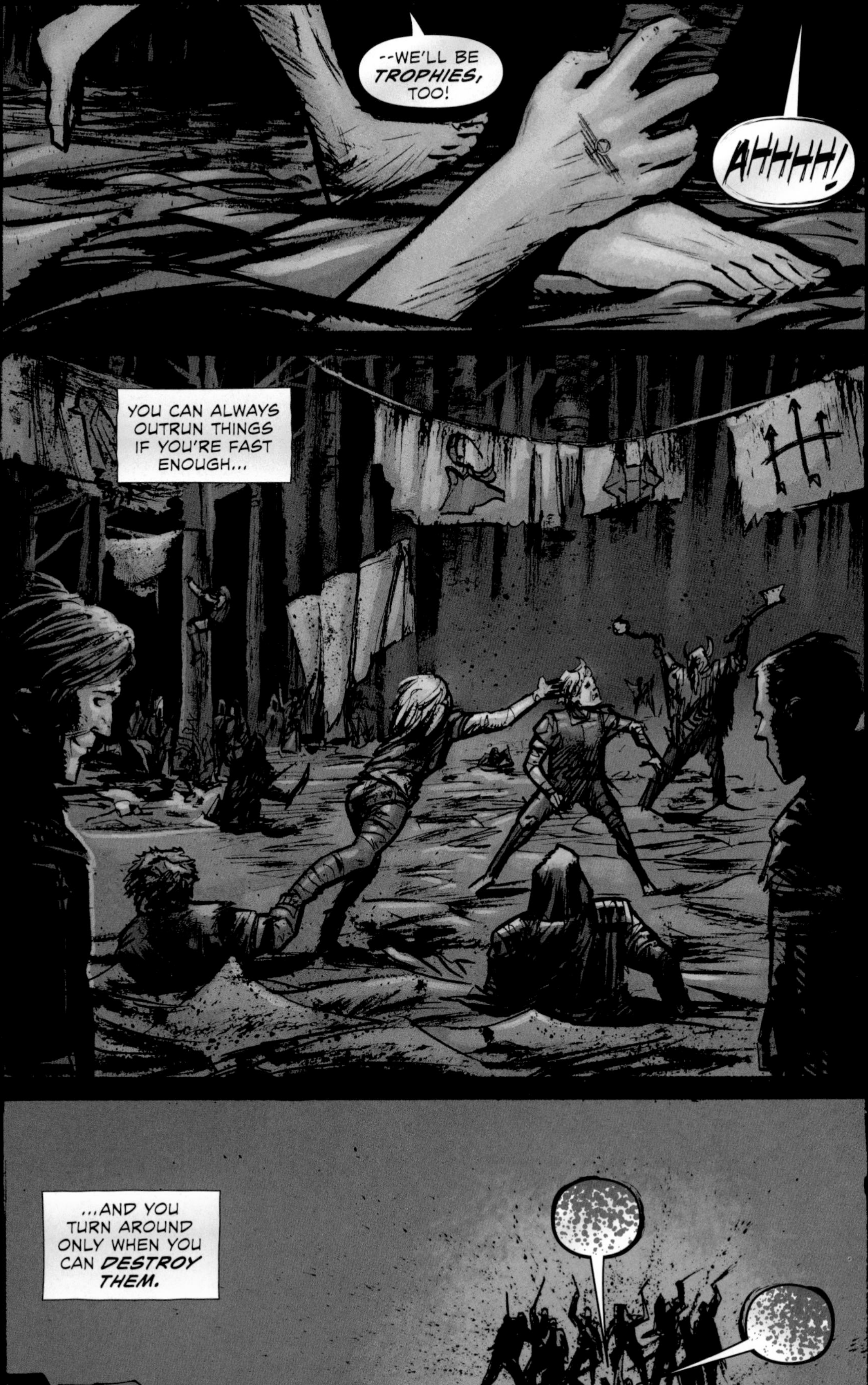
--WE'LL BE TROPHIES, TOO!
AHHHH!
YOU CAN ALWAYS OUTRUN THINGS IF YOU'RE FAST ENOUGH...
...AND YOU TURN AROUND ONLY WHEN YOU CAN DESTROY THEM.

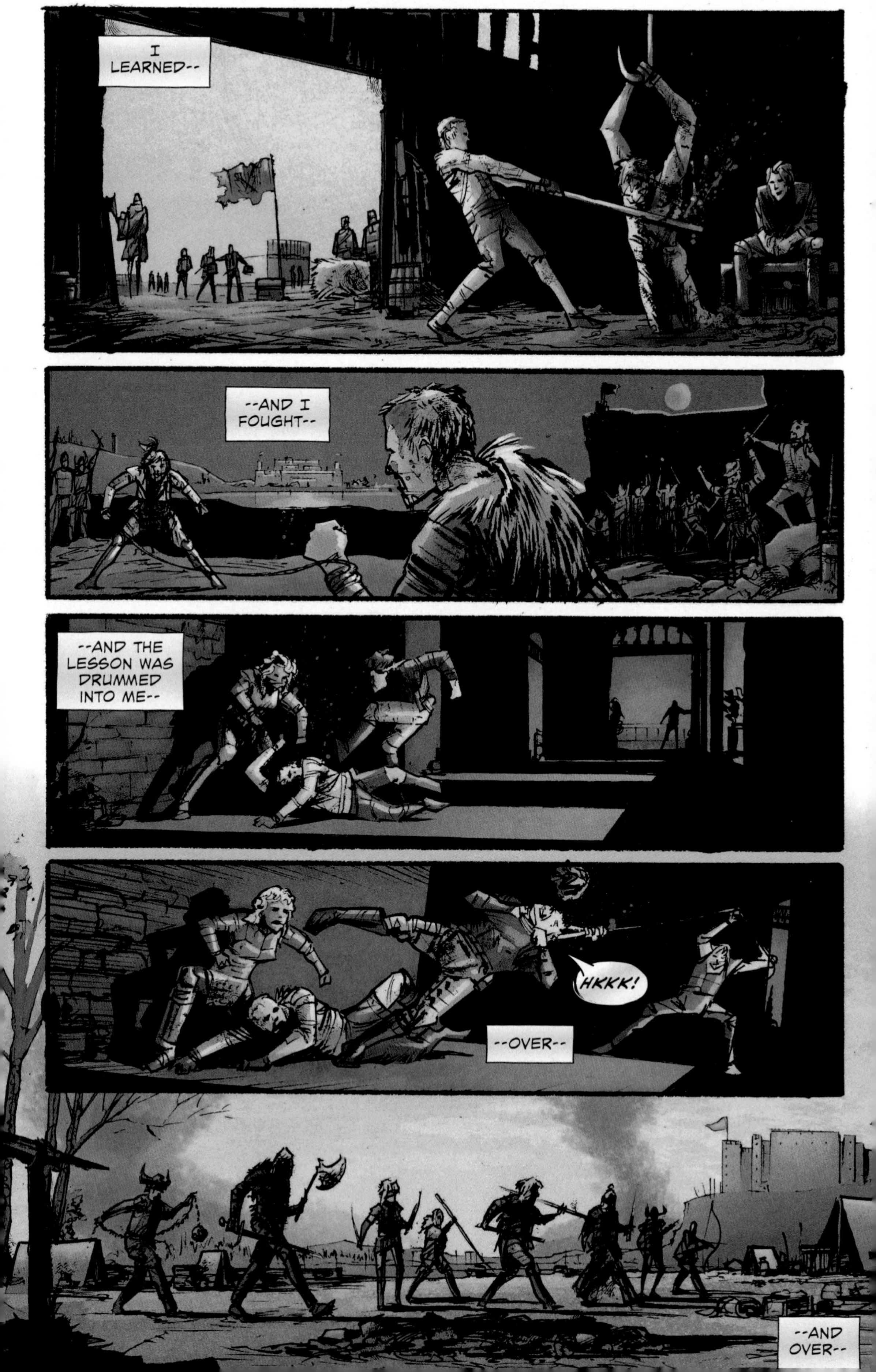
I LEARNED--
--AND I FOUGHT--
--AND THE LESSON WAS DRUMMED INTO ME--
HKKK!
--OVER--
--AND OVER--

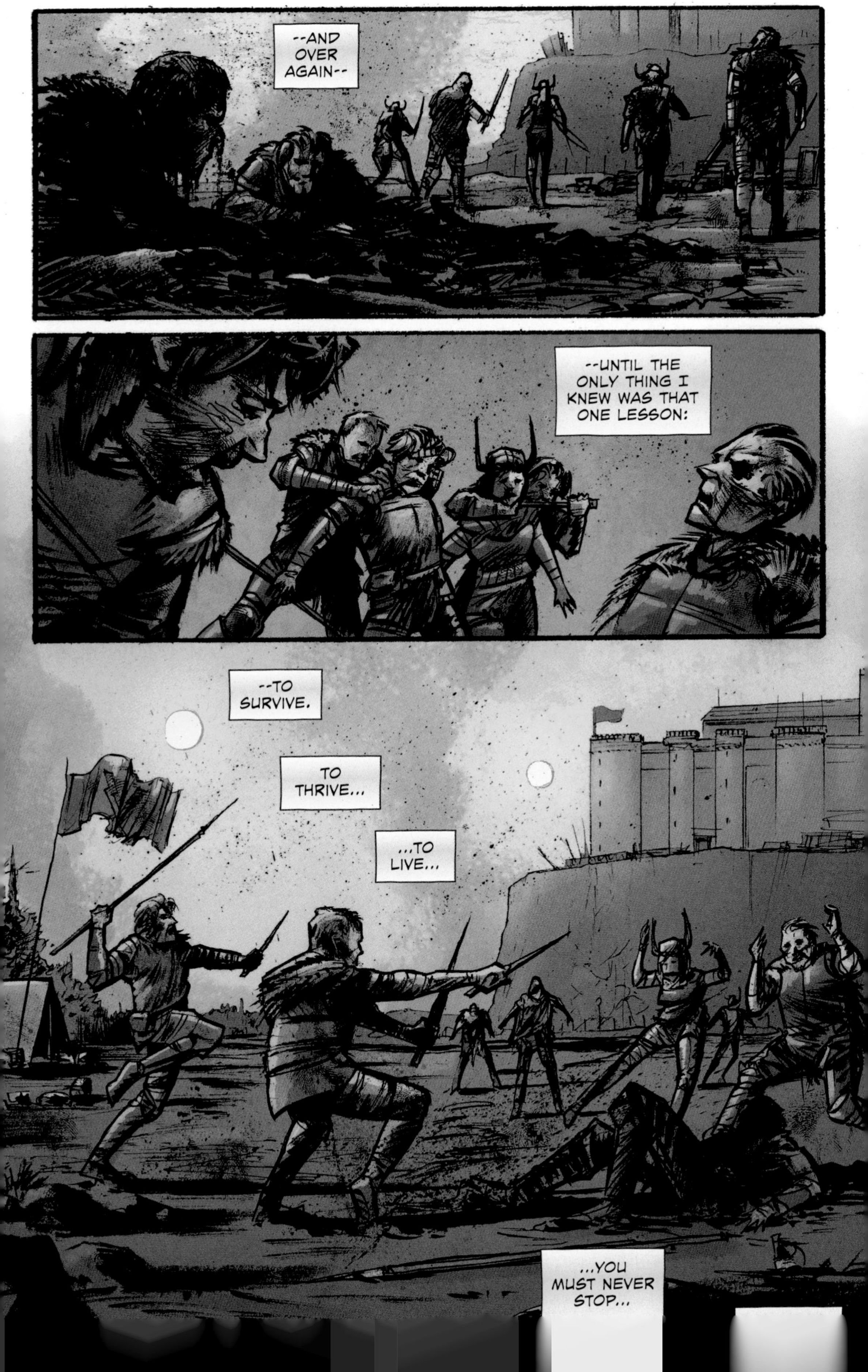
--AND OVER AGAIN--
--UNTIL THE ONLY THING I KNEW WAS THAT ONE LESSON:
--TO SURVIVE.
TO THRIVE...
...TO LIVE...
...YOU MUST NEVER STOP...

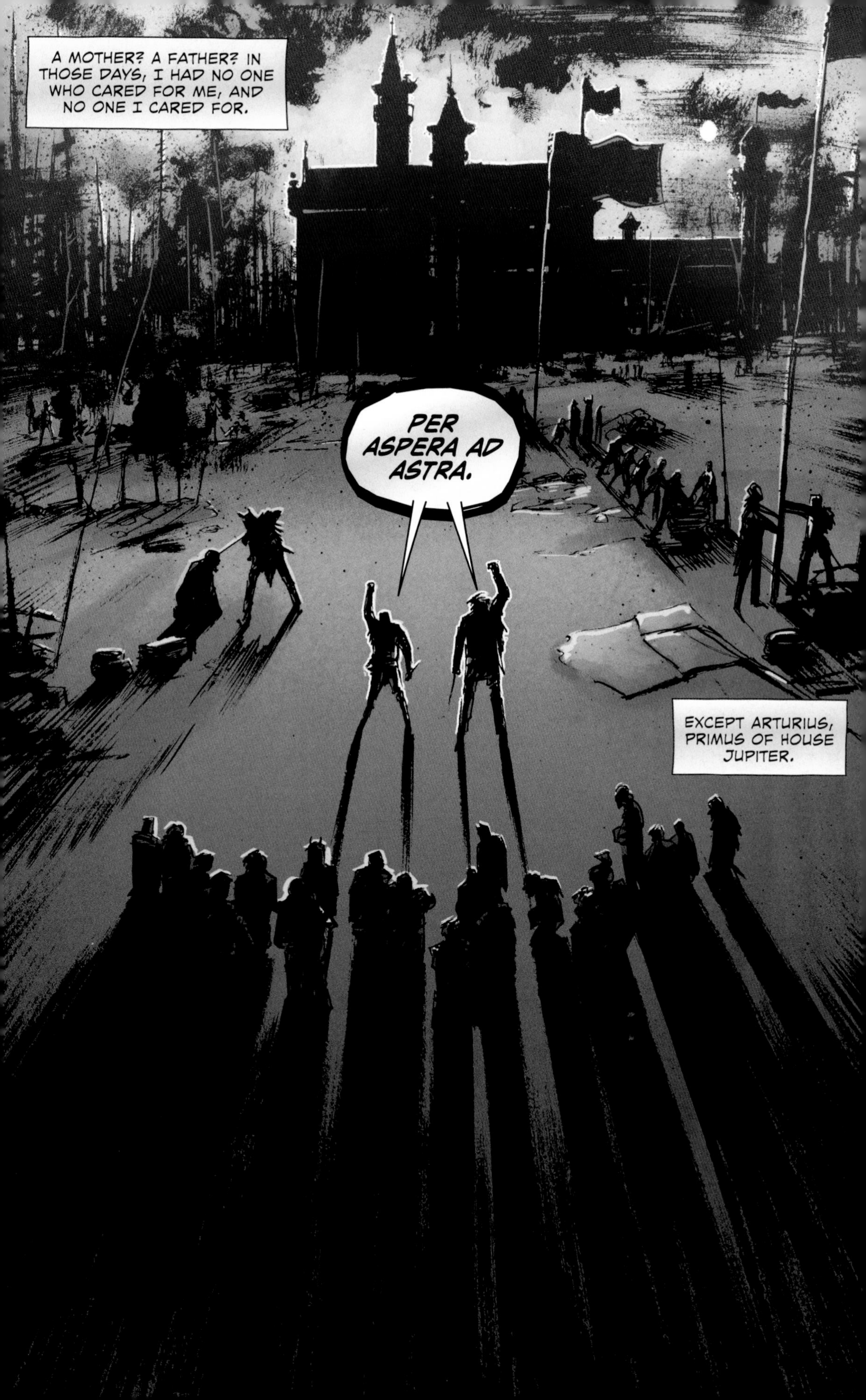
A MOTHER? A FATHER? IN THOSE DAYS, I HAD NO ONE WHO CARED FOR ME, AND NO ONE I CARED FOR.
PER ASPERA AD ASTRA.
EXCEPT ARTURIUS, PRIMUS OF HOUSE JUPITER.

DO YOU HAVE MY BACK, FITCHNER?

ALWAYS.

ARTURIUS AU VARDAN, FOR *OUTSTANDING PERFORMANCE* I AWARD YOU OUR HIGHEST HONOR-- *THE PEERLESS SCAR.*

BE PROUD--

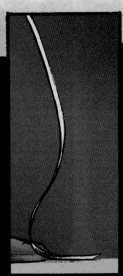

WHI-CHING

--FOR YOU TOWER ABOVE YOUR FELLOWS.

SWICK

MMF.

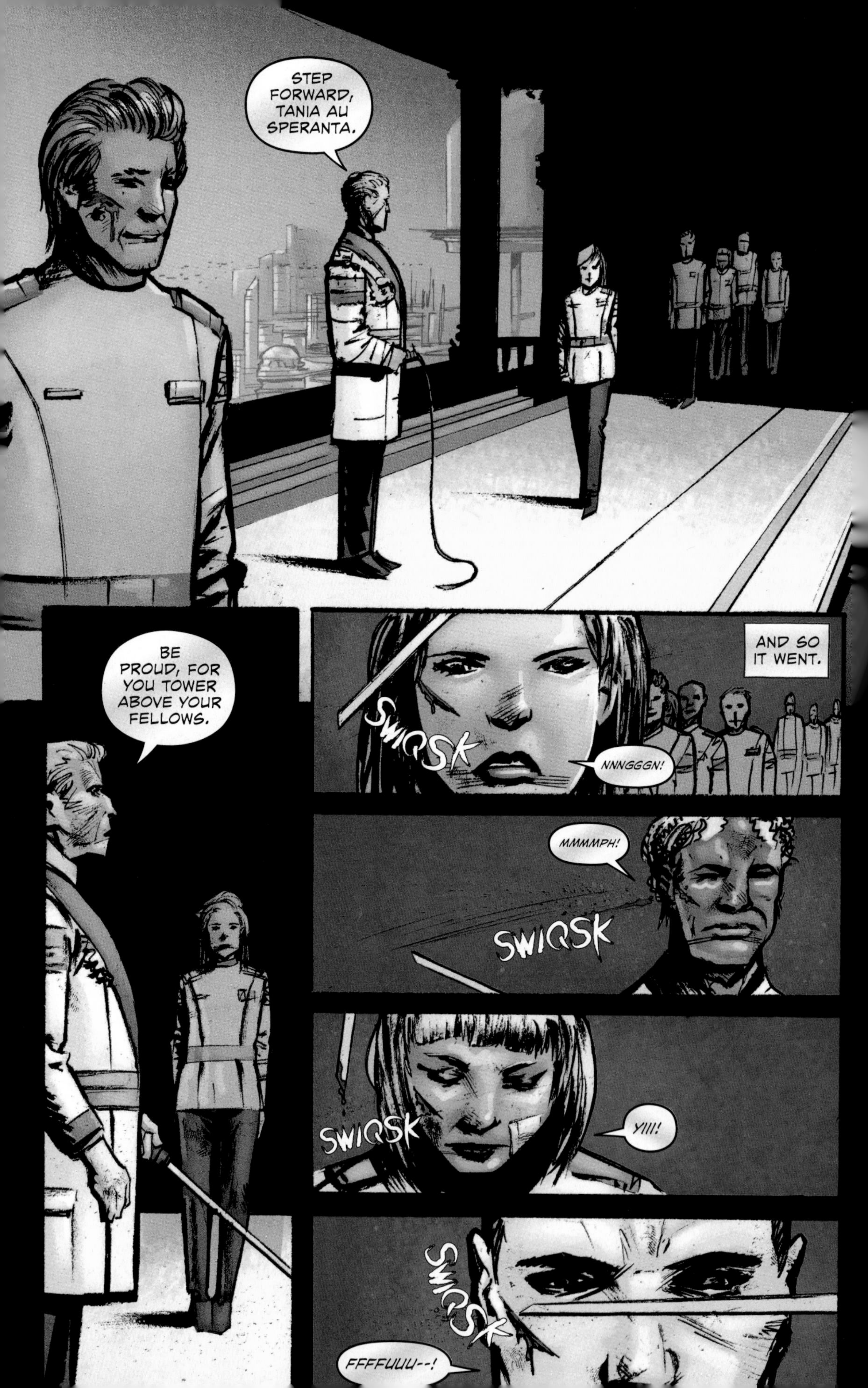
STEP FORWARD, TANIA AU SPERANTA.
BE PROUD, FOR YOU TOWER ABOVE YOUR FELLOWS.
AND SO IT WENT.
SWIQSK
NNNGGGN!
MMMMPH!
SWIQSK
SWIQSK
YIII!
SWIQSK
FFFFUUU--!

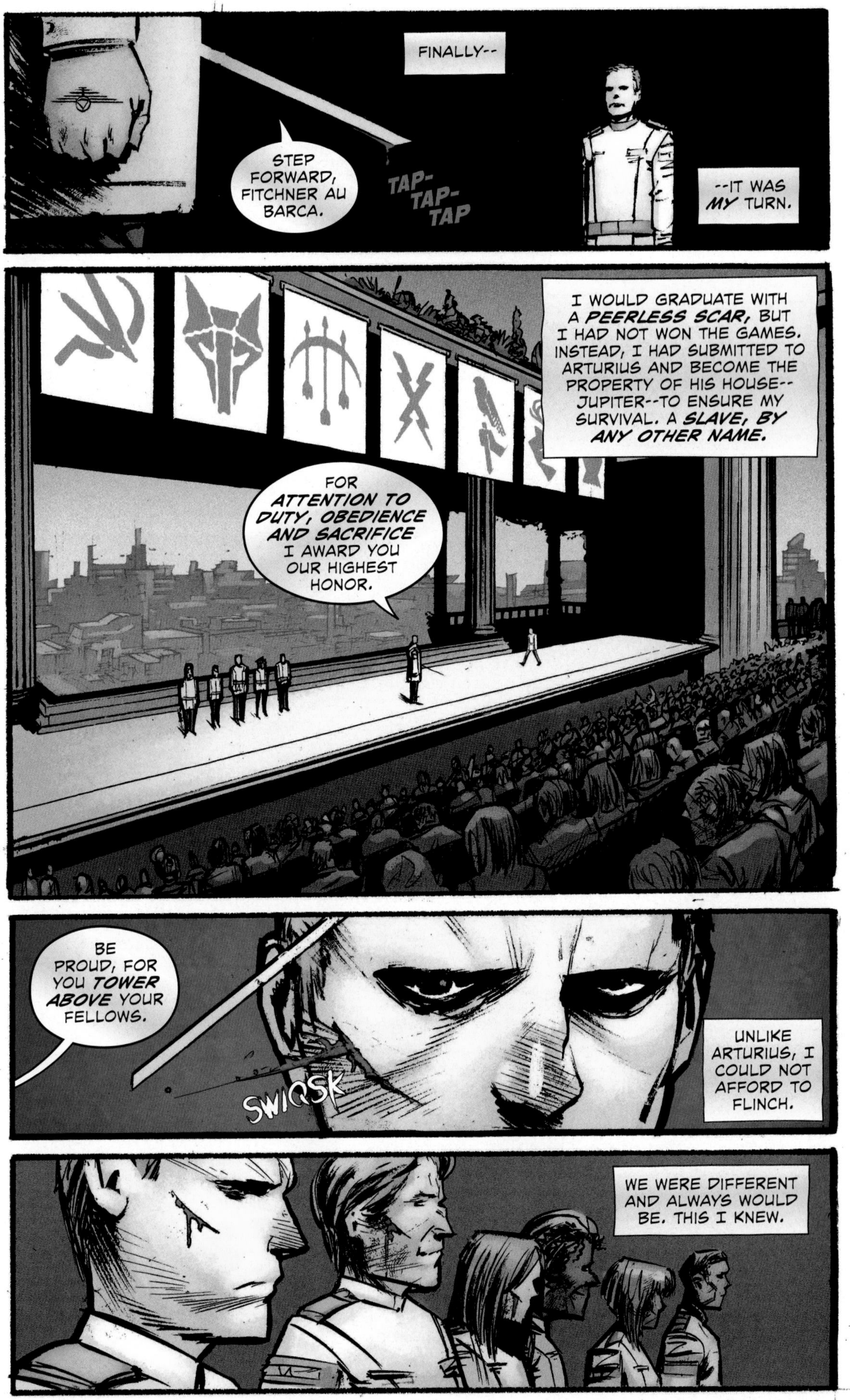

STEP FORWARD, FITCHNER AU BARCA.
TAP-TAP-TAP
FINALLY--
--IT WAS *MY* TURN.
I WOULD GRADUATE WITH A ***PEERLESS SCAR,*** BUT I HAD NOT WON THE GAMES. INSTEAD, I HAD SUBMITTED TO ARTURIUS AND BECOME THE PROPERTY OF HIS HOUSE--JUPITER--TO ENSURE MY SURVIVAL. A ***SLAVE, BY ANY OTHER NAME.***
FOR ***ATTENTION TO DUTY, OBEDIENCE AND SACRIFICE*** I AWARD YOU OUR HIGHEST HONOR.
BE PROUD, FOR YOU ***TOWER ABOVE*** YOUR FELLOWS.
SWIQSK
UNLIKE ARTURIUS, I COULD NOT AFFORD TO FLINCH.
WE WERE DIFFERENT AND ALWAYS WOULD BE. THIS I KNEW.

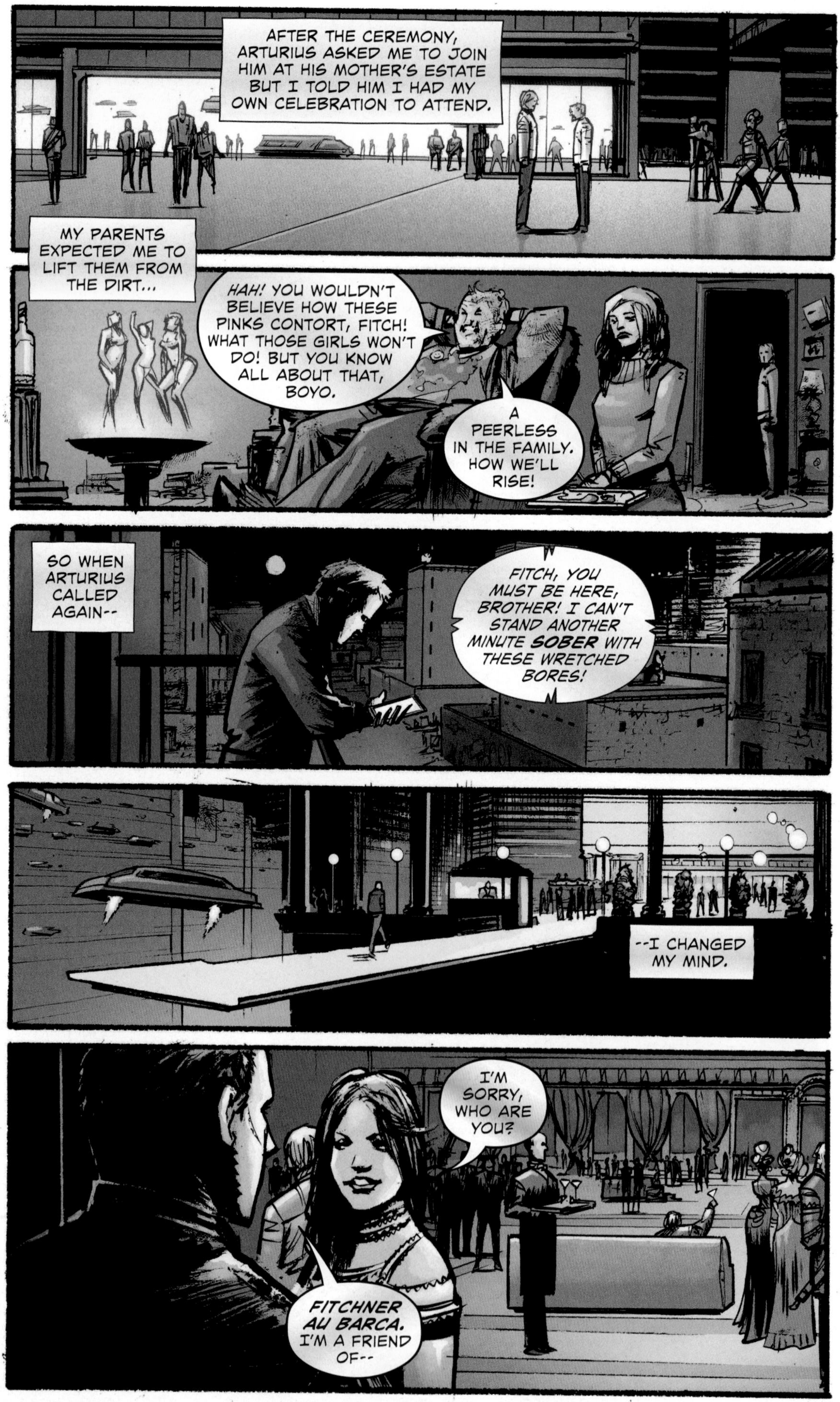
AFTER THE CEREMONY, ARTURIUS ASKED ME TO JOIN HIM AT HIS MOTHER'S ESTATE BUT I TOLD HIM I HAD MY OWN CELEBRATION TO ATTEND.
MY PARENTS EXPECTED ME TO LIFT THEM FROM THE DIRT...
HAH! YOU WOULDN'T BELIEVE HOW THESE PINKS CONTORT, FITCH! WHAT THOSE GIRLS WON'T DO! BUT YOU KNOW ALL ABOUT THAT, BOYO.
A PEERLESS IN THE FAMILY. HOW WE'LL RISE!
SO WHEN ARTURIUS CALLED AGAIN--
FITCH, YOU MUST BE HERE, BROTHER! I CAN'T STAND ANOTHER MINUTE ***SOBER*** *WITH THESE WRETCHED BORES!*
--I CHANGED MY MIND.
I'M SORRY, WHO ARE YOU?
FITCHNER AU BARCA. I'M A FRIEND OF--

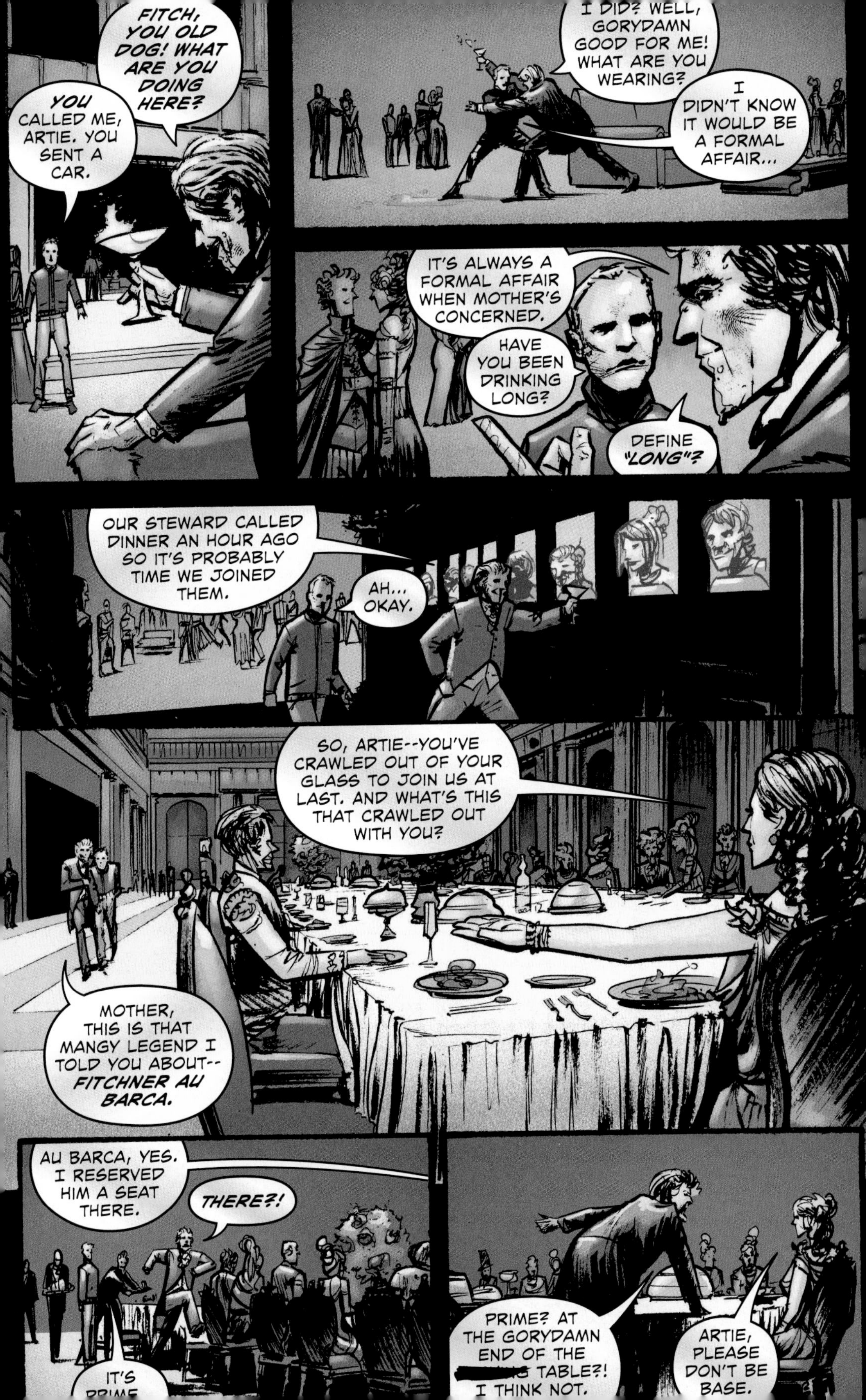
FITCH, YOU OLD DOG! WHAT ARE YOU DOING HERE?
YOU CALLED ME, ARTIE. YOU SENT A CAR.
I DID? WELL, GORYDAMN GOOD FOR ME! WHAT ARE YOU WEARING?
I DIDN'T KNOW IT WOULD BE A FORMAL AFFAIR...
IT'S ALWAYS A FORMAL AFFAIR WHEN MOTHER'S CONCERNED.
HAVE YOU BEEN DRINKING LONG?
DEFINE "LONG"?
OUR STEWARD CALLED DINNER AN HOUR AGO SO IT'S PROBABLY TIME WE JOINED THEM.
AH... OKAY.
SO, ARTIE--YOU'VE CRAWLED OUT OF YOUR GLASS TO JOIN US AT LAST. AND WHAT'S THIS THAT CRAWLED OUT WITH YOU?
MOTHER, THIS IS THAT MANGY LEGEND I TOLD YOU ABOUT--FITCHNER AU BARCA.
AU BARCA, YES. I RESERVED HIM A SEAT THERE.
THERE?!
IT'S
PRIME? AT THE GORYDAMN END OF THE [redacted] TABLE?! I THINK NOT.
ARTIE, PLEASE DON'T BE BASE.

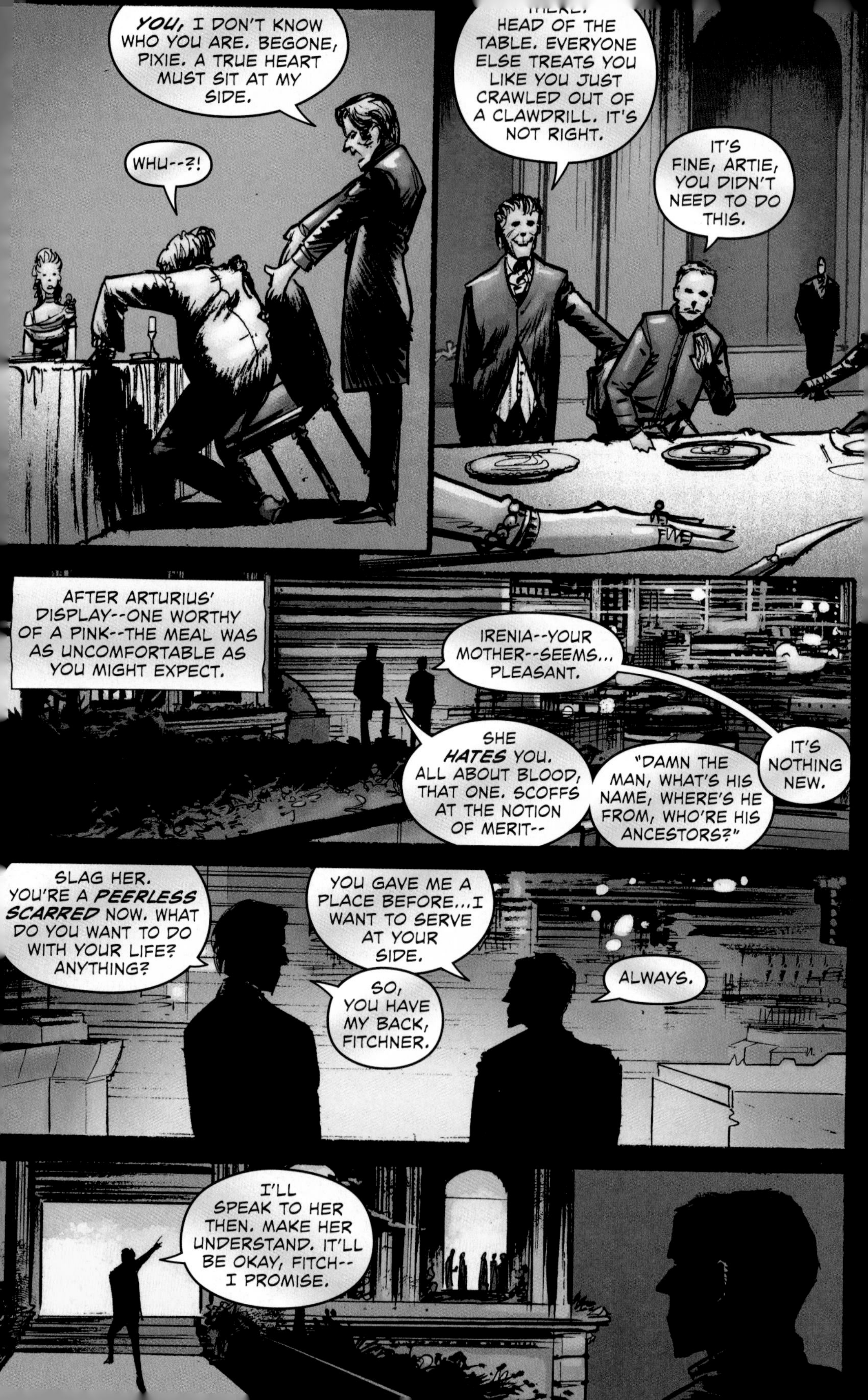
YOU, I DON'T KNOW WHO YOU ARE. BEGONE, PIXIE. A TRUE HEART MUST SIT AT MY SIDE.
WHU--?!
HEAD OF THE TABLE. EVERYONE ELSE TREATS YOU LIKE YOU JUST CRAWLED OUT OF A CLAWDRILL. IT'S NOT RIGHT.
IT'S FINE, ARTIE, YOU DIDN'T NEED TO DO THIS.
AFTER ARTURIUS' DISPLAY--ONE WORTHY OF A PINK--THE MEAL WAS AS UNCOMFORTABLE AS YOU MIGHT EXPECT.
IRENIA--YOUR MOTHER--SEEMS... PLEASANT.
IT'S NOTHING NEW.
SHE HATES YOU. ALL ABOUT BLOOD, THAT ONE. SCOFFS AT THE NOTION OF MERIT--
"DAMN THE MAN, WHAT'S HIS NAME, WHERE'S HE FROM, WHO'RE HIS ANCESTORS?"
SLAG HER. YOU'RE A PEERLESS SCARRED NOW. WHAT DO YOU WANT TO DO WITH YOUR LIFE? ANYTHING?
YOU GAVE ME A PLACE BEFORE...I WANT TO SERVE AT YOUR SIDE.
SO, YOU HAVE MY BACK, FITCHNER.
ALWAYS.
I'LL SPEAK TO HER THEN. MAKE HER UNDERSTAND. IT'LL BE OKAY, FITCH-- I PROMISE.

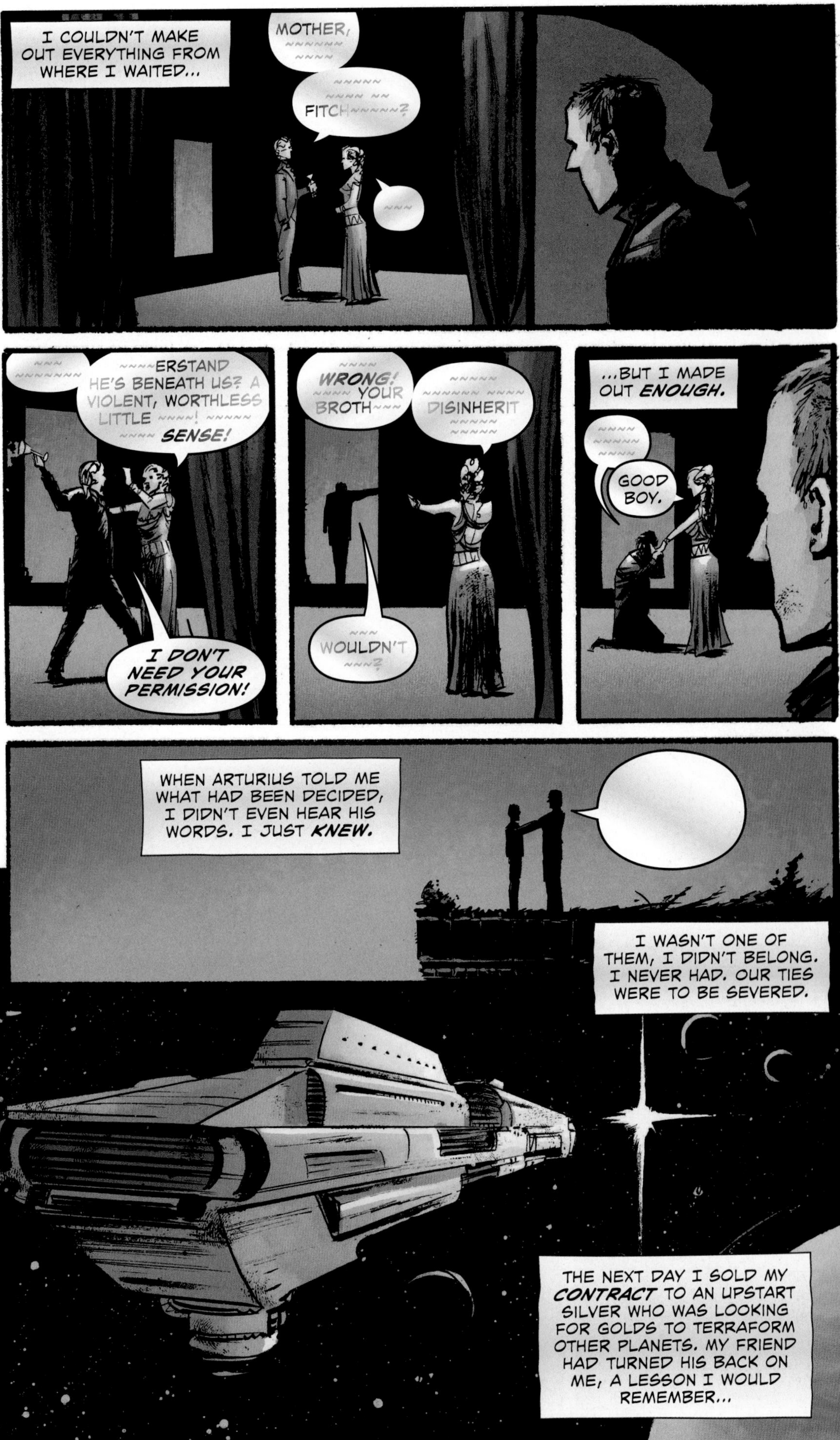
I COULDN'T MAKE OUT EVERYTHING FROM WHERE I WAITED...
MOTHER, ~~~~~~ ~~~~
~~~~~ ~~~~ ~~ FITCH~~~~~?
~~~
~~~ ~~~~~~~
~~~~ERSTAND HE'S BENEATH US? A VIOLENT, WORTHLESS LITTLE ~~~~! ~~~~~ ~~~~ SENSE!
I DON'T NEED YOUR PERMISSION!
~~~~ WRONG! ~~~~ YOUR BROTH~~~
~~~~~ ~~~~~~ ~~~~ DISINHERIT ~~~~~ ~~~~~
~~~ WOULDN'T ~~~?
...BUT I MADE OUT ENOUGH.
~~~~ ~~~~~ ~~~~
GOOD BOY.
WHEN ARTURIUS TOLD ME WHAT HAD BEEN DECIDED, I DIDN'T EVEN HEAR HIS WORDS. I JUST KNEW.
I WASN'T ONE OF THEM, I DIDN'T BELONG. I NEVER HAD. OUR TIES WERE TO BE SEVERED.
THE NEXT DAY I SOLD MY CONTRACT TO AN UPSTART SILVER WHO WAS LOOKING FOR GOLDS TO TERRAFORM OTHER PLANETS. MY FRIEND HAD TURNED HIS BACK ON ME, A LESSON I WOULD REMEMBER...

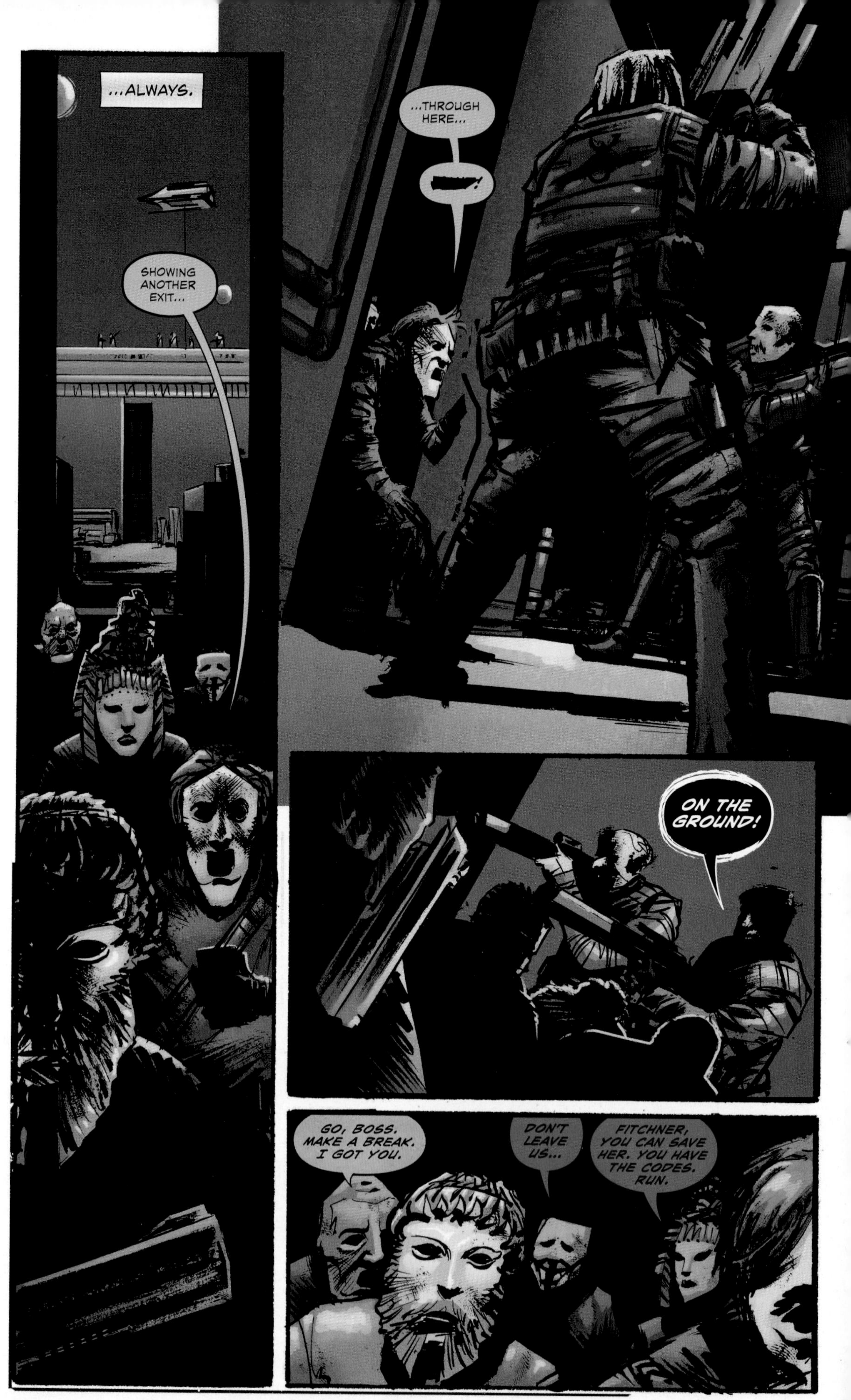
...ALWAYS.
SHOWING ANOTHER EXIT...
...THROUGH HERE...
ON THE GROUND!
GO, BOSS. MAKE A BREAK. I GOT YOU.
DON'T LEAVE US...
FITCHNER, YOU CAN SAVE HER. YOU HAVE THE CODES. RUN.

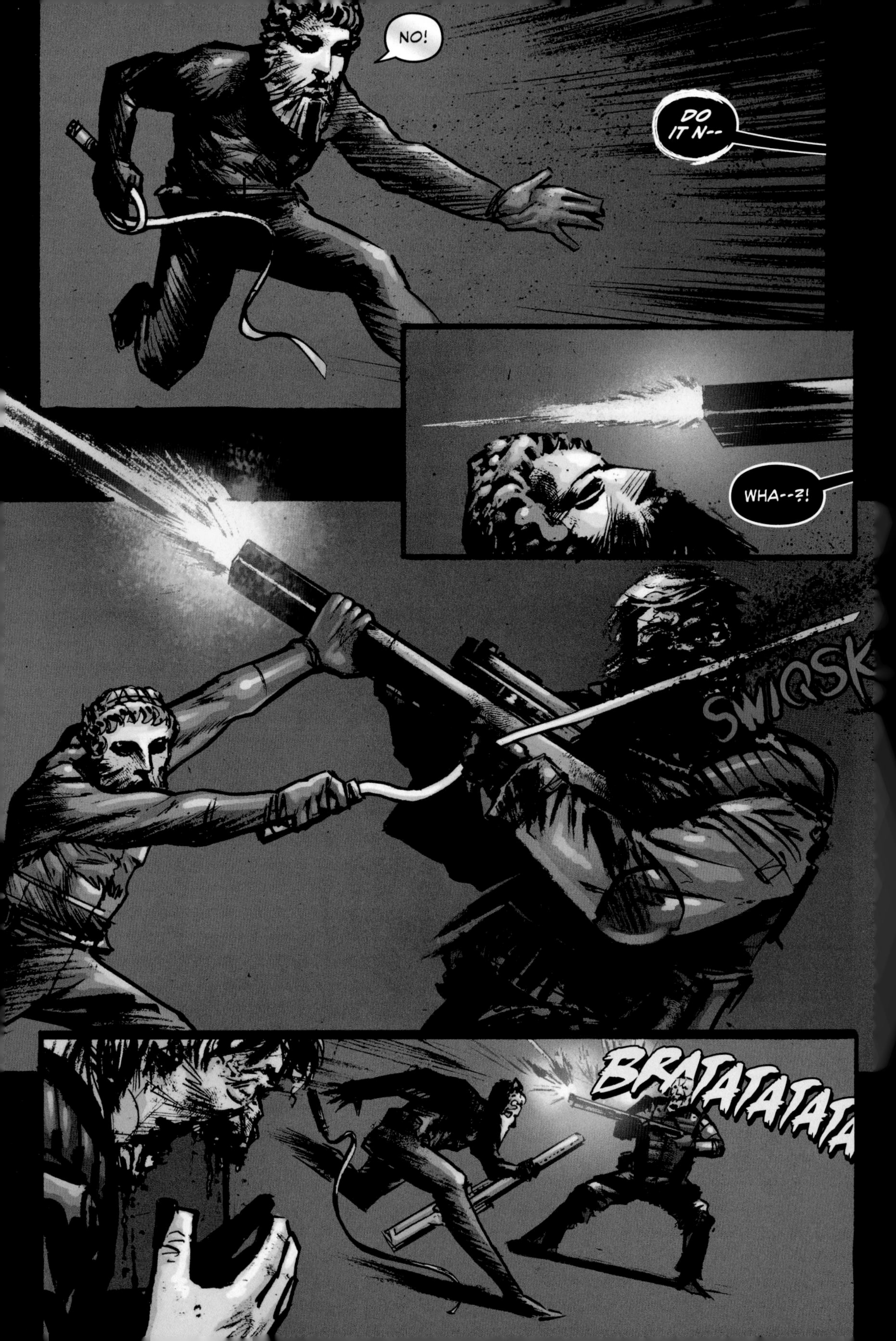
NO!
DO IT N--
WHA--?!
SWIQSK
BRATATATATA

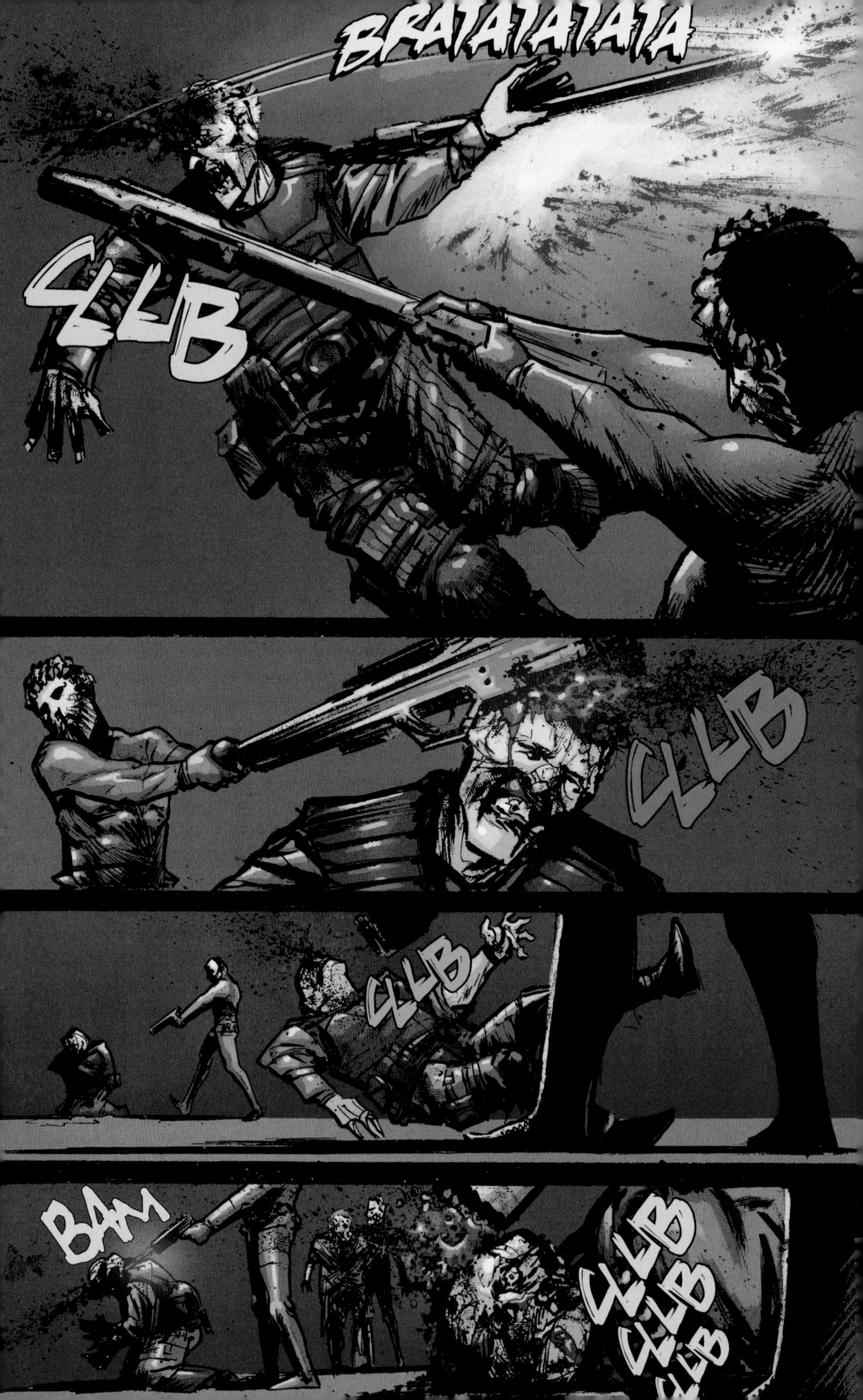
BRATATATATA
CLUB
CLUB
CLUB
BAM
CLUB
CLUB
CLUB
CLUB

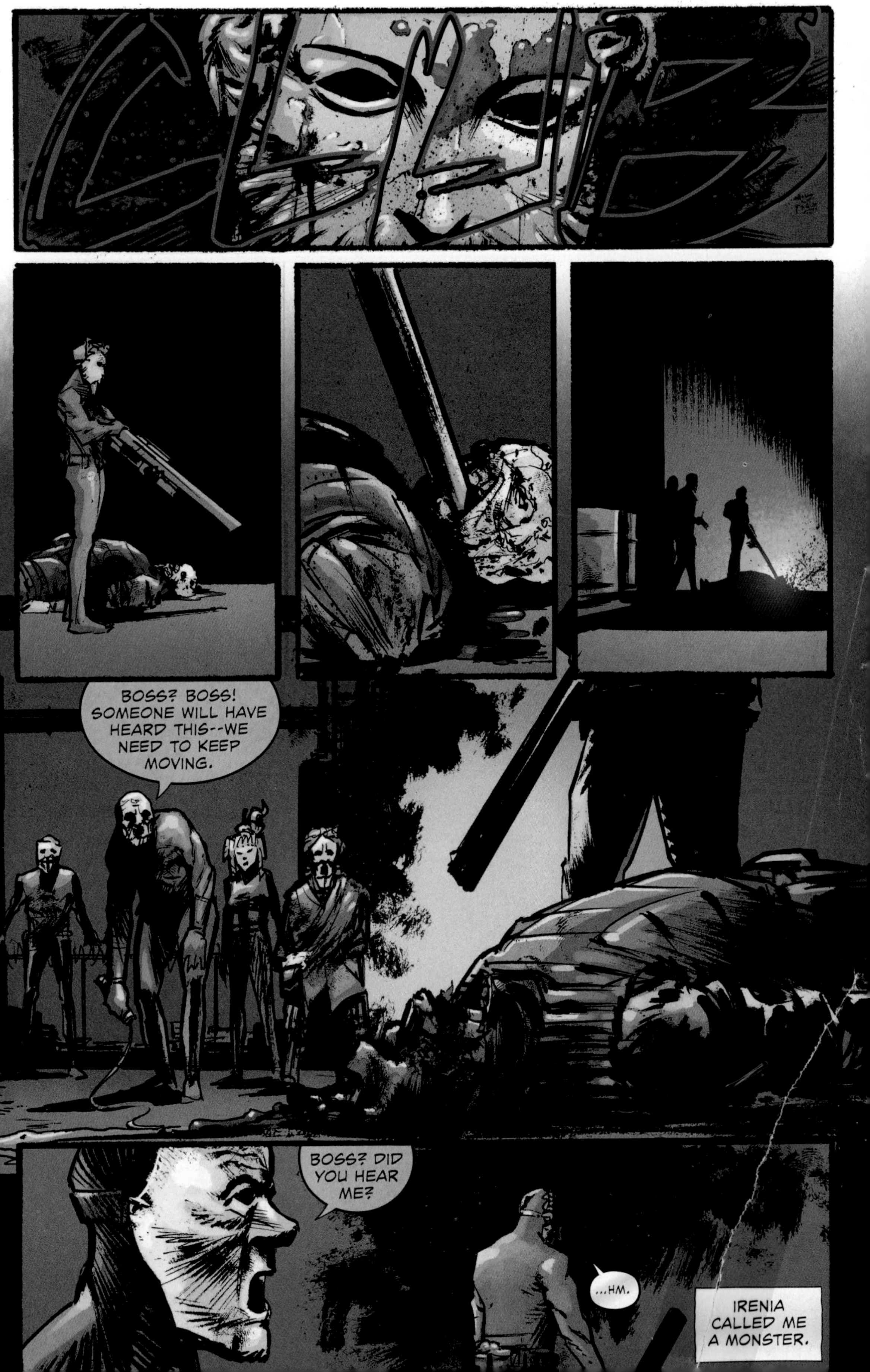
BOSS? BOSS! SOMEONE WILL HAVE HEARD THIS--WE NEED TO KEEP MOVING.
BOSS? DID YOU HEAR ME?
...HM.
IRENIA CALLED ME A MONSTER.

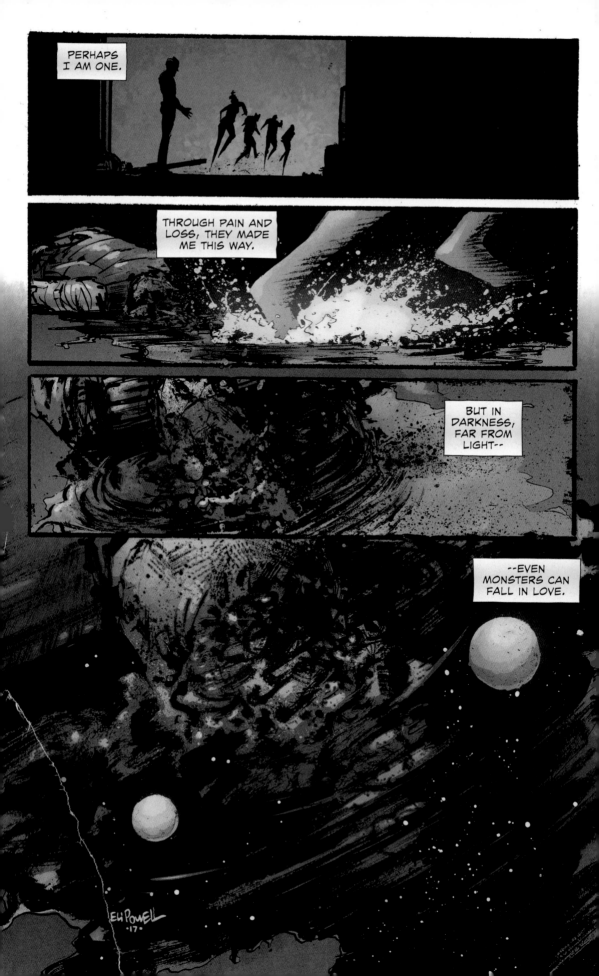

PERHAPS I AM ONE.

THROUGH PAIN AND LOSS, THEY MADE ME THIS WAY.

BUT IN DARKNESS, FAR FROM LIGHT--

--EVEN MONSTERS CAN FALL IN LOVE.

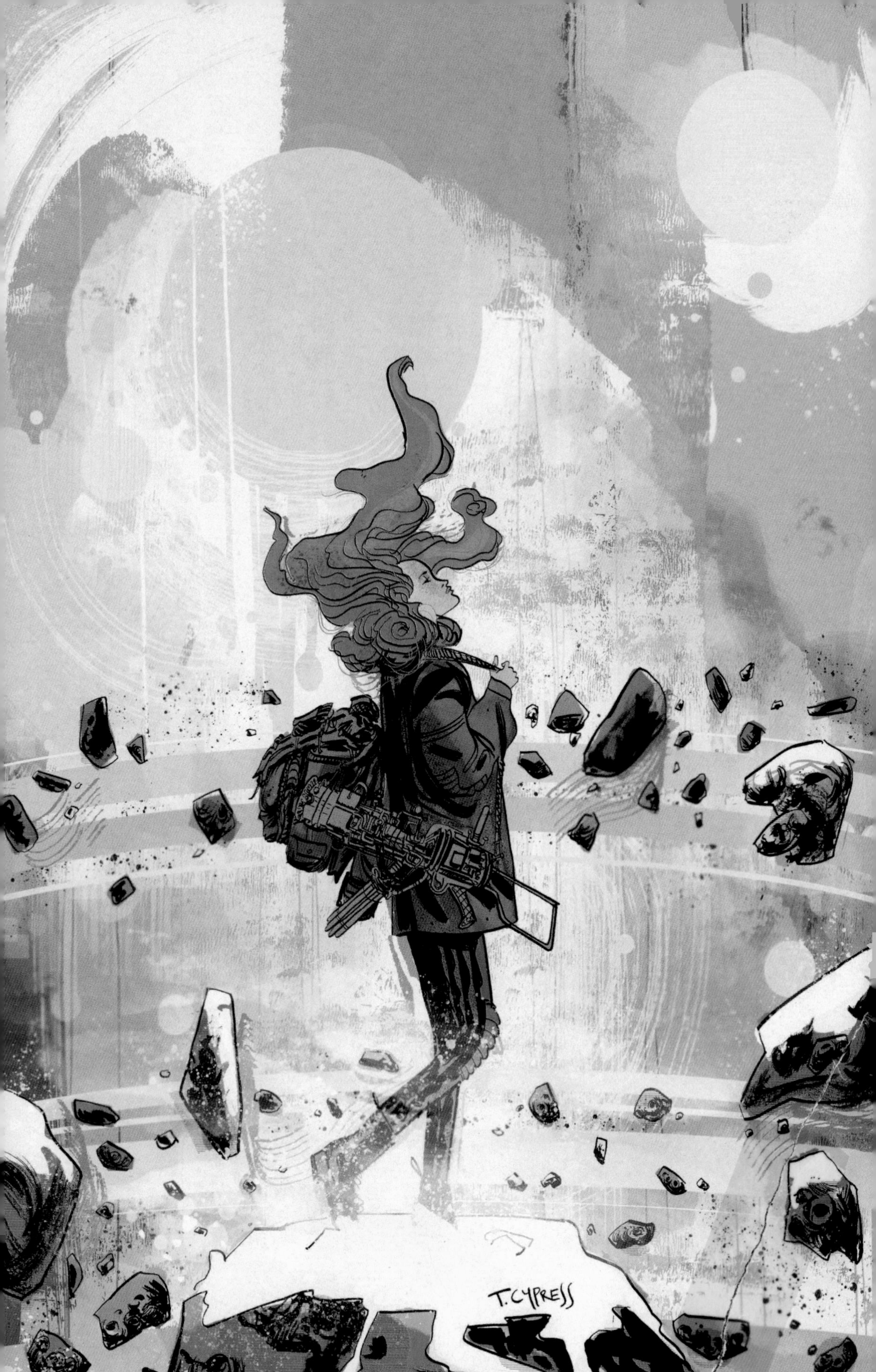
T. CYPRESS

ISSUE THREE | COVER ART BY TOBY CYPRESS

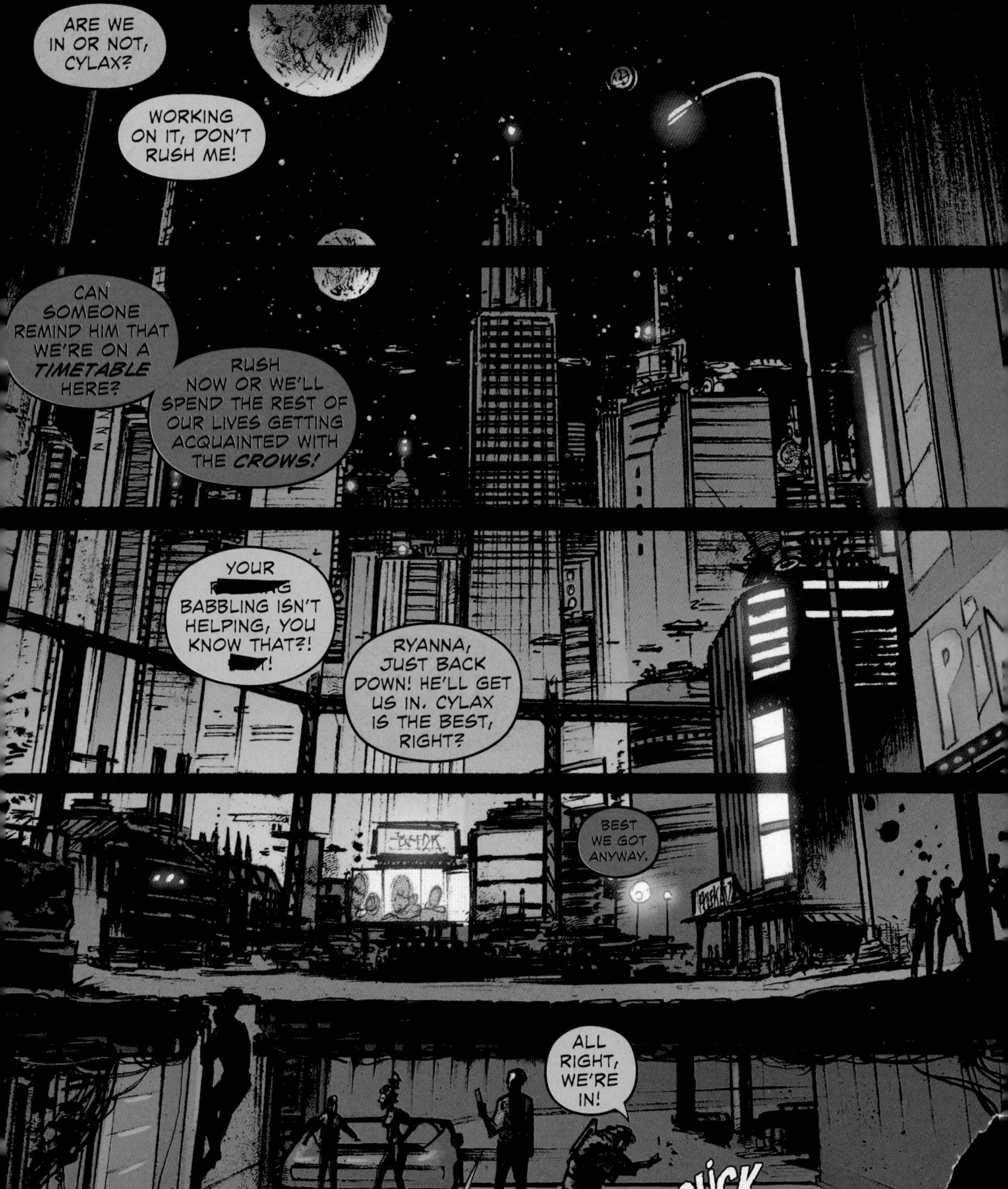
ARE WE IN OR NOT, CYLAX?
WORKING ON IT, DON'T RUSH ME!
CAN SOMEONE REMIND HIM THAT WE'RE ON A *TIMETABLE* HERE?
RUSH NOW OR WE'LL SPEND THE REST OF OUR LIVES GETTING ACQUAINTED WITH THE *CROWS!*
YOUR [redacted] BABBLING ISN'T HELPING, YOU KNOW THAT?! [redacted]!
RYANNA, JUST BACK DOWN! HE'LL GET US IN. CYLAX IS THE BEST, RIGHT?
BEST WE GOT ANYWAY.
ALL RIGHT, WE'RE IN!
STAY ALERT--
CLICK

CHAPTER 3: DROWNING ON TRITON

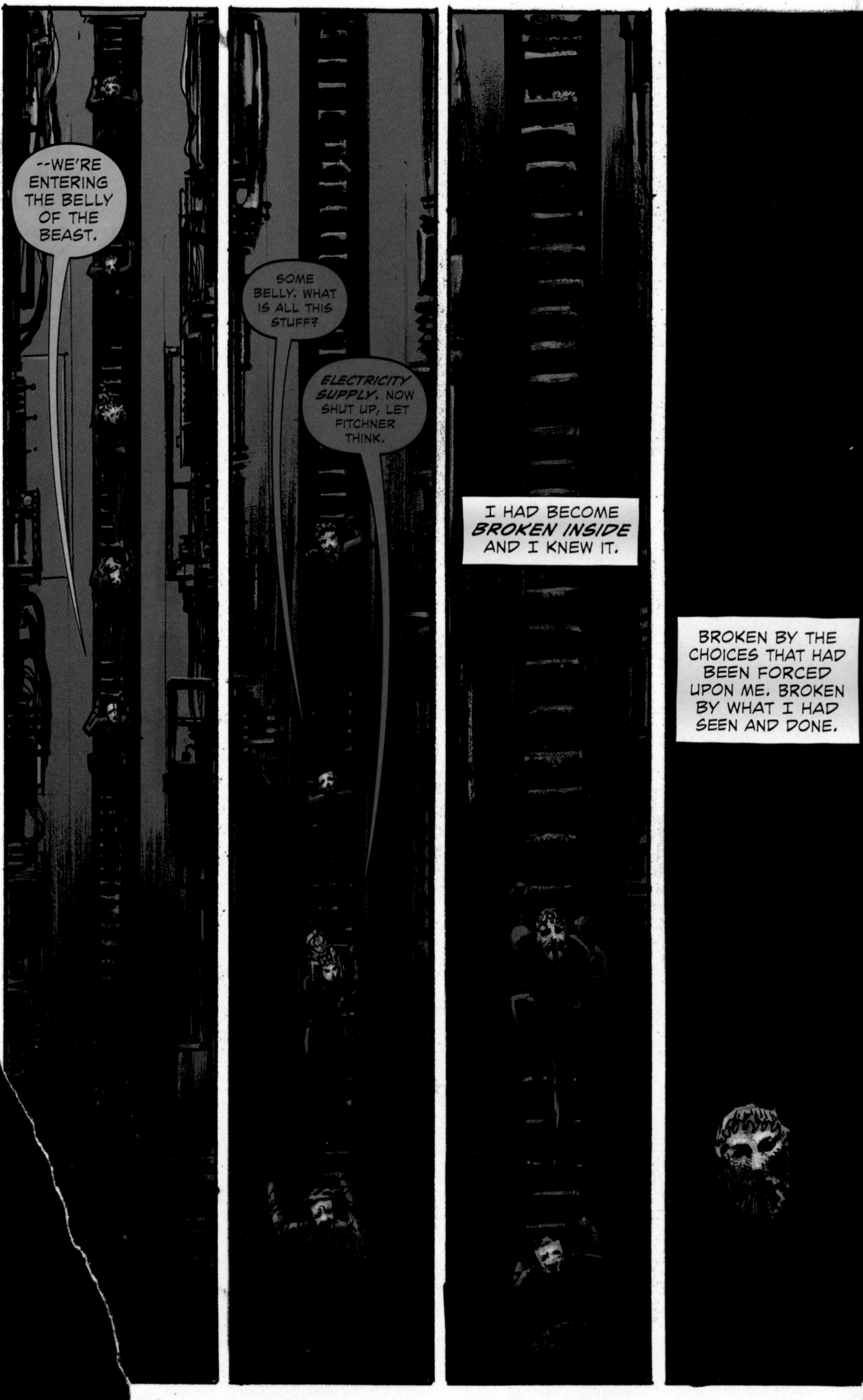
--WE'RE ENTERING THE BELLY OF THE BEAST.
SOME BELLY. WHAT IS ALL THIS STUFF?
ELECTRICITY SUPPLY. NOW SHUT UP, LET FITCHNER THINK.
I HAD BECOME BROKEN INSIDE AND I KNEW IT.
BROKEN BY THE CHOICES THAT HAD BEEN FORCED UPON ME. BROKEN BY WHAT I HAD SEEN AND DONE.

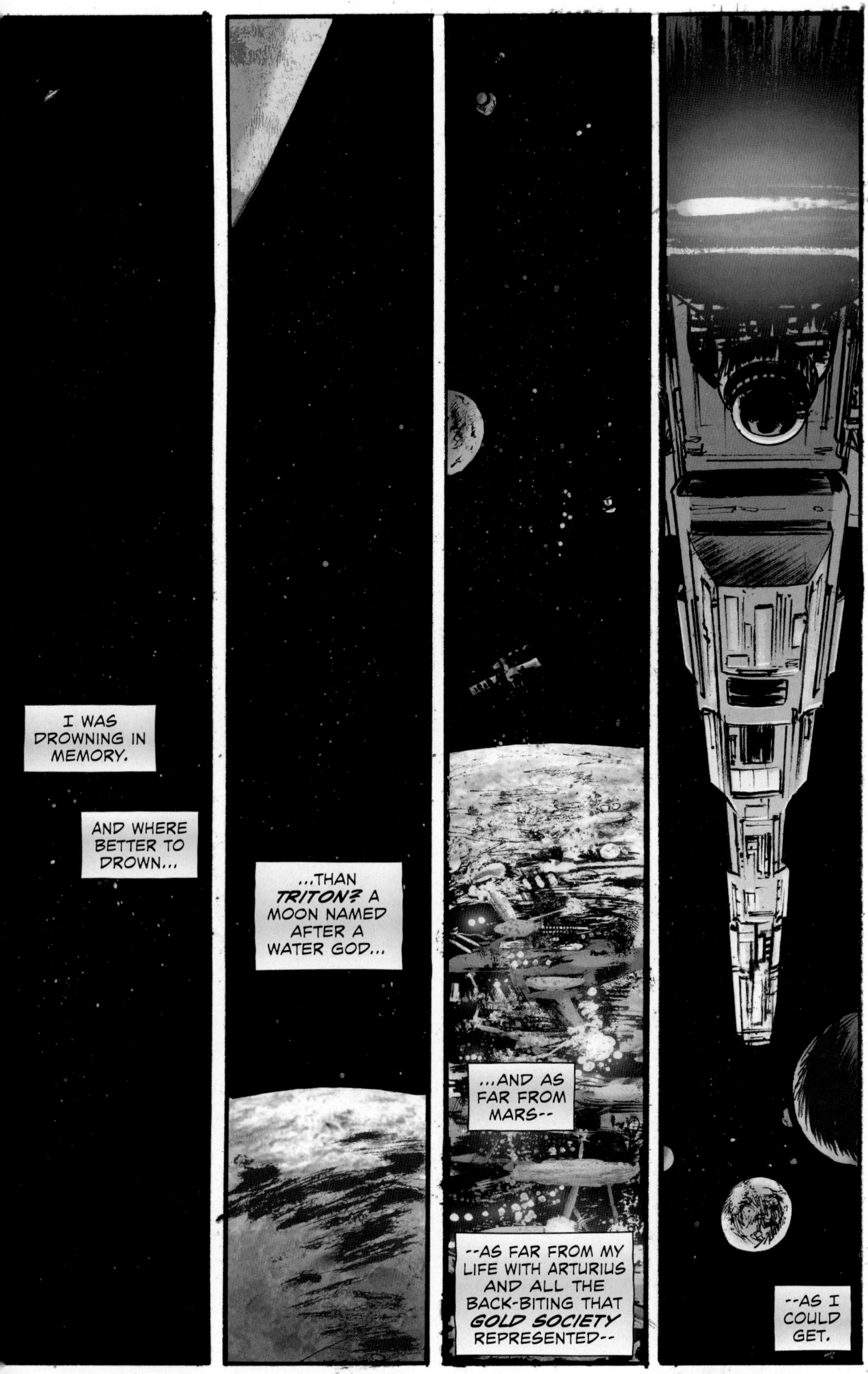
I WAS DROWNING IN MEMORY.
AND WHERE BETTER TO DROWN...
...THAN *TRITON?* A MOON NAMED AFTER A WATER GOD...
...AND AS FAR FROM MARS--
--AS FAR FROM MY LIFE WITH ARTURIUS AND ALL THE BACK-BITING THAT *GOLD SOCIETY* REPRESENTED--
--AS I COULD GET.

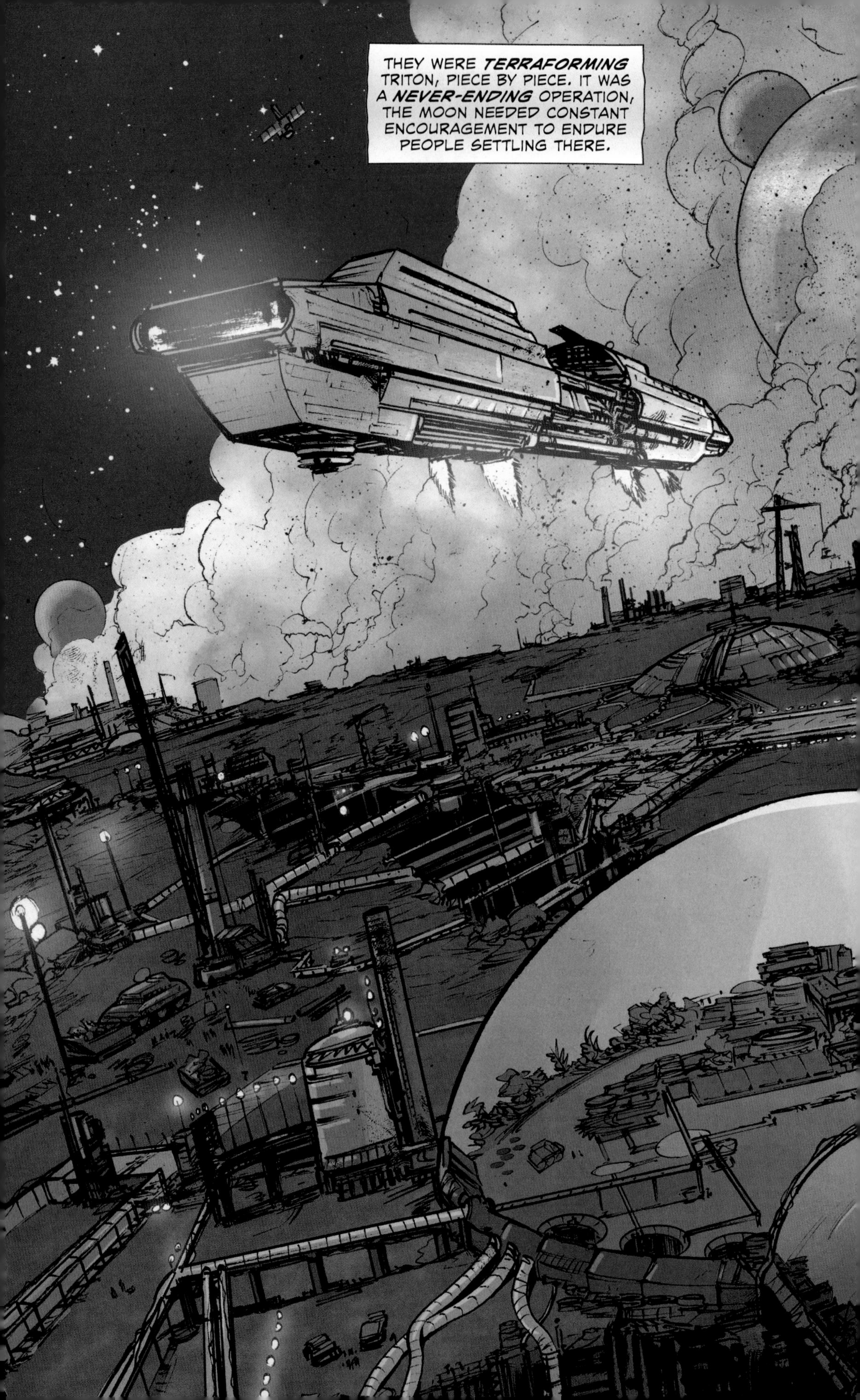
THEY WERE *TERRAFORMING* TRITON, PIECE BY PIECE. IT WAS A *NEVER-ENDING* OPERATION, THE MOON NEEDED CONSTANT ENCOURAGEMENT TO ENDURE PEOPLE SETTLING THERE.

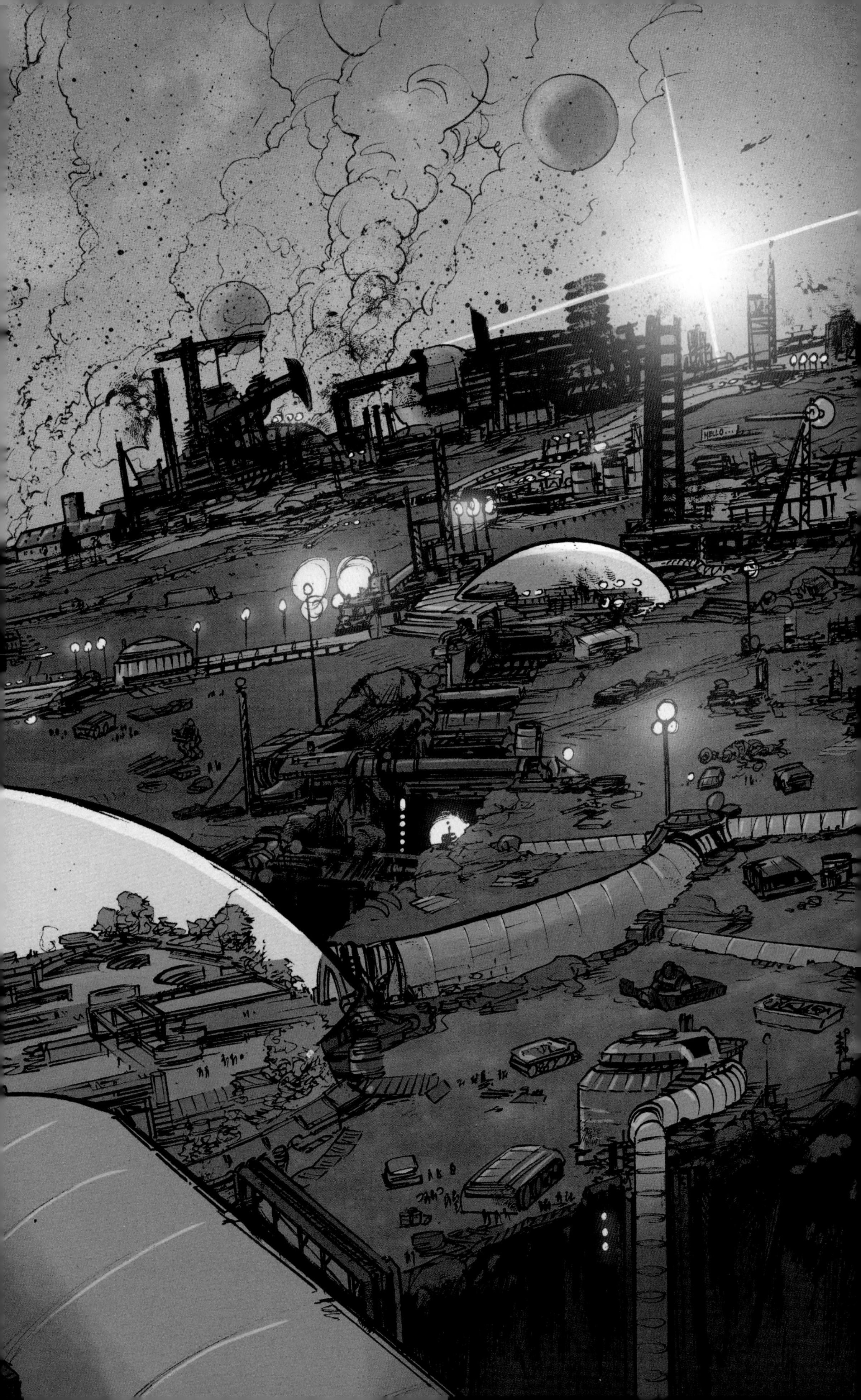
HELLO...

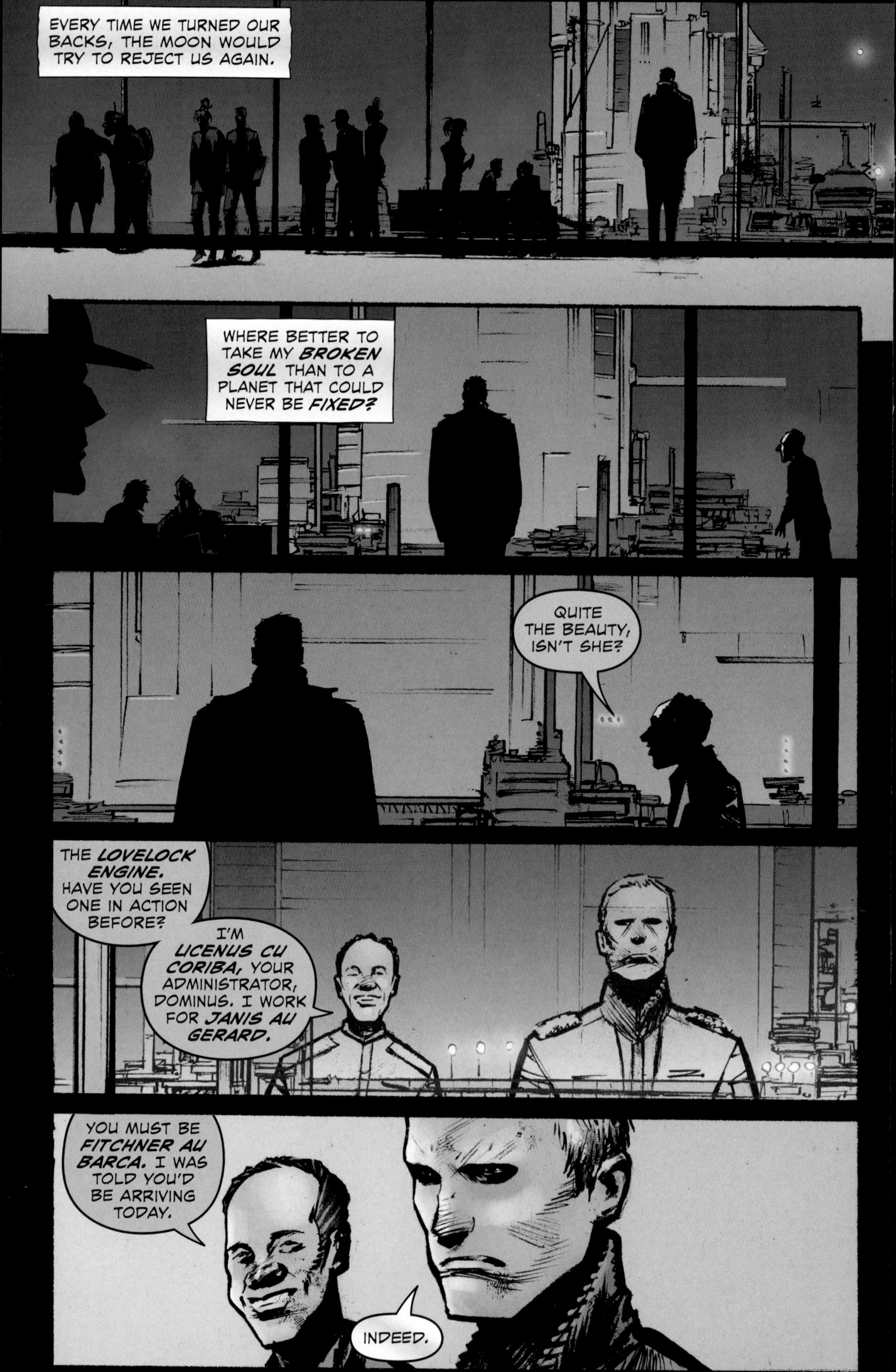
EVERY TIME WE TURNED OUR BACKS, THE MOON WOULD TRY TO REJECT US AGAIN.
WHERE BETTER TO TAKE MY BROKEN SOUL THAN TO A PLANET THAT COULD NEVER BE FIXED?
QUITE THE BEAUTY, ISN'T SHE?
THE LOVELOCK ENGINE. HAVE YOU SEEN ONE IN ACTION BEFORE?
I'M LICENUS CU CORIBA, YOUR ADMINISTRATOR, DOMINUS. I WORK FOR JANIS AU GERARD.
YOU MUST BE FITCHNER AU BARCA. I WAS TOLD YOU'D BE ARRIVING TODAY.
INDEED.

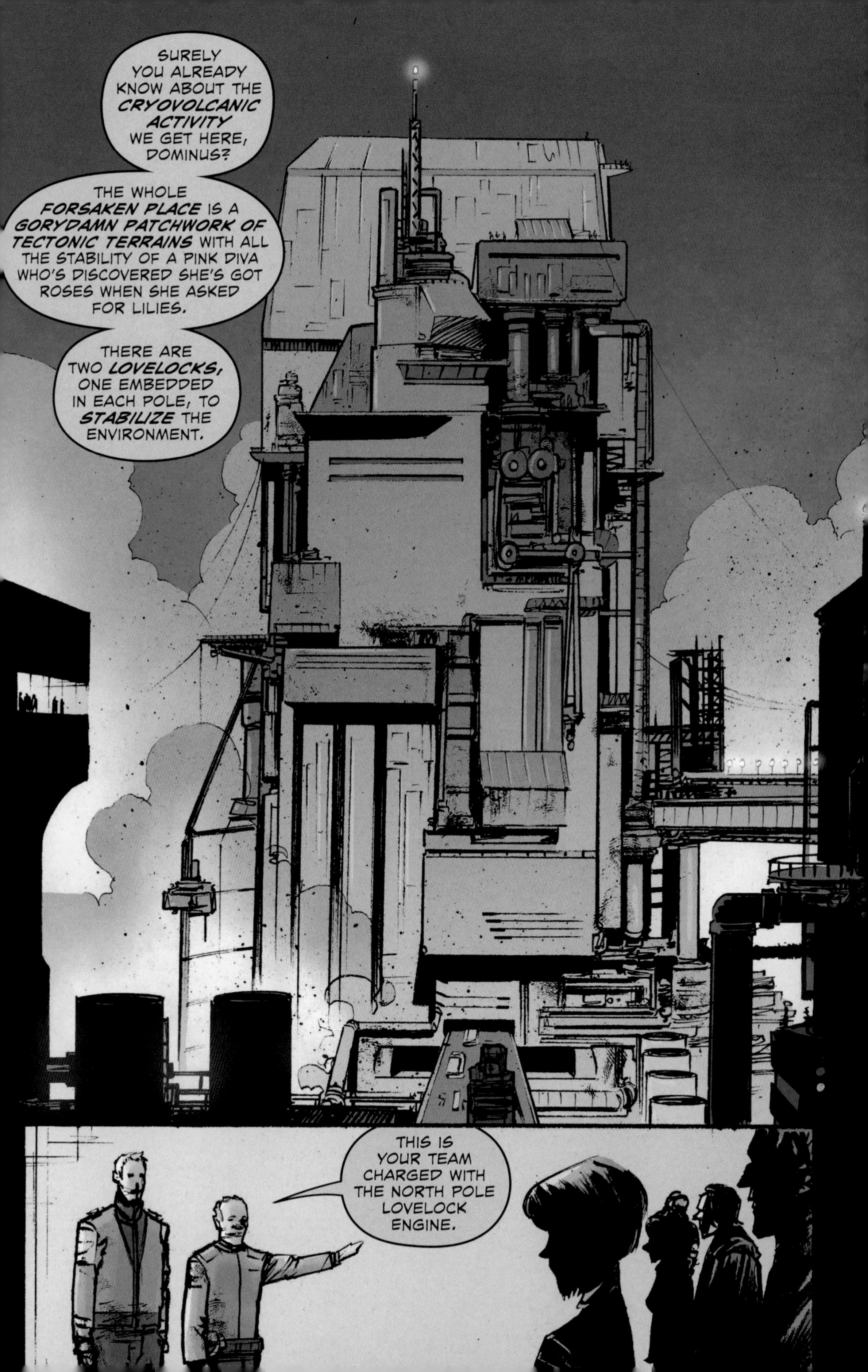
SURELY YOU ALREADY KNOW ABOUT THE CRYOVOLCANIC ACTIVITY WE GET HERE, DOMINUS?
THE WHOLE FORSAKEN PLACE IS A GORYDAMN PATCHWORK OF TECTONIC TERRAINS WITH ALL THE STABILITY OF A PINK DIVA WHO'S DISCOVERED SHE'S GOT ROSES WHEN SHE ASKED FOR LILIES.
THERE ARE TWO LOVELOCKS, ONE EMBEDDED IN EACH POLE, TO STABILIZE THE ENVIRONMENT.
THIS IS YOUR TEAM CHARGED WITH THE NORTH POLE LOVELOCK ENGINE.

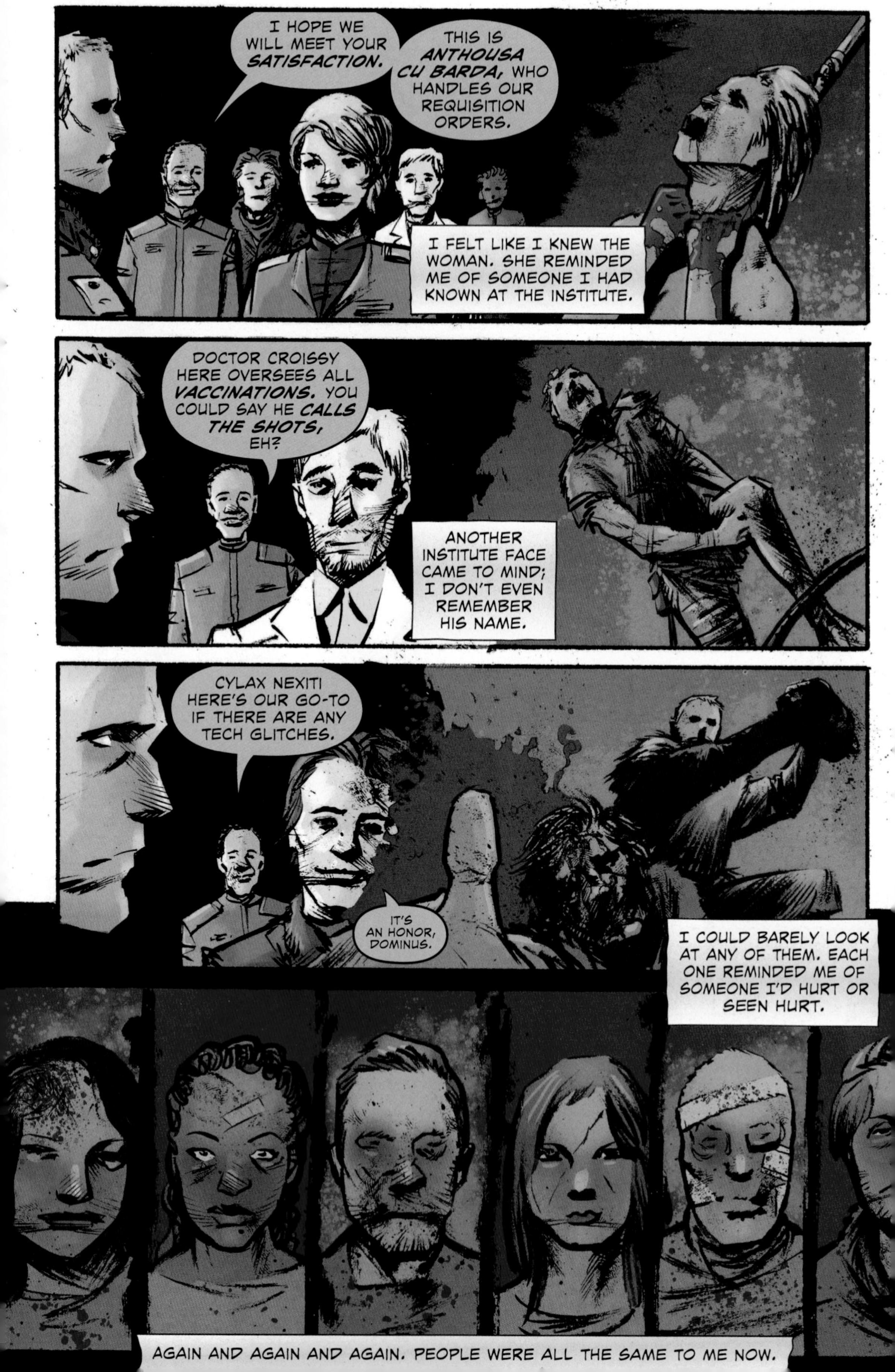

I HOPE WE WILL MEET YOUR *SATISFACTION.*
THIS IS *ANTHOUSA CU BARDA,* WHO HANDLES OUR REQUISITION ORDERS.
I FELT LIKE I KNEW THE WOMAN. SHE REMINDED ME OF SOMEONE I HAD KNOWN AT THE INSTITUTE.
DOCTOR CROISSY HERE OVERSEES ALL *VACCINATIONS.* YOU COULD SAY HE *CALLS THE SHOTS,* EH?
ANOTHER INSTITUTE FACE CAME TO MIND; I DON'T EVEN REMEMBER HIS NAME.
CYLAX NEXITI HERE'S OUR GO-TO IF THERE ARE ANY TECH GLITCHES.
IT'S AN HONOR, DOMINUS.
I COULD BARELY LOOK AT ANY OF THEM. EACH ONE REMINDED ME OF SOMEONE I'D HURT OR SEEN HURT.
AGAIN AND AGAIN AND AGAIN. PEOPLE WERE ALL THE SAME TO ME NOW.

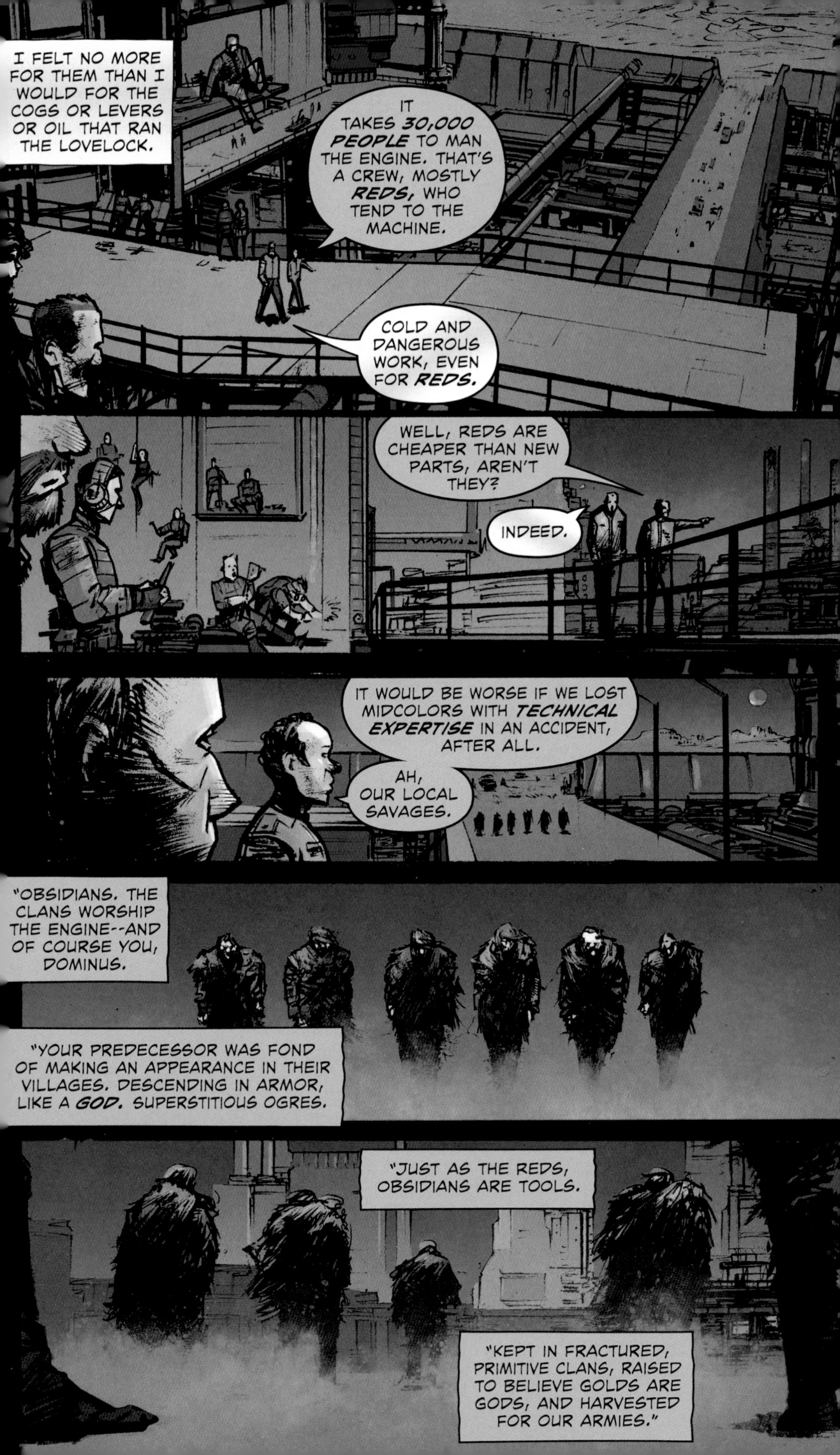
I FELT NO MORE FOR THEM THAN I WOULD FOR THE COGS OR LEVERS OR OIL THAT RAN THE LOVELOCK.
IT TAKES *30,000 PEOPLE* TO MAN THE ENGINE. THAT'S A CREW, MOSTLY *REDS,* WHO TEND TO THE MACHINE.
COLD AND DANGEROUS WORK, EVEN FOR *REDS.*
WELL, REDS ARE CHEAPER THAN NEW PARTS, AREN'T THEY?
INDEED.
IT WOULD BE WORSE IF WE LOST MIDCOLORS WITH *TECHNICAL EXPERTISE* IN AN ACCIDENT, AFTER ALL.
AH, OUR LOCAL SAVAGES.
"OBSIDIANS. THE CLANS WORSHIP THE ENGINE--AND OF COURSE YOU, DOMINUS.
"YOUR PREDECESSOR WAS FOND OF MAKING AN APPEARANCE IN THEIR VILLAGES. DESCENDING IN ARMOR, LIKE A *GOD.* SUPERSTITIOUS OGRES.
"JUST AS THE REDS, OBSIDIANS ARE TOOLS.
"KEPT IN FRACTURED, PRIMITIVE CLANS, RAISED TO BELIEVE GOLDS ARE GODS, AND HARVESTED FOR OUR ARMIES."

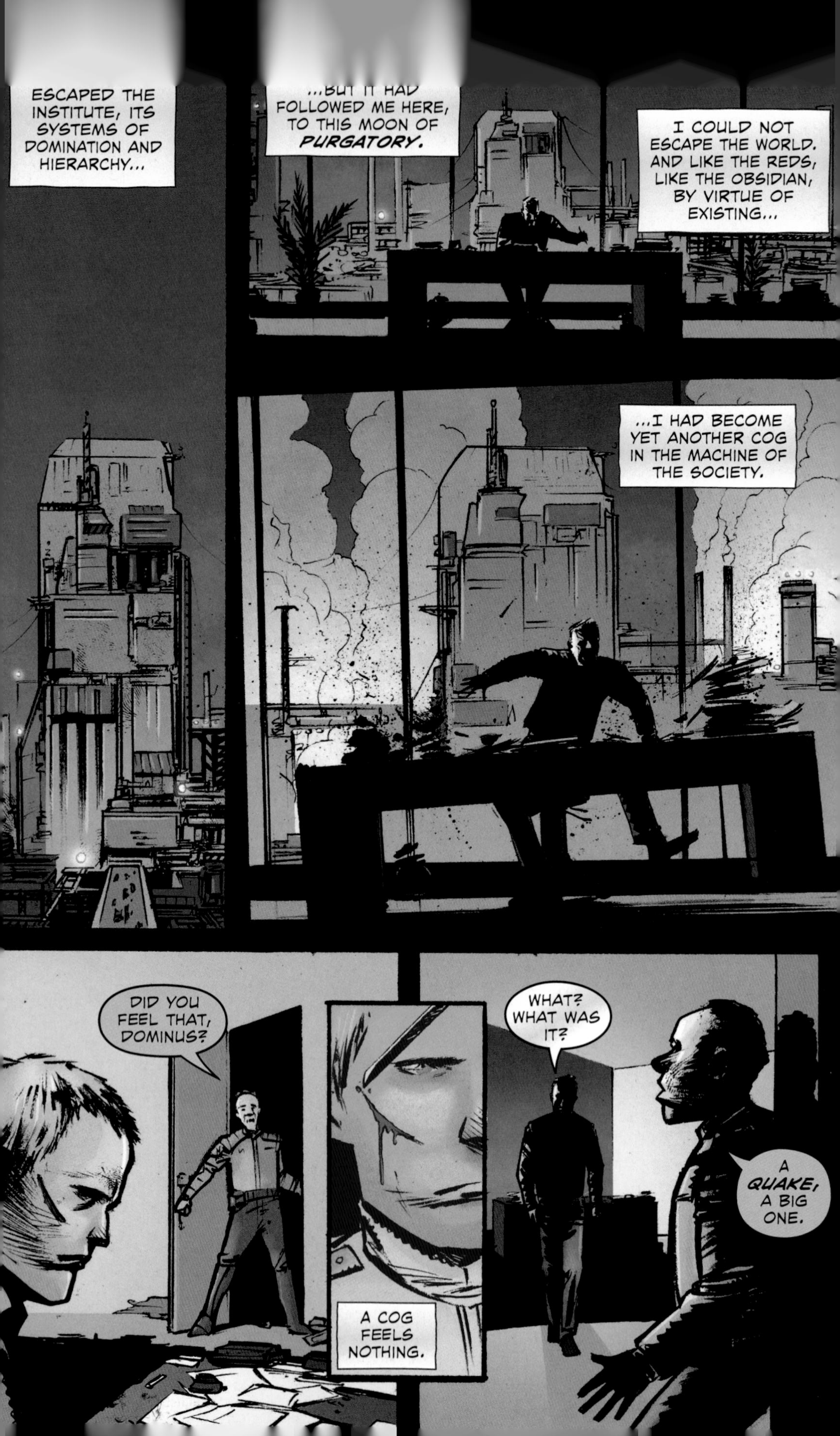
ESCAPED THE INSTITUTE, ITS SYSTEMS OF DOMINATION AND HIERARCHY...
...BUT IT HAD FOLLOWED ME HERE, TO THIS MOON OF *PURGATORY.*
I COULD NOT ESCAPE THE WORLD. AND LIKE THE REDS, LIKE THE OBSIDIAN, BY VIRTUE OF EXISTING...
...I HAD BECOME YET ANOTHER COG IN THE MACHINE OF THE SOCIETY.
DID YOU FEEL THAT, DOMINUS?
A COG FEELS NOTHING.
WHAT? WHAT WAS IT?
A *QUAKE,* A BIG ONE.

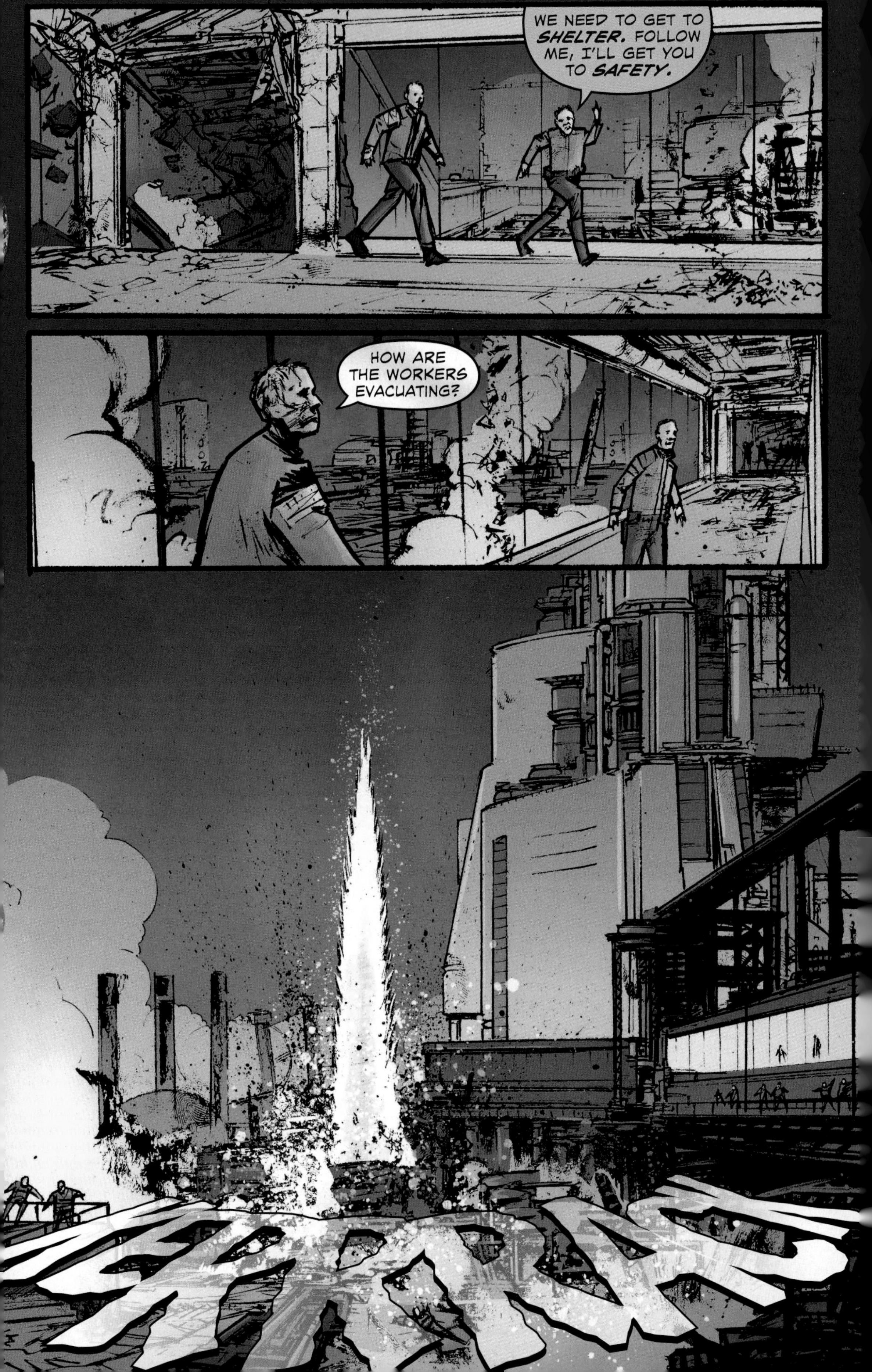
WE NEED TO GET TO SHELTER. FOLLOW ME, I'LL GET YOU TO SAFETY.
HOW ARE THE WORKERS EVACUATING?

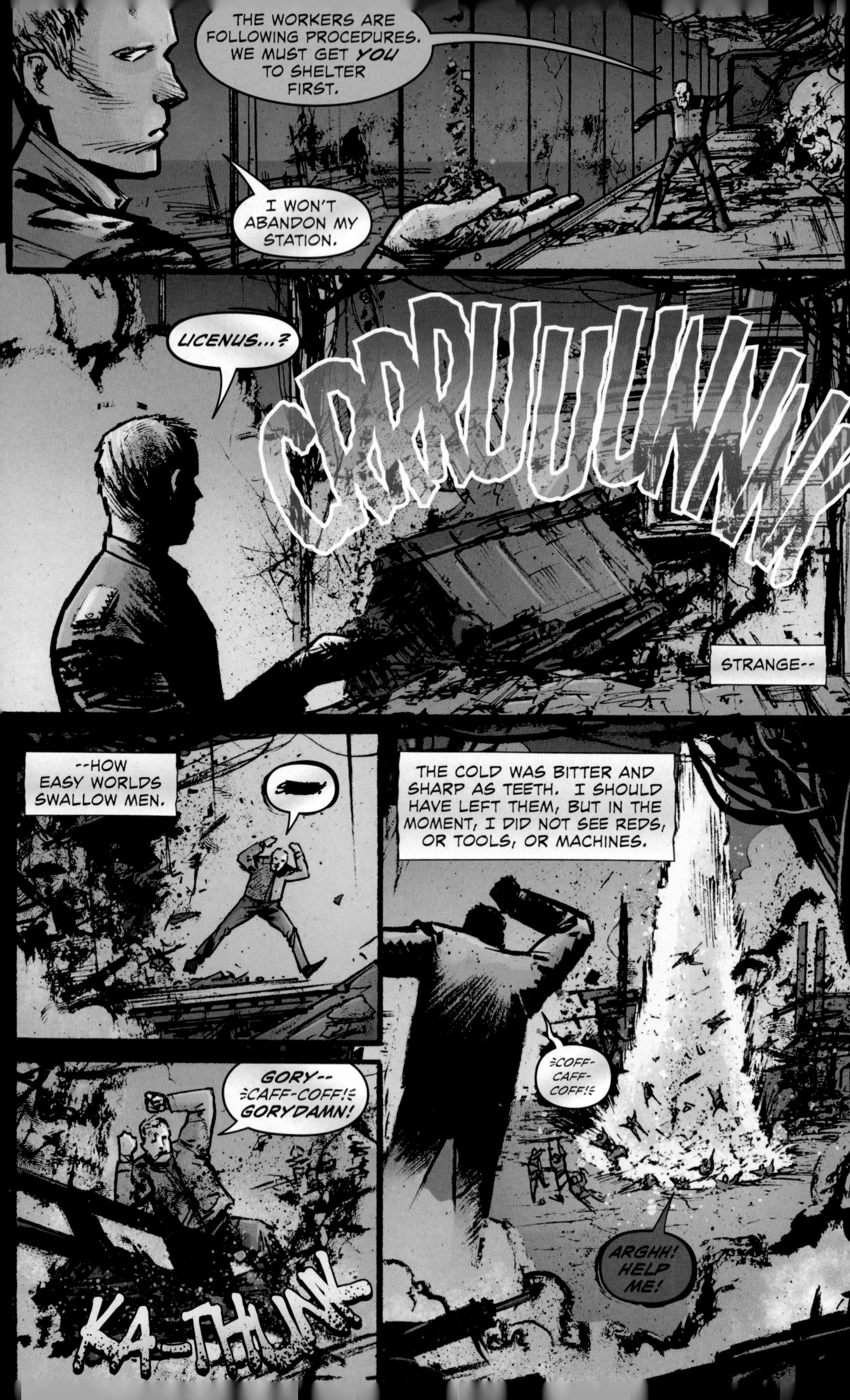
THE WORKERS ARE FOLLOWING PROCEDURES. WE MUST GET *YOU* TO SHELTER FIRST.
I WON'T ABANDON MY STATION.
LICENUS...?
CRRUUUNNN
STRANGE--
--HOW EASY WORLDS SWALLOW MEN.
GORY-- ≈CAFF-COFF!≈ GORYDAMN!
KA-THUNK
THE COLD WAS BITTER AND SHARP AS TEETH. I SHOULD HAVE LEFT THEM, BUT IN THE MOMENT, I DID NOT SEE REDS, OR TOOLS, OR MACHINES.
≈COFF-CAFF-COFF!≈
ARGHH! HELP ME!

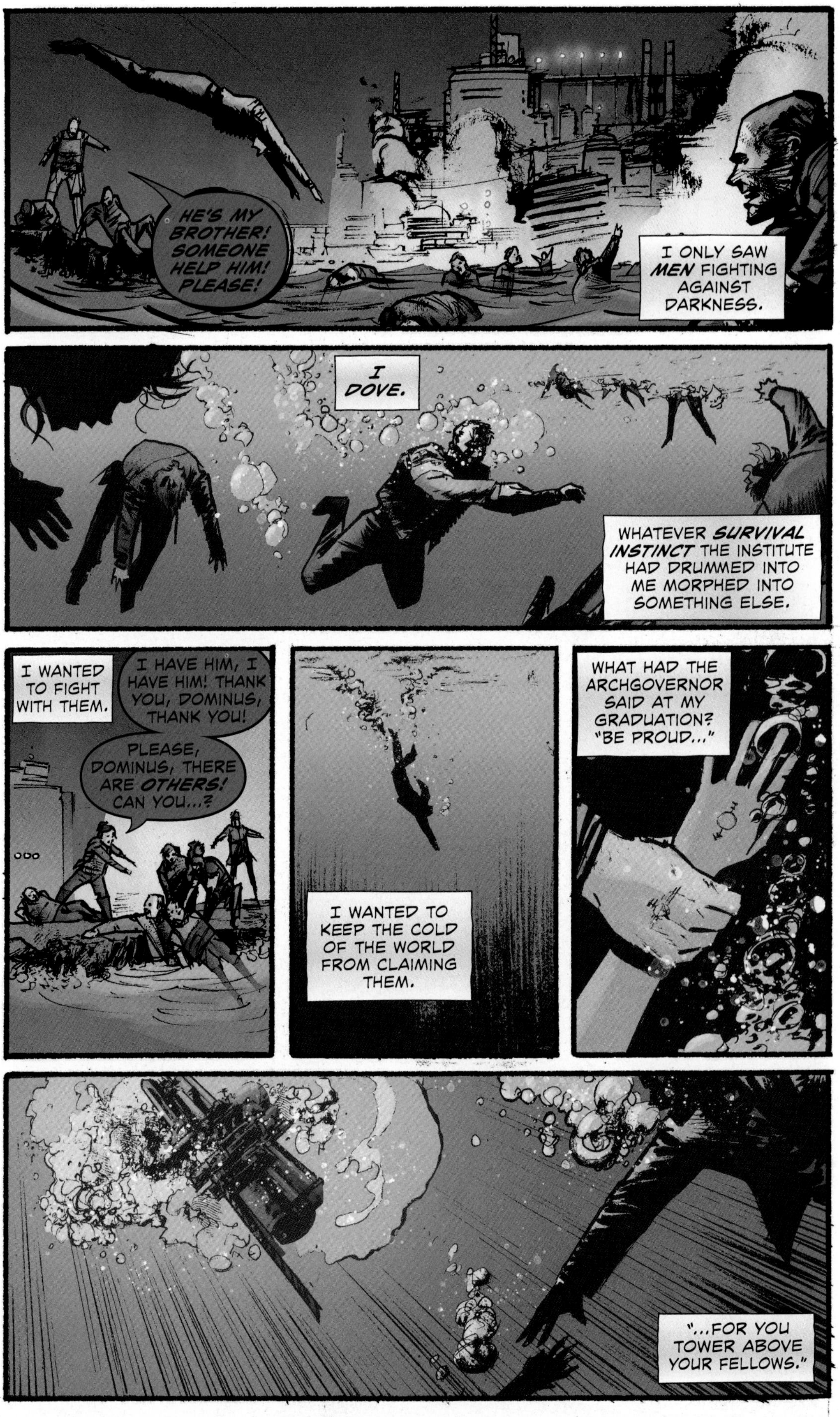
HE'S MY BROTHER! SOMEONE HELP HIM! PLEASE!
I ONLY SAW MEN FIGHTING AGAINST DARKNESS.
I DOVE.
WHATEVER SURVIVAL INSTINCT THE INSTITUTE HAD DRUMMED INTO ME MORPHED INTO SOMETHING ELSE.
I WANTED TO FIGHT WITH THEM.
I HAVE HIM, I HAVE HIM! THANK YOU, DOMINUS, THANK YOU!
PLEASE, DOMINUS, THERE ARE OTHERS! CAN YOU...?
I WANTED TO KEEP THE COLD OF THE WORLD FROM CLAIMING THEM.
WHAT HAD THE ARCHGOVERNOR SAID AT MY GRADUATION? "BE PROUD..."
"...FOR YOU TOWER ABOVE YOUR FELLOWS."

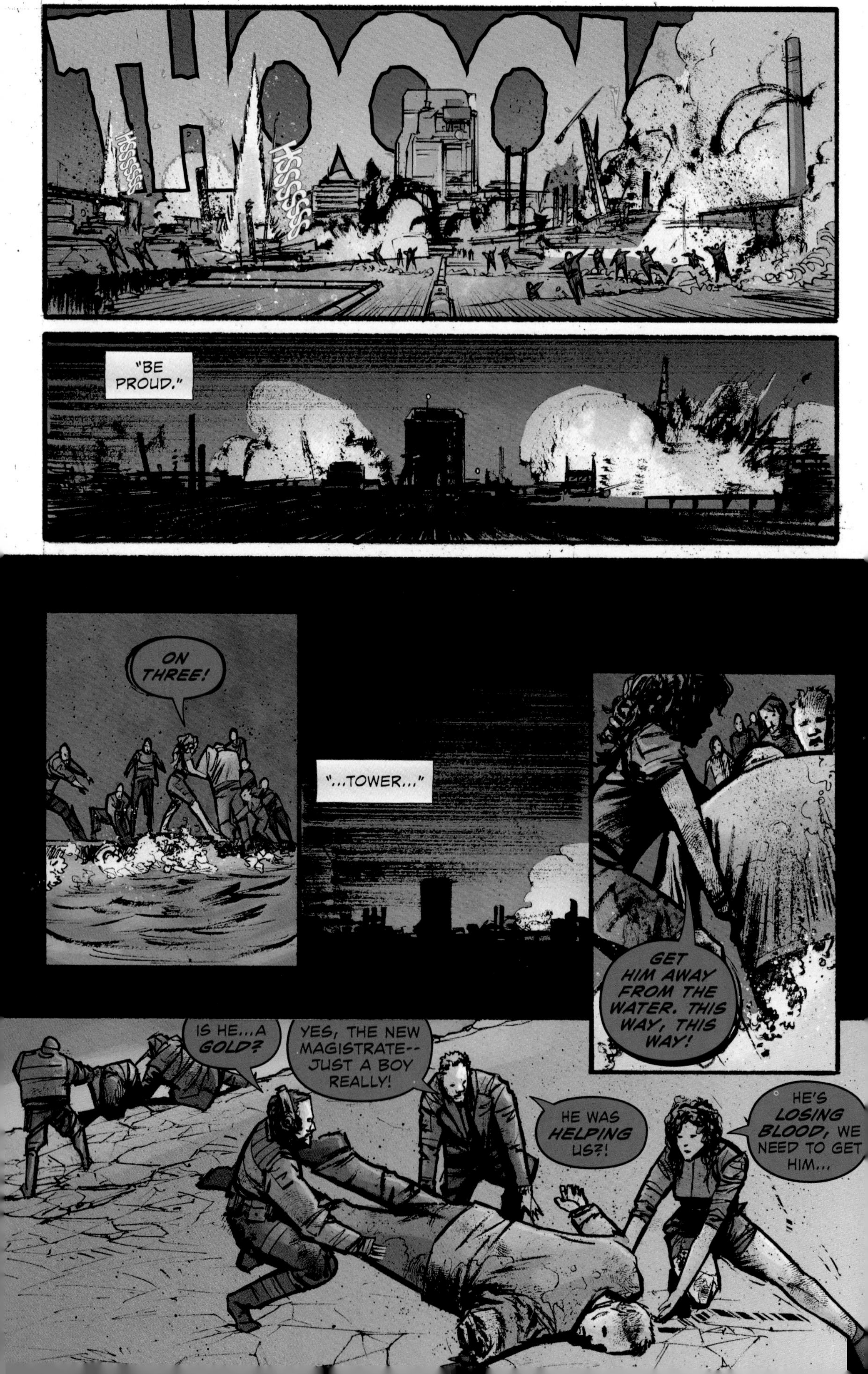
THOOOM
HSSSSS
HSSSSSS
"BE PROUD."
ON THREE!
"...TOWER..."
GET HIM AWAY FROM THE WATER. THIS WAY, THIS WAY!
IS HE...A GOLD?
YES, THE NEW MAGISTRATE-- JUST A BOY REALLY!
HE WAS HELPING US?!
HE'S LOSING BLOOD, WE NEED TO GET HIM...

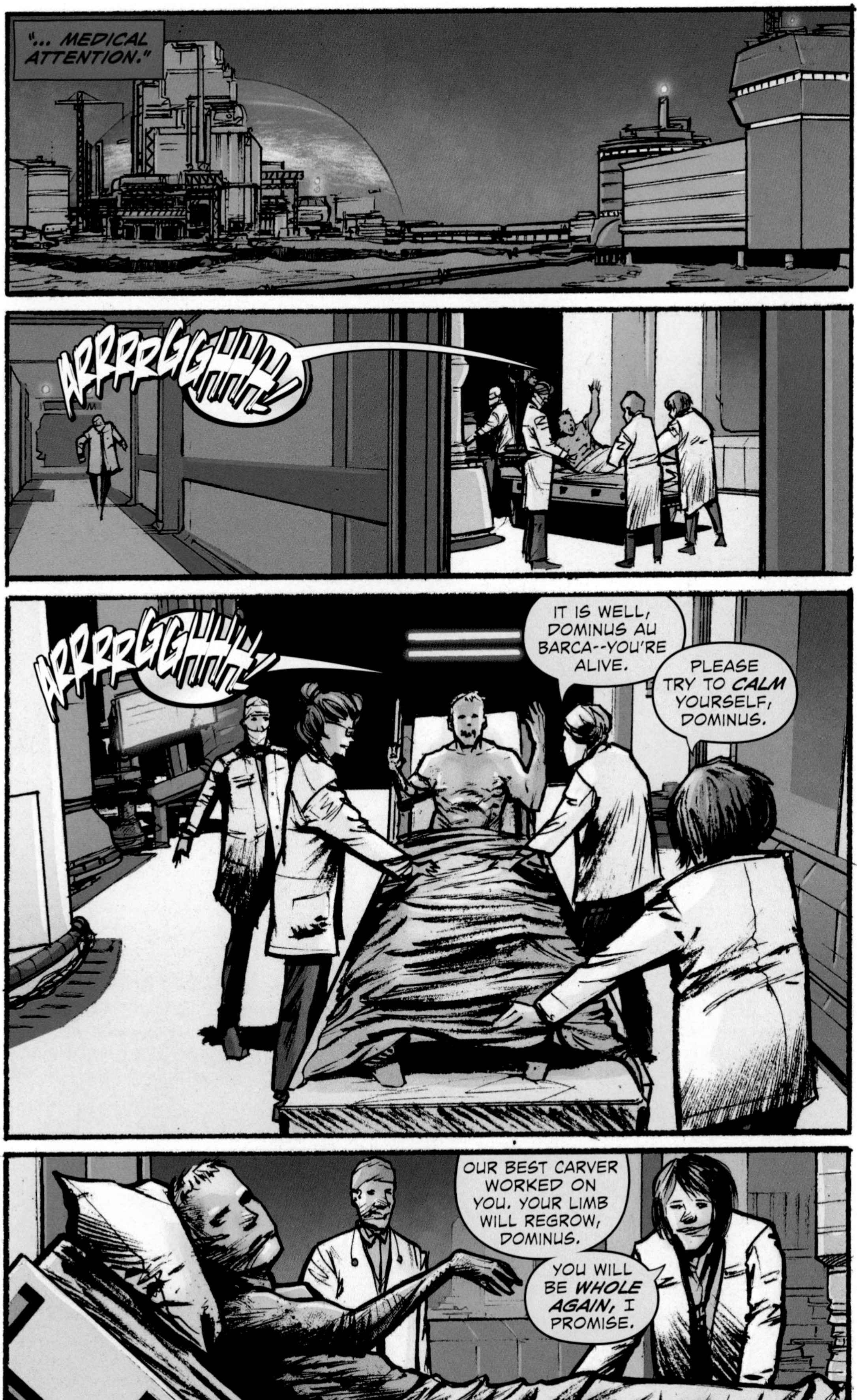
"... MEDICAL ATTENTION."
ARRRRGGHHH!
ARRRRGGHHH!
IT IS WELL, DOMINUS AU BARCA--YOU'RE ALIVE.
PLEASE TRY TO *CALM* YOURSELF, DOMINUS.
OUR BEST CARVER WORKED ON YOU. YOUR LIMB WILL REGROW, DOMINUS.
YOU WILL BE *WHOLE AGAIN,* I PROMISE.

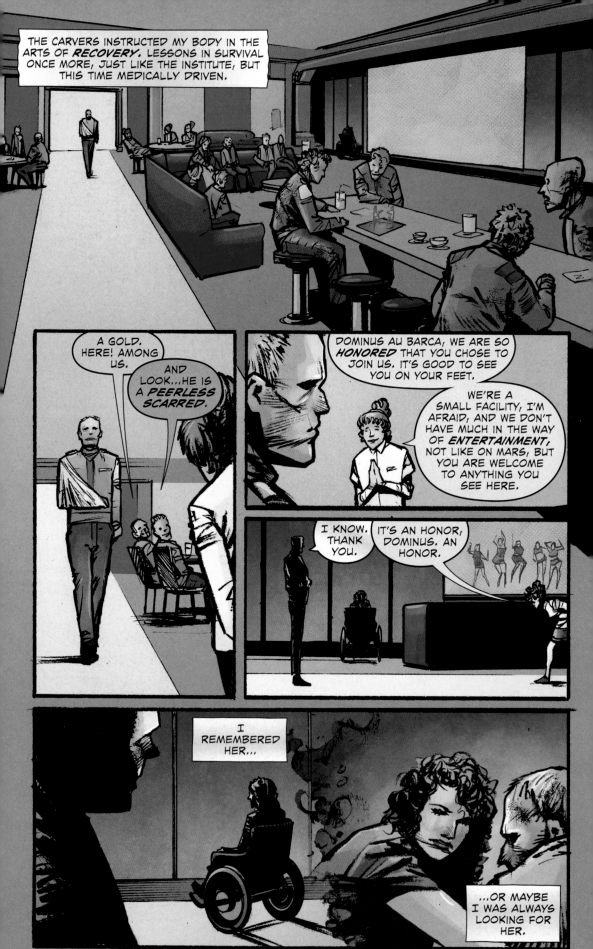

THE CARVERS INSTRUCTED MY BODY IN THE ARTS OF *RECOVERY*. LESSONS IN SURVIVAL ONCE MORE, JUST LIKE THE INSTITUTE, BUT THIS TIME MEDICALLY DRIVEN.

A GOLD. HERE! AMONG US.

AND LOOK...HE IS A *PEERLESS SCARRED*.

DOMINUS AU BARCA, WE ARE SO *HONORED* THAT YOU CHOSE TO JOIN US. IT'S GOOD TO SEE YOU ON YOUR FEET.

WE'RE A SMALL FACILITY, I'M AFRAID, AND WE DON'T HAVE MUCH IN THE WAY OF *ENTERTAINMENT*, NOT LIKE ON MARS, BUT YOU ARE WELCOME TO ANYTHING YOU SEE HERE.

I KNOW. THANK YOU.

IT'S AN HONOR, DOMINUS. AN HONOR.

I REMEMBERED HER...

...OR MAYBE I WAS ALWAYS LOOKING FOR HER.

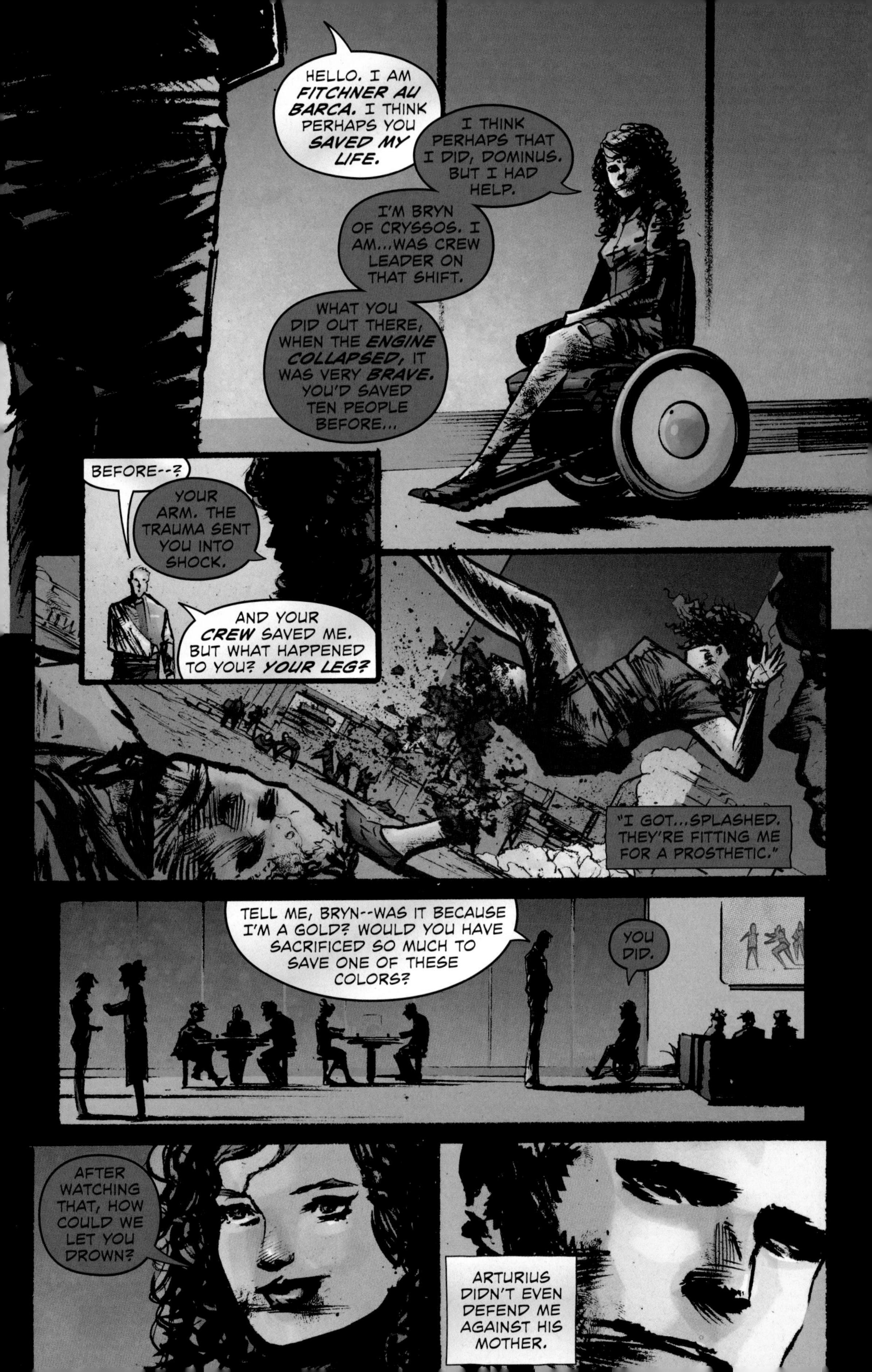
HELLO. I AM FITCHNER AU BARCA. I THINK PERHAPS YOU SAVED MY LIFE.
I THINK PERHAPS THAT I DID, DOMINUS. BUT I HAD HELP.
I'M BRYN OF CRYSSOS. I AM...WAS CREW LEADER ON THAT SHIFT.
WHAT YOU DID OUT THERE, WHEN THE ENGINE COLLAPSED, IT WAS VERY BRAVE. YOU'D SAVED TEN PEOPLE BEFORE...
BEFORE--?
YOUR ARM. THE TRAUMA SENT YOU INTO SHOCK.
AND YOUR CREW SAVED ME. BUT WHAT HAPPENED TO YOU? YOUR LEG?
"I GOT...SPLASHED. THEY'RE FITTING ME FOR A PROSTHETIC."
TELL ME, BRYN--WAS IT BECAUSE I'M A GOLD? WOULD YOU HAVE SACRIFICED SO MUCH TO SAVE ONE OF THESE COLORS?
YOU DID.
AFTER WATCHING THAT, HOW COULD WE LET YOU DROWN?
ARTURIUS DIDN'T EVEN DEFEND ME AGAINST HIS MOTHER.

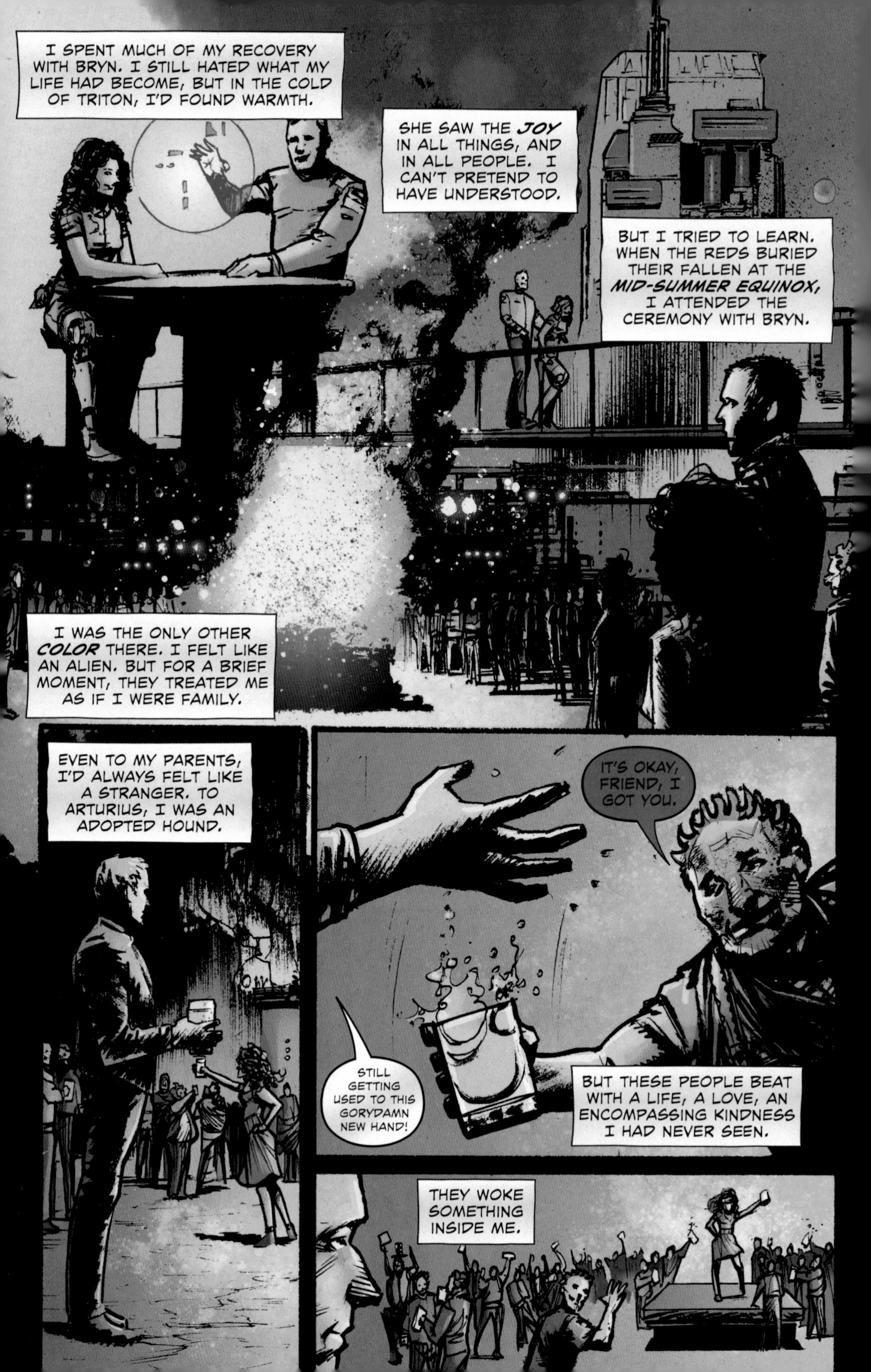
I SPENT MUCH OF MY RECOVERY WITH BRYN. I STILL HATED WHAT MY LIFE HAD BECOME, BUT IN THE COLD OF TRITON, I'D FOUND WARMTH.
SHE SAW THE *JOY* IN ALL THINGS, AND IN ALL PEOPLE. I CAN'T PRETEND TO HAVE UNDERSTOOD.
BUT I TRIED TO LEARN. WHEN THE REDS BURIED THEIR FALLEN AT THE *MID-SUMMER EQUINOX,* I ATTENDED THE CEREMONY WITH BRYN.
I WAS THE ONLY OTHER *COLOR* THERE. I FELT LIKE AN ALIEN. BUT FOR A BRIEF MOMENT, THEY TREATED ME AS IF I WERE FAMILY.
EVEN TO MY PARENTS, I'D ALWAYS FELT LIKE A STRANGER. TO ARTURIUS, I WAS AN ADOPTED HOUND.
IT'S OKAY, FRIEND, I GOT YOU.
STILL GETTING USED TO THIS GORYDAMN NEW HAND!
BUT THESE PEOPLE BEAT WITH A LIFE, A LOVE, AN ENCOMPASSING KINDNESS I HAD NEVER SEEN.
THEY WOKE SOMETHING INSIDE ME.

BUMP

I WASN'T LOOKING WHERE--

NO HARM DONE. JUST A LITTLE SPILT WINE.

THEN YOU SHALL HAVE MINE, DOMINUS. AFTER ALL, IT WAS MY MISTAKE.

HER MISTAKE?

AS IF *HER TOUCH* COULD EVER BE A MISTAKE.

I'M *SCARED,* DOMI--

FITCHNER. YOU CALL ME FITCHNER.

FITCHNER.

OUR AFFAIR COULD *NEVER* BE PUBLIC, OF COURSE.

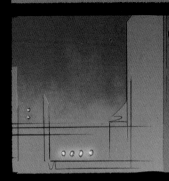

JANIS AU GERARD HAD DIED IN THE ACCIDENT, AND I HAD BEEN PROMOTED TO GOVERNOR OF THE NORTH LOVELOCK ENGINE IN HIS PLACE.

IF ANYONE HAD KNOWN I WAS *INVOLVED* WITH A RED I WOULD HAVE BEEN BRANDED A TRAITOR.

IMPRISONED, OR *WORSE.*

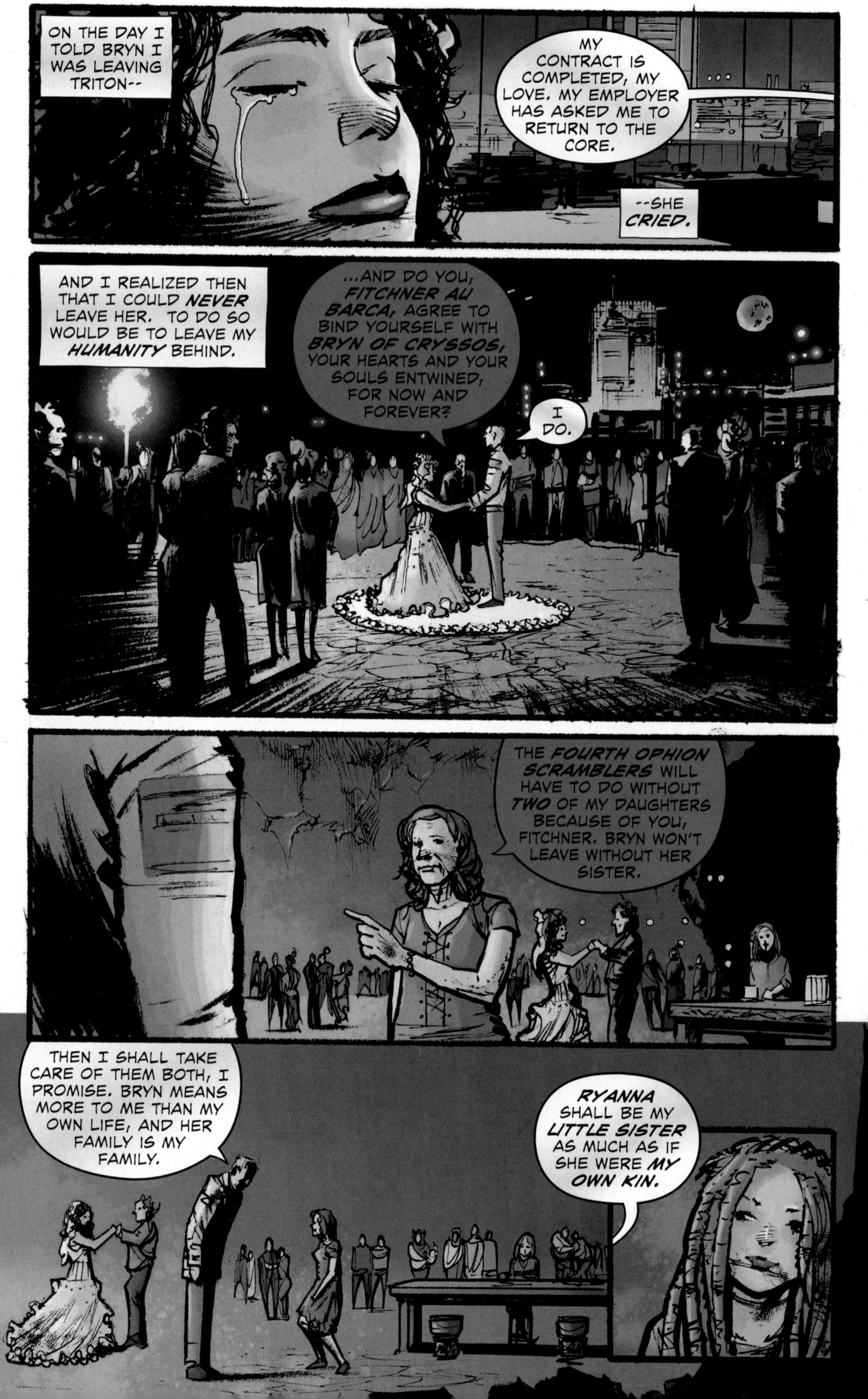
ON THE DAY I TOLD BRYN I WAS LEAVING TRITON--
MY CONTRACT IS COMPLETED, MY LOVE. MY EMPLOYER HAS ASKED ME TO RETURN TO THE CORE.
--SHE *CRIED.*
AND I REALIZED THEN THAT I COULD *NEVER* LEAVE HER. TO DO SO WOULD BE TO LEAVE MY *HUMANITY* BEHIND.
...AND DO YOU, *FITCHNER AU BARCA,* AGREE TO BIND YOURSELF WITH *BRYN OF CRYSSOS,* YOUR HEARTS AND YOUR SOULS ENTWINED, FOR NOW AND FOREVER?
I DO.
THE *FOURTH OPHION SCRAMBLERS* WILL HAVE TO DO WITHOUT *TWO* OF MY DAUGHTERS BECAUSE OF YOU, FITCHNER. BRYN WON'T LEAVE WITHOUT HER SISTER.
THEN I SHALL TAKE CARE OF THEM BOTH, I PROMISE. BRYN MEANS MORE TO ME THAN MY OWN LIFE, AND HER FAMILY IS MY FAMILY.
RYANNA SHALL BE MY *LITTLE SISTER* AS MUCH AS IF SHE WERE *MY OWN KIN.*

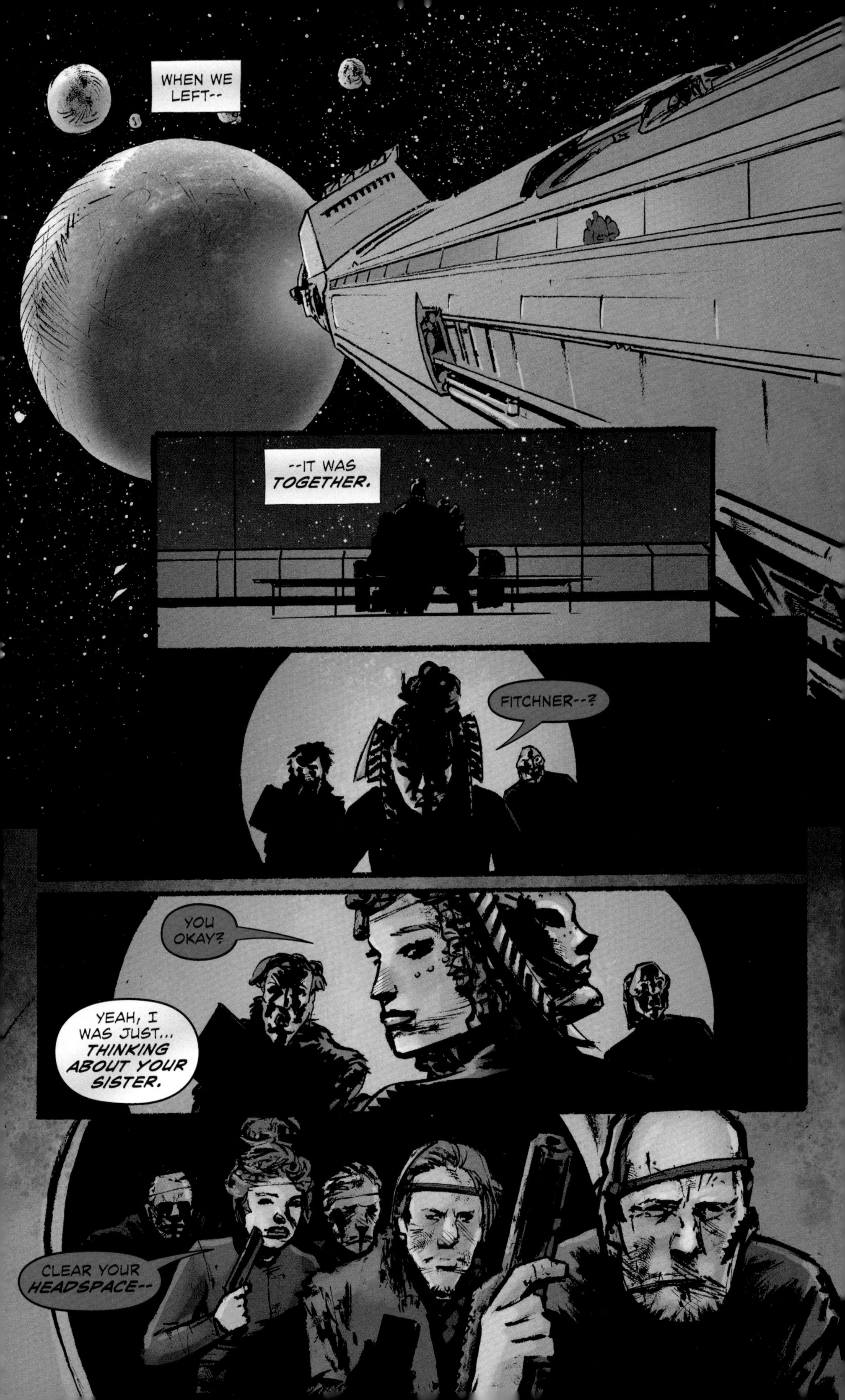
WHEN WE LEFT--
--IT WAS TOGETHER.
FITCHNER--?
YOU OKAY?
YEAH, I WAS JUST... THINKING ABOUT YOUR SISTER.
CLEAR YOUR HEADSPACE--

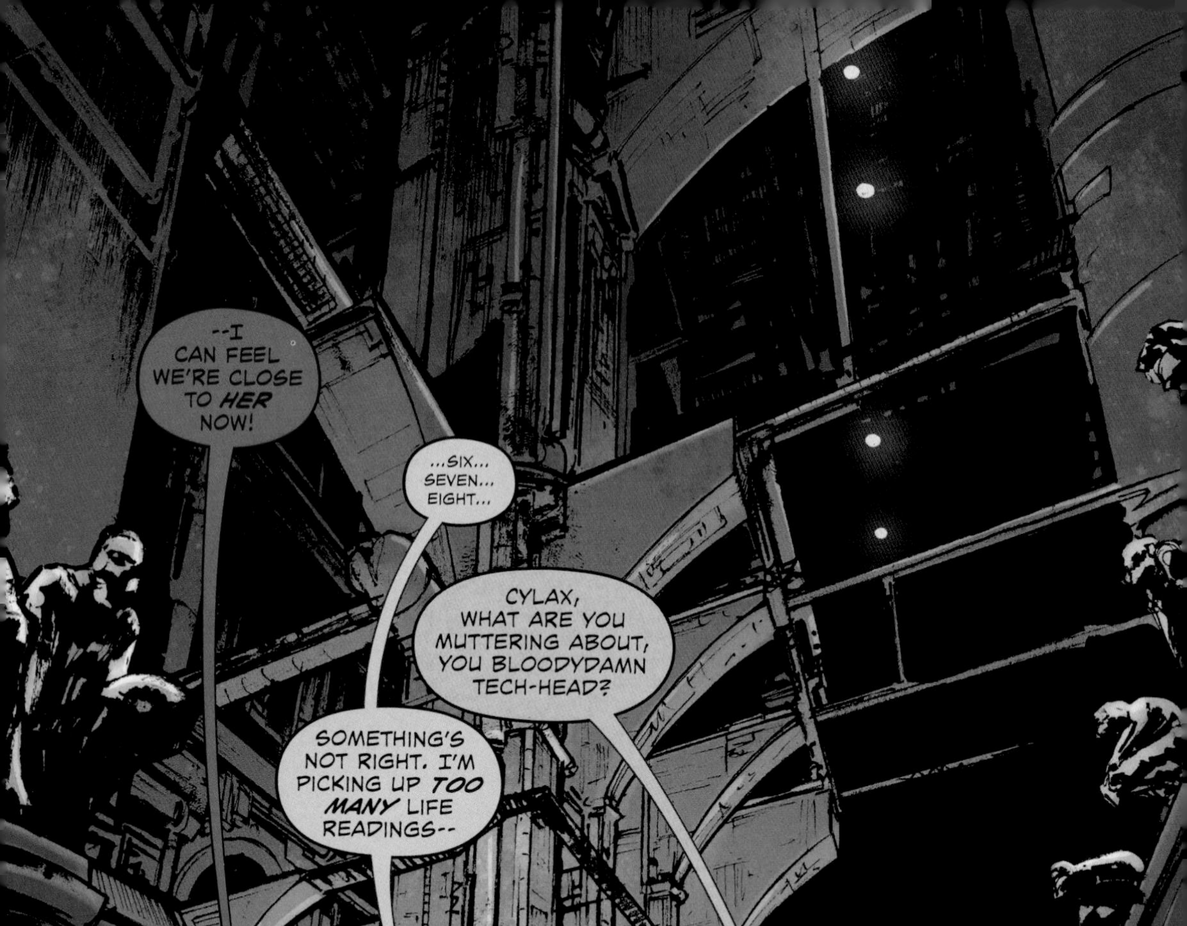
--I CAN FEEL WE'RE CLOSE TO *HER* NOW!
...SIX... SEVEN... EIGHT...
CYLAX, WHAT ARE YOU MUTTERING ABOUT, YOU BLOODYDAMN TECH-HEAD?
SOMETHING'S NOT RIGHT. I'M PICKING UP *TOO MANY* LIFE READINGS--

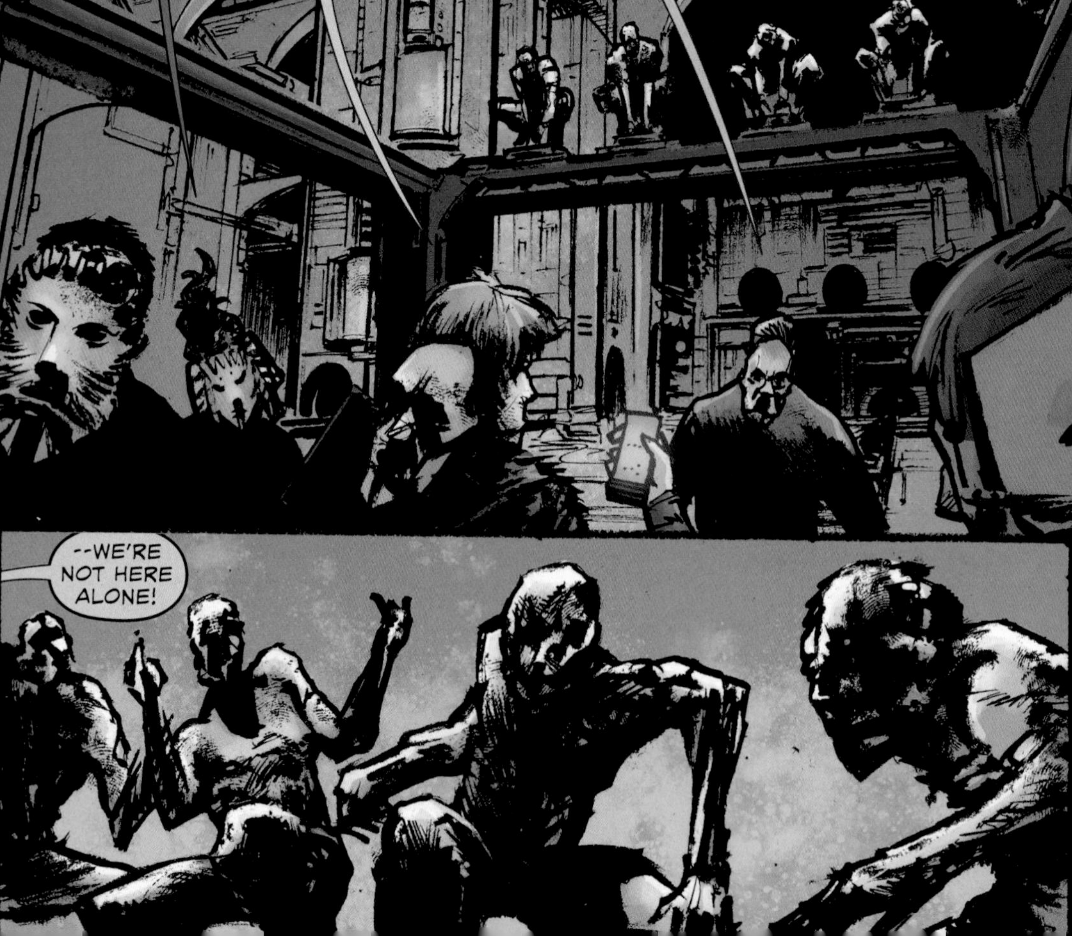
--WE'RE NOT HERE ALONE!

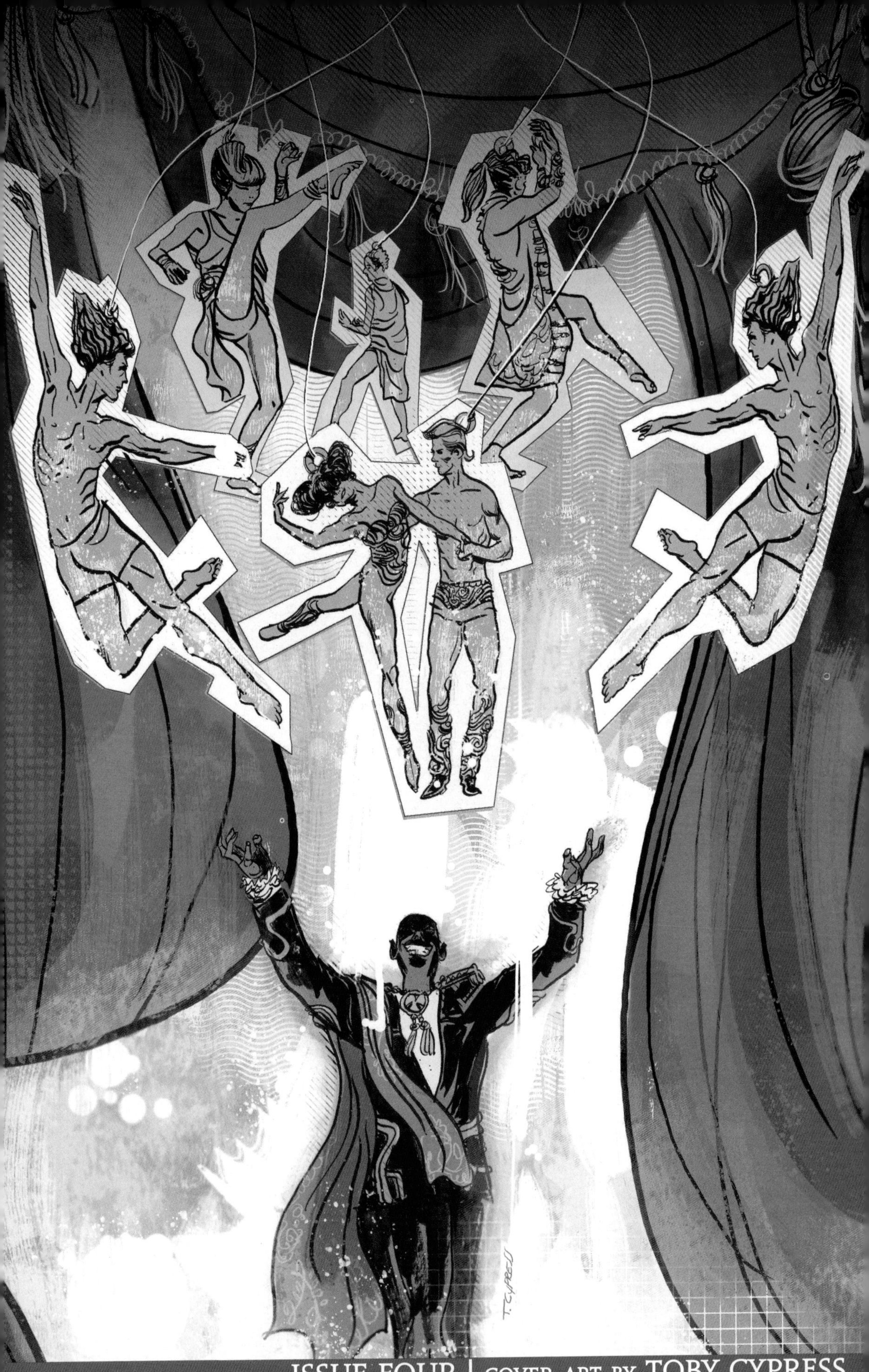
T. CYPRESS

ISSUE FOUR | COVER ART BY TOBY CYPRESS

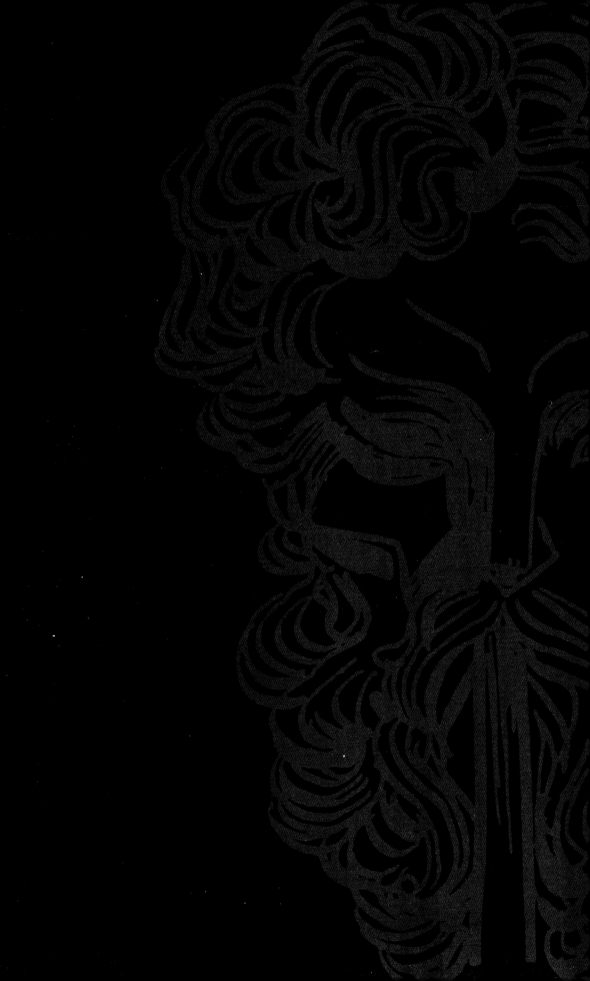

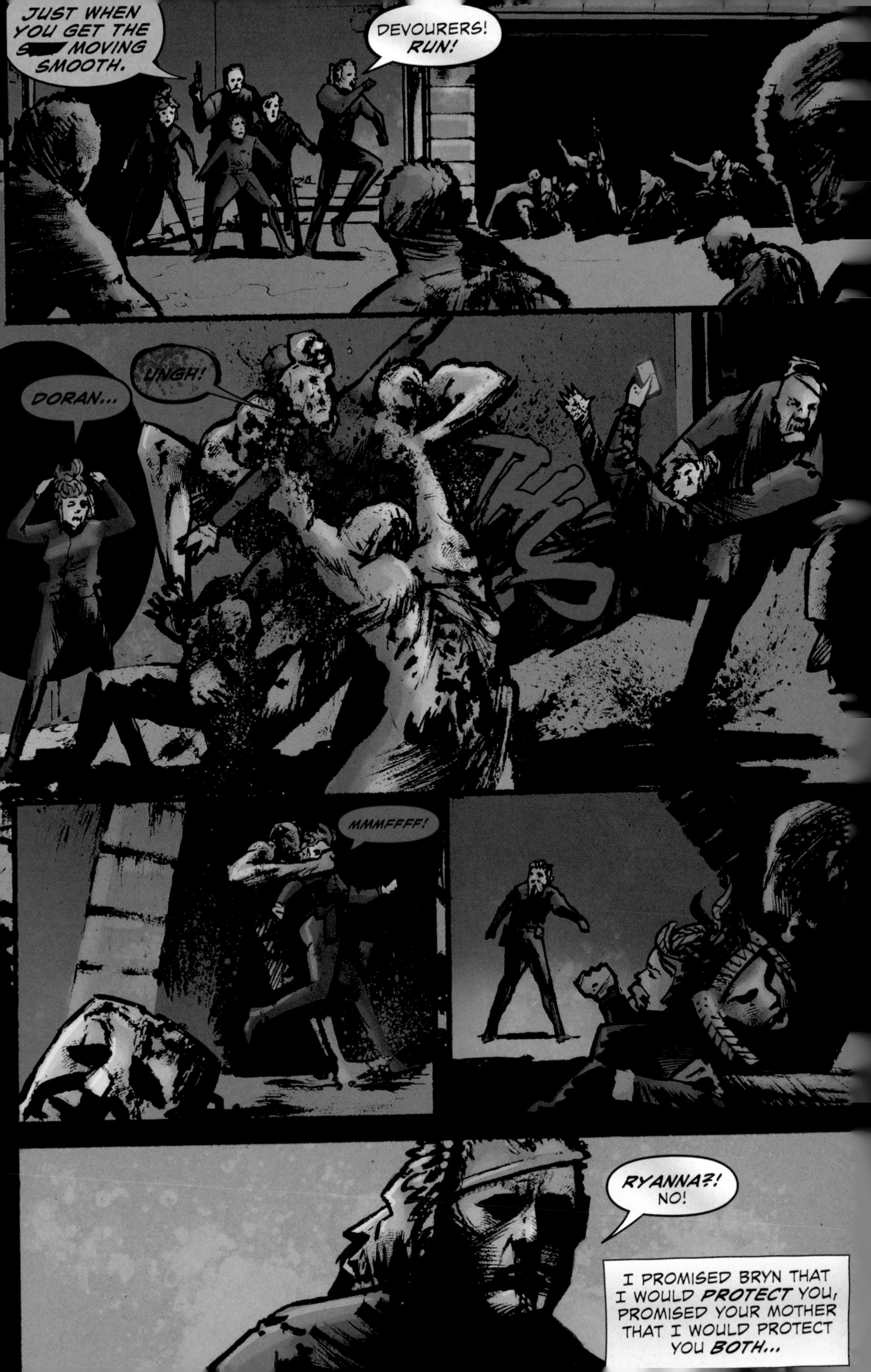
JUST WHEN YOU GET THE S[redacted] MOVING SMOOTH.
DEVOURERS! RUN!
DORAN...
UNGH!
MMMFFFF!
RYANNA?! NO!
I PROMISED BRYN THAT I WOULD PROTECT YOU, PROMISED YOUR MOTHER THAT I WOULD PROTECT YOU BOTH...

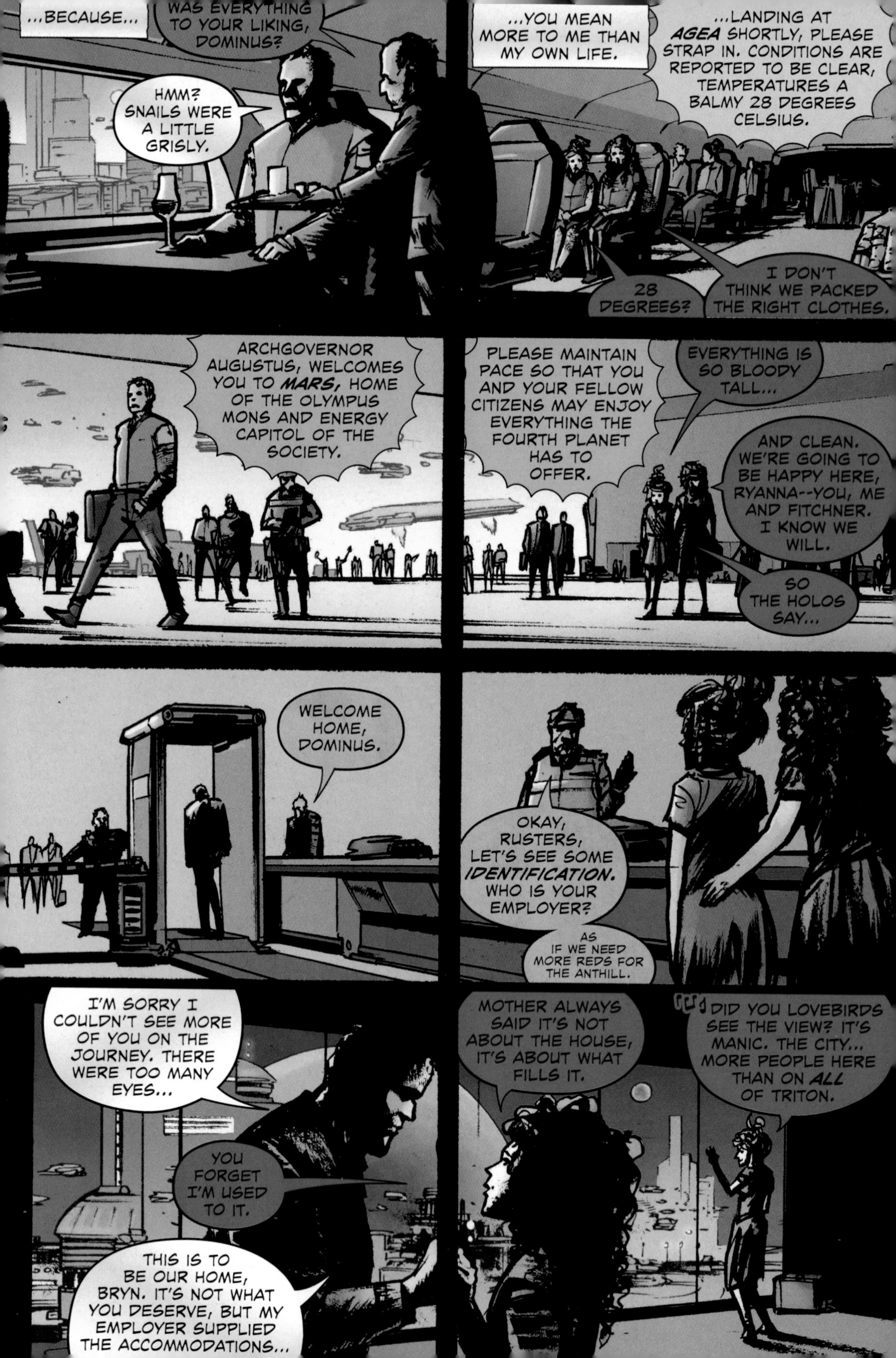
...BECAUSE...
WAS EVERYTHING TO YOUR LIKING, DOMINUS?
HMM? SNAILS WERE A LITTLE GRISLY.
...YOU MEAN MORE TO ME THAN MY OWN LIFE.
...LANDING AT AGEA SHORTLY, PLEASE STRAP IN. CONDITIONS ARE REPORTED TO BE CLEAR, TEMPERATURES A BALMY 28 DEGREES CELSIUS.
28 DEGREES?
I DON'T THINK WE PACKED THE RIGHT CLOTHES.
ARCHGOVERNOR AUGUSTUS, WELCOMES YOU TO MARS, HOME OF THE OLYMPUS MONS AND ENERGY CAPITOL OF THE SOCIETY.
PLEASE MAINTAIN PACE SO THAT YOU AND YOUR FELLOW CITIZENS MAY ENJOY EVERYTHING THE FOURTH PLANET HAS TO OFFER.
EVERYTHING IS SO BLOODY TALL...
AND CLEAN. WE'RE GOING TO BE HAPPY HERE, RYANNA--YOU, ME AND FITCHNER. I KNOW WE WILL.
SO THE HOLOS SAY...
WELCOME HOME, DOMINUS.
OKAY, RUSTERS, LET'S SEE SOME IDENTIFICATION. WHO IS YOUR EMPLOYER?
AS IF WE NEED MORE REDS FOR THE ANTHILL.
I'M SORRY I COULDN'T SEE MORE OF YOU ON THE JOURNEY. THERE WERE TOO MANY EYES...
YOU FORGET I'M USED TO IT.
THIS IS TO BE OUR HOME, BRYN. IT'S NOT WHAT YOU DESERVE, BUT MY EMPLOYER SUPPLIED THE ACCOMMODATIONS...
MOTHER ALWAYS SAID IT'S NOT ABOUT THE HOUSE, IT'S ABOUT WHAT FILLS IT.
DID YOU LOVEBIRDS SEE THE VIEW? IT'S MANIC. THE CITY... MORE PEOPLE HERE THAN ON ALL OF TRITON.

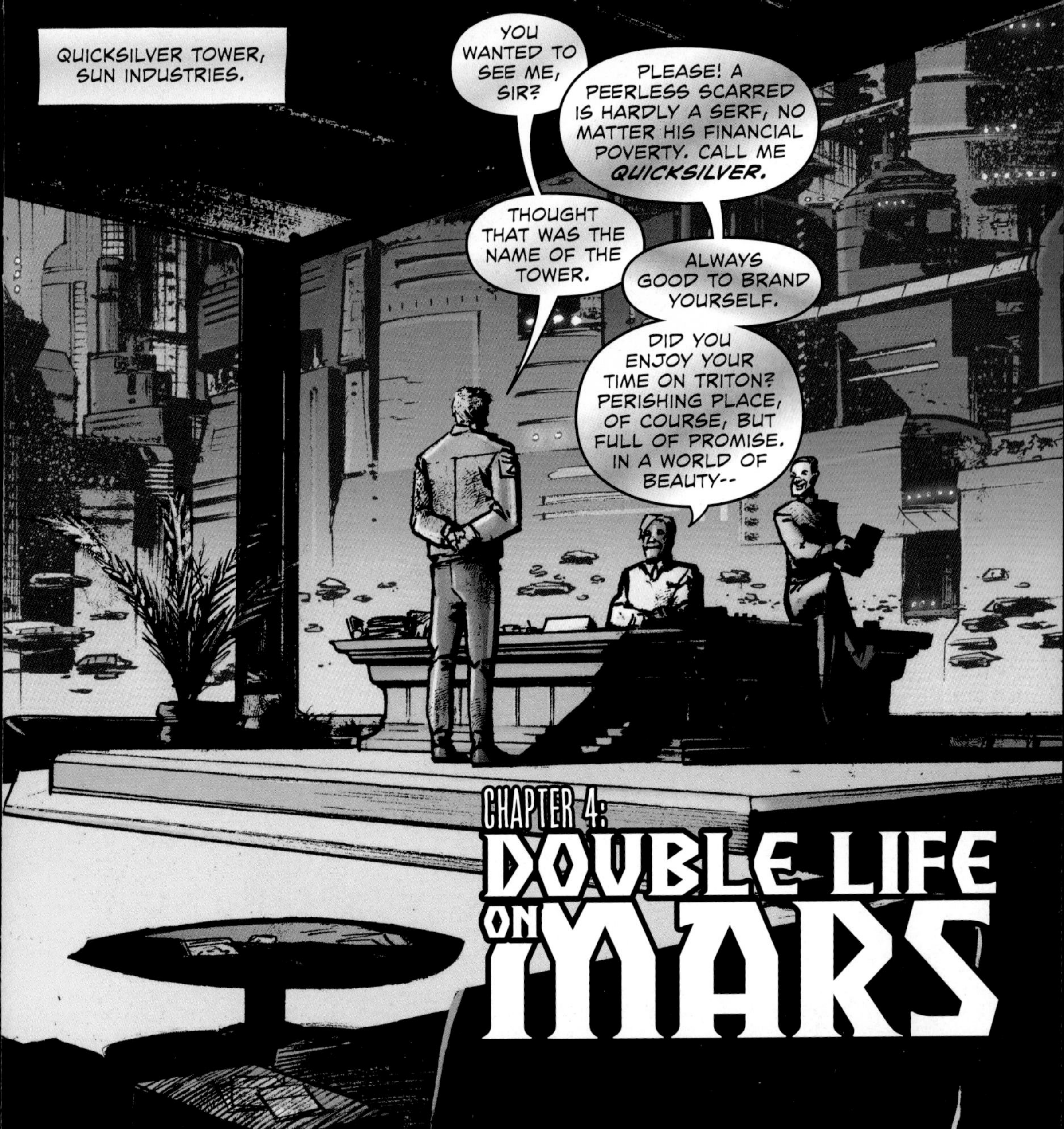
QUICKSILVER TOWER, SUN INDUSTRIES.
YOU WANTED TO SEE ME, SIR?
PLEASE! A PEERLESS SCARRED IS HARDLY A SERF, NO MATTER HIS FINANCIAL POVERTY. CALL ME *QUICKSILVER.*
THOUGHT THAT WAS THE NAME OF THE TOWER.
ALWAYS GOOD TO BRAND YOURSELF.
DID YOU ENJOY YOUR TIME ON TRITON? PERISHING PLACE, OF COURSE, BUT FULL OF PROMISE. IN A WORLD OF BEAUTY--
CHAPTER 4:
DOUBLE LIFE ON MARS

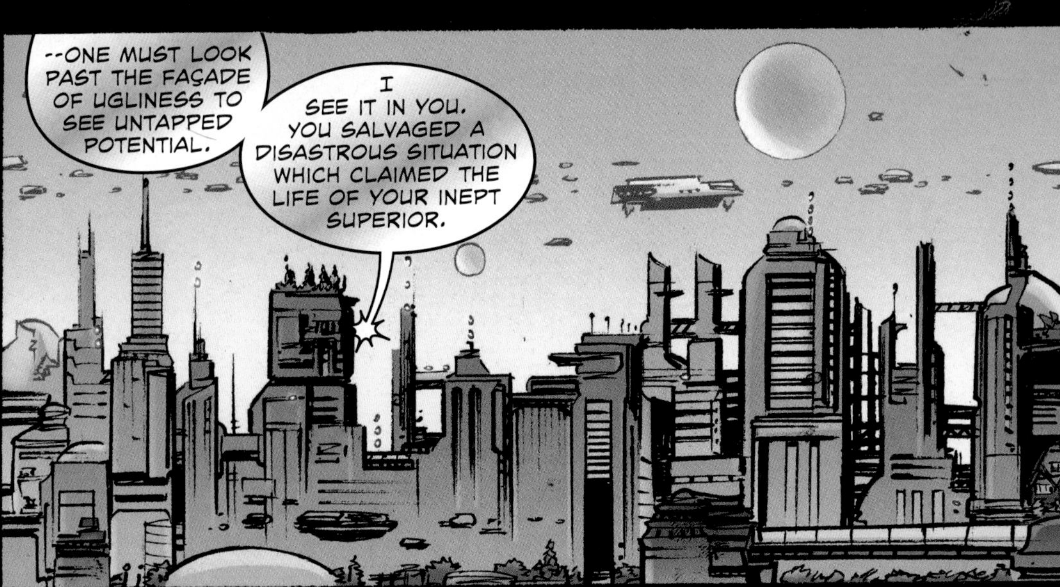
--ONE MUST LOOK PAST THE FAÇADE OF UGLINESS TO SEE UNTAPPED POTENTIAL.
I SEE IT IN YOU. YOU SALVAGED A DISASTROUS SITUATION WHICH CLAIMED THE LIFE OF YOUR INEPT SUPERIOR.

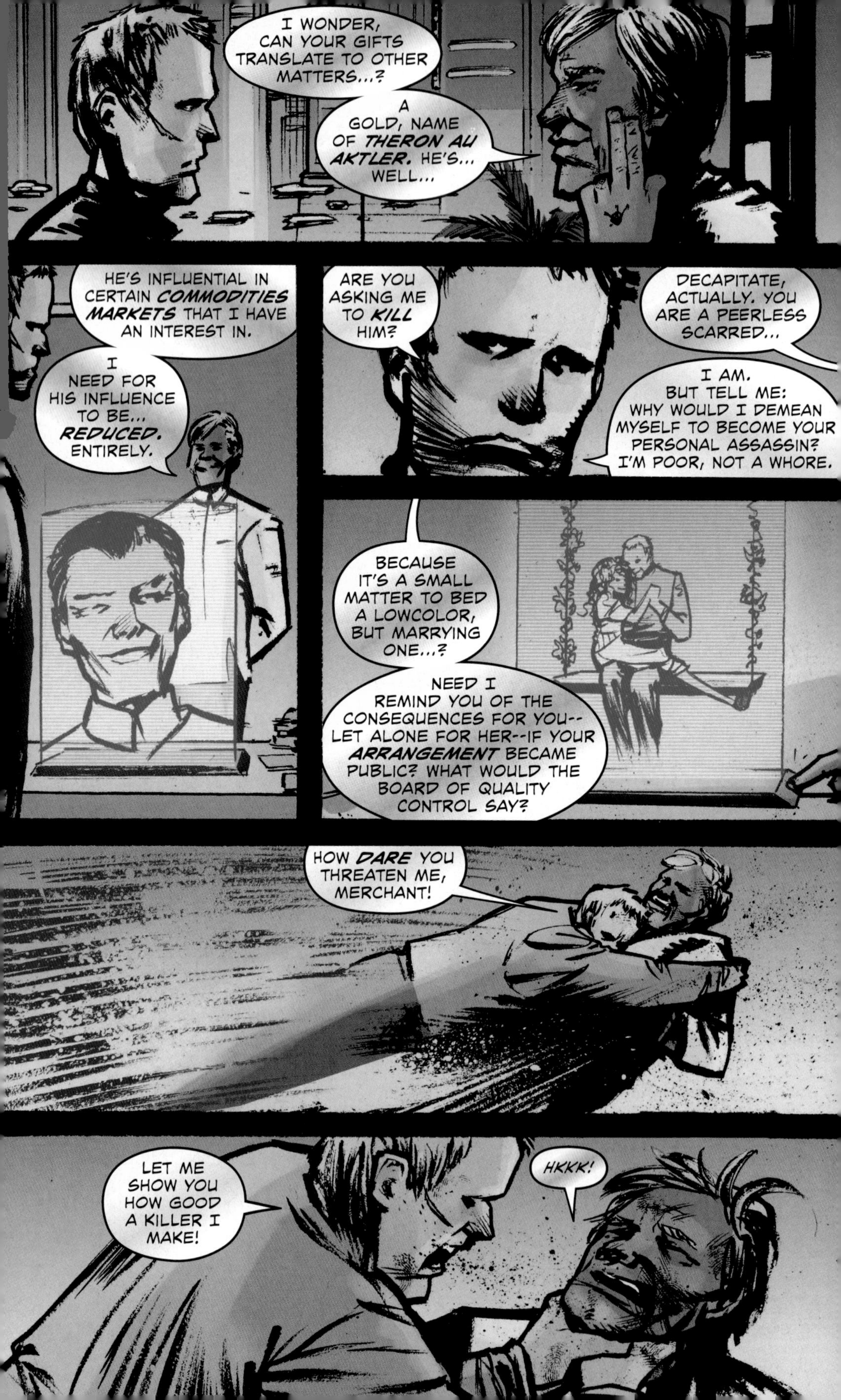
I WONDER, CAN YOUR GIFTS TRANSLATE TO OTHER MATTERS...?
A GOLD, NAME OF THERON AU AKTLER. HE'S... WELL...
HE'S INFLUENTIAL IN CERTAIN COMMODITIES MARKETS THAT I HAVE AN INTEREST IN.
I NEED FOR HIS INFLUENCE TO BE... REDUCED. ENTIRELY.
ARE YOU ASKING ME TO KILL HIM?
DECAPITATE, ACTUALLY. YOU ARE A PEERLESS SCARRED...
I AM. BUT TELL ME: WHY WOULD I DEMEAN MYSELF TO BECOME YOUR PERSONAL ASSASSIN? I'M POOR, NOT A WHORE.
BECAUSE IT'S A SMALL MATTER TO BED A LOWCOLOR, BUT MARRYING ONE...?
NEED I REMIND YOU OF THE CONSEQUENCES FOR YOU--LET ALONE FOR HER--IF YOUR ARRANGEMENT BECAME PUBLIC? WHAT WOULD THE BOARD OF QUALITY CONTROL SAY?
HOW DARE YOU THREATEN ME, MERCHANT!
LET ME SHOW YOU HOW GOOD A KILLER I MAKE!
HKKK!

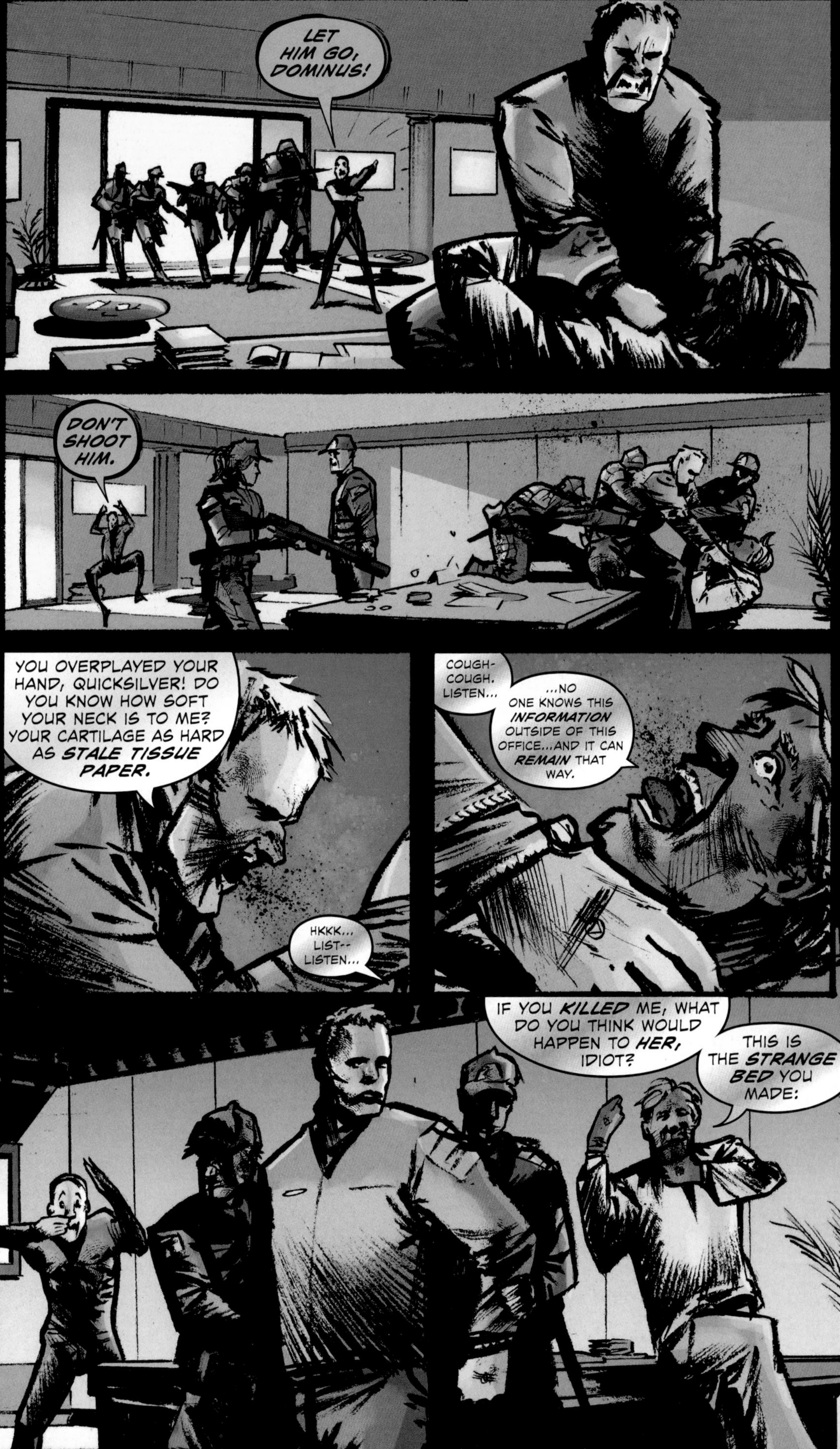
LET HIM GO, DOMINUS!
DON'T SHOOT HIM.
YOU OVERPLAYED YOUR HAND, QUICKSILVER! DO YOU KNOW HOW SOFT YOUR NECK IS TO ME? YOUR CARTILAGE AS HARD AS STALE TISSUE PAPER.
HKKK... LIST-- LISTEN...
COUGH-COUGH. LISTEN...
...NO ONE KNOWS THIS INFORMATION OUTSIDE OF THIS OFFICE...AND IT CAN REMAIN THAT WAY.
IF YOU KILLED ME, WHAT DO YOU THINK WOULD HAPPEN TO HER, IDIOT?
THIS IS THE STRANGE BED YOU MADE:

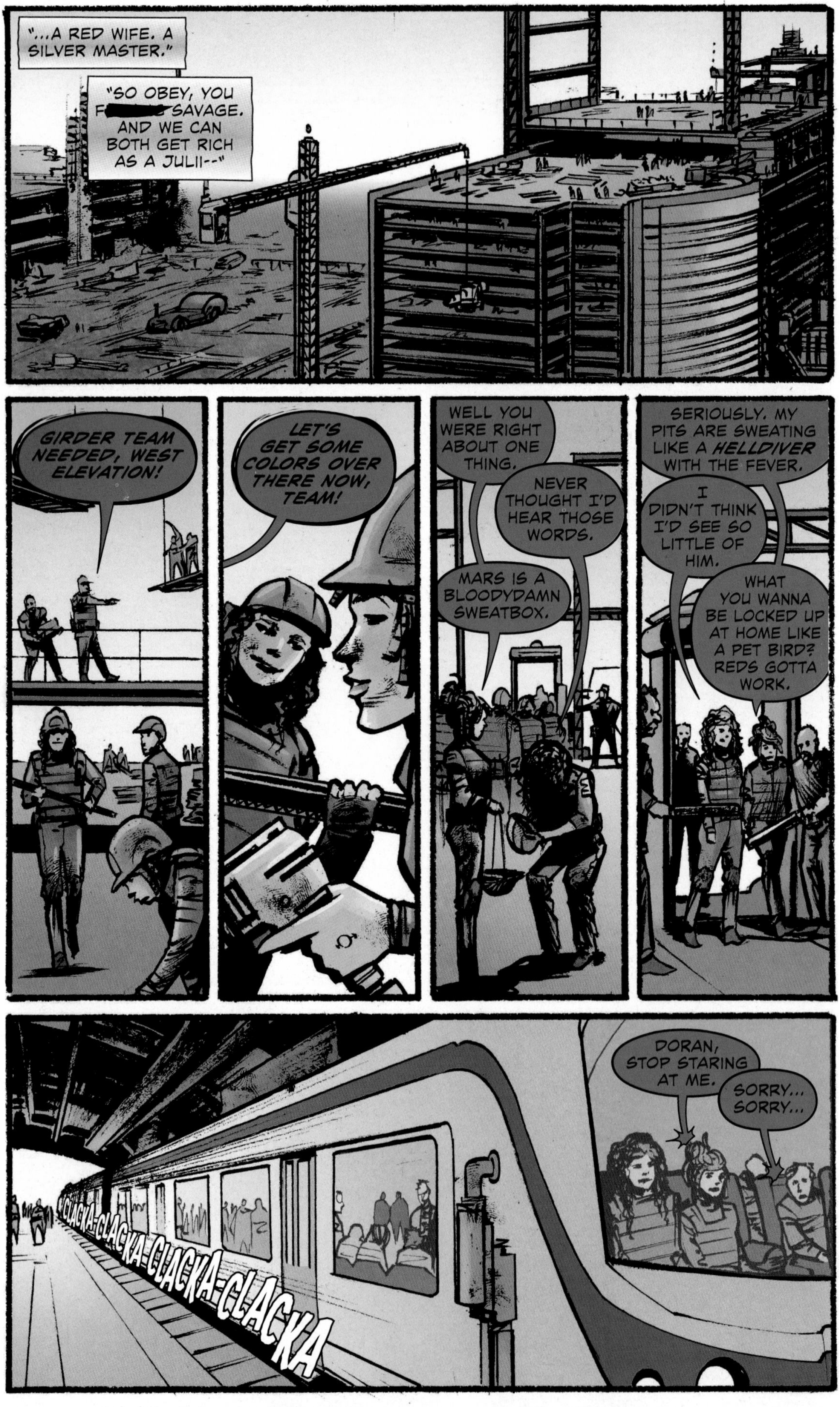
"...A RED WIFE. A SILVER MASTER."
"SO OBEY, YOU F[redacted] SAVAGE. AND WE CAN BOTH GET RICH AS A JULII--"
GIRDER TEAM NEEDED, WEST ELEVATION!
LET'S GET SOME COLORS OVER THERE NOW, TEAM!
WELL YOU WERE RIGHT ABOUT ONE THING.
NEVER THOUGHT I'D HEAR THOSE WORDS.
MARS IS A BLOODYDAMN SWEATBOX.
SERIOUSLY. MY PITS ARE SWEATING LIKE A HELLDIVER WITH THE FEVER.
I DIDN'T THINK I'D SEE SO LITTLE OF HIM.
WHAT YOU WANNA BE LOCKED UP AT HOME LIKE A PET BIRD? REDS GOTTA WORK.
CLACKA-CLACKA-CLACKA-CLACKA
DORAN, STOP STARING AT ME.
SORRY... SORRY...

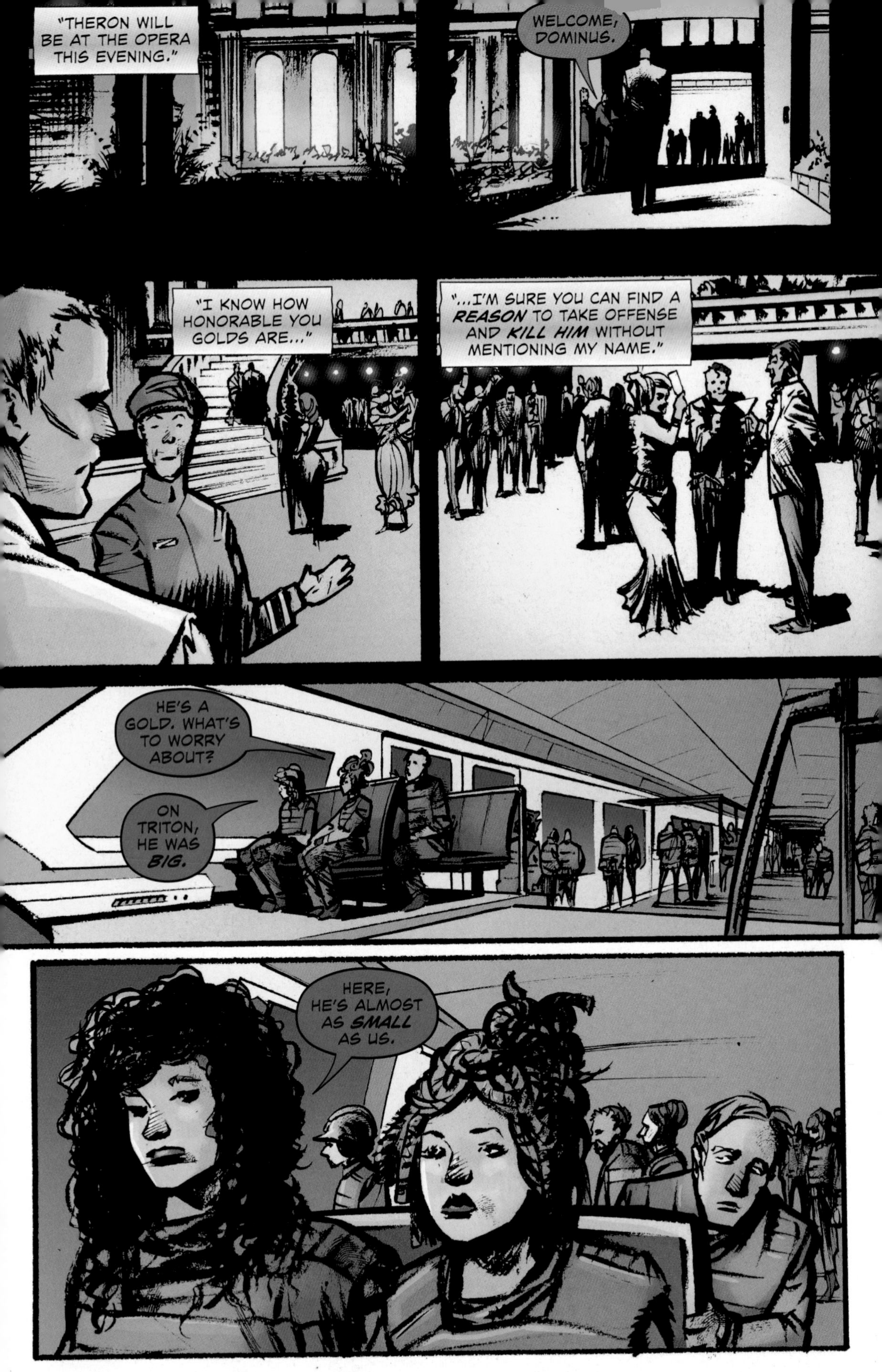
"THERON WILL BE AT THE OPERA THIS EVENING."
WELCOME, DOMINUS.
"I KNOW HOW HONORABLE YOU GOLDS ARE..."
"...I'M SURE YOU CAN FIND A *REASON* TO TAKE OFFENSE AND *KILL HIM* WITHOUT MENTIONING MY NAME."
HE'S A GOLD. WHAT'S TO WORRY ABOUT?
ON TRITON, HE WAS *BIG*.
HERE, HE'S ALMOST AS *SMALL* AS US.

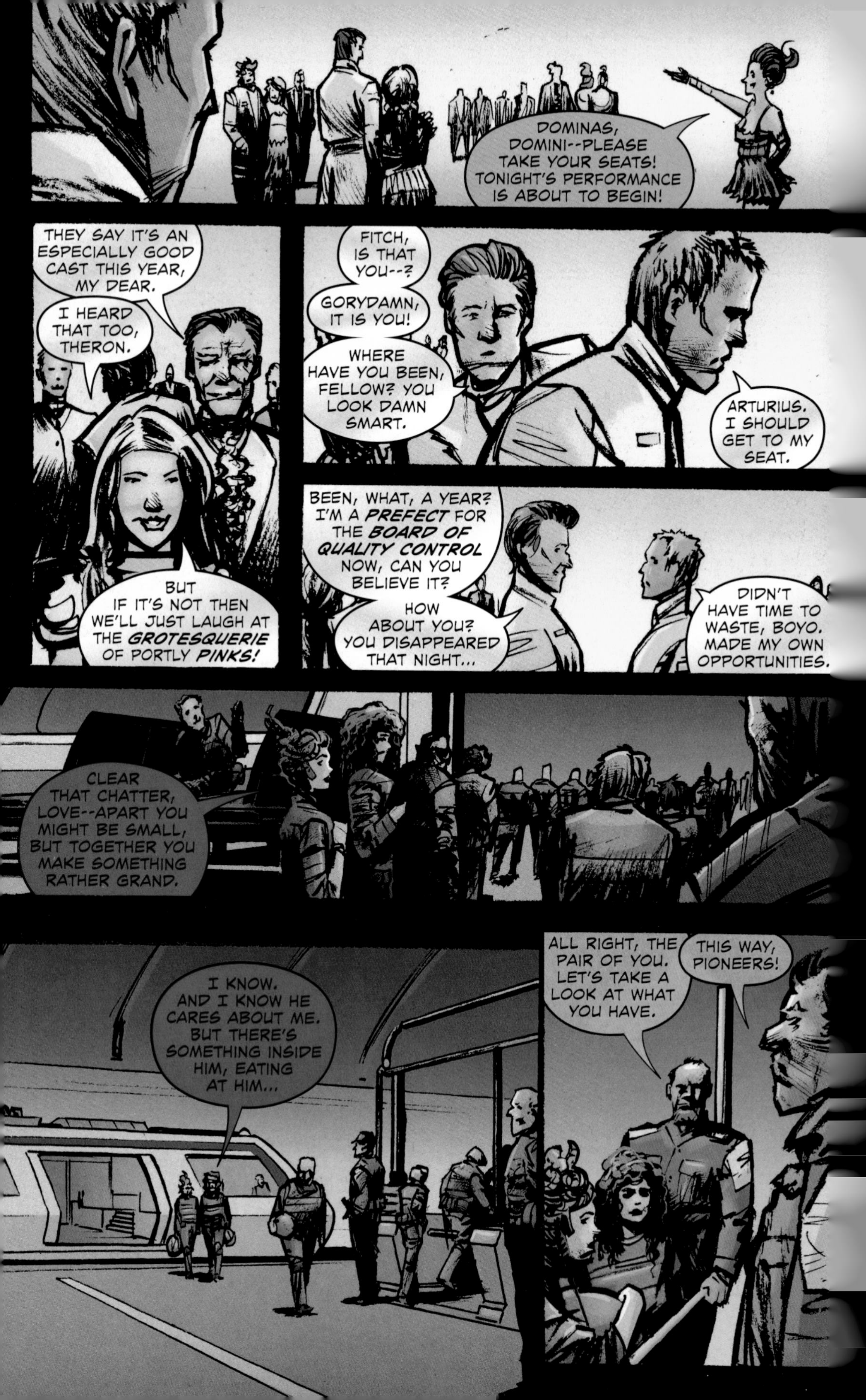
DOMINAS, DOMINI--PLEASE TAKE YOUR SEATS! TONIGHT'S PERFORMANCE IS ABOUT TO BEGIN!
THEY SAY IT'S AN ESPECIALLY GOOD CAST THIS YEAR, MY DEAR.
I HEARD THAT TOO, THERON.
BUT IF IT'S NOT THEN WE'LL JUST LAUGH AT THE *GROTESQUERIE* OF PORTLY *PINKS!*
FITCH, IS THAT YOU--?
GORYDAMN, IT IS YOU!
WHERE HAVE YOU BEEN, FELLOW? YOU LOOK DAMN SMART.
ARTURIUS. I SHOULD GET TO MY SEAT.
BEEN, WHAT, A YEAR? I'M A *PREFECT* FOR THE *BOARD OF QUALITY CONTROL* NOW, CAN YOU BELIEVE IT?
HOW ABOUT YOU? YOU DISAPPEARED THAT NIGHT...
DIDN'T HAVE TIME TO WASTE, BOYO. MADE MY OWN OPPORTUNITIES.
CLEAR THAT CHATTER, LOVE--APART YOU MIGHT BE SMALL, BUT TOGETHER YOU MAKE SOMETHING RATHER GRAND.
I KNOW. AND I KNOW HE CARES ABOUT ME. BUT THERE'S SOMETHING INSIDE HIM, EATING AT HIM...
ALL RIGHT, THE PAIR OF YOU. LET'S TAKE A LOOK AT WHAT YOU HAVE.
THIS WAY, PIONEERS!

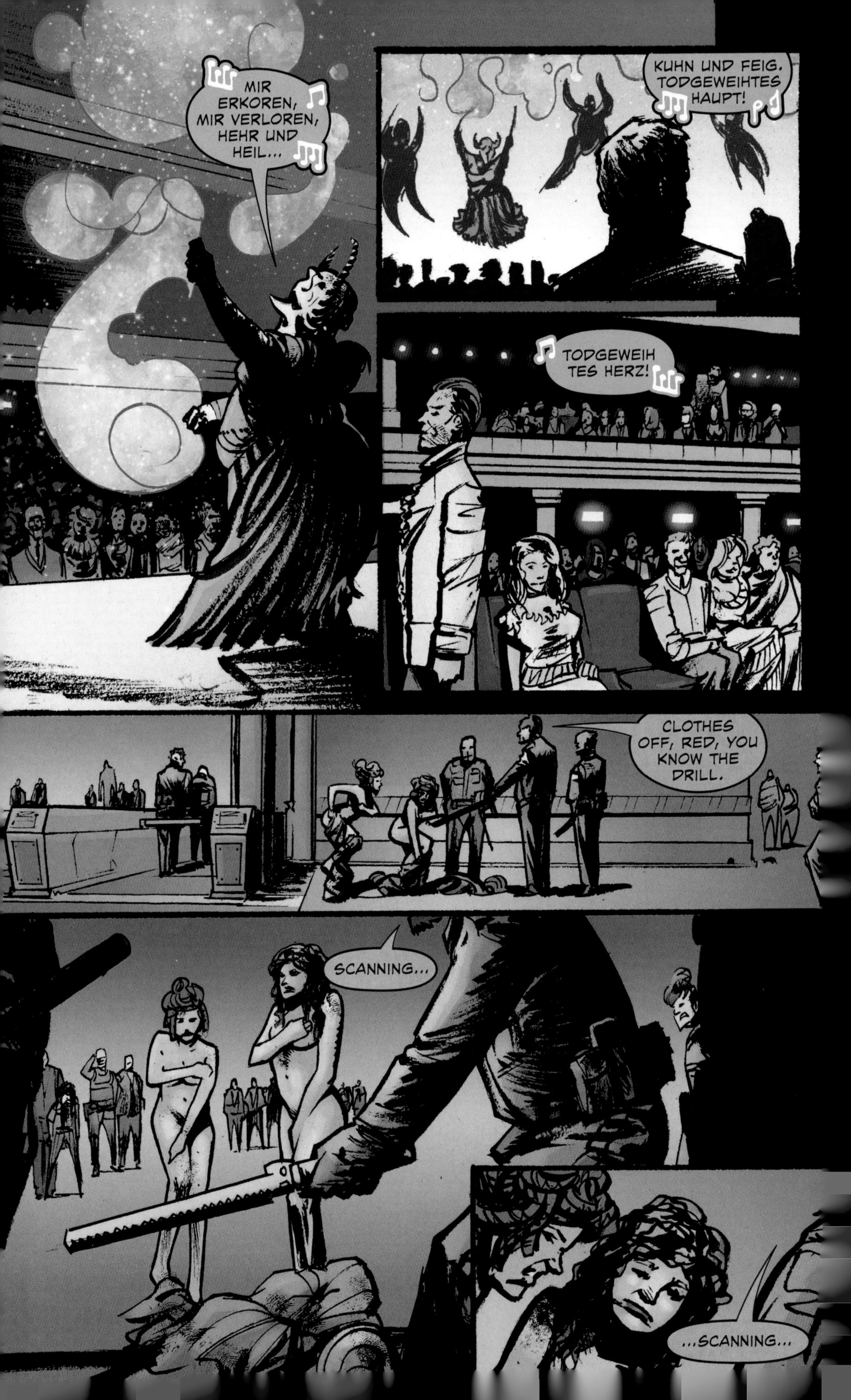
MIR ERKOREN, MIR VERLOREN, HEHR UND HEIL...
KUHN UND FEIG. TODGEWEIHTES HAUPT!
TODGEWEIH TES HERZ!
CLOTHES OFF, RED, YOU KNOW THE DRILL.
SCANNING...
...SCANNING...

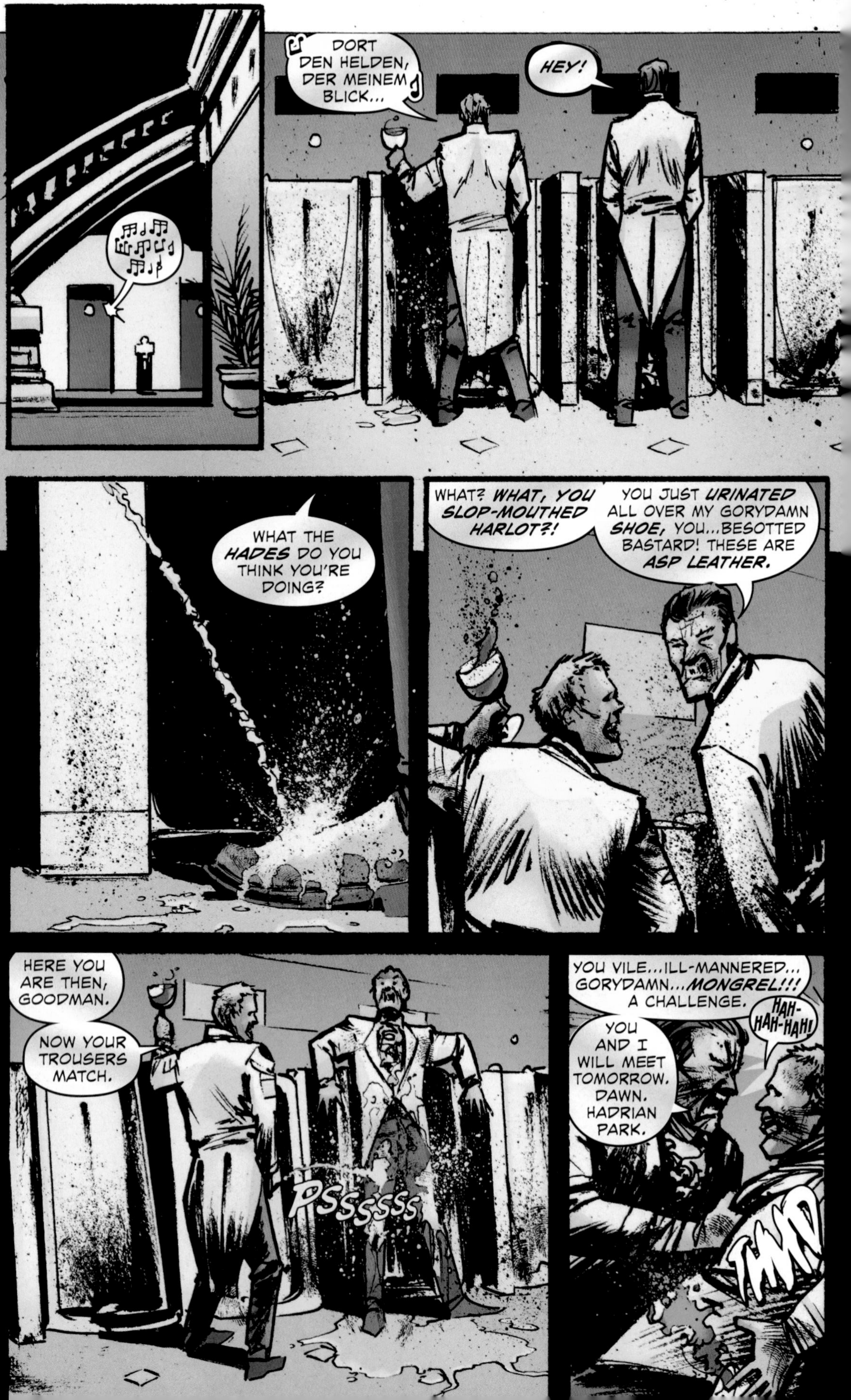
DORT DEN HELDEN, DER MEINEM BLICK...
HEY!
WHAT THE HADES DO YOU THINK YOU'RE DOING?
WHAT? WHAT, YOU SLOP-MOUTHED HARLOT?!
YOU JUST URINATED ALL OVER MY GORYDAMN SHOE, YOU...BESOTTED BASTARD! THESE ARE ASP LEATHER.
HERE YOU ARE THEN, GOODMAN.
NOW YOUR TROUSERS MATCH.
PSSSSSS
YOU VILE...ILL-MANNERED... GORYDAMN...MONGREL!!! A CHALLENGE.
HAH-HAH-HAH!
YOU AND I WILL MEET TOMORROW. DAWN. HADRIAN PARK.
THMP

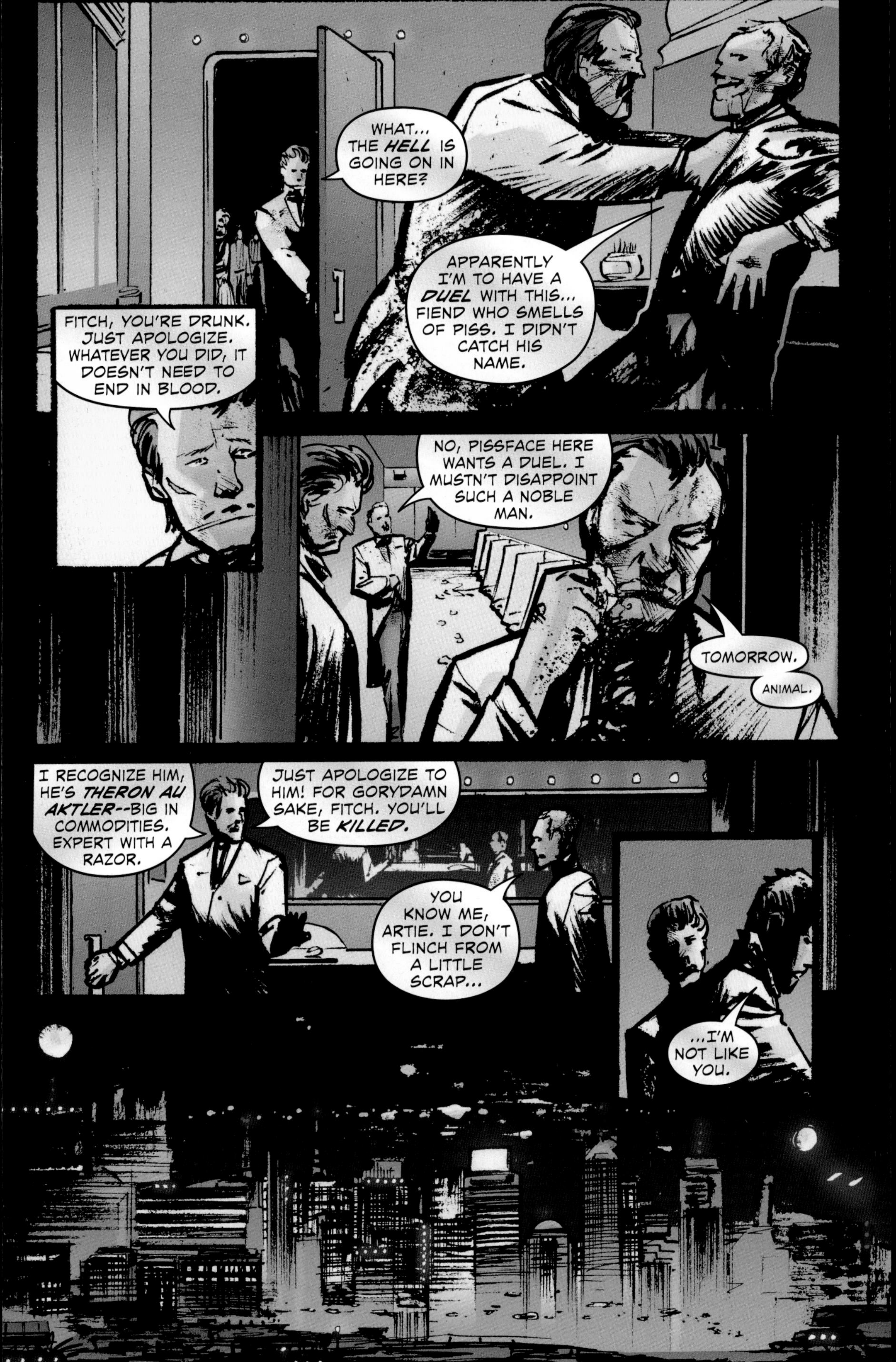
WHAT... THE *HELL* IS GOING ON IN HERE?
APPARENTLY I'M TO HAVE A *DUEL* WITH THIS... FIEND WHO SMELLS OF PISS. I DIDN'T CATCH HIS NAME.
FITCH, YOU'RE DRUNK. JUST APOLOGIZE. WHATEVER YOU DID, IT DOESN'T NEED TO END IN BLOOD.
NO, PISSFACE HERE WANTS A DUEL. I MUSTN'T DISAPPOINT SUCH A NOBLE MAN.
TOMORROW.
ANIMAL.
I RECOGNIZE HIM, HE'S *THERON AU AKTLER*--BIG IN COMMODITIES. EXPERT WITH A RAZOR.
JUST APOLOGIZE TO HIM! FOR GORYDAMN SAKE, FITCH. YOU'LL BE *KILLED.*
YOU KNOW ME, ARTIE. I DON'T FLINCH FROM A LITTLE SCRAP...
...I'M NOT LIKE YOU.

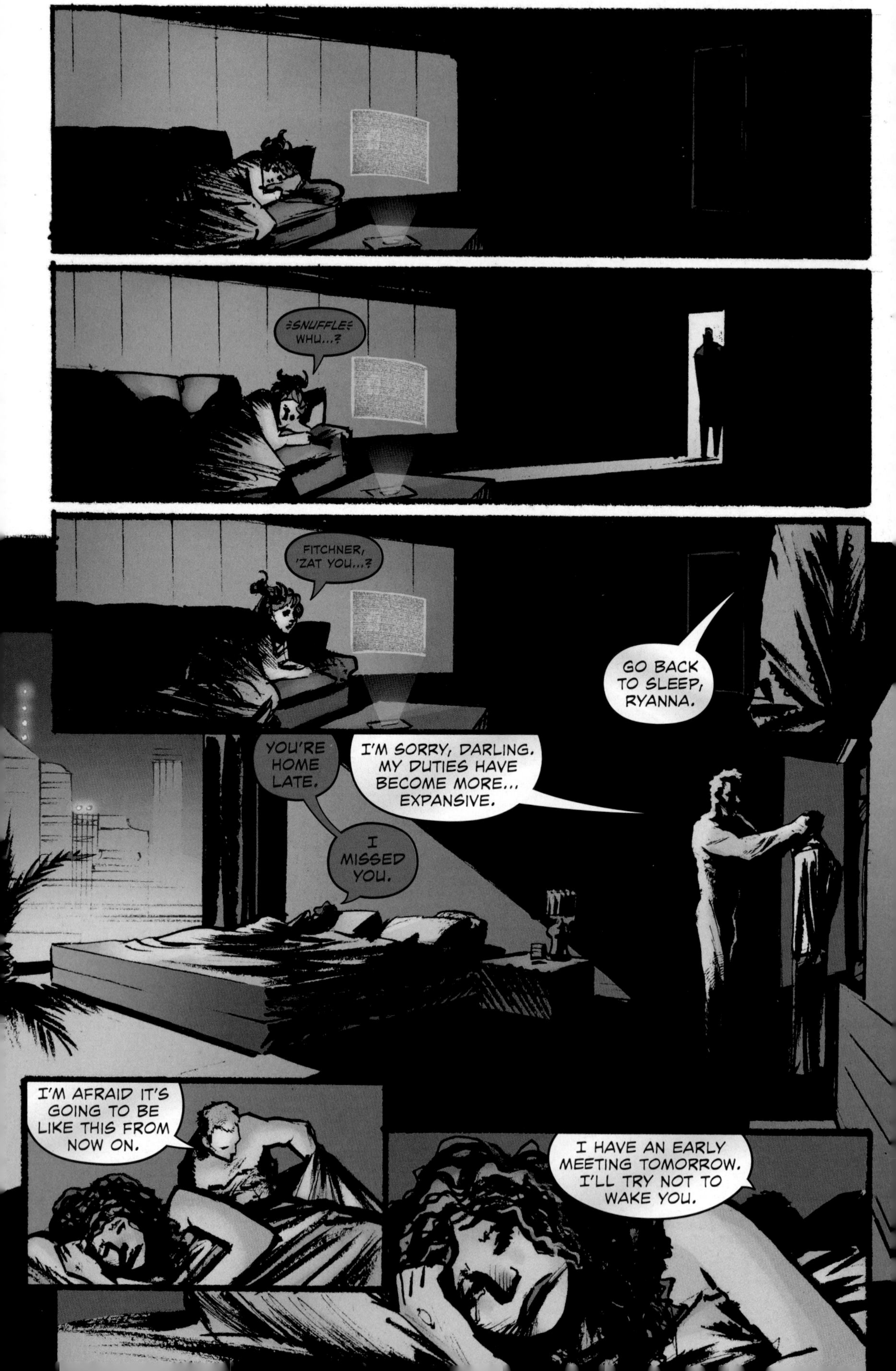

SNUFFLE WHU...?
FITCHNER, 'ZAT YOU...?
GO BACK TO SLEEP, RYANNA.
YOU'RE HOME LATE.
I'M SORRY, DARLING. MY DUTIES HAVE BECOME MORE... EXPANSIVE.
I MISSED YOU.
I'M AFRAID IT'S GOING TO BE LIKE THIS FROM NOW ON.
I HAVE AN EARLY MEETING TOMORROW. I'LL TRY NOT TO WAKE YOU.

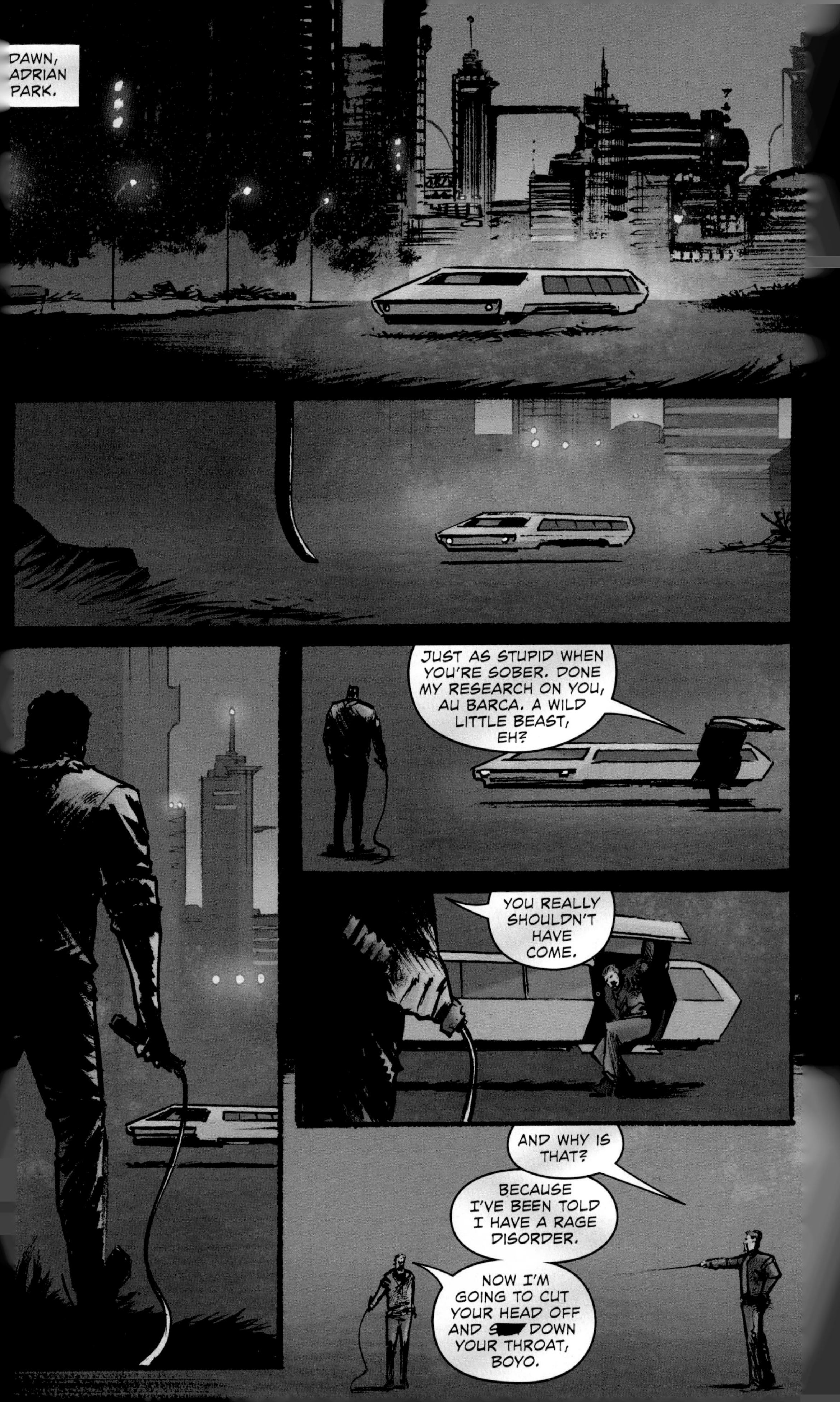
DAWN, ADRIAN PARK.
JUST AS STUPID WHEN YOU'RE SOBER. DONE MY RESEARCH ON YOU, AU BARCA. A WILD LITTLE BEAST, EH?
YOU REALLY SHOULDN'T HAVE COME.
AND WHY IS THAT?
BECAUSE I'VE BEEN TOLD I HAVE A RAGE DISORDER.
NOW I'M GOING TO CUT YOUR HEAD OFF AND S[redacted] DOWN YOUR THROAT, BOYO.

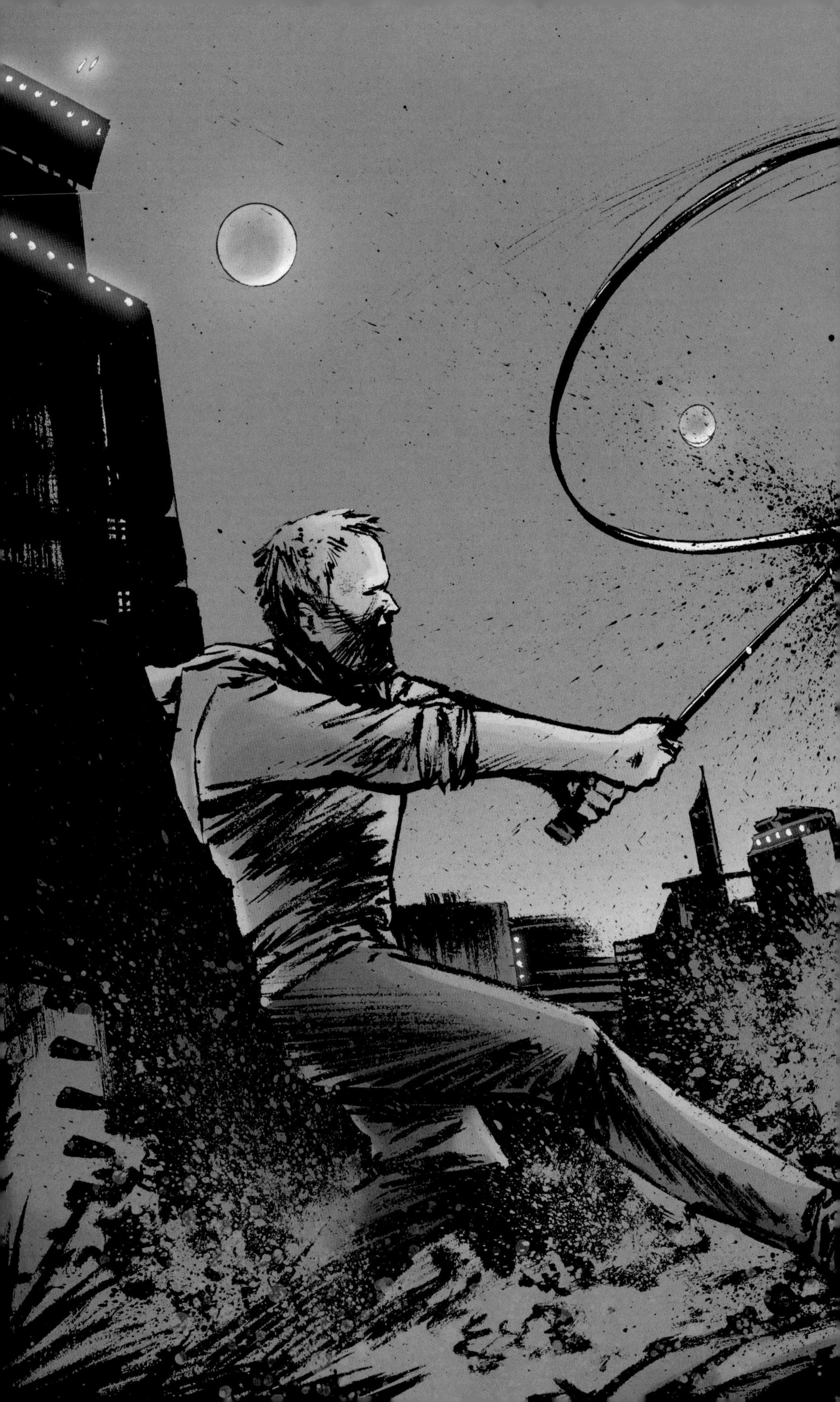

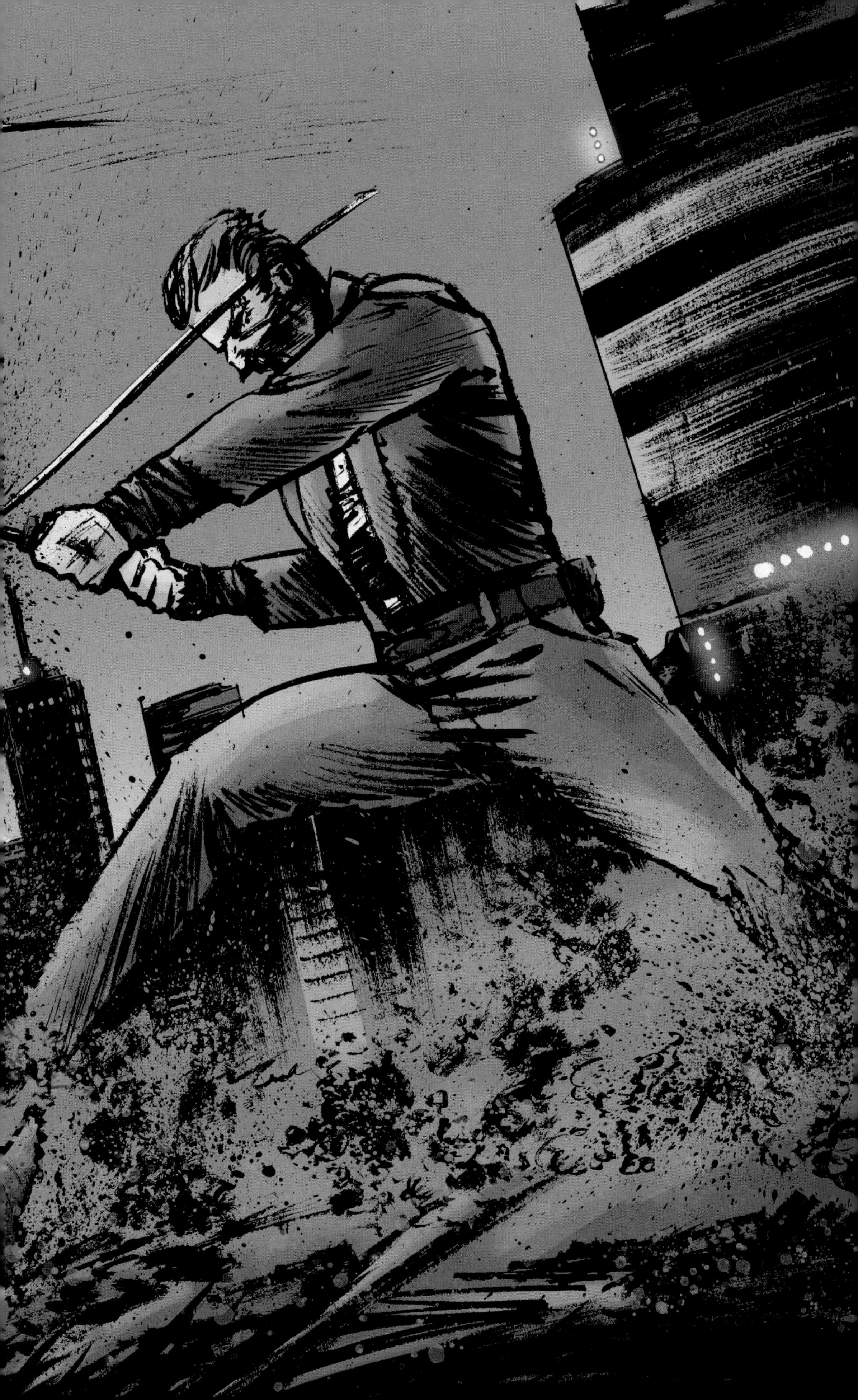

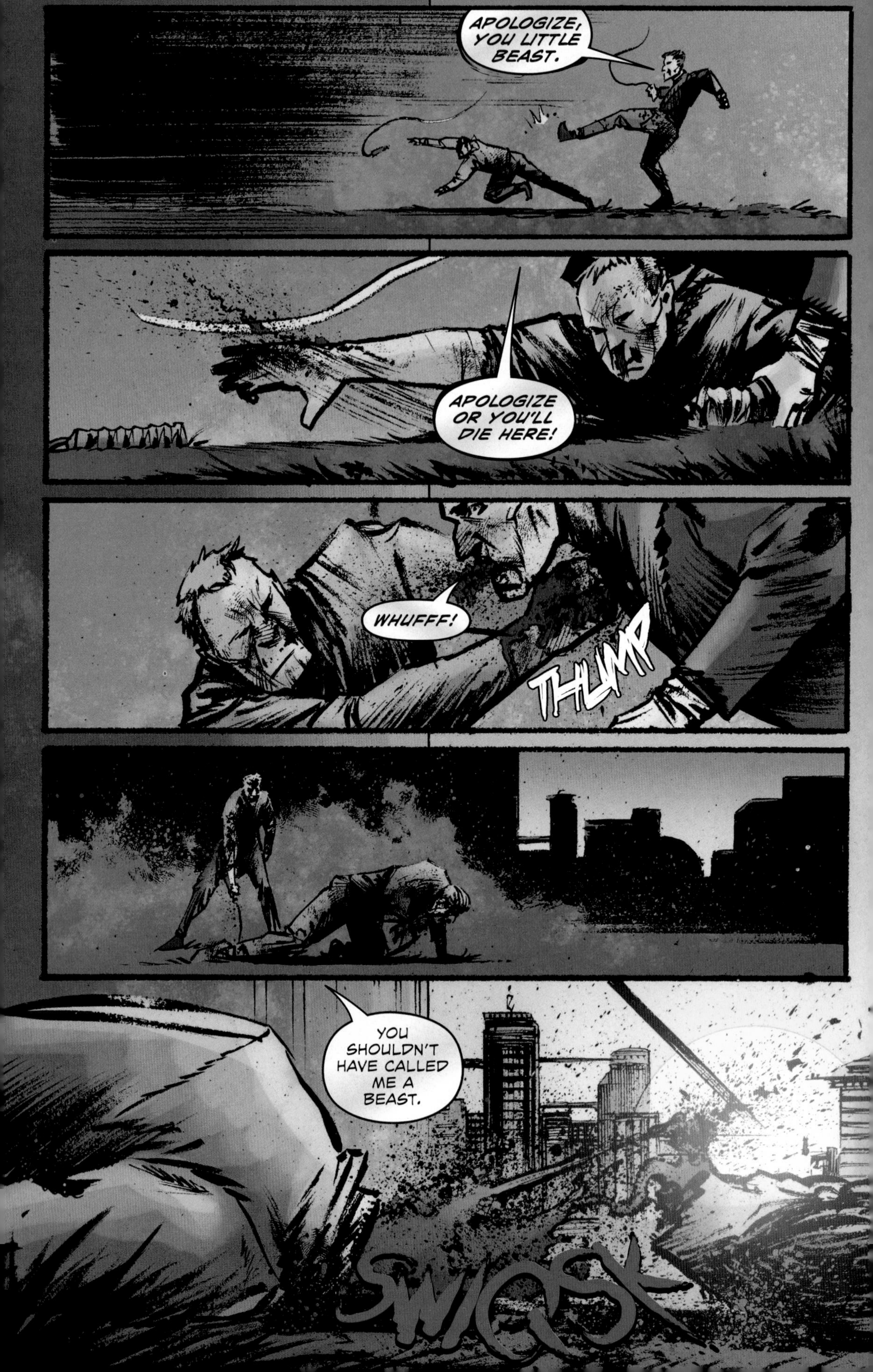
APOLOGIZE, YOU LITTLE BEAST.
APOLOGIZE OR YOU'LL DIE HERE!
WHUFFF!
THUMP
YOU SHOULDN'T HAVE CALLED ME A BEAST.
SWOOSH

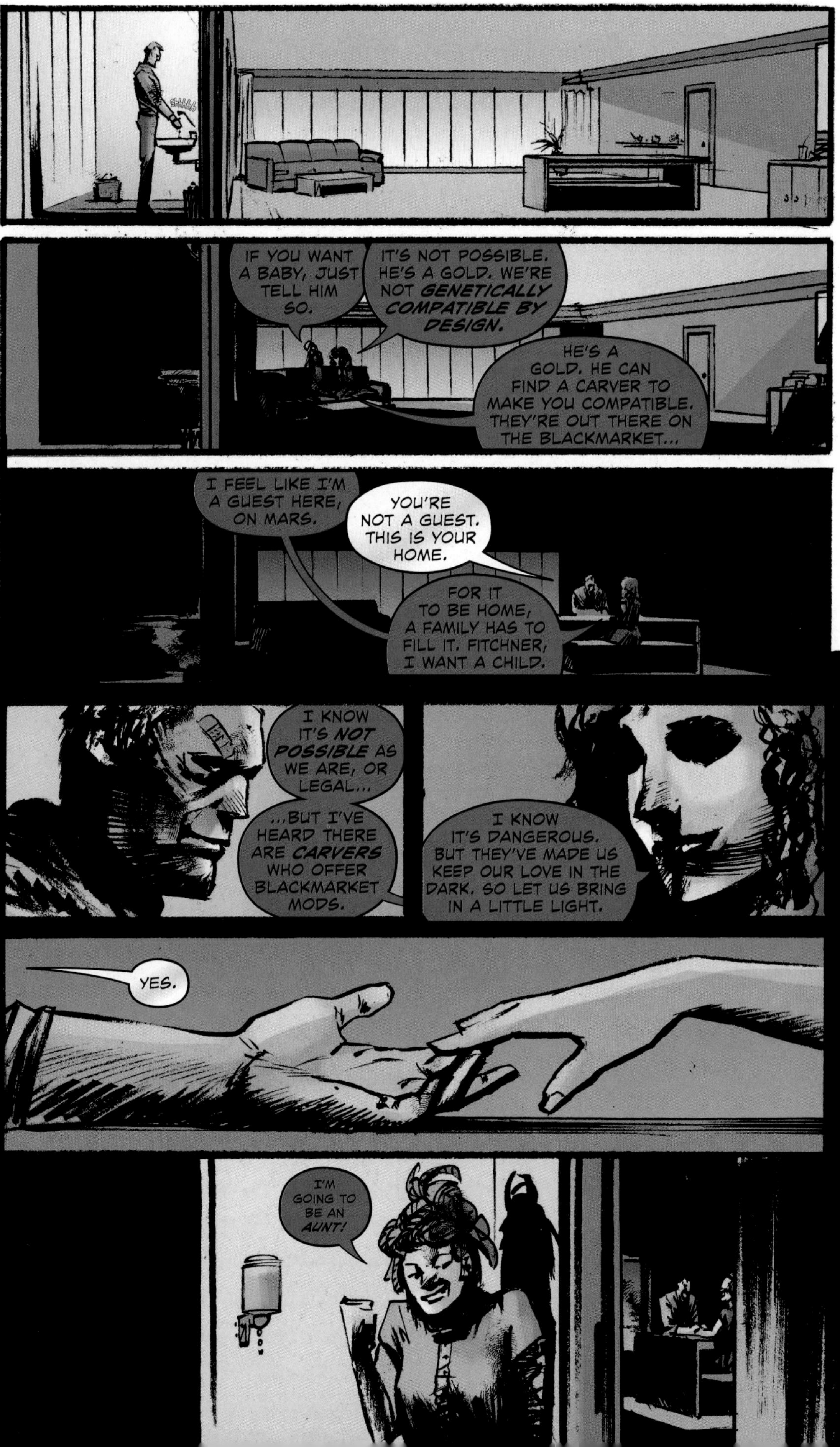
Shhhhh
IF YOU WANT A BABY, JUST TELL HIM SO.
IT'S NOT POSSIBLE. HE'S A GOLD. WE'RE NOT *GENETICALLY COMPATIBLE BY DESIGN.*
HE'S A GOLD. HE CAN FIND A CARVER TO MAKE YOU COMPATIBLE. THEY'RE OUT THERE ON THE BLACKMARKET...
I FEEL LIKE I'M A GUEST HERE, ON MARS.
YOU'RE NOT A GUEST. THIS IS YOUR HOME.
FOR IT TO BE HOME, A FAMILY HAS TO FILL IT. FITCHNER, I WANT A CHILD.
I KNOW IT'S *NOT POSSIBLE* AS WE ARE, OR LEGAL...
...BUT I'VE HEARD THERE ARE *CARVERS* WHO OFFER BLACKMARKET MODS.
I KNOW IT'S DANGEROUS. BUT THEY'VE MADE US KEEP OUR LOVE IN THE DARK. SO LET US BRING IN A LITTLE LIGHT.
YES.
I'M GOING TO BE AN *AUNT!*

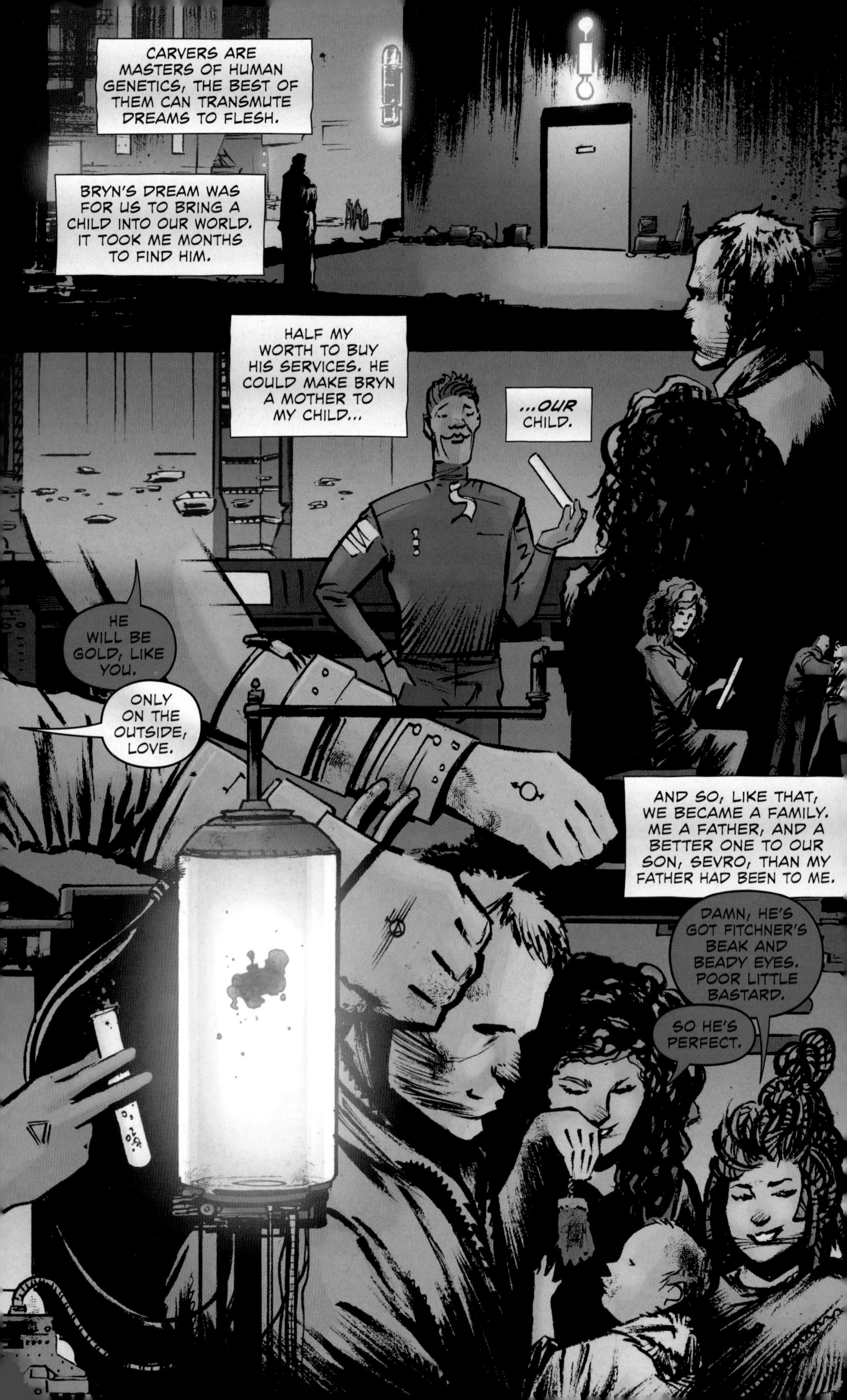
CARVERS ARE MASTERS OF HUMAN GENETICS, THE BEST OF THEM CAN TRANSMUTE DREAMS TO FLESH.
BRYN'S DREAM WAS FOR US TO BRING A CHILD INTO OUR WORLD. IT TOOK ME MONTHS TO FIND HIM.
HALF MY WORTH TO BUY HIS SERVICES. HE COULD MAKE BRYN A MOTHER TO MY CHILD...
...OUR CHILD.
HE WILL BE GOLD, LIKE YOU.
ONLY ON THE OUTSIDE, LOVE.
AND SO, LIKE THAT, WE BECAME A FAMILY. ME A FATHER, AND A BETTER ONE TO OUR SON, SEVRO, THAN MY FATHER HAD BEEN TO ME.
DAMN, HE'S GOT FITCHNER'S BEAK AND BEADY EYES. POOR LITTLE BASTARD.
SO HE'S PERFECT.

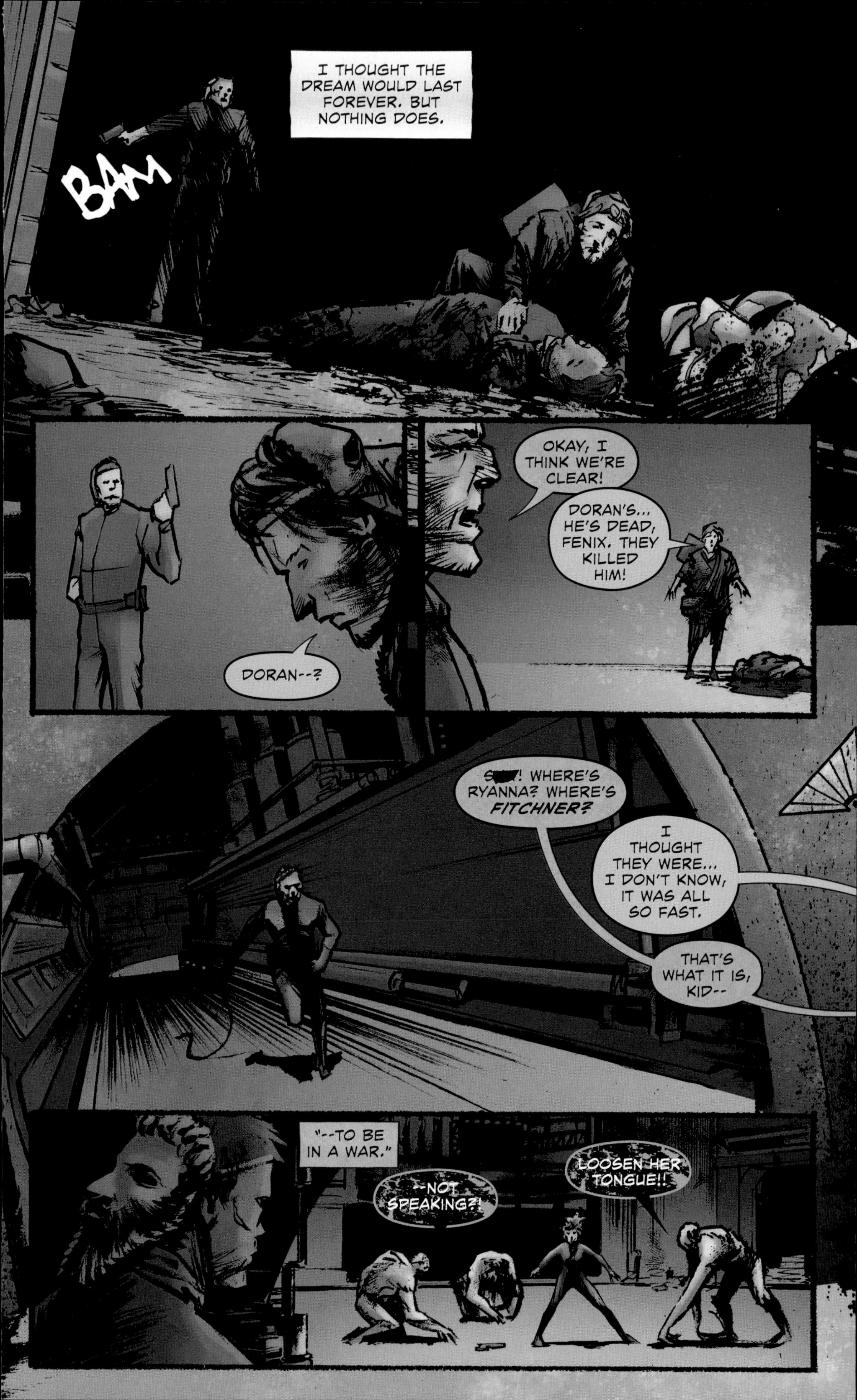
I THOUGHT THE DREAM WOULD LAST FOREVER. BUT NOTHING DOES.
BAM
DORAN--?
OKAY, I THINK WE'RE CLEAR!
DORAN'S... HE'S DEAD, FENIX. THEY KILLED HIM!
S[redacted]! WHERE'S RYANNA? WHERE'S *FITCHNER?*
I THOUGHT THEY WERE... I DON'T KNOW, IT WAS ALL SO FAST.
THAT'S WHAT IT IS, KID--
"--TO BE IN A WAR."
--NOT SPEAKING?!
LOOSEN HER TONGUE!!

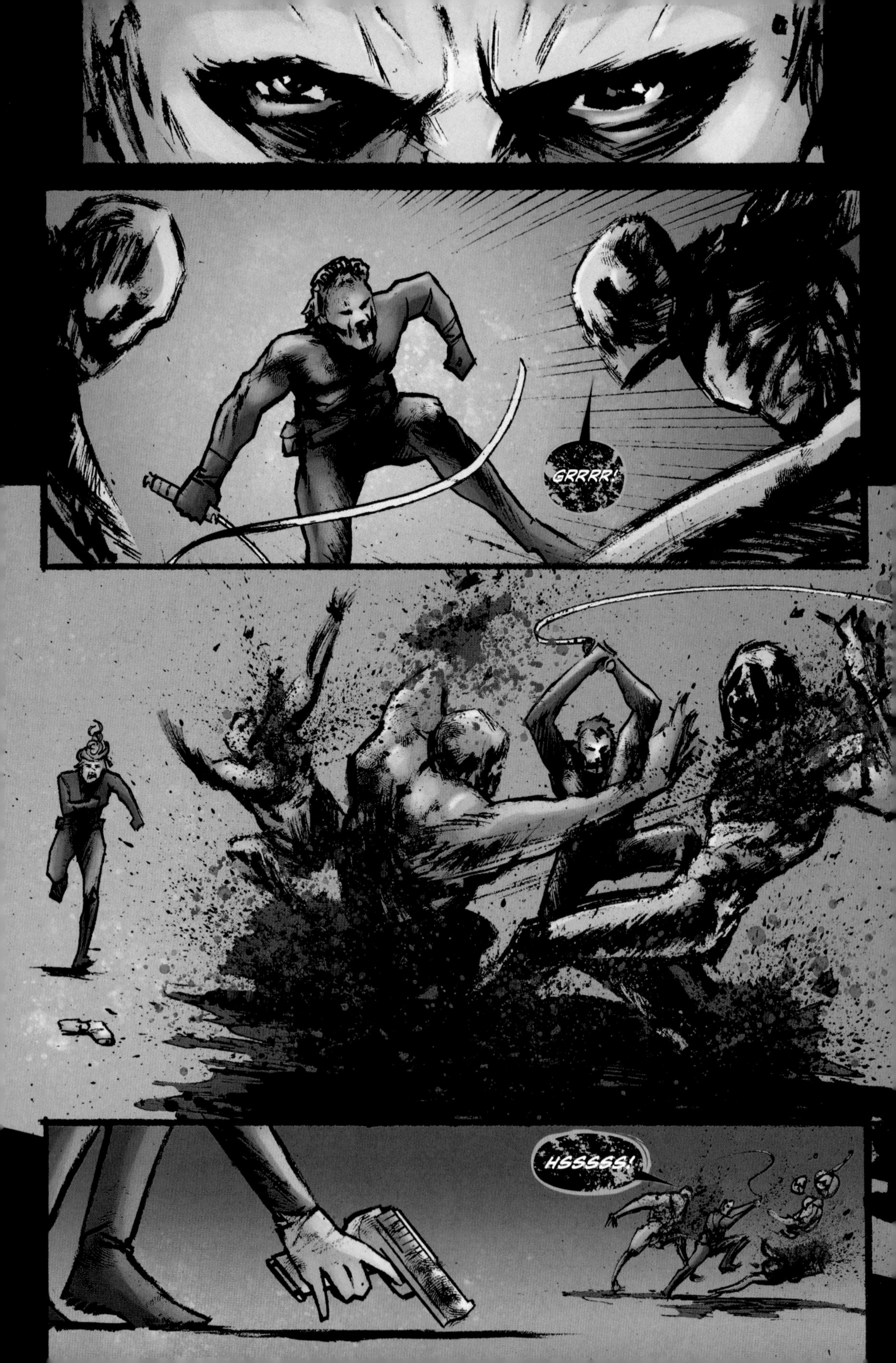
GRRRR!
HSSSSS!

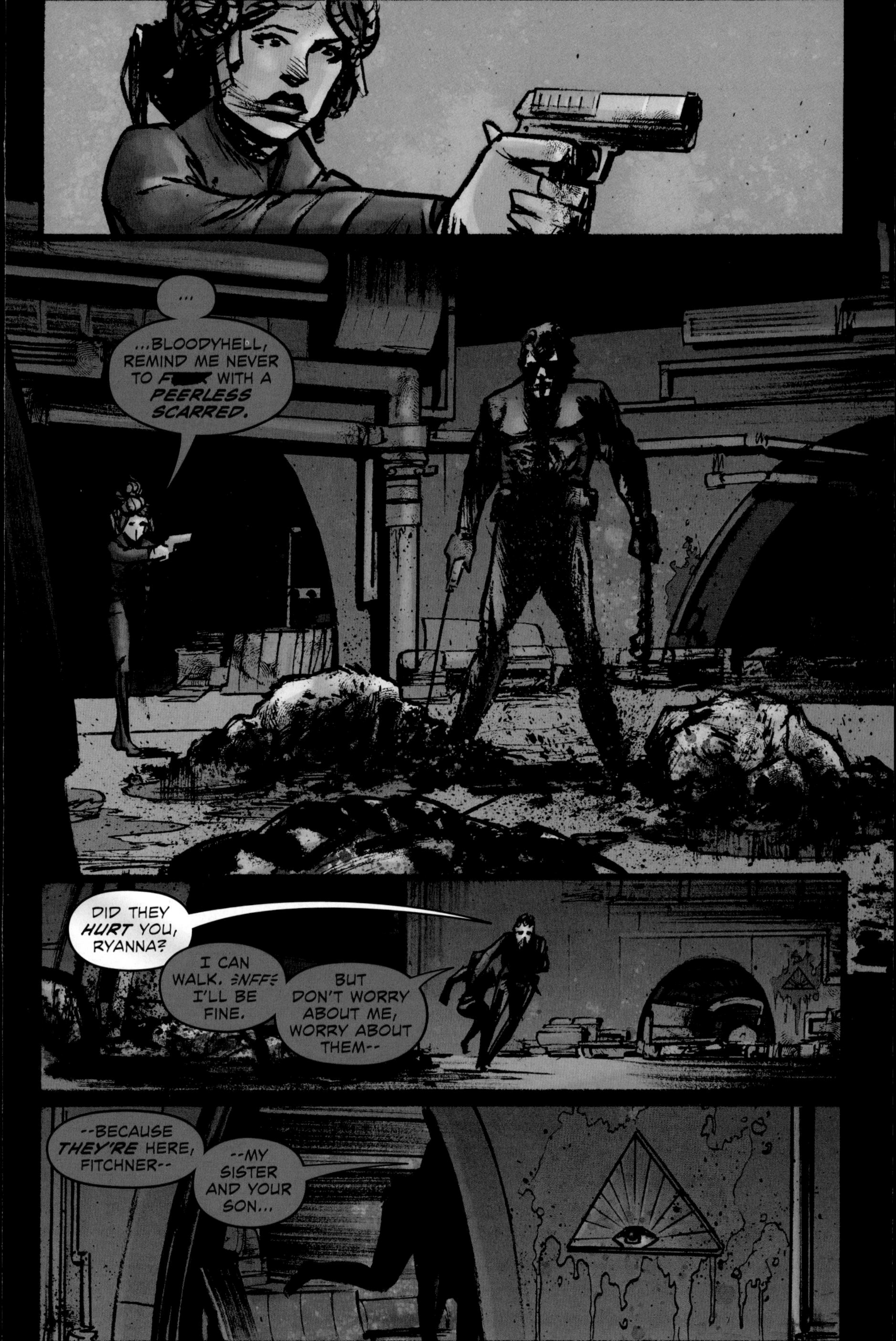
...
...BLOODYHELL, REMIND ME NEVER TO F[redacted] WITH A *PEERLESS SCARRED.*
DID THEY *HURT* YOU, RYANNA?
I CAN WALK. SNFF I'LL BE FINE.
BUT DON'T WORRY ABOUT ME, WORRY ABOUT THEM--
--BECAUSE *THEY'RE* HERE, FITCHNER--
--MY SISTER AND YOUR SON...

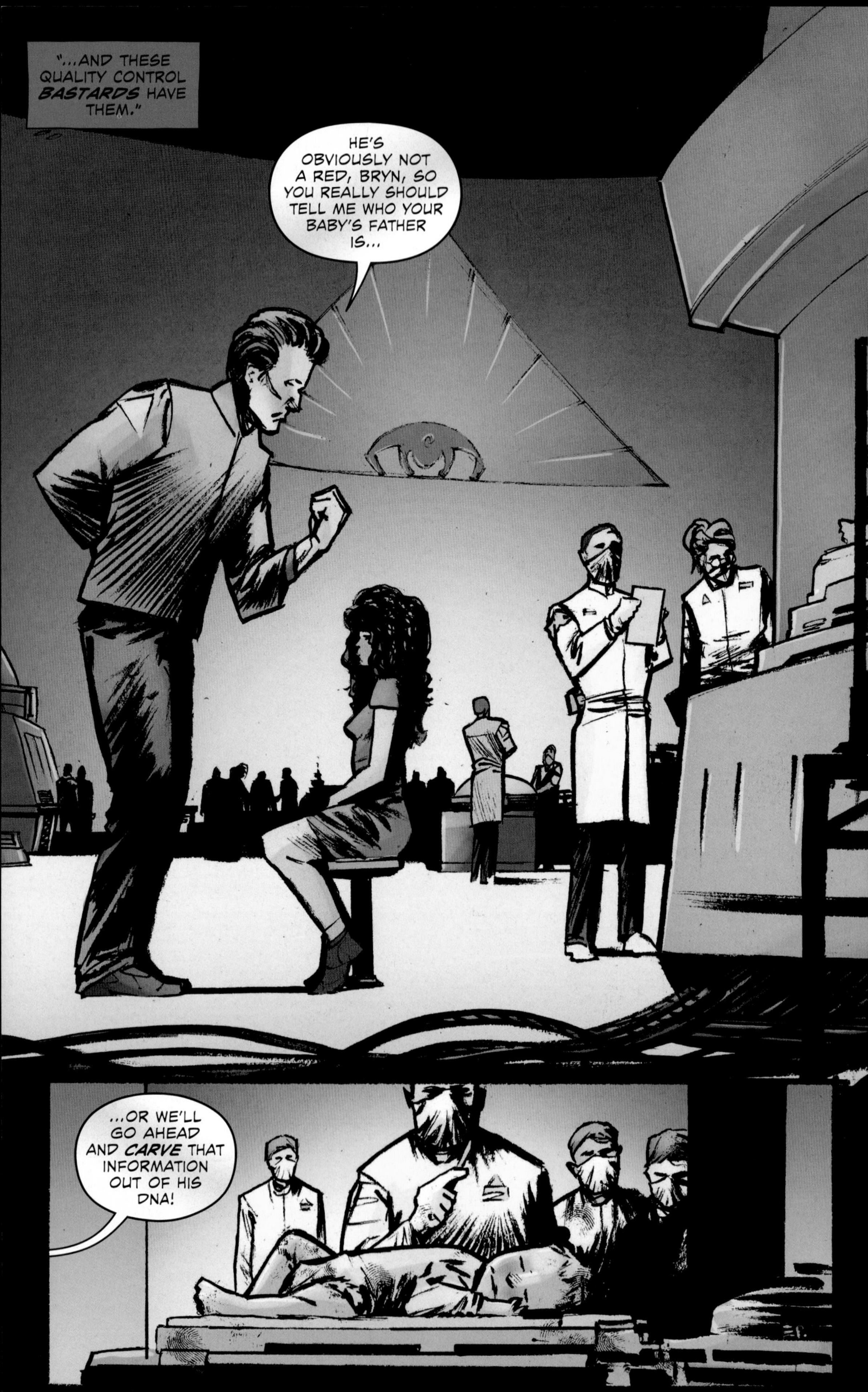
"...AND THESE QUALITY CONTROL BASTARDS HAVE THEM."
HE'S OBVIOUSLY NOT A RED, BRYN, SO YOU REALLY SHOULD TELL ME WHO YOUR BABY'S FATHER IS...
...OR WE'LL GO AHEAD AND CARVE THAT INFORMATION OUT OF HIS DNA!

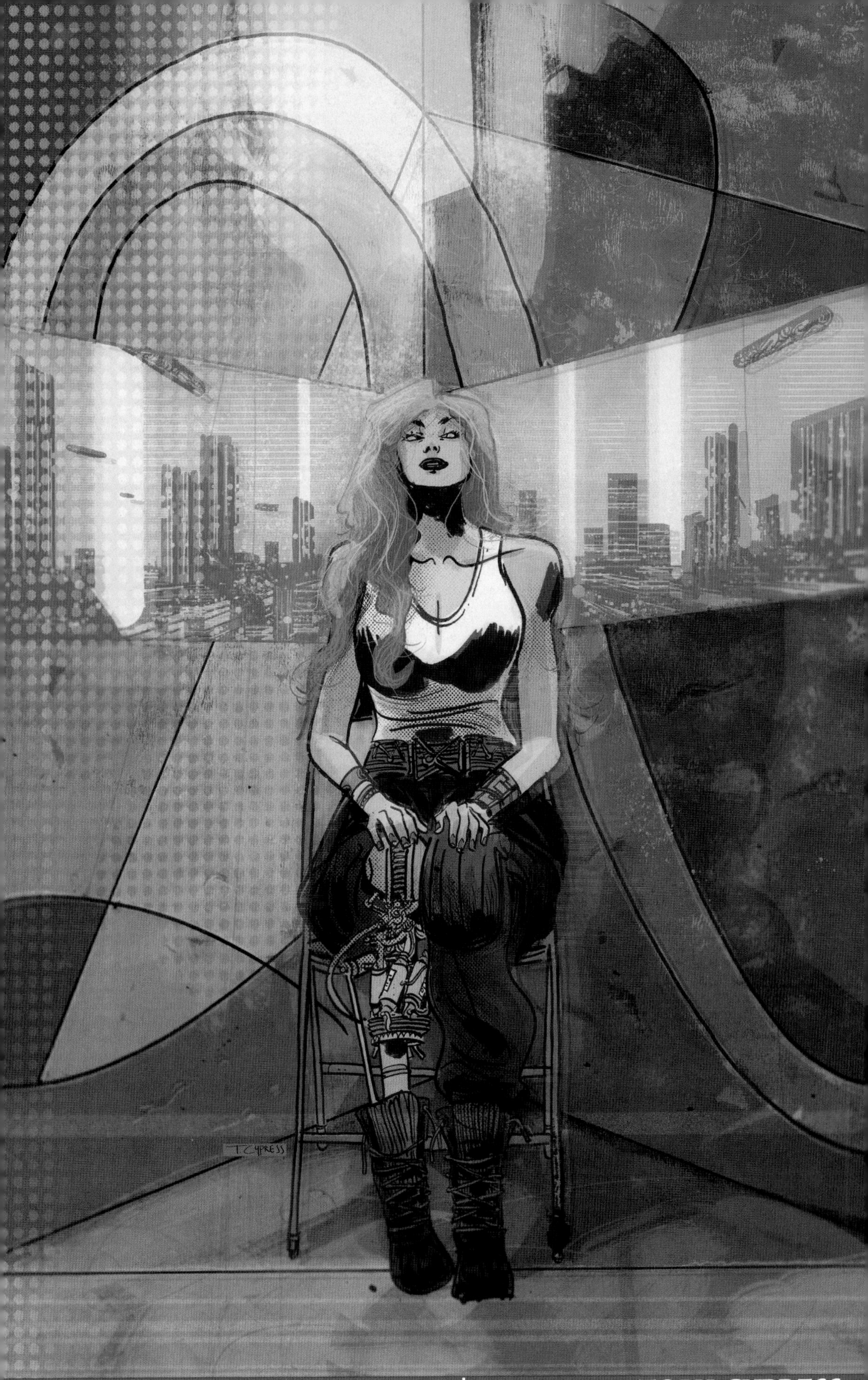
T. CYPRESS

ISSUE FIVE | COVER ART BY TOBY CYPRESS

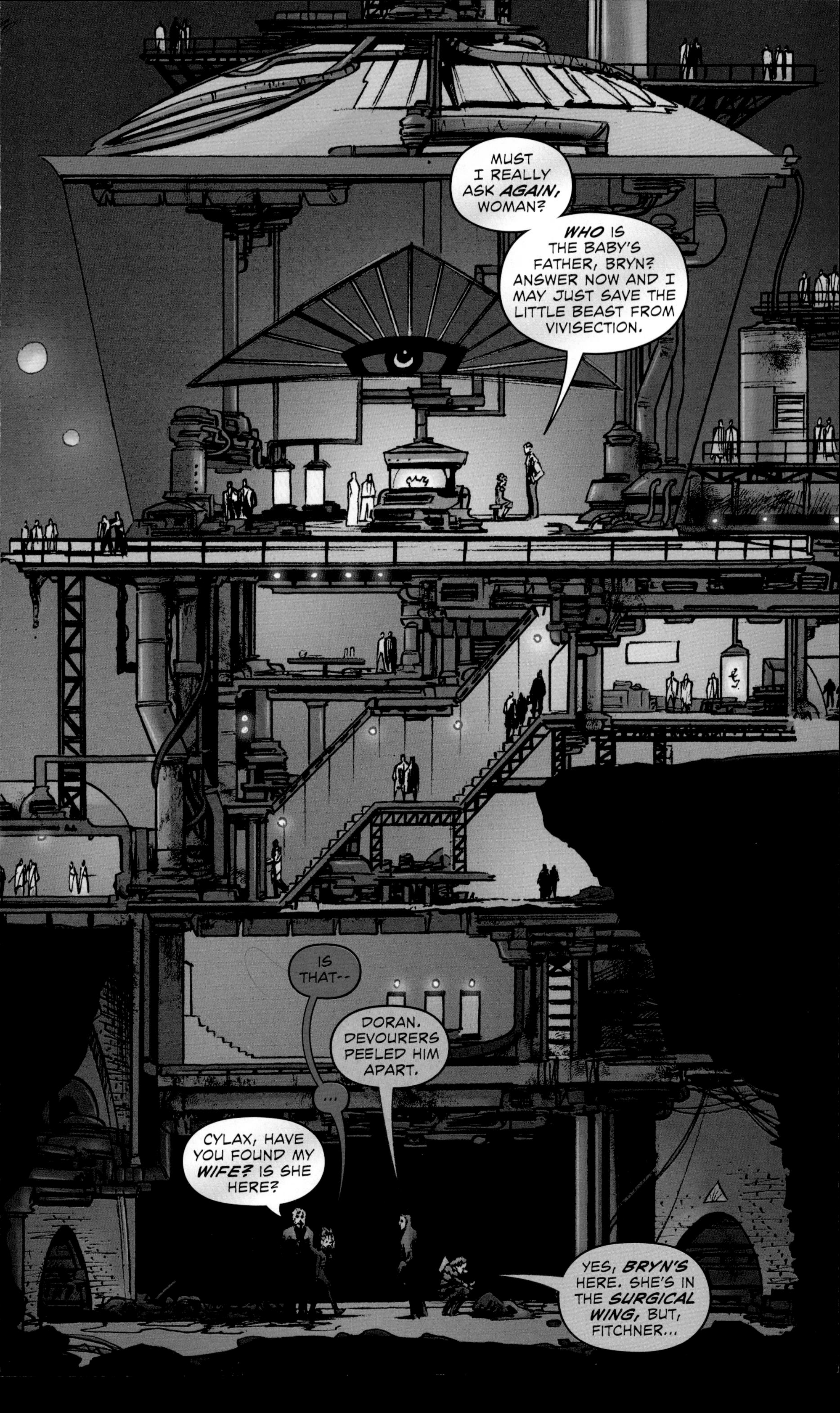
MUST I REALLY ASK *AGAIN,* WOMAN?
WHO IS THE BABY'S FATHER, BRYN? ANSWER NOW AND I MAY JUST SAVE THE LITTLE BEAST FROM VIVISECTION.
IS THAT--
DORAN. DEVOURERS PEELED HIM APART.
...
CYLAX, HAVE YOU FOUND MY *WIFE?* IS SHE HERE?
YES, *BRYN'S* HERE. SHE'S IN THE *SURGICAL WING,* BUT, FITCHNER...

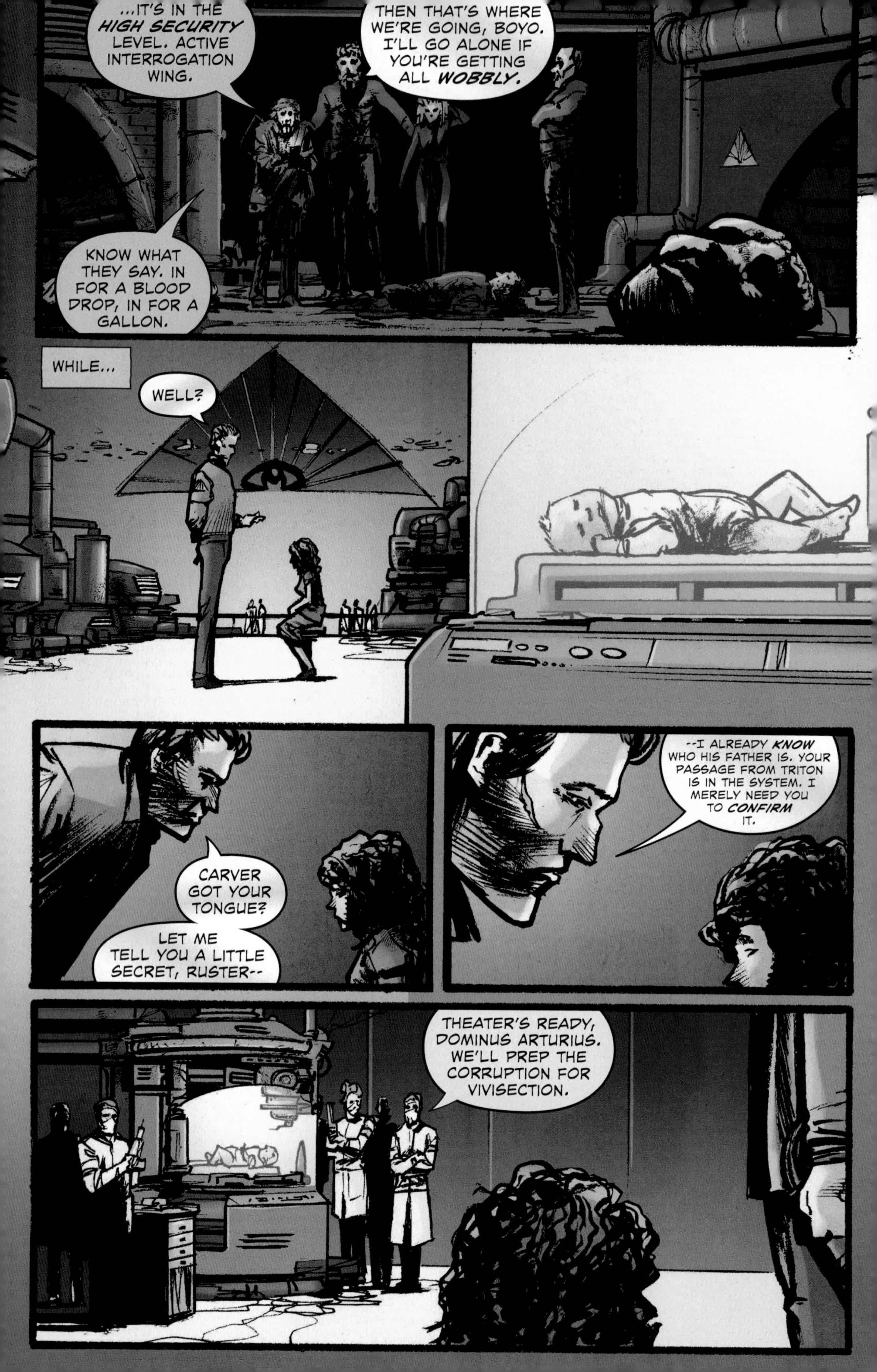
...IT'S IN THE HIGH SECURITY LEVEL. ACTIVE INTERROGATION WING.
THEN THAT'S WHERE WE'RE GOING, BOYO. I'LL GO ALONE IF YOU'RE GETTING ALL WOBBLY.
KNOW WHAT THEY SAY. IN FOR A BLOOD DROP, IN FOR A GALLON.
WHILE...
WELL?
CARVER GOT YOUR TONGUE?
LET ME TELL YOU A LITTLE SECRET, RUSTER--
--I ALREADY KNOW WHO HIS FATHER IS. YOUR PASSAGE FROM TRITON IS IN THE SYSTEM. I MERELY NEED YOU TO CONFIRM IT.
THEATER'S READY, DOMINUS ARTURIUS. WE'LL PREP THE CORRUPTION FOR VIVISECTION.

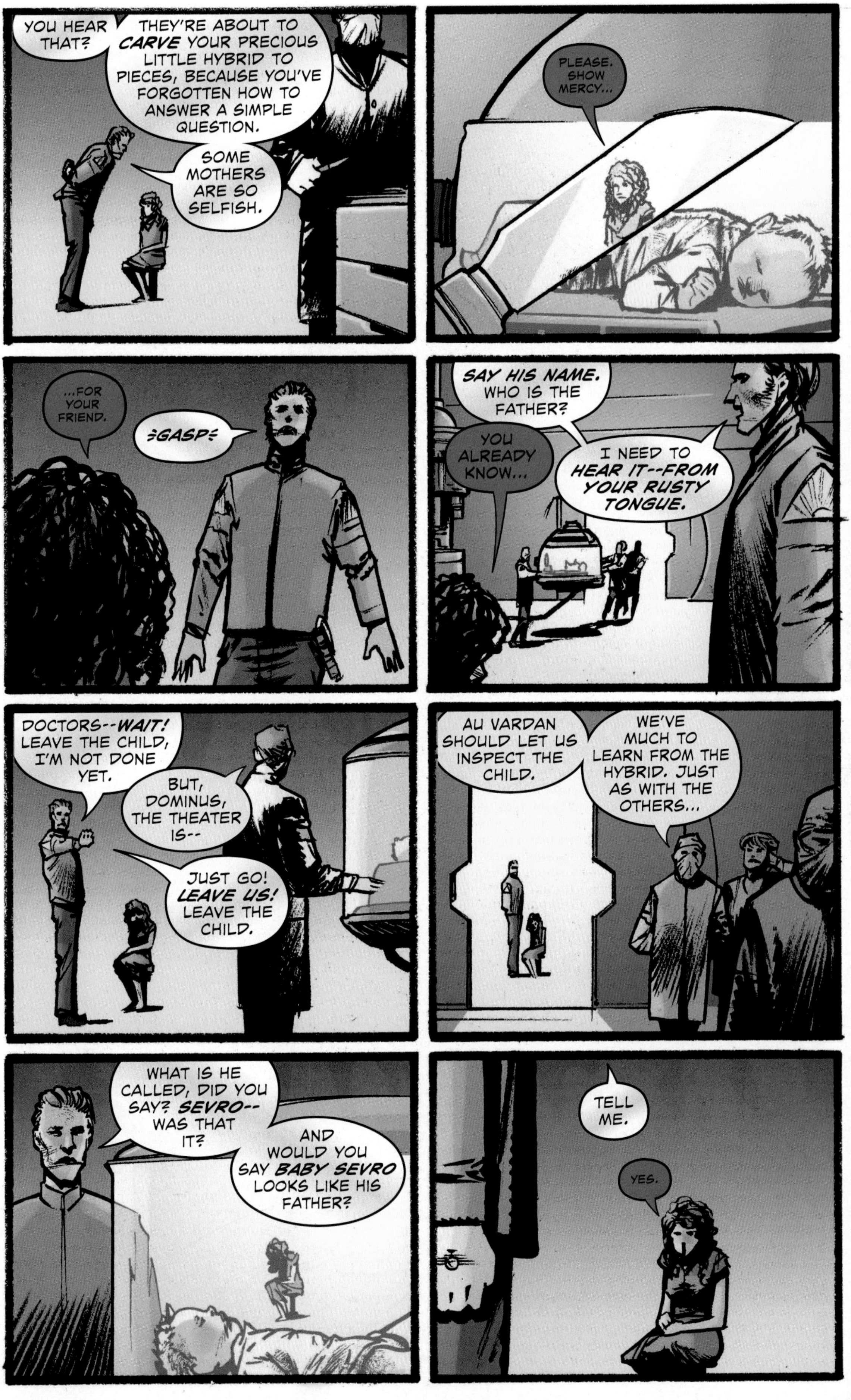
YOU HEAR THAT?
THEY'RE ABOUT TO CARVE YOUR PRECIOUS LITTLE HYBRID TO PIECES, BECAUSE YOU'VE FORGOTTEN HOW TO ANSWER A SIMPLE QUESTION.
SOME MOTHERS ARE SO SELFISH.
PLEASE. SHOW MERCY...
...FOR YOUR FRIEND.
GASP
SAY HIS NAME. WHO IS THE FATHER?
YOU ALREADY KNOW...
I NEED TO HEAR IT--FROM YOUR RUSTY TONGUE.
DOCTORS--WAIT! LEAVE THE CHILD, I'M NOT DONE YET.
BUT, DOMINUS, THE THEATER IS--
JUST GO! LEAVE US! LEAVE THE CHILD.
AU VARDAN SHOULD LET US INSPECT THE CHILD.
WE'VE MUCH TO LEARN FROM THE HYBRID. JUST AS WITH THE OTHERS...
WHAT IS HE CALLED, DID YOU SAY? SEVRO--WAS THAT IT?
AND WOULD YOU SAY BABY SEVRO LOOKS LIKE HIS FATHER?
TELL ME.
YES.

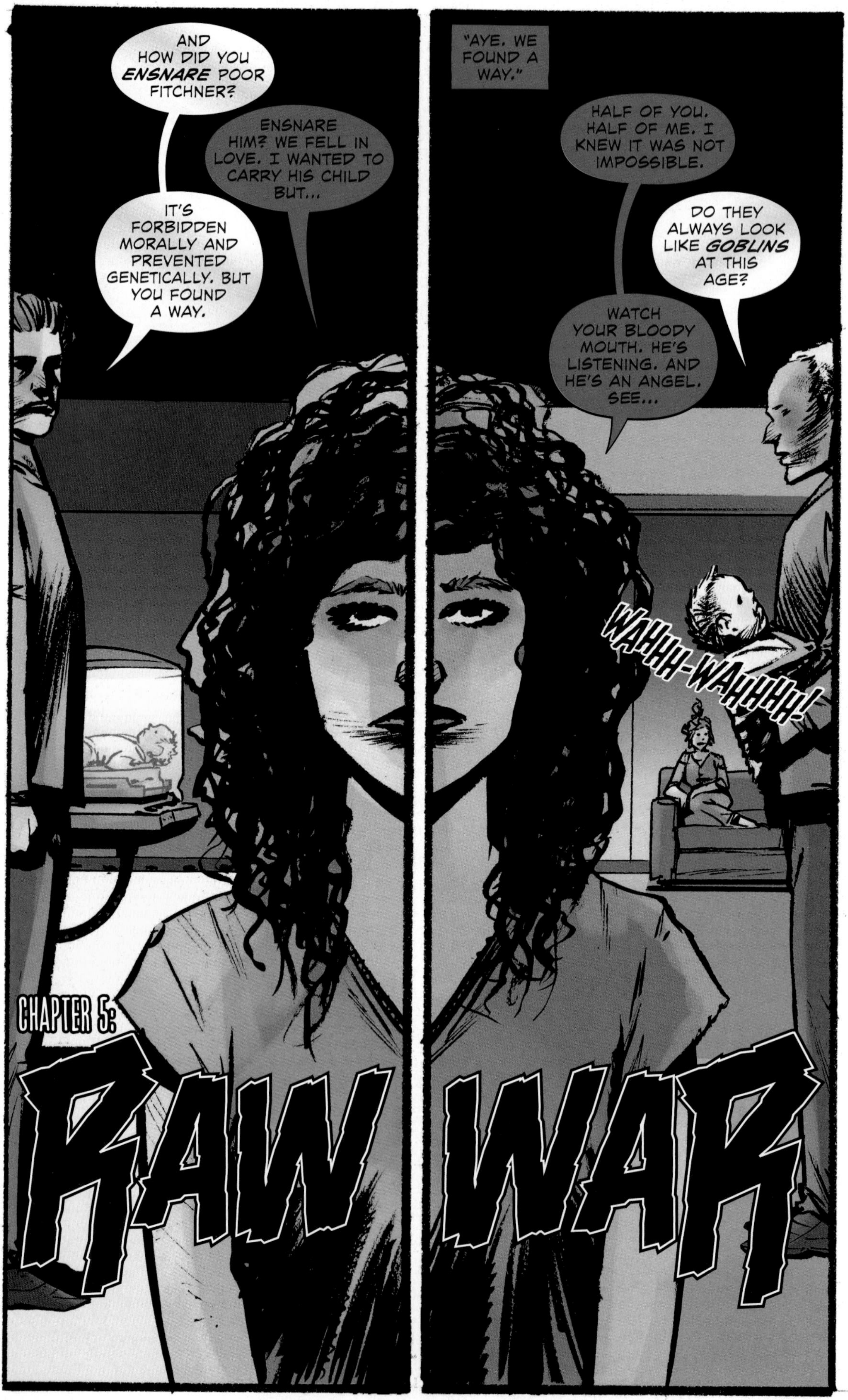
AND HOW DID YOU ENSNARE POOR FITCHNER?
ENSNARE HIM? WE FELL IN LOVE. I WANTED TO CARRY HIS CHILD BUT...
IT'S FORBIDDEN MORALLY AND PREVENTED GENETICALLY. BUT YOU FOUND A WAY.
CHAPTER 5:
RAW WAR
"AYE. WE FOUND A WAY."
HALF OF YOU. HALF OF ME. I KNEW IT WAS NOT IMPOSSIBLE.
DO THEY ALWAYS LOOK LIKE GOBLINS AT THIS AGE?
WATCH YOUR BLOODY MOUTH. HE'S LISTENING. AND HE'S AN ANGEL. SEE...
WAHHH-WAHHHH!

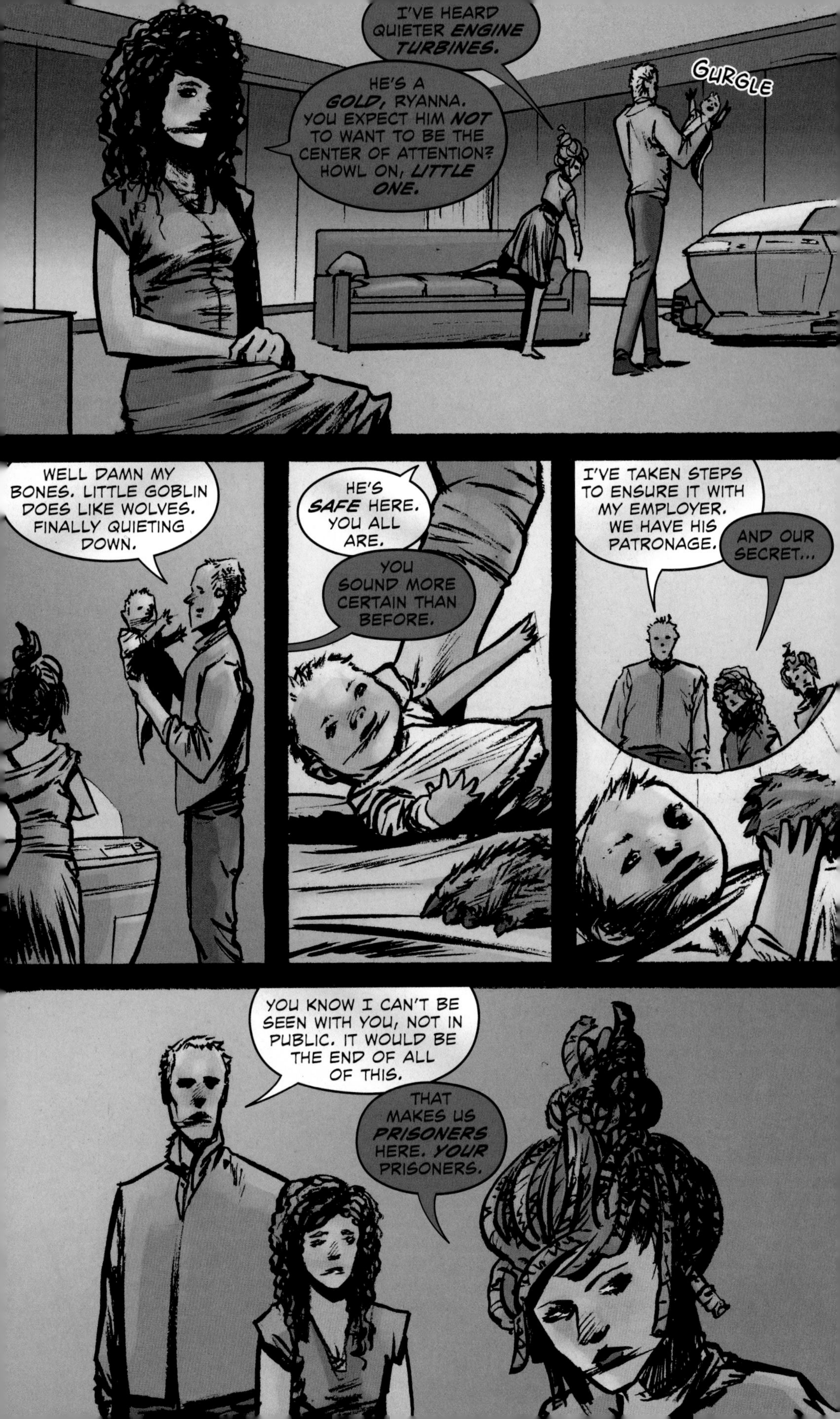
I'VE HEARD QUIETER ENGINE TURBINES.
GURGLE
HE'S A GOLD, RYANNA. YOU EXPECT HIM NOT TO WANT TO BE THE CENTER OF ATTENTION? HOWL ON, LITTLE ONE.
WELL DAMN MY BONES. LITTLE GOBLIN DOES LIKE WOLVES. FINALLY QUIETING DOWN.
HE'S SAFE HERE. YOU ALL ARE.
YOU SOUND MORE CERTAIN THAN BEFORE.
I'VE TAKEN STEPS TO ENSURE IT WITH MY EMPLOYER. WE HAVE HIS PATRONAGE.
AND OUR SECRET...
YOU KNOW I CAN'T BE SEEN WITH YOU, NOT IN PUBLIC. IT WOULD BE THE END OF ALL OF THIS.
THAT MAKES US PRISONERS HERE. YOUR PRISONERS.

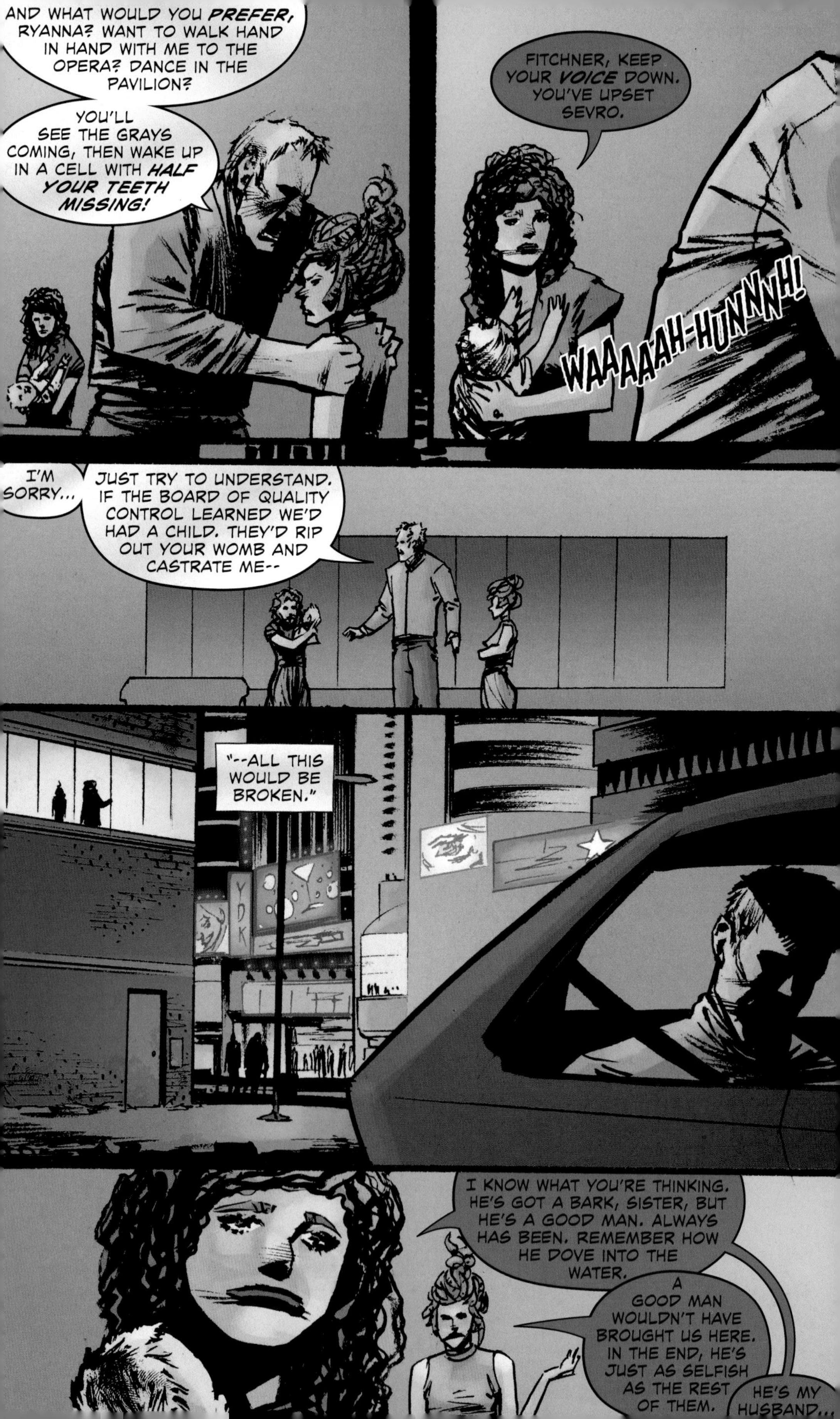
AND WHAT WOULD YOU PREFER, RYANNA? WANT TO WALK HAND IN HAND WITH ME TO THE OPERA? DANCE IN THE PAVILION?
YOU'LL SEE THE GRAYS COMING, THEN WAKE UP IN A CELL WITH HALF YOUR TEETH MISSING!
FITCHNER, KEEP YOUR VOICE DOWN. YOU'VE UPSET SEVRO.
WAAAAAH-HUNNNH!
I'M SORRY...
JUST TRY TO UNDERSTAND. IF THE BOARD OF QUALITY CONTROL LEARNED WE'D HAD A CHILD. THEY'D RIP OUT YOUR WOMB AND CASTRATE ME--
"--ALL THIS WOULD BE BROKEN."
I KNOW WHAT YOU'RE THINKING. HE'S GOT A BARK, SISTER, BUT HE'S A GOOD MAN. ALWAYS HAS BEEN. REMEMBER HOW HE DOVE INTO THE WATER.
A GOOD MAN WOULDN'T HAVE BROUGHT US HERE. IN THE END, HE'S JUST AS SELFISH AS THE REST OF THEM.
HE'S MY HUSBAND...

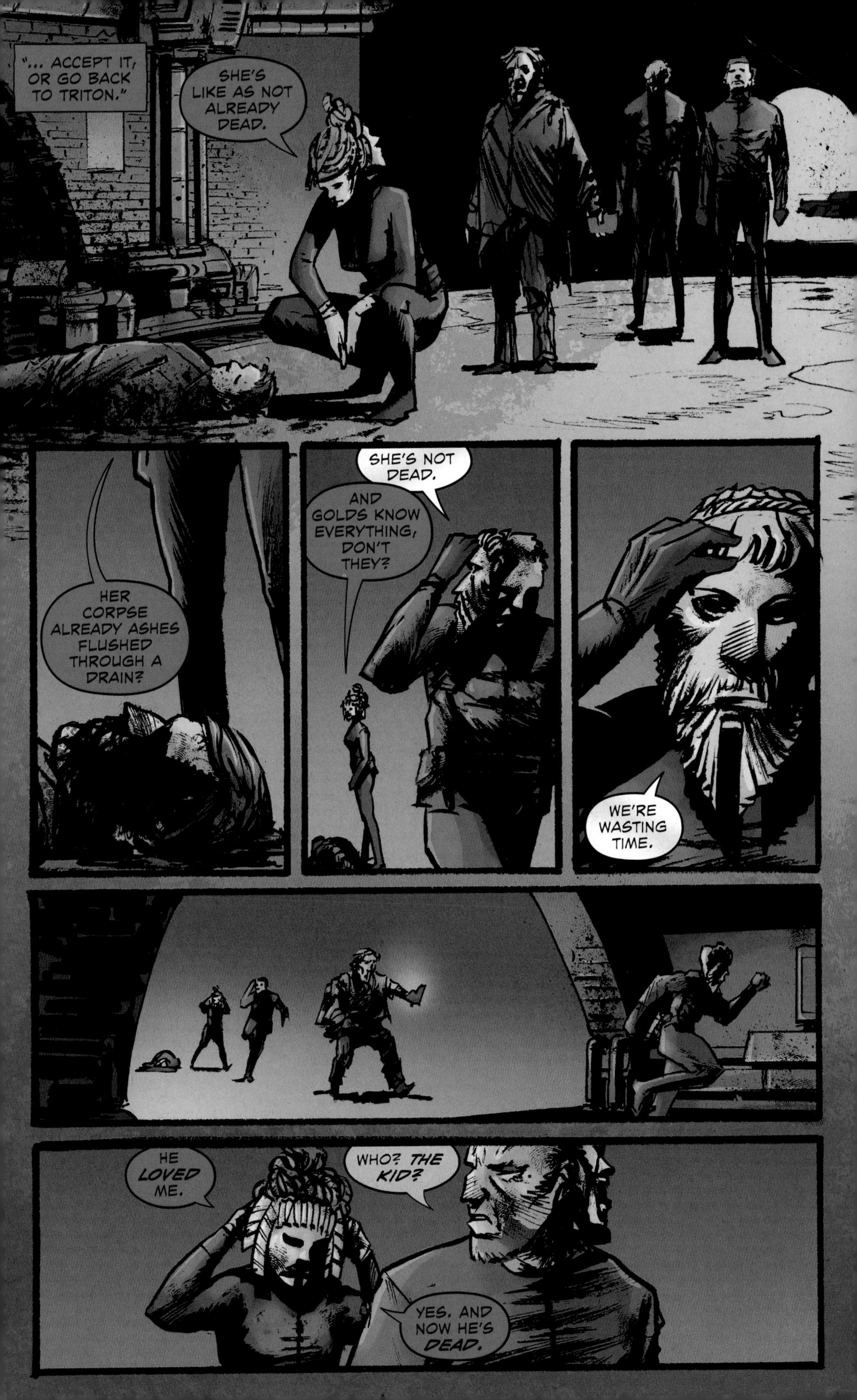
"... ACCEPT IT, OR GO BACK TO TRITON."
SHE'S LIKE AS NOT ALREADY DEAD.
HER CORPSE ALREADY ASHES FLUSHED THROUGH A DRAIN?
SHE'S NOT DEAD.
AND GOLDS KNOW EVERYTHING, DON'T THEY?
WE'RE WASTING TIME.
HE *LOVED* ME.
WHO? *THE KID?*
YES. AND NOW HE'S *DEAD.*

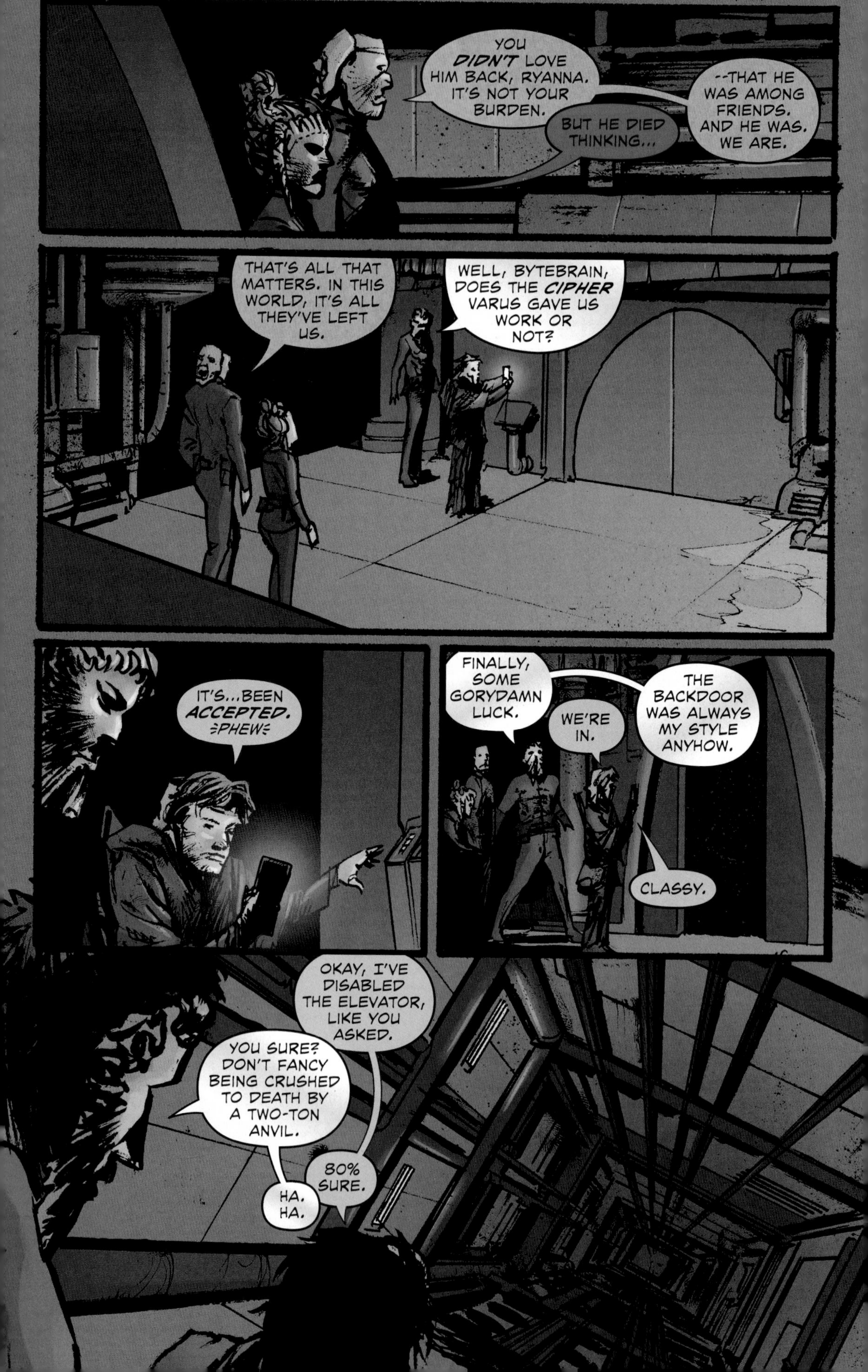
YOU DIDN'T LOVE HIM BACK, RYANNA. IT'S NOT YOUR BURDEN.
BUT HE DIED THINKING...
--THAT HE WAS AMONG FRIENDS. AND HE WAS. WE ARE.
THAT'S ALL THAT MATTERS. IN THIS WORLD, IT'S ALL THEY'VE LEFT US.
WELL, BYTEBRAIN, DOES THE CIPHER VARUS GAVE US WORK OR NOT?
IT'S...BEEN ACCEPTED. PHEW
FINALLY, SOME GORYDAMN LUCK.
WE'RE IN.
THE BACKDOOR WAS ALWAYS MY STYLE ANYHOW.
CLASSY.
OKAY, I'VE DISABLED THE ELEVATOR, LIKE YOU ASKED.
YOU SURE? DON'T FANCY BEING CRUSHED TO DEATH BY A TWO-TON ANVIL.
80% SURE.
HA. HA.

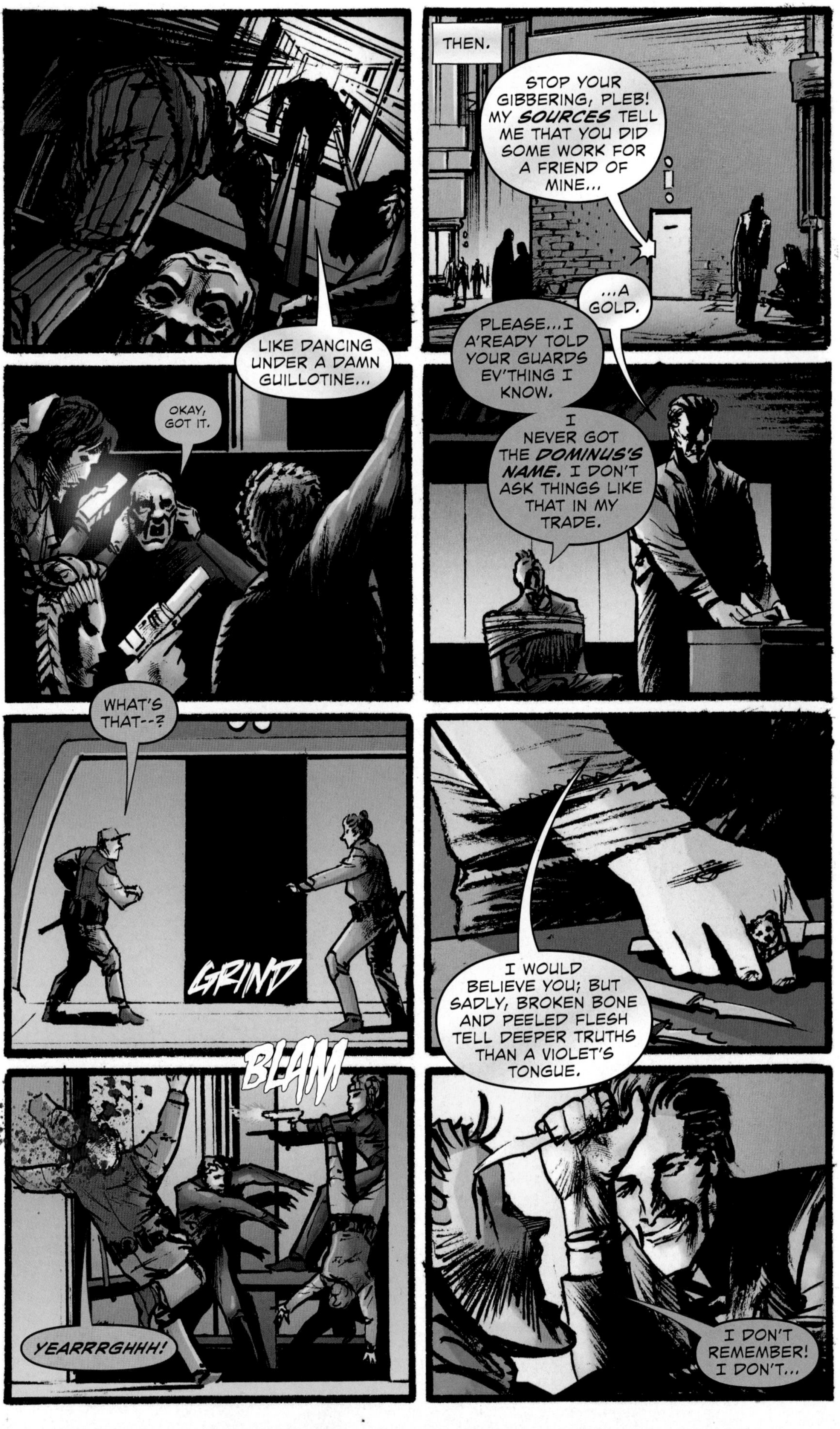

LIKE DANCING UNDER A DAMN GUILLOTINE...
THEN.
STOP YOUR GIBBERING, PLEB! MY SOURCES TELL ME THAT YOU DID SOME WORK FOR A FRIEND OF MINE...
OKAY, GOT IT.
...A GOLD.
PLEASE...I A'READY TOLD YOUR GUARDS EV'THING I KNOW.
I NEVER GOT THE DOMINUS'S NAME. I DON'T ASK THINGS LIKE THAT IN MY TRADE.
WHAT'S THAT--?
GRIND
I WOULD BELIEVE YOU; BUT SADLY, BROKEN BONE AND PEELED FLESH TELL DEEPER TRUTHS THAN A VIOLET'S TONGUE.
BLAM
YEARRRGHHH!
I DON'T REMEMBER! I DON'T...

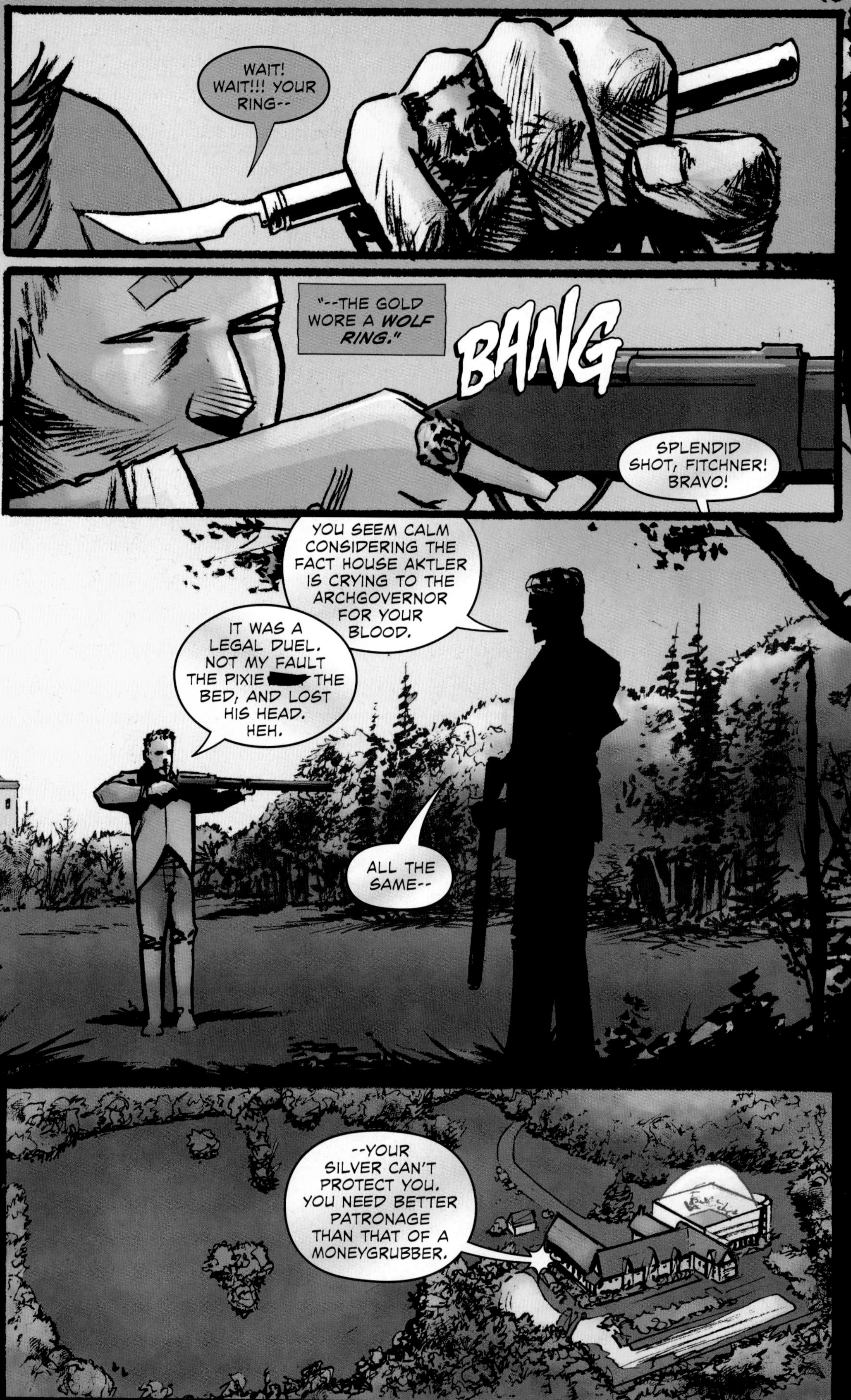
WAIT! WAIT!!! YOUR RING--
"--THE GOLD WORE A *WOLF RING.*"
BANG
SPLENDID SHOT, FITCHNER! BRAVO!
YOU SEEM CALM CONSIDERING THE FACT HOUSE AKTLER IS CRYING TO THE ARCHGOVERNOR FOR YOUR BLOOD.
IT WAS A LEGAL DUEL. NOT MY FAULT THE PIXIE [redacted] THE BED, AND LOST HIS HEAD. HEH.
ALL THE SAME--
--YOUR SILVER CAN'T PROTECT YOU. YOU NEED BETTER PATRONAGE THAN THAT OF A MONEYGRUBBER.

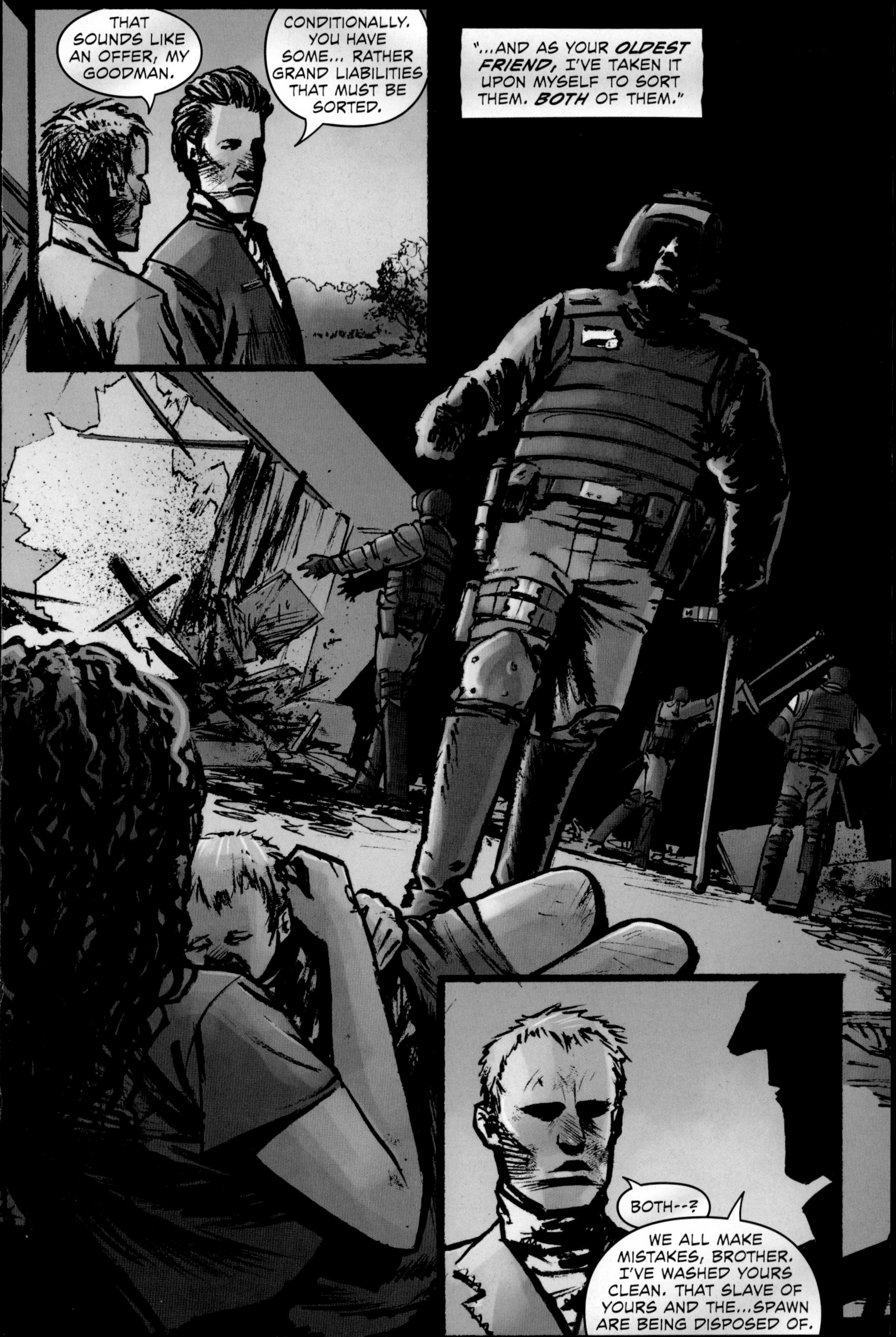
THAT SOUNDS LIKE AN OFFER, MY GOODMAN.
CONDITIONALLY. YOU HAVE SOME... RATHER GRAND LIABILITIES THAT MUST BE SORTED.
"...AND AS YOUR OLDEST FRIEND, I'VE TAKEN IT UPON MYSELF TO SORT THEM. BOTH OF THEM."
BOTH--?
WE ALL MAKE MISTAKES, BROTHER. I'VE WASHED YOURS CLEAN. THAT SLAVE OF YOURS AND THE...SPAWN ARE BEING DISPOSED OF.

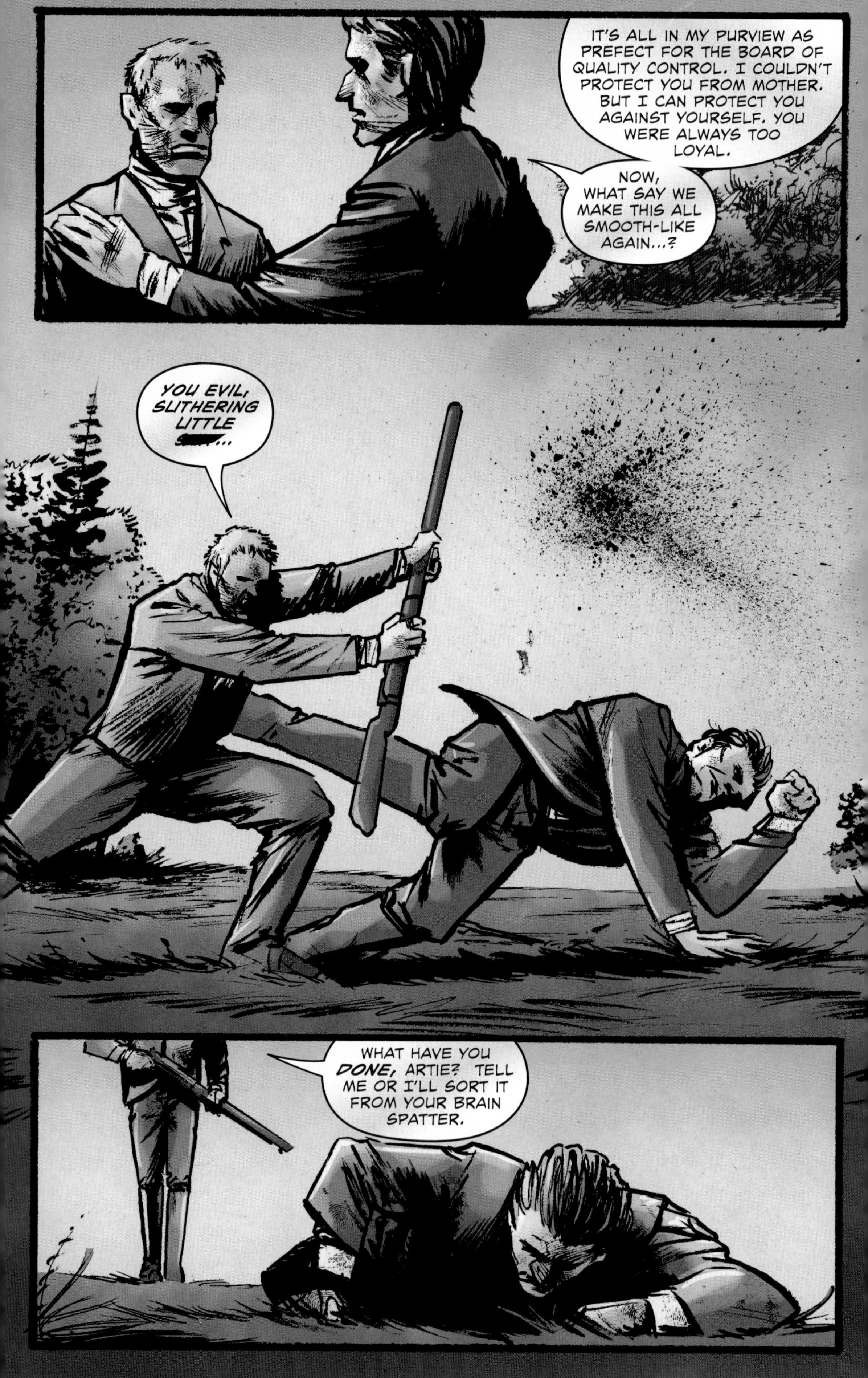
IT'S ALL IN MY PURVIEW AS PREFECT FOR THE BOARD OF QUALITY CONTROL. I COULDN'T PROTECT YOU FROM MOTHER. BUT I CAN PROTECT YOU AGAINST YOURSELF. YOU WERE ALWAYS TOO LOYAL.
NOW, WHAT SAY WE MAKE THIS ALL SMOOTH-LIKE AGAIN...?
YOU EVIL, SLITHERING LITTLE [redacted]...
WHAT HAVE YOU DONE, ARTIE? TELL ME OR I'LL SORT IT FROM YOUR BRAIN SPATTER.

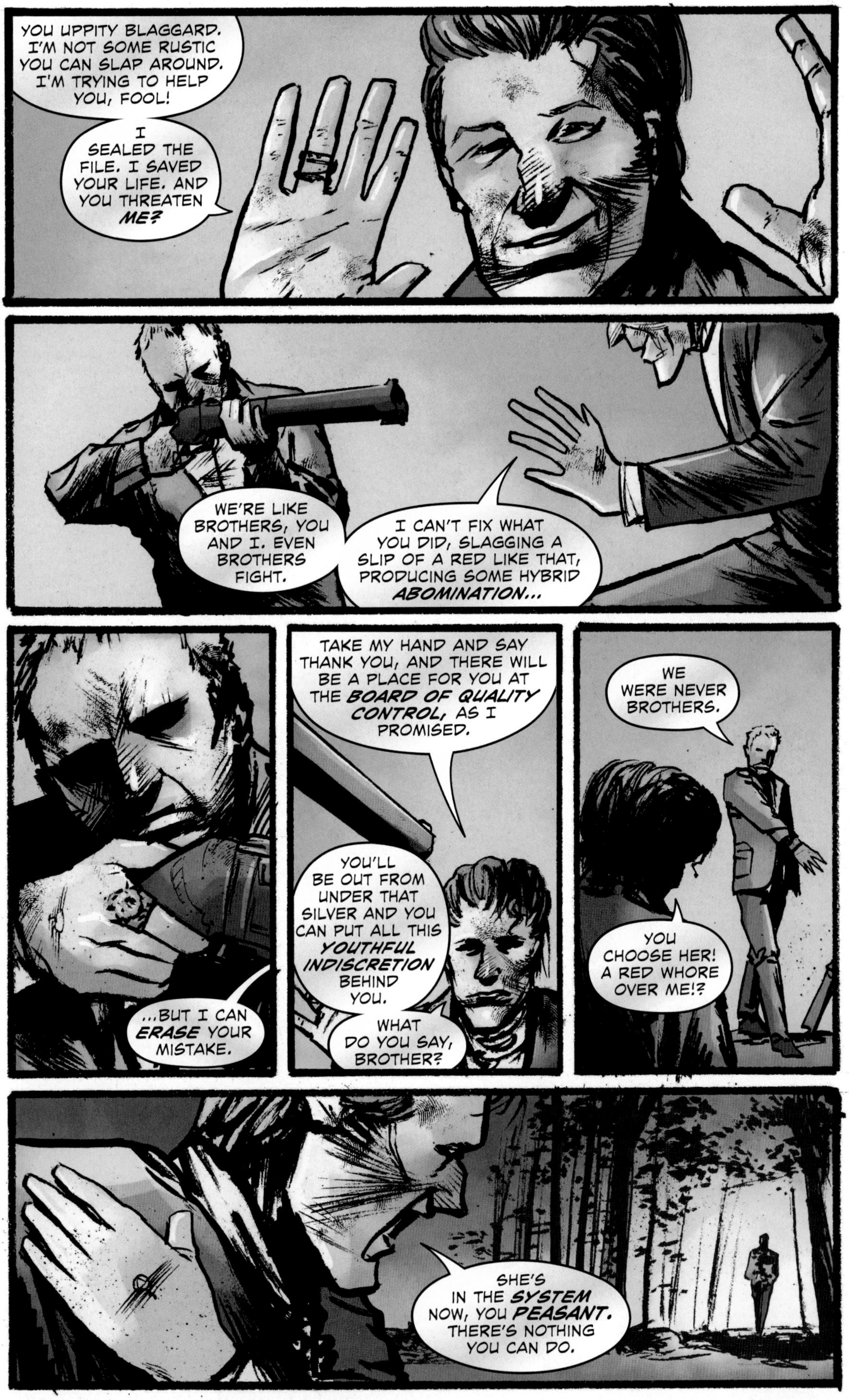
YOU UPPITY BLAGGARD. I'M NOT SOME RUSTIC YOU CAN SLAP AROUND. I'M TRYING TO HELP YOU, FOOL!
I SEALED THE FILE. I SAVED YOUR LIFE. AND YOU THREATEN *ME?*
WE'RE LIKE BROTHERS, YOU AND I. EVEN BROTHERS FIGHT.
I CAN'T FIX WHAT YOU DID, SLAGGING A SLIP OF A RED LIKE THAT, PRODUCING SOME HYBRID *ABOMINATION...*
...BUT I CAN *ERASE* YOUR MISTAKE.
TAKE MY HAND AND SAY THANK YOU, AND THERE WILL BE A PLACE FOR YOU AT THE *BOARD OF QUALITY CONTROL,* AS I PROMISED.
YOU'LL BE OUT FROM UNDER THAT SILVER AND YOU CAN PUT ALL THIS *YOUTHFUL INDISCRETION* BEHIND YOU.
WHAT DO YOU SAY, BROTHER?
WE WERE NEVER BROTHERS.
YOU CHOOSE HER! A RED WHORE OVER ME!?
SHE'S IN THE *SYSTEM* NOW, YOU *PEASANT.* THERE'S NOTHING YOU CAN DO.

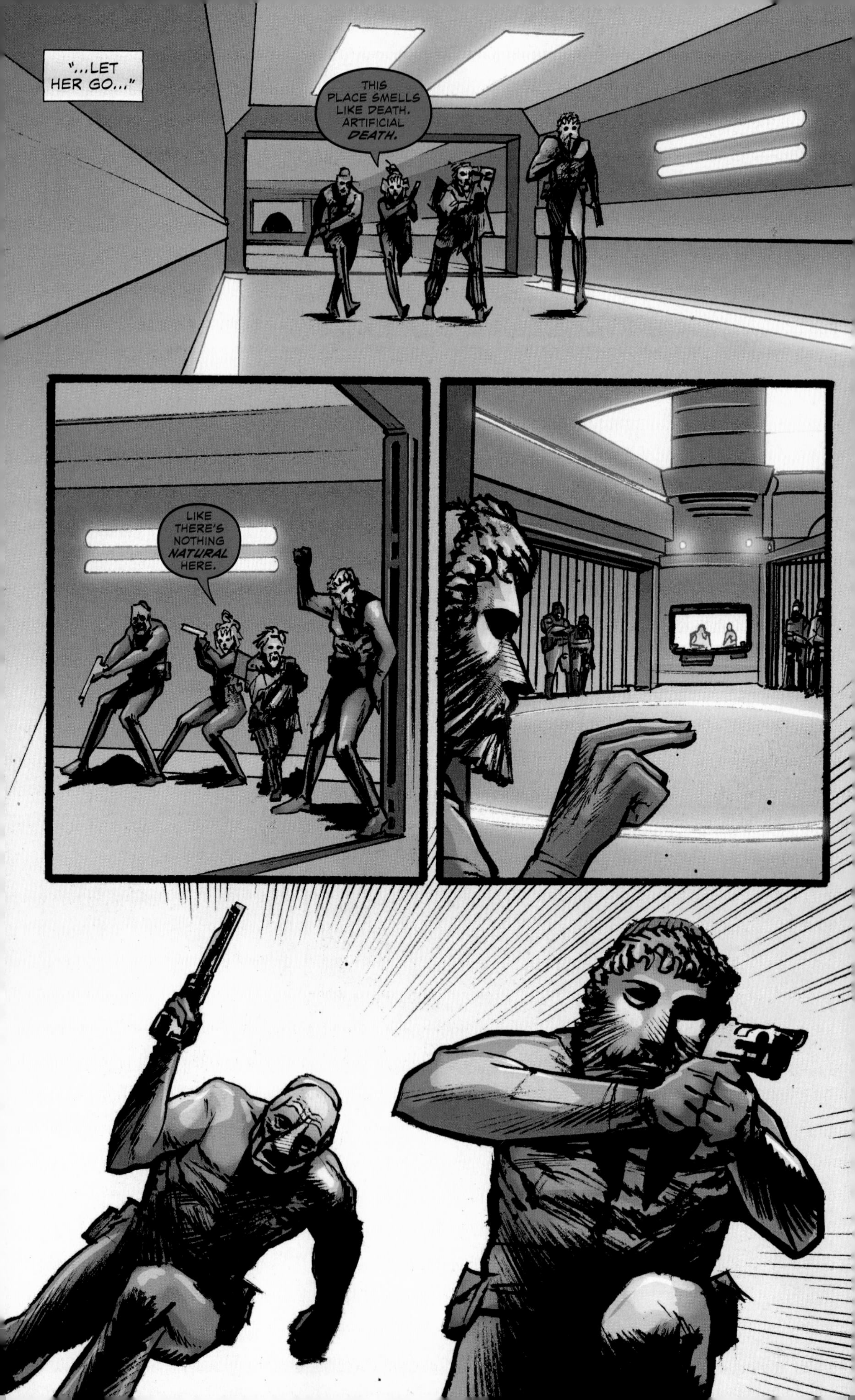
"...LET HER GO..."
THIS PLACE SMELLS LIKE DEATH. ARTIFICIAL *DEATH.*
LIKE THERE'S NOTHING *NATURAL* HERE.

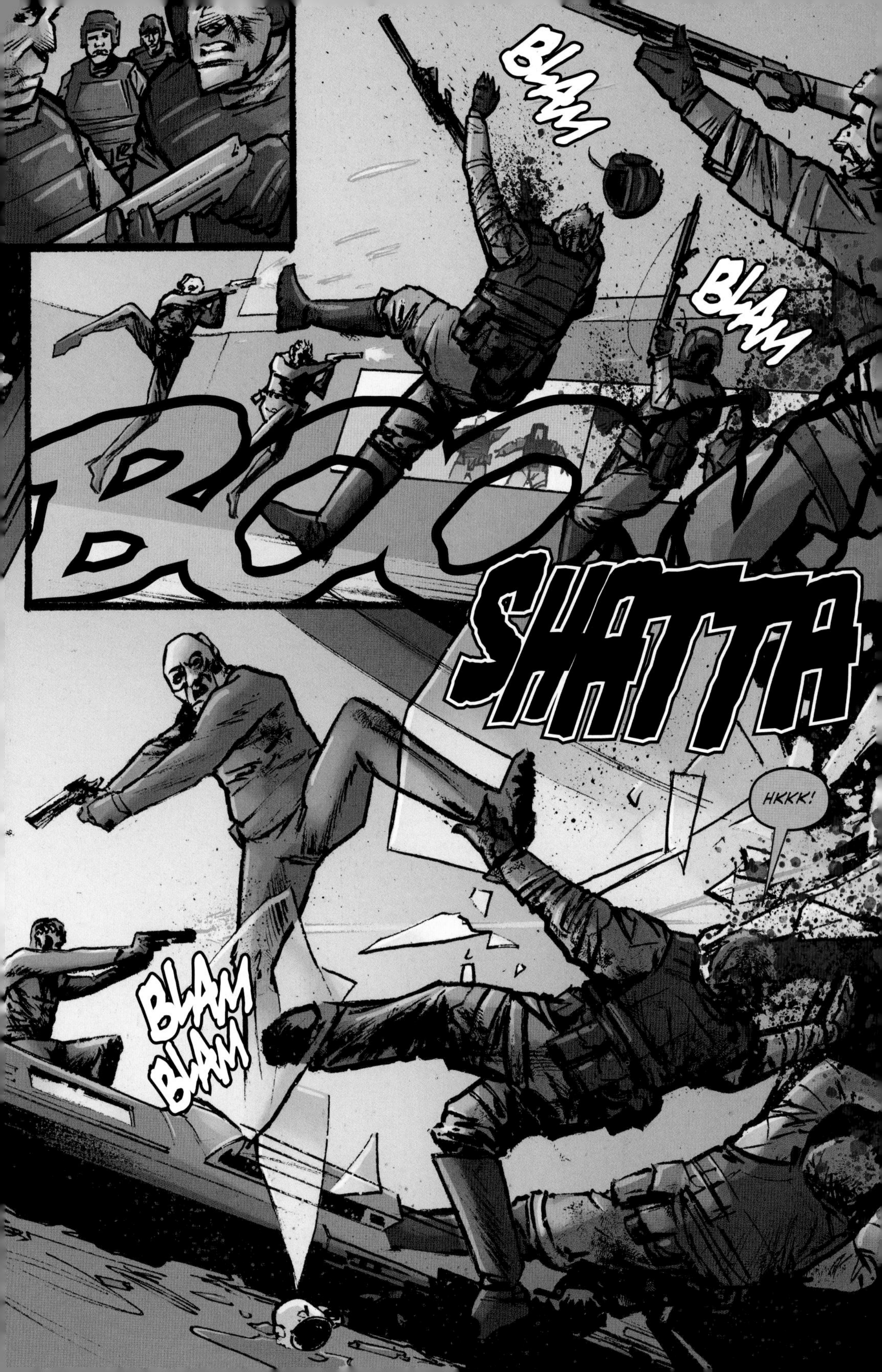
BLAM
BLAM
BOO
SHATTA
HKKK!
BLAM
BLAM

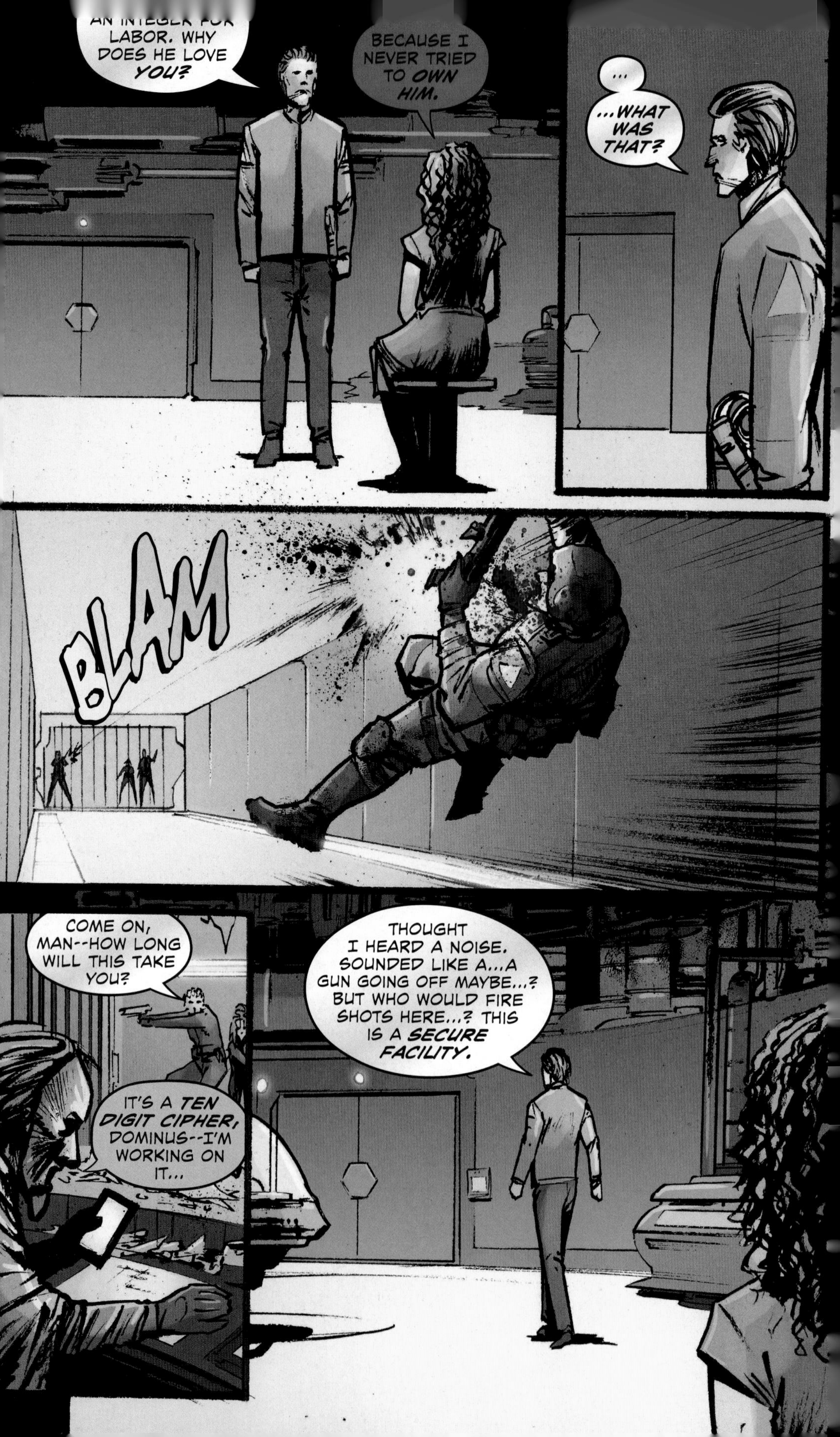
AN INTEGER FOR LABOR. WHY DOES HE LOVE *YOU?*
BECAUSE I NEVER TRIED TO *OWN HIM.*
...
...*WHAT WAS THAT?*
BLAM
COME ON, MAN--HOW LONG WILL THIS TAKE YOU?
IT'S A *TEN DIGIT CIPHER,* DOMINUS--I'M WORKING ON IT...
THOUGHT I HEARD A NOISE. SOUNDED LIKE A...A GUN GOING OFF MAYBE...? BUT WHO WOULD FIRE SHOTS HERE...? THIS IS A *SECURE FACILITY.*

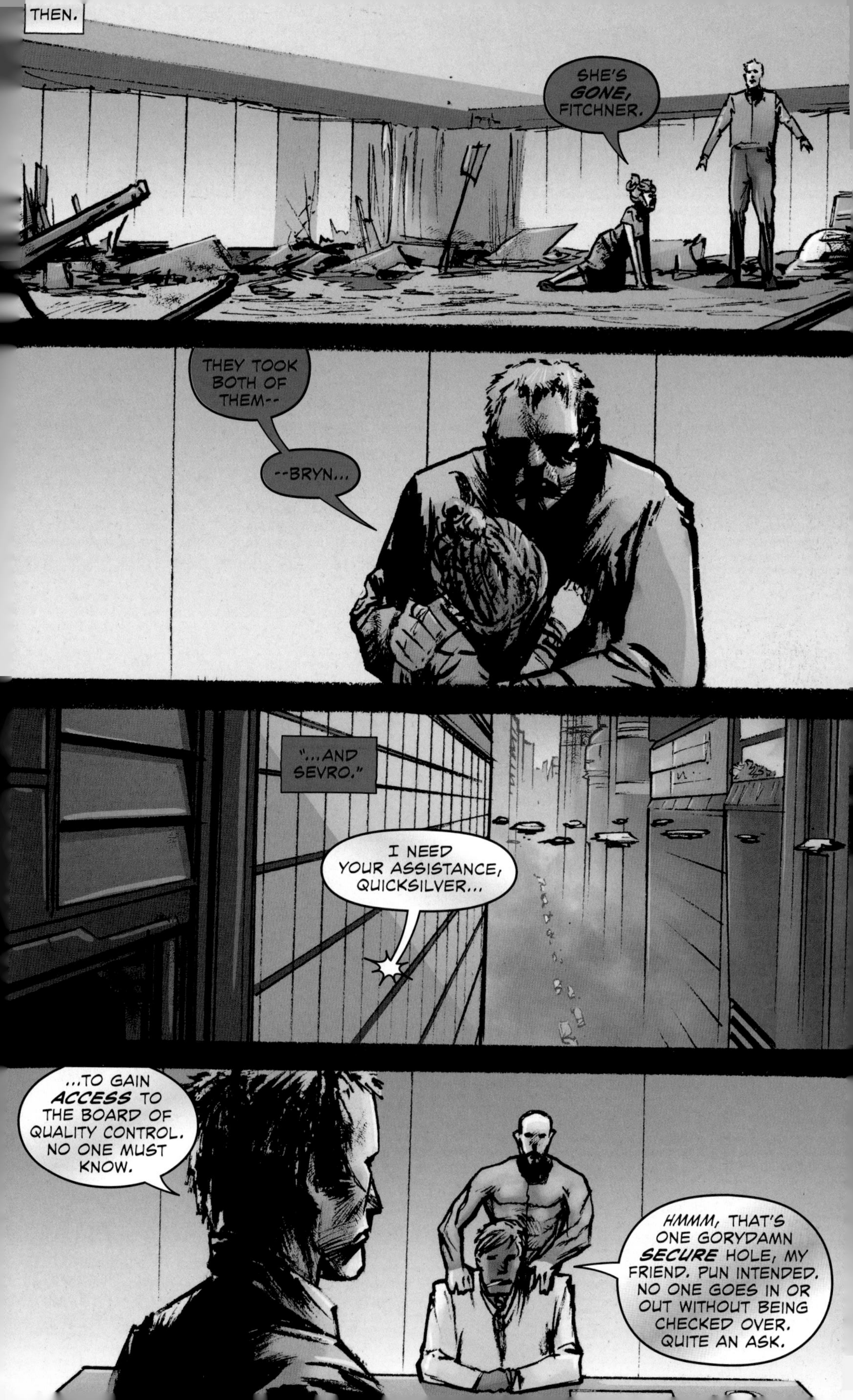
THEN.
SHE'S GONE, FITCHNER.
THEY TOOK BOTH OF THEM--
--BRYN...
"...AND SEVRO."
I NEED YOUR ASSISTANCE, QUICKSILVER...
...TO GAIN ACCESS TO THE BOARD OF QUALITY CONTROL. NO ONE MUST KNOW.
HMMM, THAT'S ONE GORYDAMN SECURE HOLE, MY FRIEND. PUN INTENDED. NO ONE GOES IN OR OUT WITHOUT BEING CHECKED OVER. QUITE AN ASK.

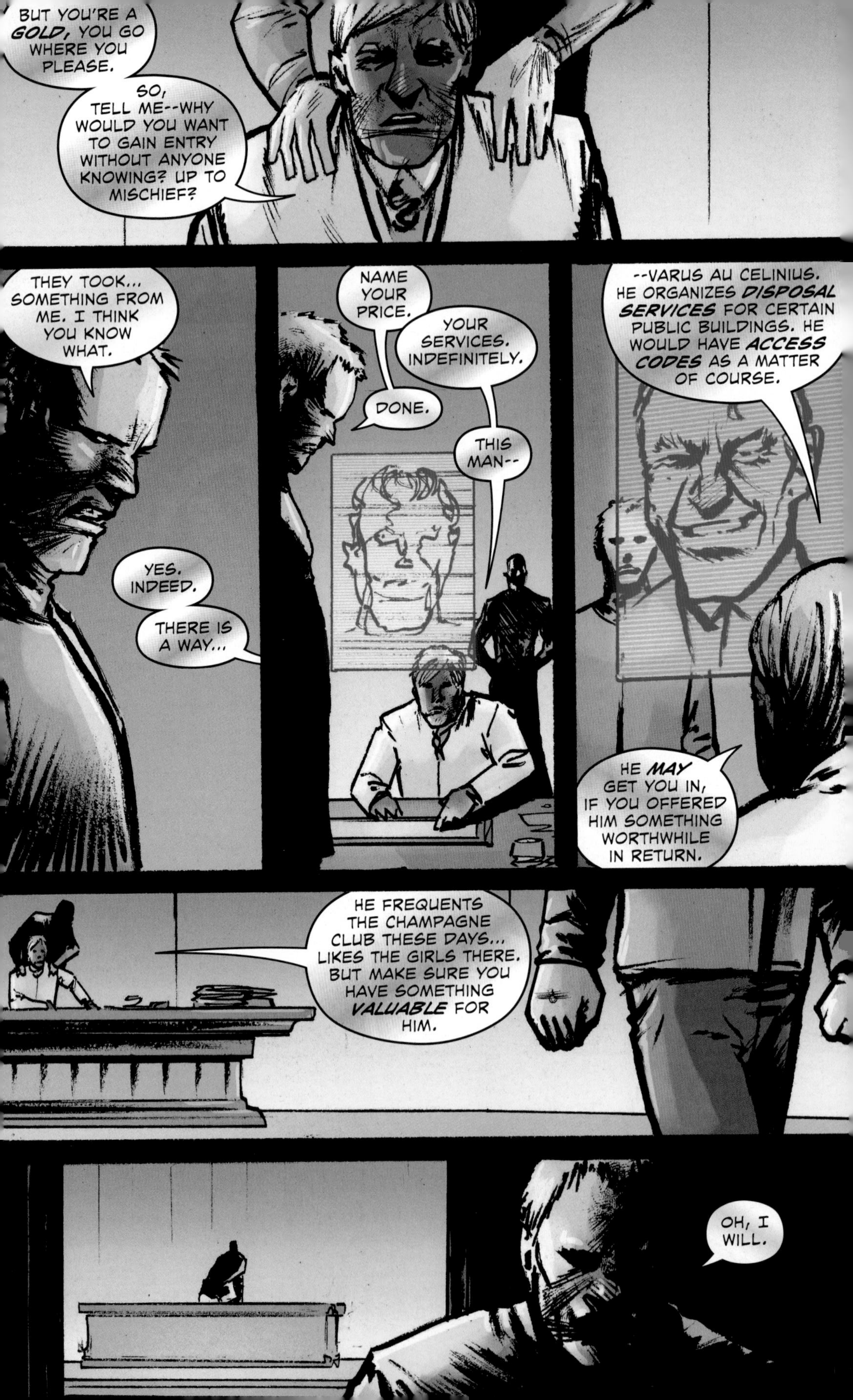
BUT YOU'RE A GOLD, YOU GO WHERE YOU PLEASE.
SO, TELL ME--WHY WOULD YOU WANT TO GAIN ENTRY WITHOUT ANYONE KNOWING? UP TO MISCHIEF?
THEY TOOK... SOMETHING FROM ME. I THINK YOU KNOW WHAT.
YES. INDEED.
THERE IS A WAY...
NAME YOUR PRICE.
YOUR SERVICES. INDEFINITELY.
DONE.
THIS MAN--
--VARUS AU CELINIUS. HE ORGANIZES DISPOSAL SERVICES FOR CERTAIN PUBLIC BUILDINGS. HE WOULD HAVE ACCESS CODES AS A MATTER OF COURSE.
HE MAY GET YOU IN, IF YOU OFFERED HIM SOMETHING WORTHWHILE IN RETURN.
HE FREQUENTS THE CHAMPAGNE CLUB THESE DAYS... LIKES THE GIRLS THERE. BUT MAKE SURE YOU HAVE SOMETHING VALUABLE FOR HIM.
OH, I WILL.

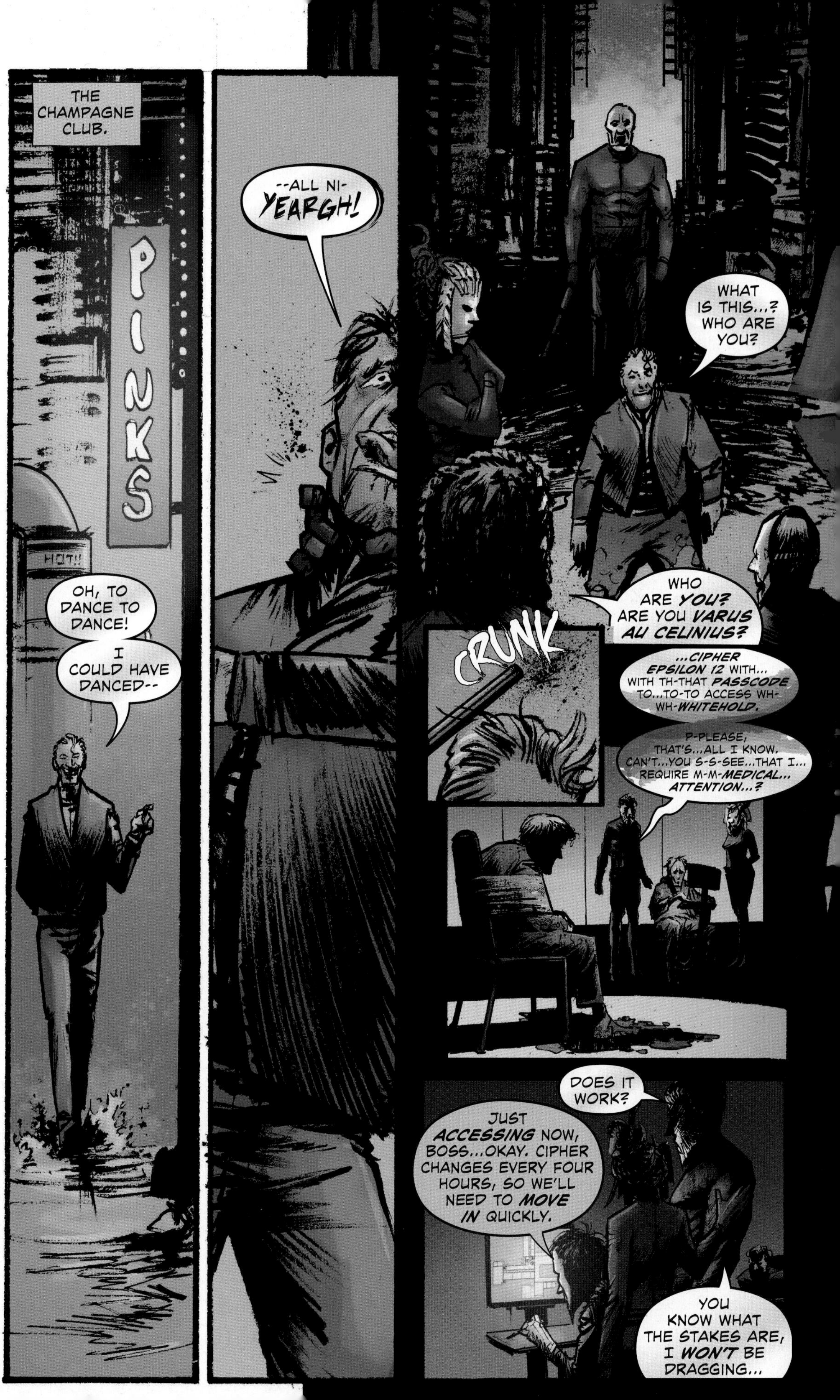
THE CHAMPAGNE CLUB.
PINKS
HOT!!
OH, TO DANCE TO DANCE!
I COULD HAVE DANCED--
--ALL NI-YEARGH!
WHAT IS THIS...? WHO ARE YOU?
WHO ARE YOU? ARE YOU VARUS AU CELINIUS?
CRUNK
...CIPHER EPSILON 12 WITH... WITH TH-THAT PASSCODE TO...TO-TO ACCESS WH-WH-WHITEHOLD.
P-PLEASE, THAT'S...ALL I KNOW. CAN'T...YOU S-S-SEE...THAT I... REQUIRE M-M-MEDICAL... ATTENTION...?
DOES IT WORK?
JUST ACCESSING NOW, BOSS...OKAY. CIPHER CHANGES EVERY FOUR HOURS, SO WE'LL NEED TO MOVE IN QUICKLY.
YOU KNOW WHAT THE STAKES ARE, I WON'T BE DRAGGING...

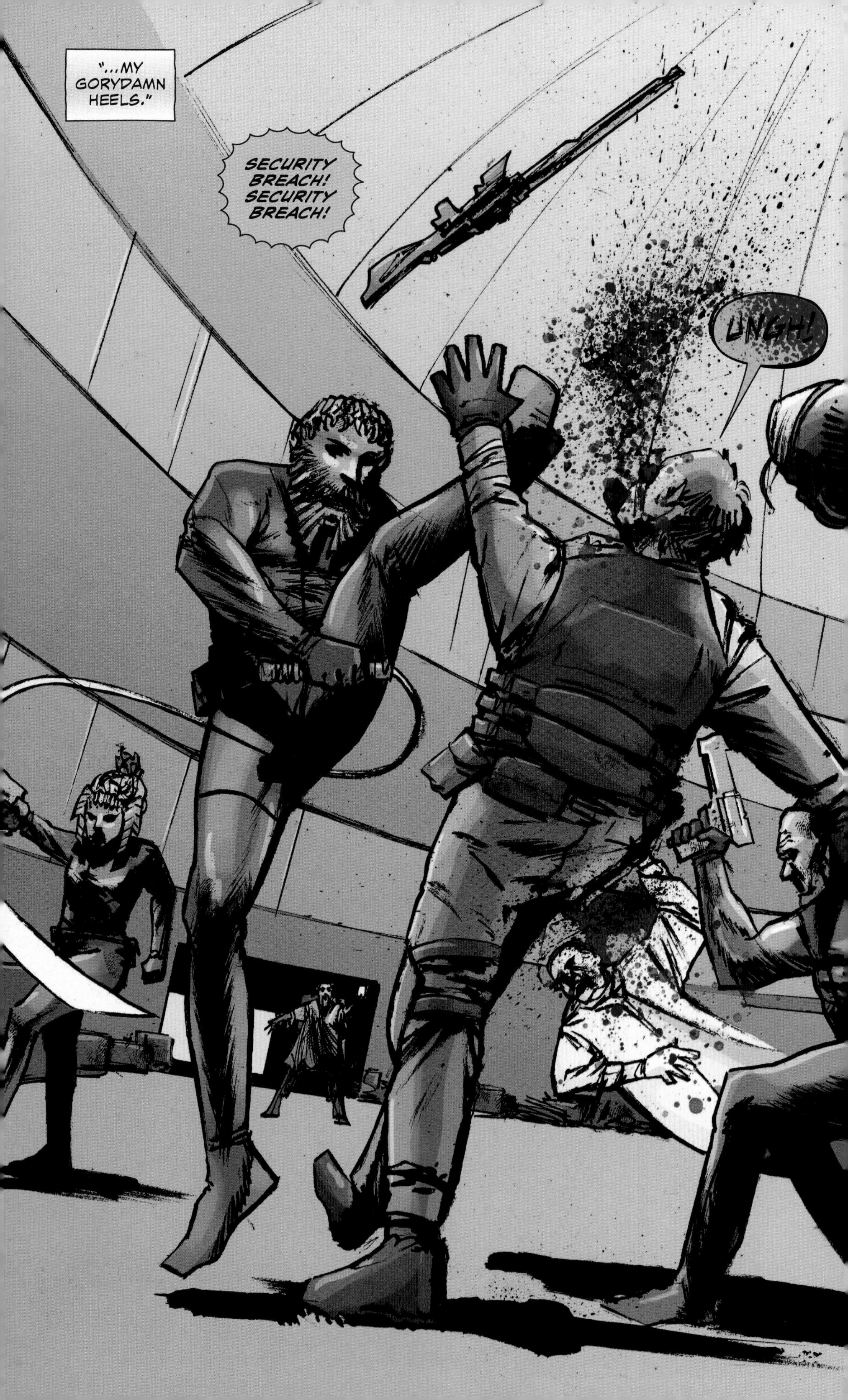
"...MY GORYDAMN HEELS."
SECURITY BREACH! SECURITY BREACH!
UNGH!

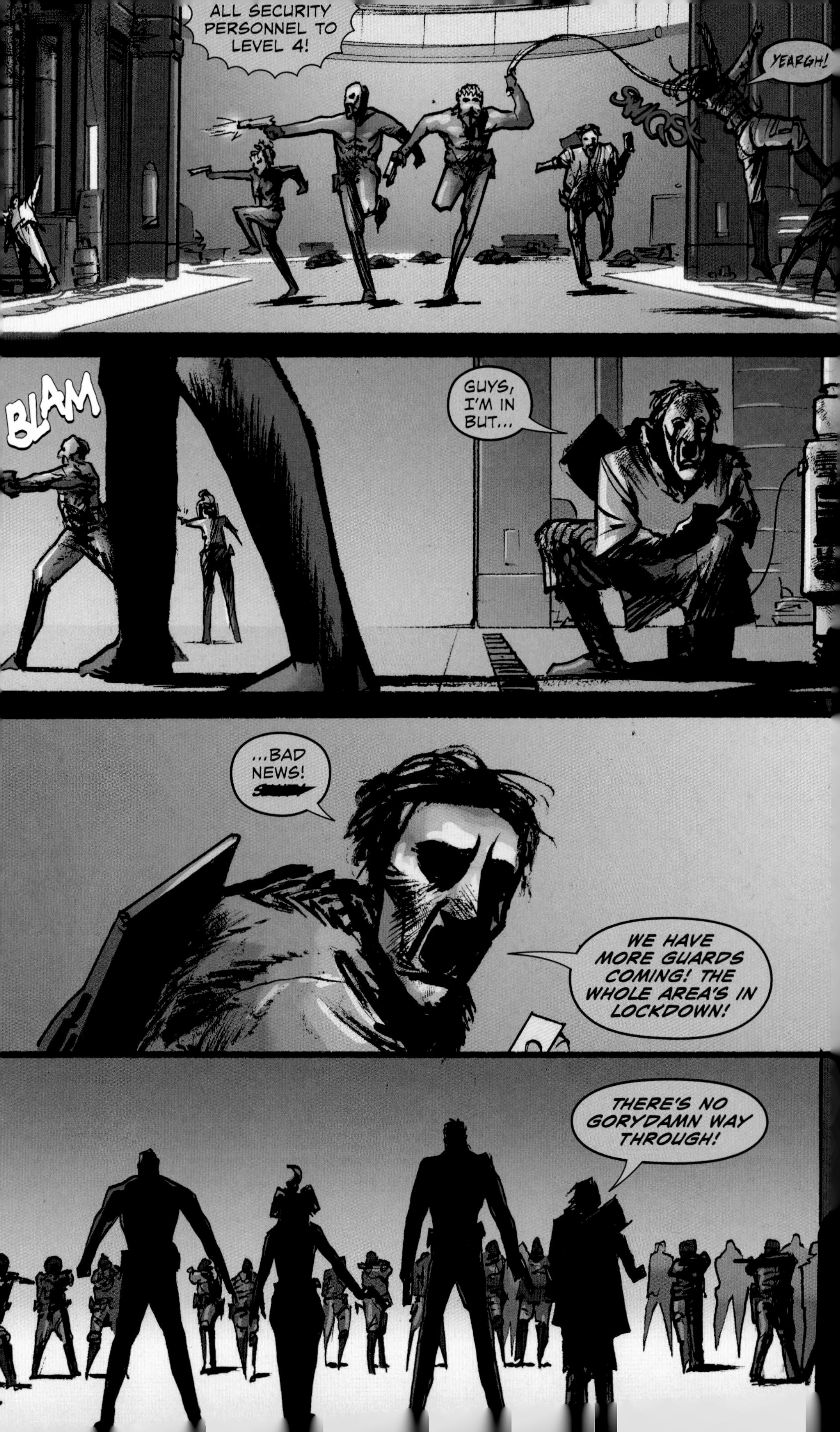
ALL SECURITY PERSONNEL TO LEVEL 4!
SWQSK
YEARGH!
BLAM
GUYS, I'M IN BUT...
...BAD NEWS!
WE HAVE MORE GUARDS COMING! THE WHOLE AREA'S IN LOCKDOWN!
THERE'S NO GORYDAMN WAY THROUGH!

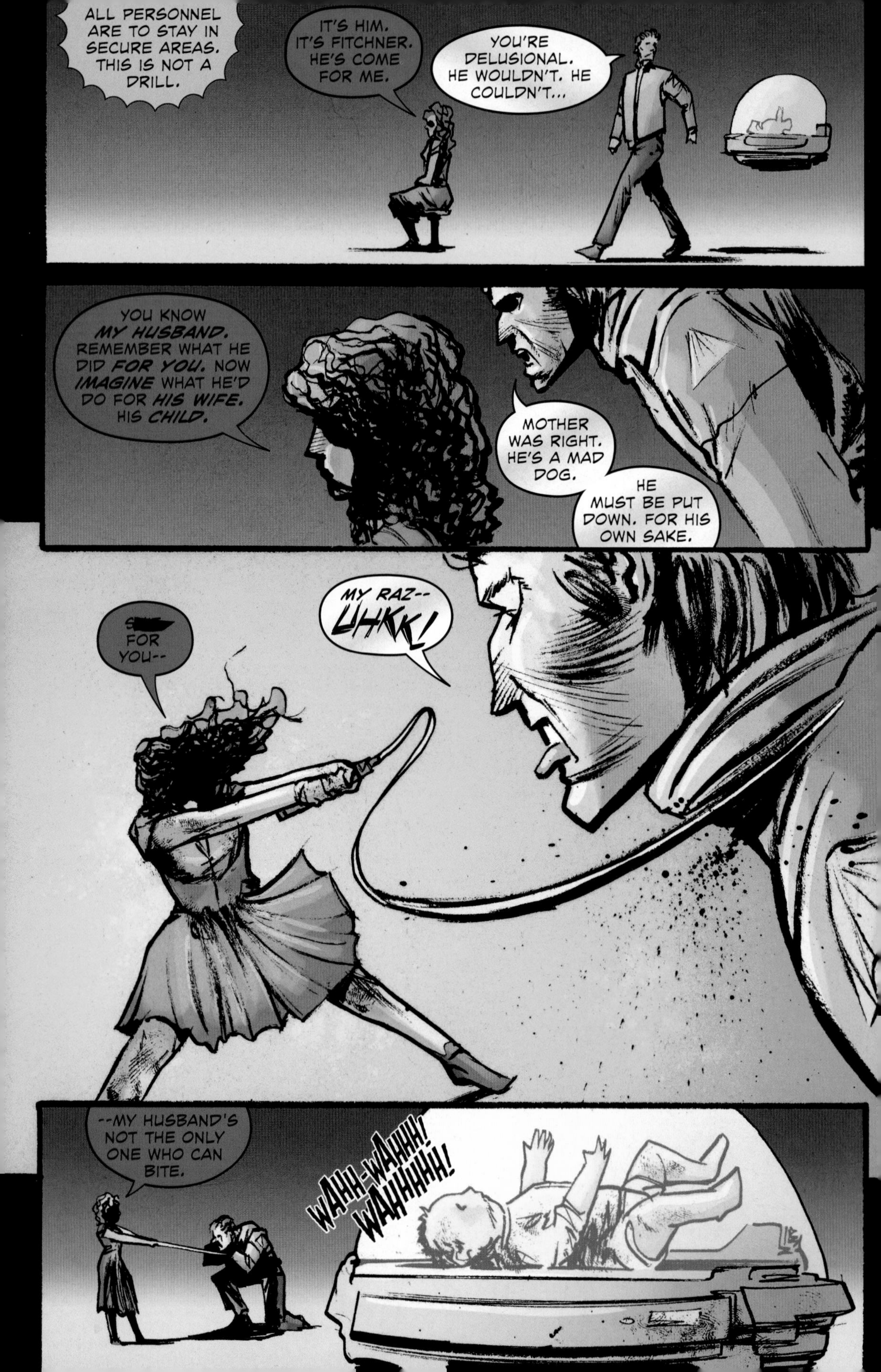
ALL PERSONNEL ARE TO STAY IN SECURE AREAS. THIS IS NOT A DRILL.
IT'S HIM. IT'S FITCHNER. HE'S COME FOR ME.
YOU'RE DELUSIONAL. HE WOULDN'T. HE COULDN'T...
YOU KNOW MY HUSBAND. REMEMBER WHAT HE DID FOR YOU. NOW IMAGINE WHAT HE'D DO FOR HIS WIFE. HIS CHILD.
MOTHER WAS RIGHT. HE'S A MAD DOG.
HE MUST BE PUT DOWN. FOR HIS OWN SAKE.
[redacted] FOR YOU--
MY RAZ-- UHKK!
--MY HUSBAND'S NOT THE ONLY ONE WHO CAN BITE.
WAHH-WAHHH! WAHHHHH!

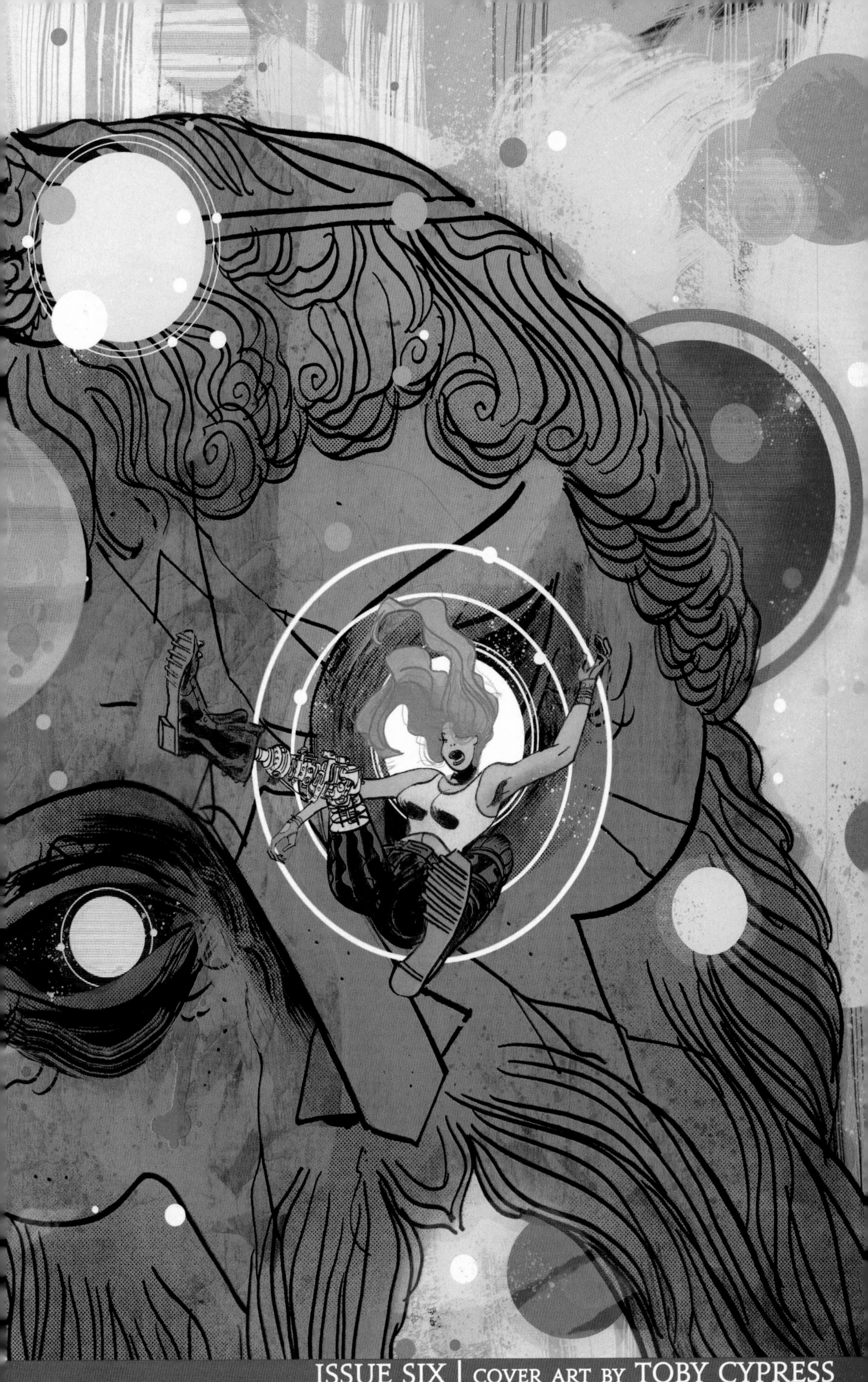

ISSUE SIX | COVER ART BY TOBY CYPRESS

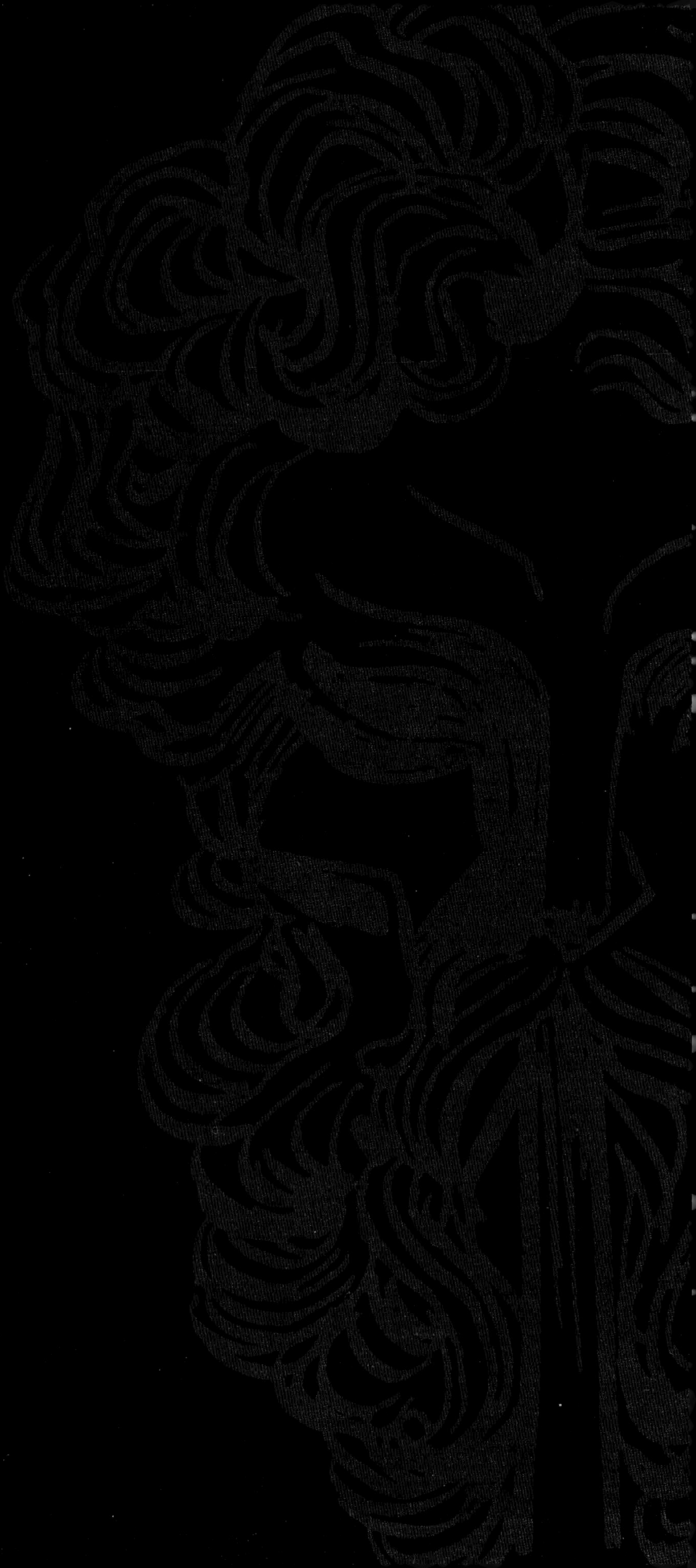

ALL PERSONNEL ARE TO STAY IN SECURE AREAS. THIS IS NOT A DRILL.
YOU HEAR THAT? SOUNDS LIKE MY HUSBAND IS COMING...
...EITHER TO COLLECT ME...
...OR TO KILL YOU!
YOU'D BETTER DECIDE FASTLIKE WHICH, BEFORE HE DECIDES FOR YOU!
WHERE WILL YOU GO, BRYN? THERE'S NOWHERE YOU CAN RUN.
ANYWHERE BUT HERE.
THE...STUD WORKS THE DOORS.
IT'S KEYED TO MY SECURITY PROTOCOLS, SO IT WILL LET YOU GO ANYWHERE.
TAKE IT AND LEAVE.
BUT UNDERSTAND THAT THE SOCIETY WILL HUNT YOU. FIND YOU. AND KILL YOU BOTH.
WHACK
I'LL TAKE MY CHANCES.
UNGK!
WHACK

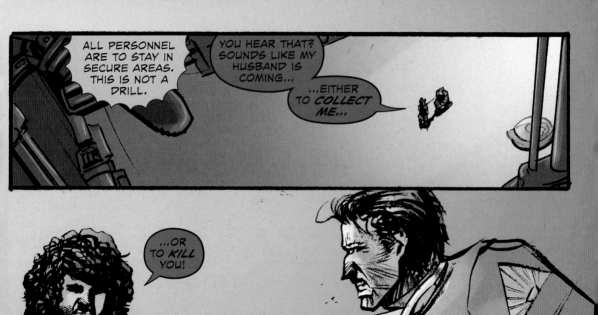

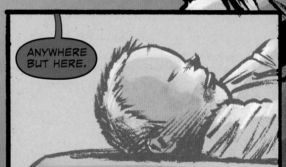

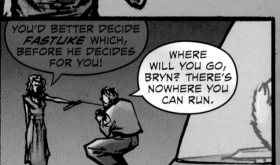

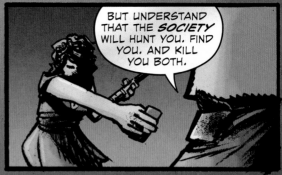

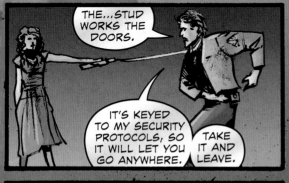

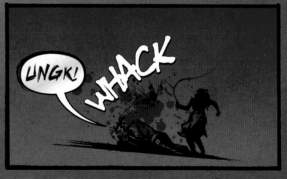

BETTER ME AND SEVRO LEAVE HERE ALIVE, DOMINUS...
...THAN STAY HERE FOR OUR OWN BLOODYDAMN *VIVISECTION!*
GOODBYE, DOMINUS.
IF MY HUSBAND FINDS YOU BEFORE HE FINDS ME, TELL HIM I HAVE SEVRO...
...AND HE MAY LET YOU LIVE.

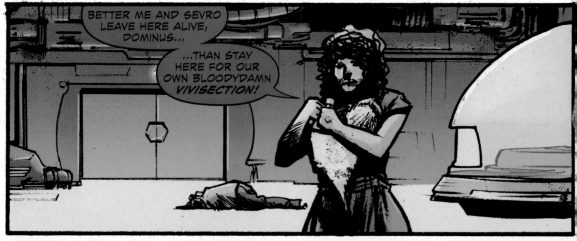

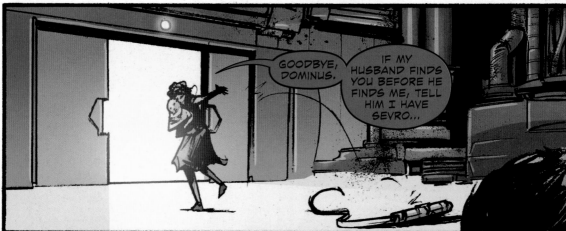

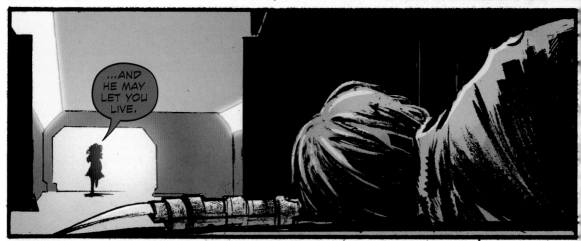

CHAPTER 6:

BIRTH OF A MYTH...

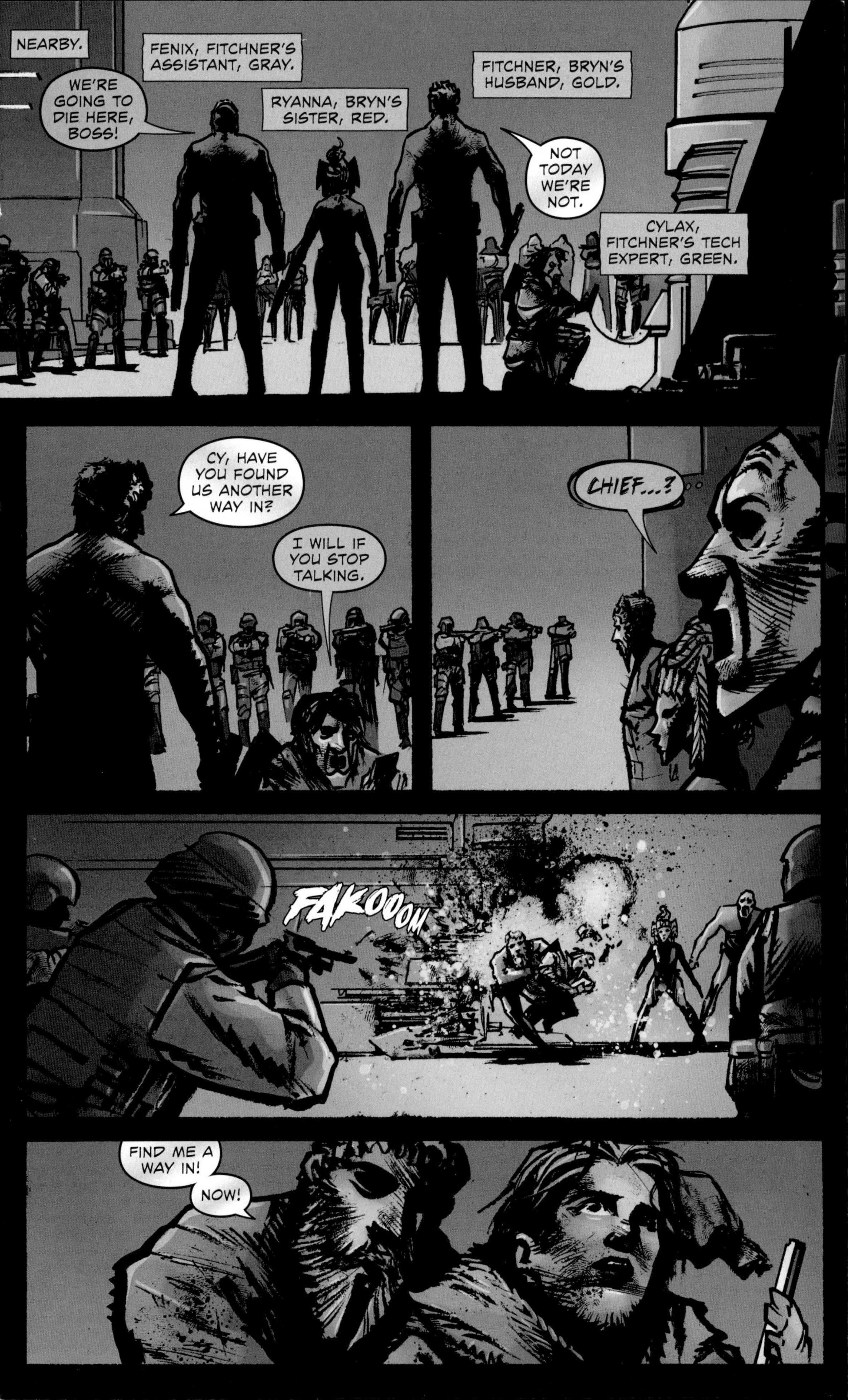
NEARBY.
FENIX, FITCHNER'S ASSISTANT, GRAY.
WE'RE GOING TO DIE HERE, BOSS!
RYANNA, BRYN'S SISTER, RED.
FITCHNER, BRYN'S HUSBAND, GOLD.
NOT TODAY WE'RE NOT.
CYLAX, FITCHNER'S TECH EXPERT, GREEN.
CY, HAVE YOU FOUND US ANOTHER WAY IN?
I WILL IF YOU STOP TALKING.
CHIEF...?
FAKOOOM
FIND ME A WAY IN!
NOW!

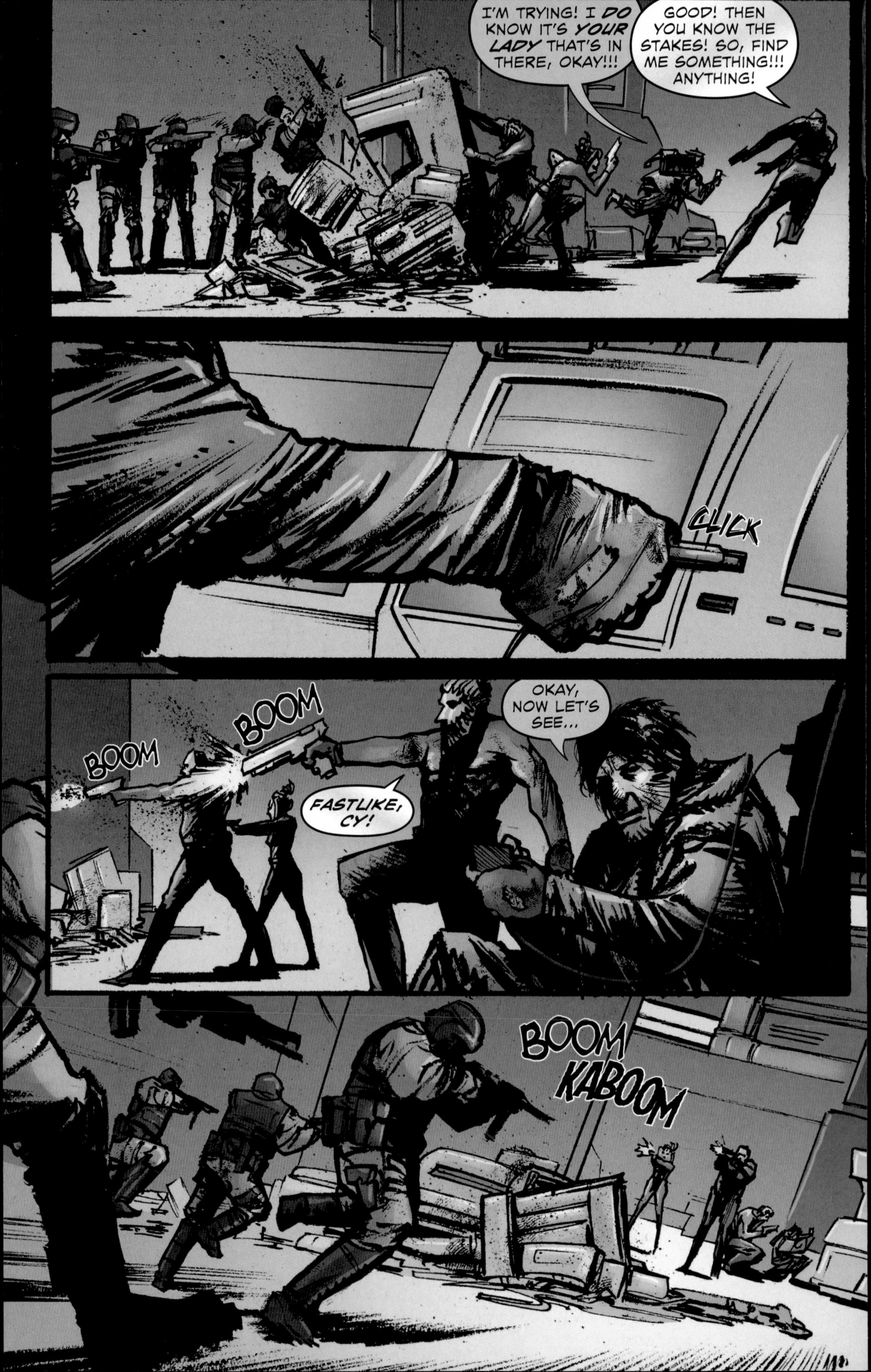
I'M TRYING! I DO KNOW IT'S YOUR LADY THAT'S IN THERE, OKAY!!!
GOOD! THEN YOU KNOW THE STAKES! SO, FIND ME SOMETHING!!! ANYTHING!
CLICK
BOOM
BOOM
FASTLIKE, CY!
OKAY, NOW LET'S SEE...
BOOM
KABOOM

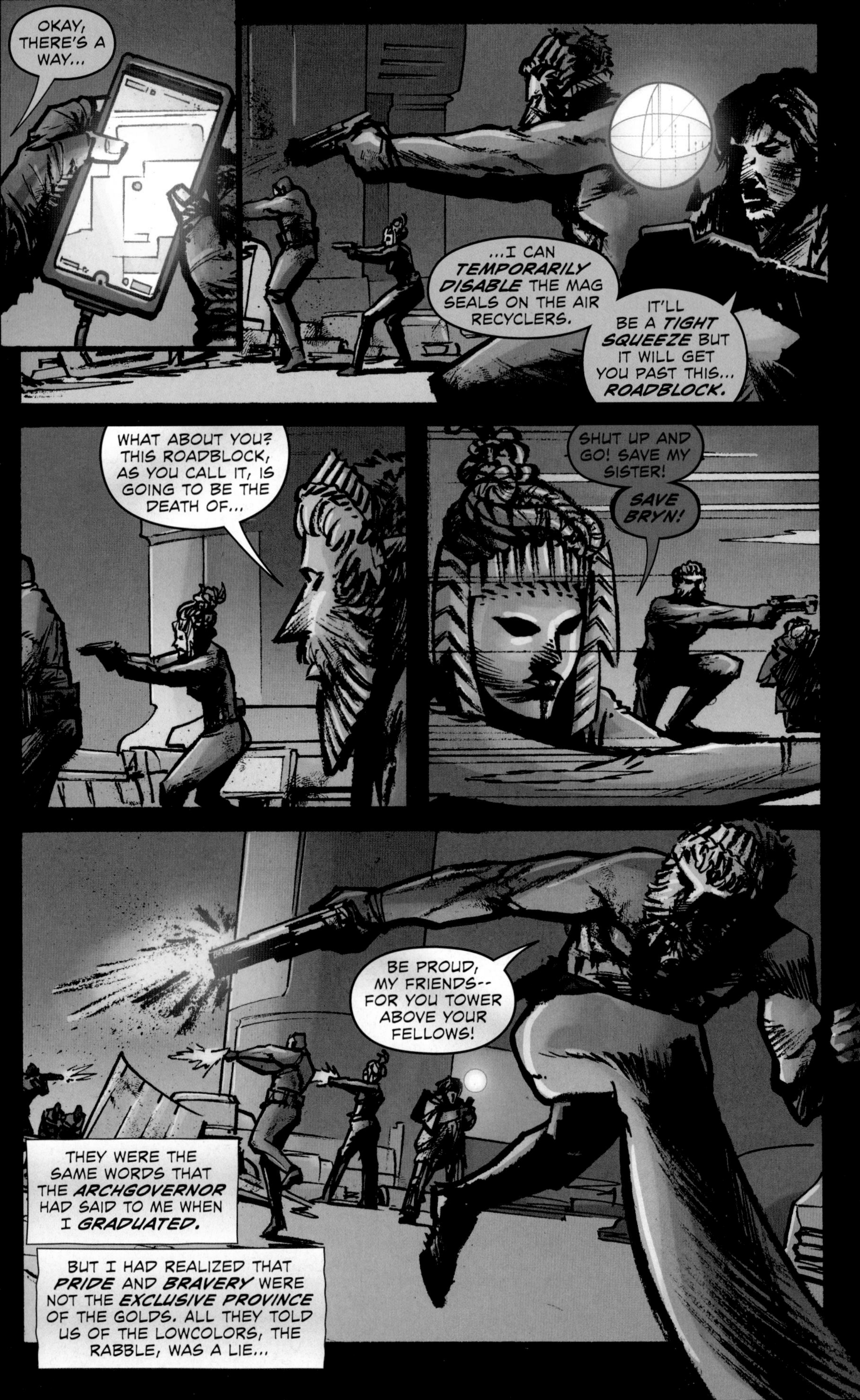
OKAY, THERE'S A WAY...
...I CAN TEMPORARILY DISABLE THE MAG SEALS ON THE AIR RECYCLERS.
IT'LL BE A TIGHT SQUEEZE BUT IT WILL GET YOU PAST THIS... ROADBLOCK.
WHAT ABOUT YOU? THIS ROADBLOCK, AS YOU CALL IT, IS GOING TO BE THE DEATH OF...
SHUT UP AND GO! SAVE MY SISTER!
SAVE BRYN!
BE PROUD, MY FRIENDS-- FOR YOU TOWER ABOVE YOUR FELLOWS!
THEY WERE THE SAME WORDS THAT THE ARCHGOVERNOR HAD SAID TO ME WHEN I GRADUATED.
BUT I HAD REALIZED THAT PRIDE AND BRAVERY WERE NOT THE EXCLUSIVE PROVINCE OF THE GOLDS. ALL THEY TOLD US OF THE LOWCOLORS, THE RABBLE, WAS A LIE...

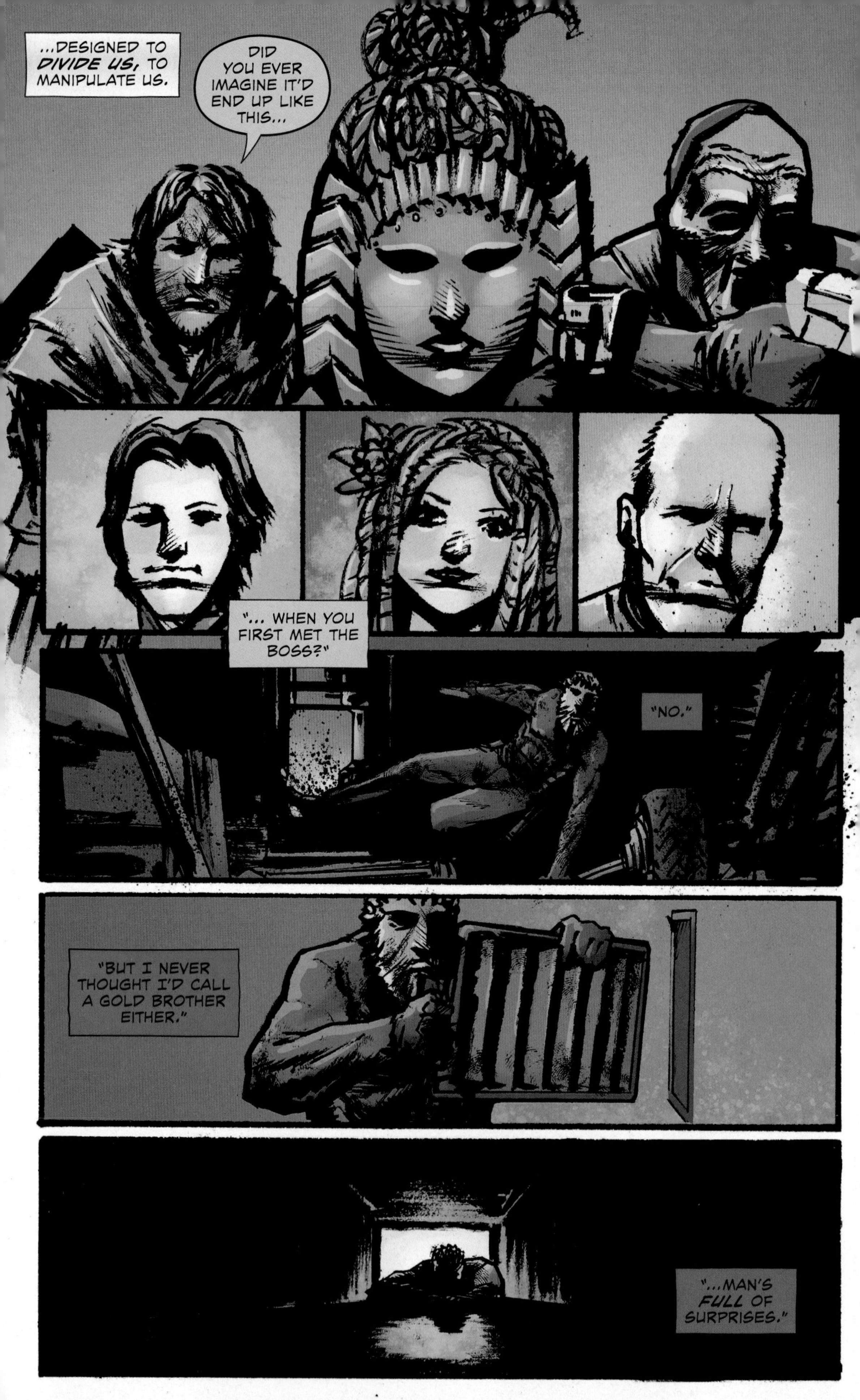
...DESIGNED TO *DIVIDE US,* TO MANIPULATE US.
DID YOU EVER IMAGINE IT'D END UP LIKE THIS...
"... WHEN YOU FIRST MET THE BOSS?"
"NO."
"BUT I NEVER THOUGHT I'D CALL A GOLD BROTHER EITHER."
"...MAN'S *FULL* OF SURPRISES."

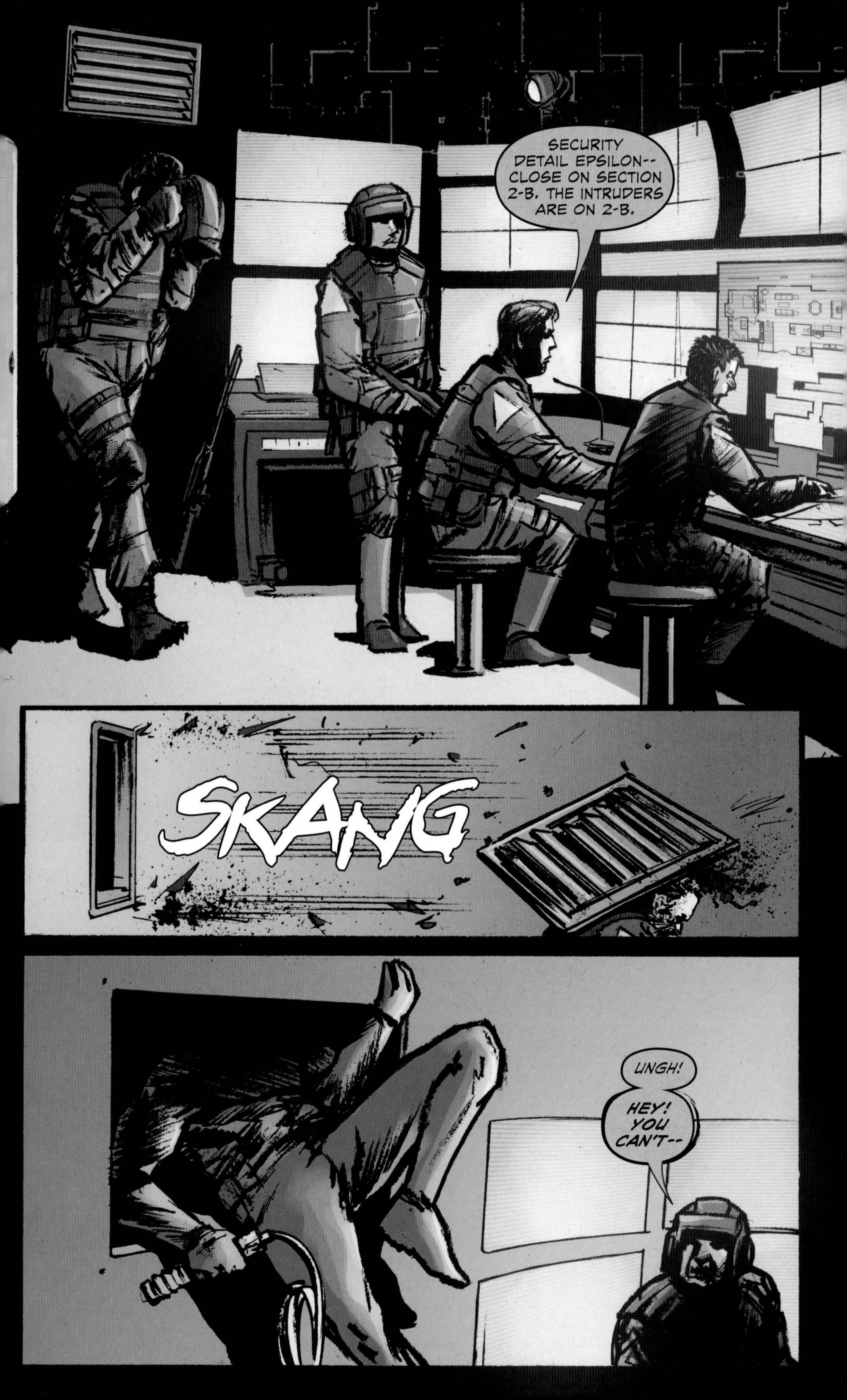
SECURITY DETAIL EPSILON-- CLOSE ON SECTION 2-B. THE INTRUDERS ARE ON 2-B.
SKANG
UNGH!
HEY! YOU CAN'T--

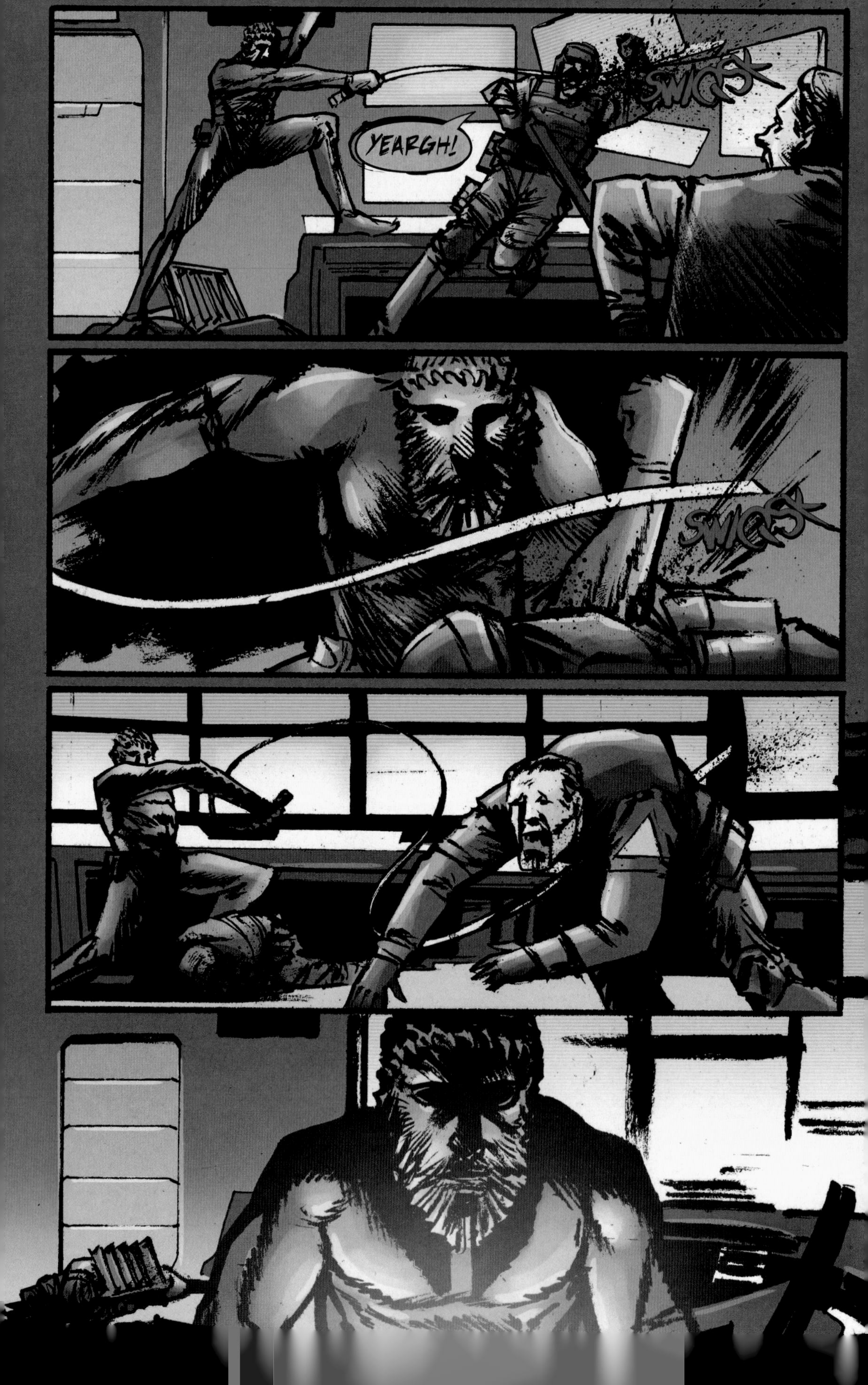
YEARGH!
SWICCK
SWICCK

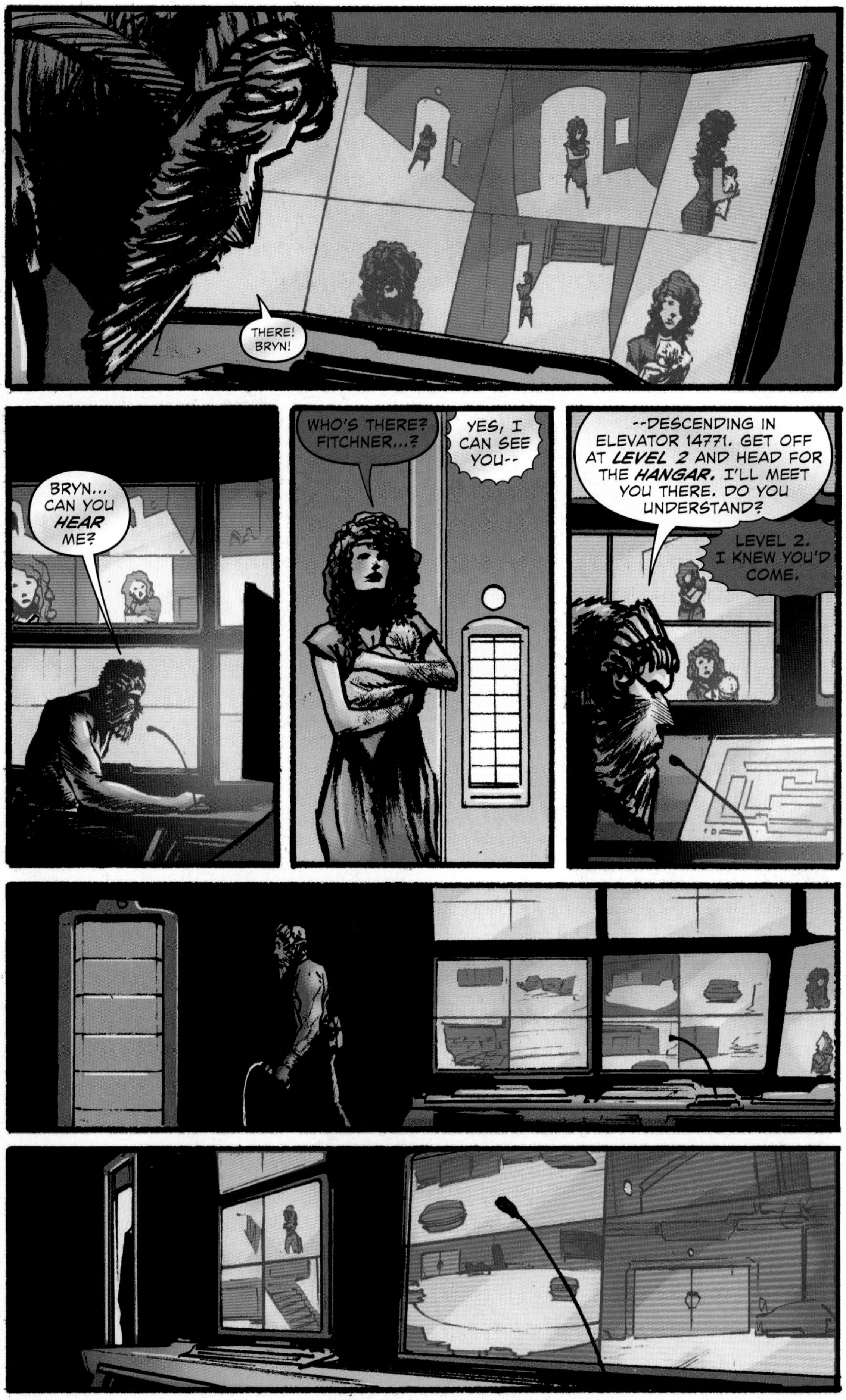
THERE! BRYN!
BRYN... CAN YOU *HEAR* ME?
WHO'S THERE? FITCHNER...?
YES, I CAN SEE YOU--
--DESCENDING IN ELEVATOR 14771. GET OFF AT *LEVEL 2* AND HEAD FOR THE *HANGAR.* I'LL MEET YOU THERE. DO YOU UNDERSTAND?
LEVEL 2. I KNEW YOU'D COME.

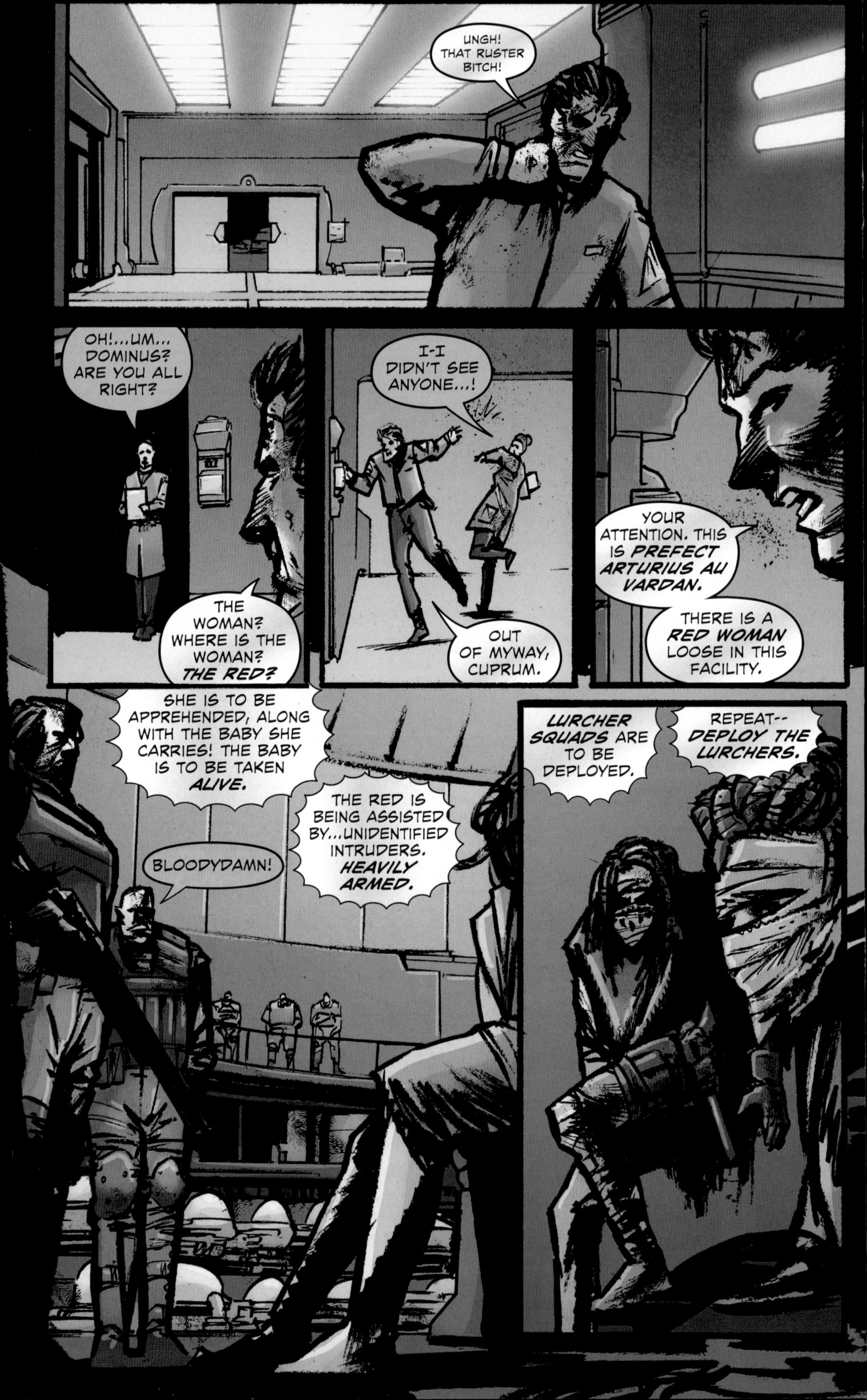
UNGH! THAT RUSTER BITCH!
OH!...UM... DOMINUS? ARE YOU ALL RIGHT?
THE WOMAN? WHERE IS THE WOMAN? THE RED?
I-I DIDN'T SEE ANYONE...!
OUT OF MYWAY, CUPRUM.
YOUR ATTENTION. THIS IS PREFECT ARTURIUS AU VARDAN.
THERE IS A RED WOMAN LOOSE IN THIS FACILITY.
SHE IS TO BE APPREHENDED, ALONG WITH THE BABY SHE CARRIES! THE BABY IS TO BE TAKEN ALIVE.
BLOODYDAMN!
THE RED IS BEING ASSISTED BY...UNIDENTIFIED INTRUDERS. HEAVILY ARMED.
LURCHER SQUADS ARE TO BE DEPLOYED.
REPEAT-- DEPLOY THE LURCHERS.

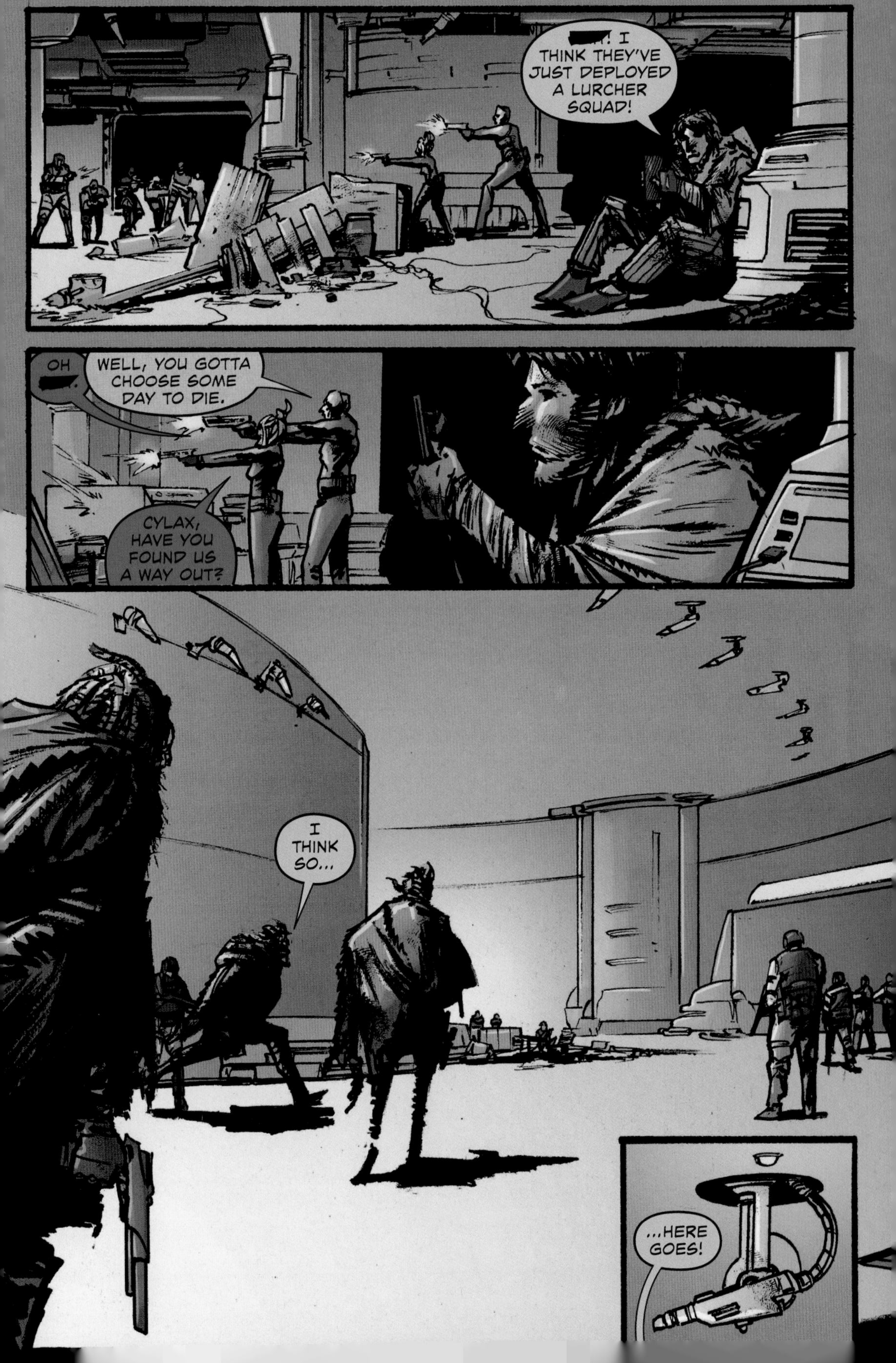
[redacted]! I THINK THEY'VE JUST DEPLOYED A LURCHER SQUAD!
OH [redacted].
WELL, YOU GOTTA CHOOSE SOME DAY TO DIE.
CYLAX, HAVE YOU FOUND US A WAY OUT?
I THINK SO...
...HERE GOES!

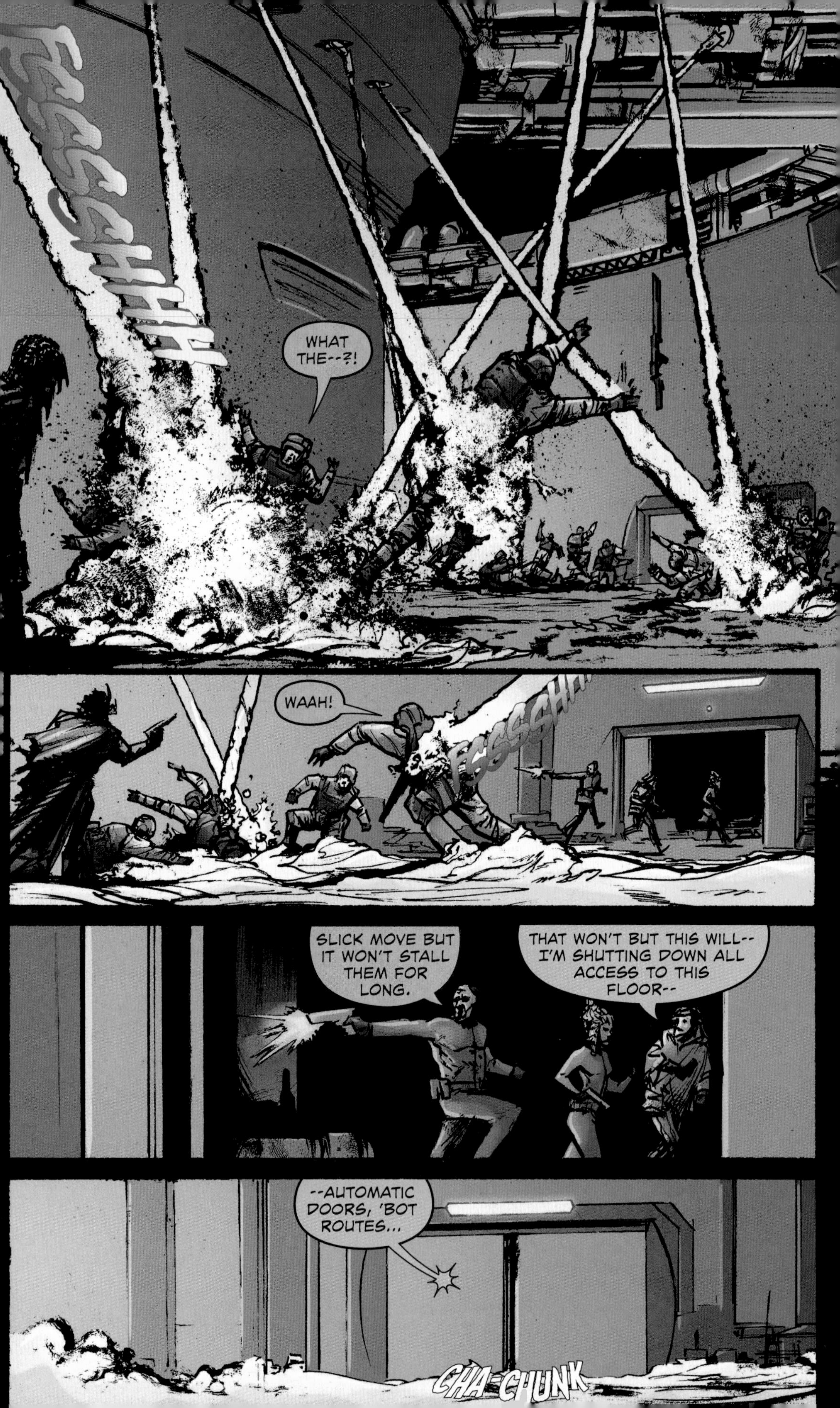
FSSSHHH
WHAT THE--?!
WAAH!
FSSSHH
SLICK MOVE BUT IT WON'T STALL THEM FOR LONG.
THAT WON'T BUT THIS WILL-- I'M SHUTTING DOWN ALL ACCESS TO THIS FLOOR--
--AUTOMATIC DOORS, 'BOT ROUTES...
CHA-CHUNK

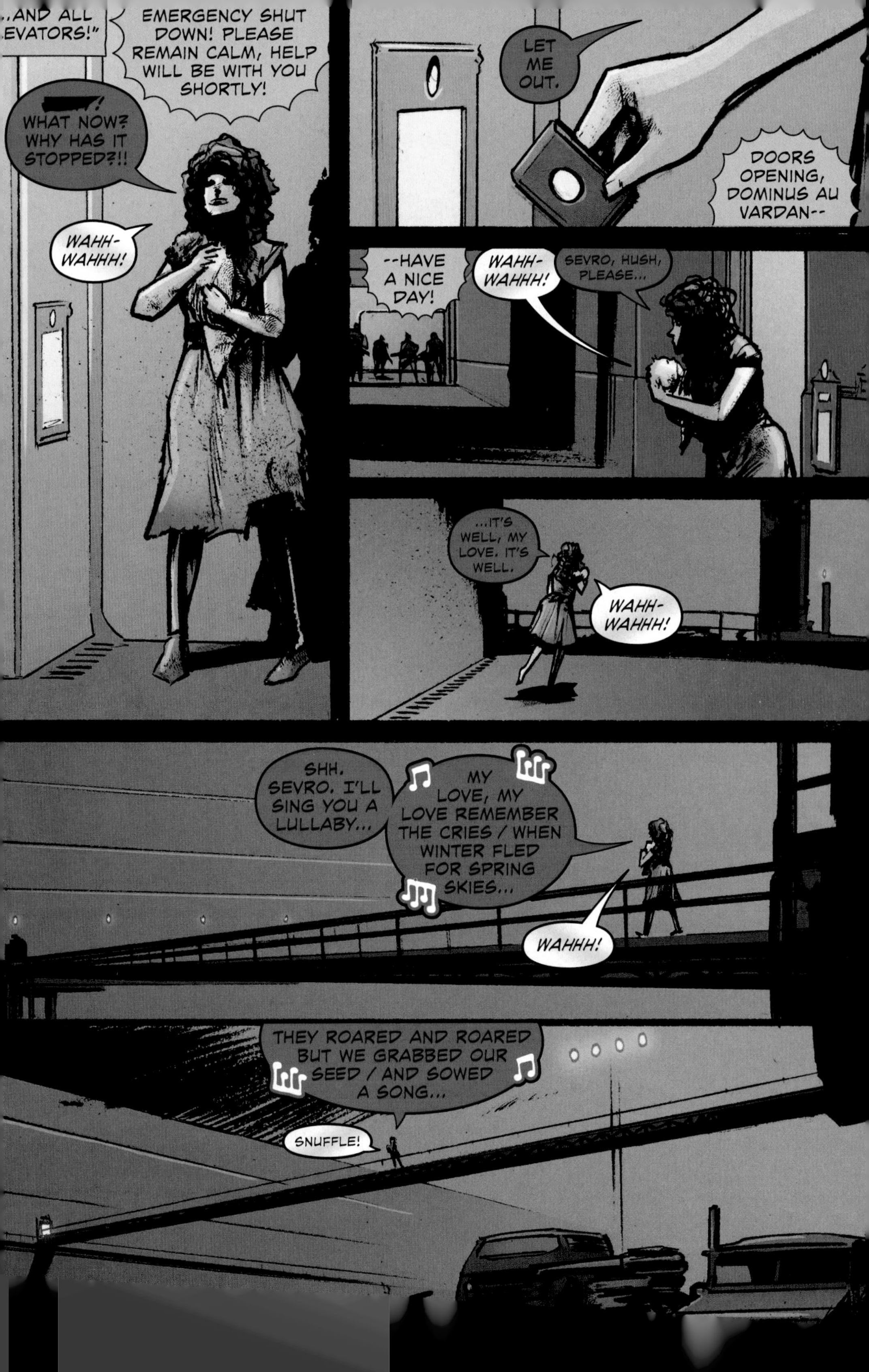

.AND ALL EVATORS!"
EMERGENCY SHUT DOWN! PLEASE REMAIN CALM, HELP WILL BE WITH YOU SHORTLY!
[redacted]! WHAT NOW? WHY HAS IT STOPPED?!!
WAHH-WAHHH!
LET ME OUT.
DOORS OPENING, DOMINUS AU VARDAN--
--HAVE A NICE DAY!
WAHH-WAHHH!
SEVRO, HUSH, PLEASE...
...IT'S WELL, MY LOVE. IT'S WELL.
WAHH-WAHHH!
SHH. SEVRO. I'LL SING YOU A LULLABY...
MY LOVE, MY LOVE REMEMBER THE CRIES / WHEN WINTER FLED FOR SPRING SKIES...
WAHHH!
THEY ROARED AND ROARED BUT WE GRABBED OUR SEED / AND SOWED A SONG...
SNUFFLE!

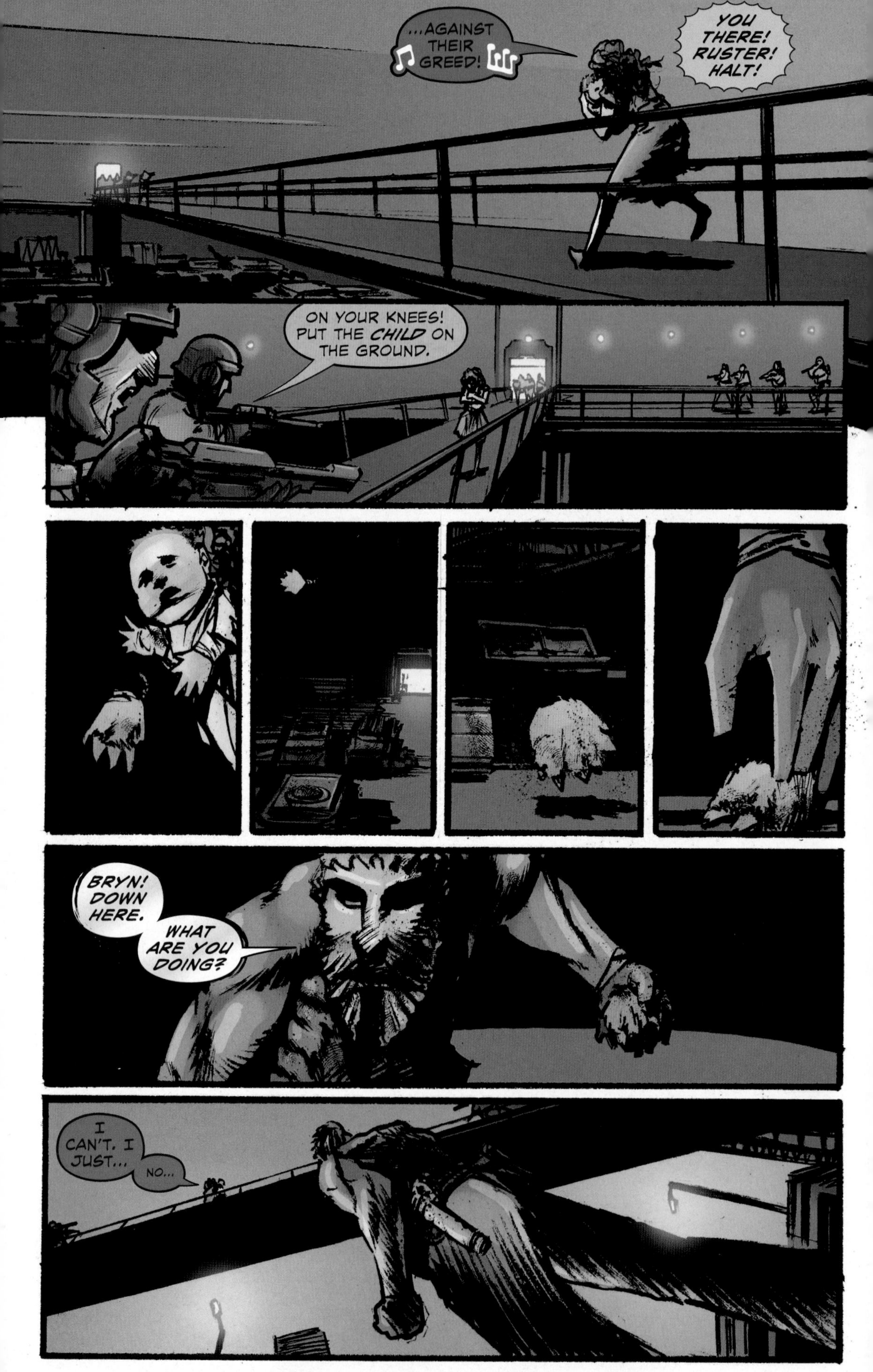
...AGAINST THEIR GREED!
YOU THERE! RUSTER! HALT!
ON YOUR KNEES! PUT THE *CHILD* ON THE GROUND.
BRYN! DOWN HERE.
WHAT ARE YOU DOING?
I CAN'T. I JUST...
NO...

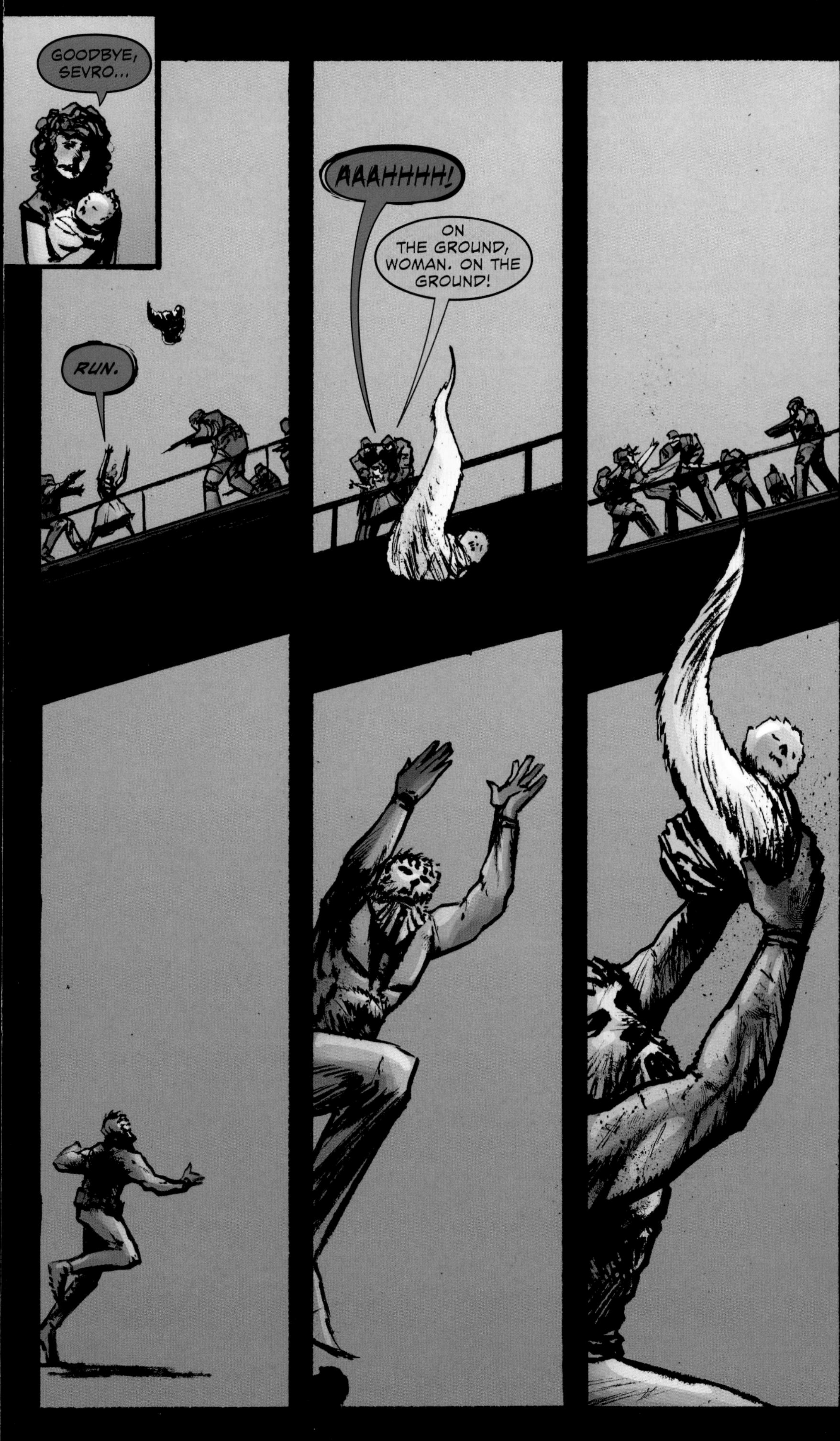
GOODBYE, SEVRO...
RUN.
AAAHHHH!
ON THE GROUND, WOMAN. ON THE GROUND!

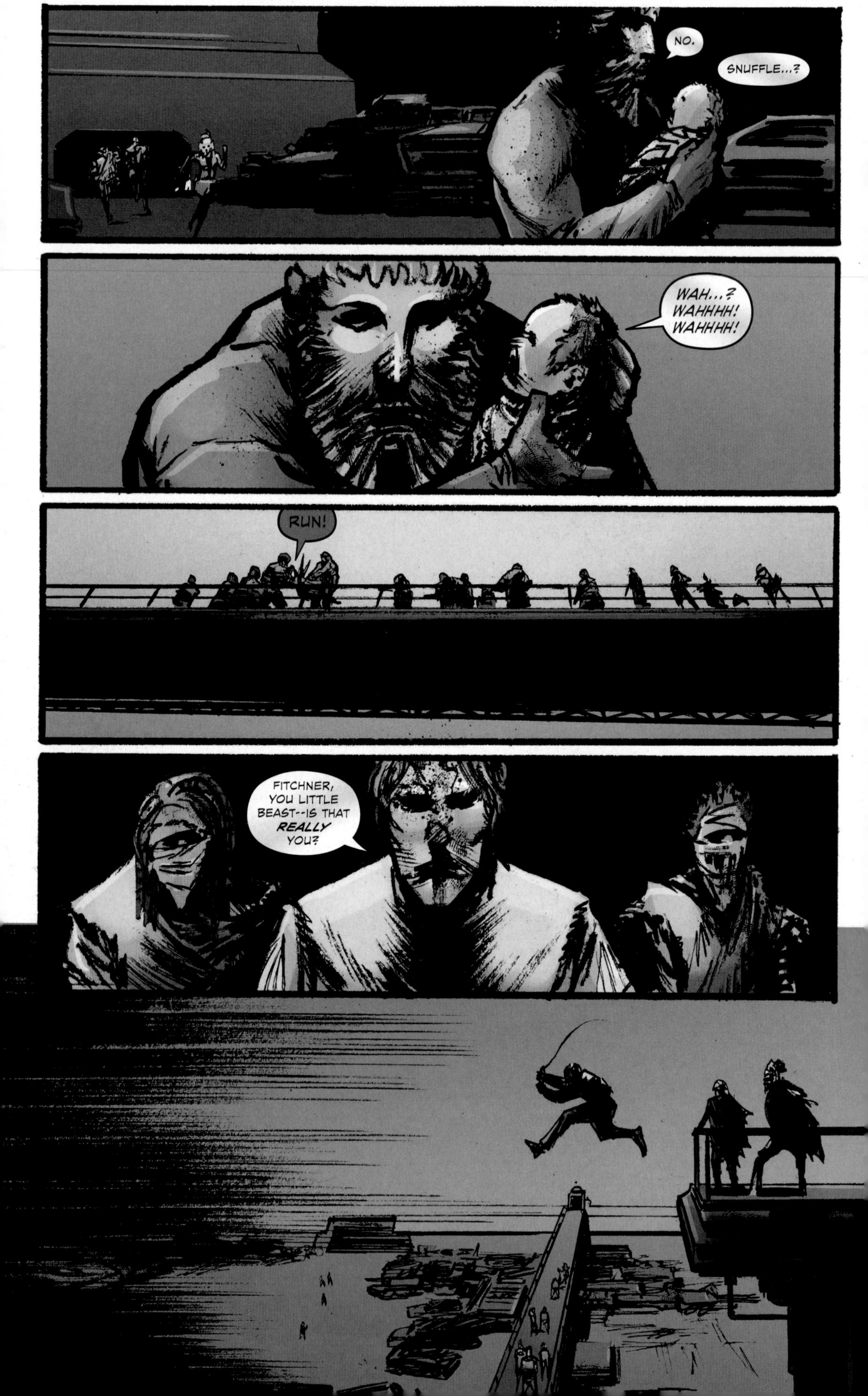
NO.
SNUFFLE...?
WAH...? WAHHHH! WAHHHH!
RUN!
FITCHNER, YOU LITTLE BEAST--IS THAT *REALLY* YOU?

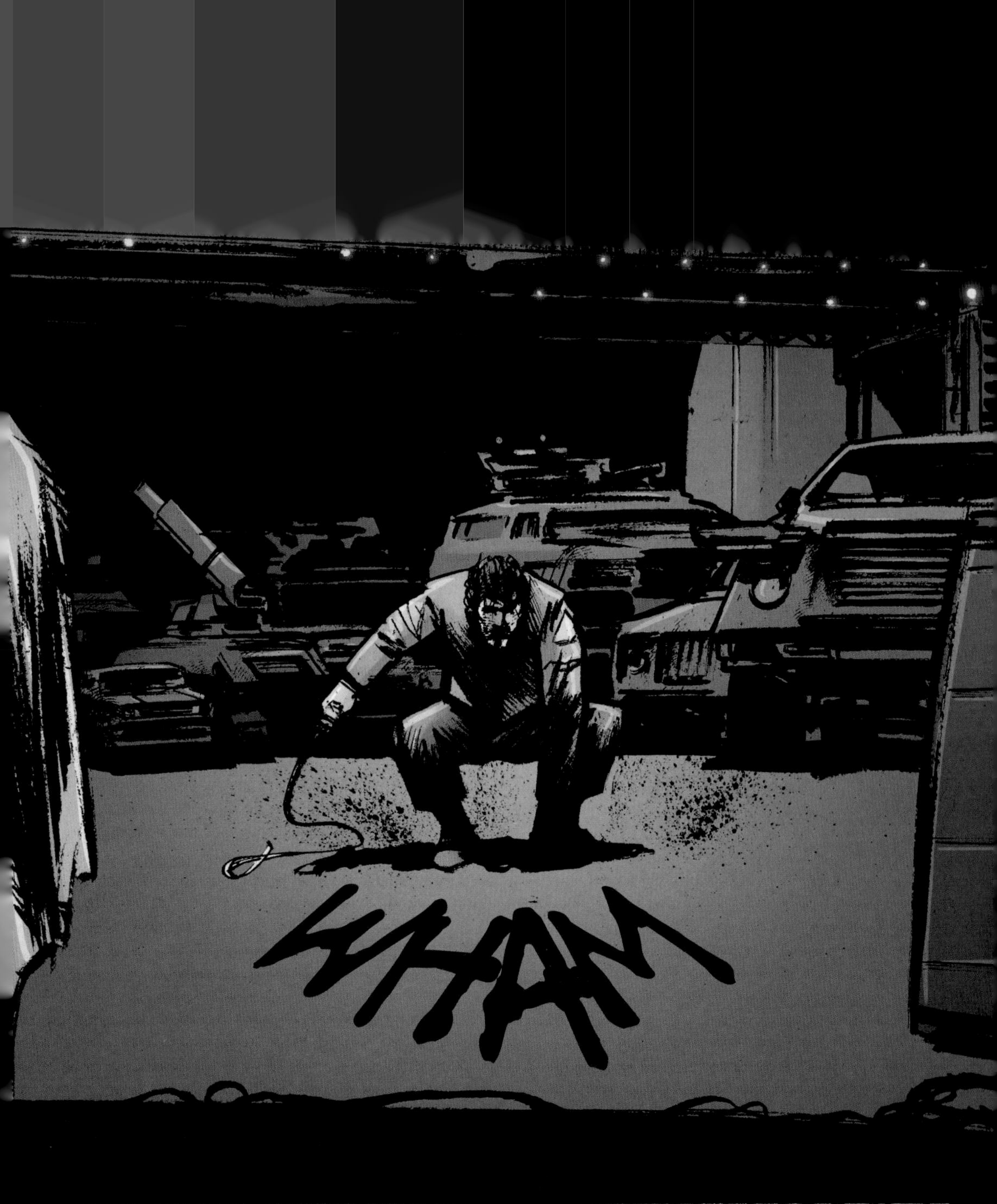
WHAM

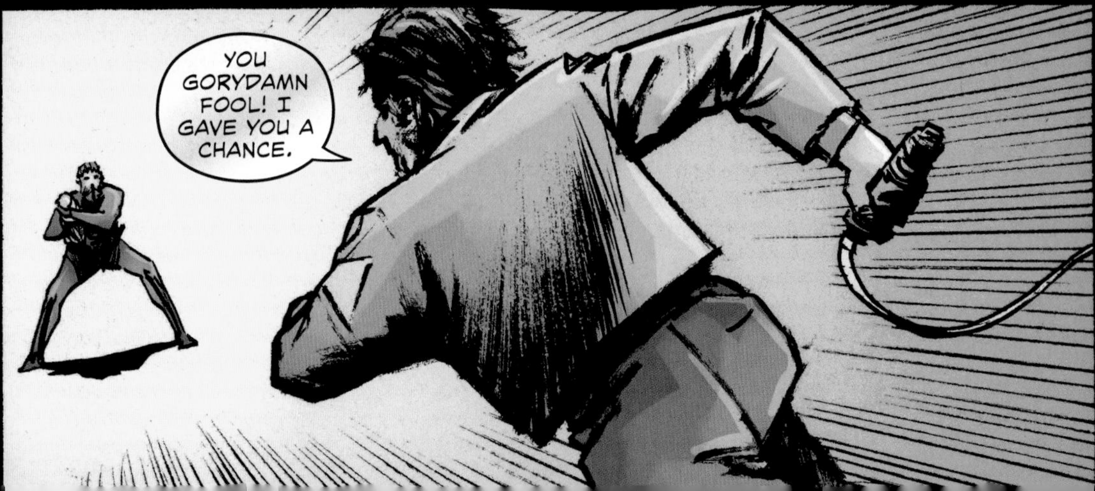
YOU GORYDAMN FOOL! I GAVE YOU A CHANCE.

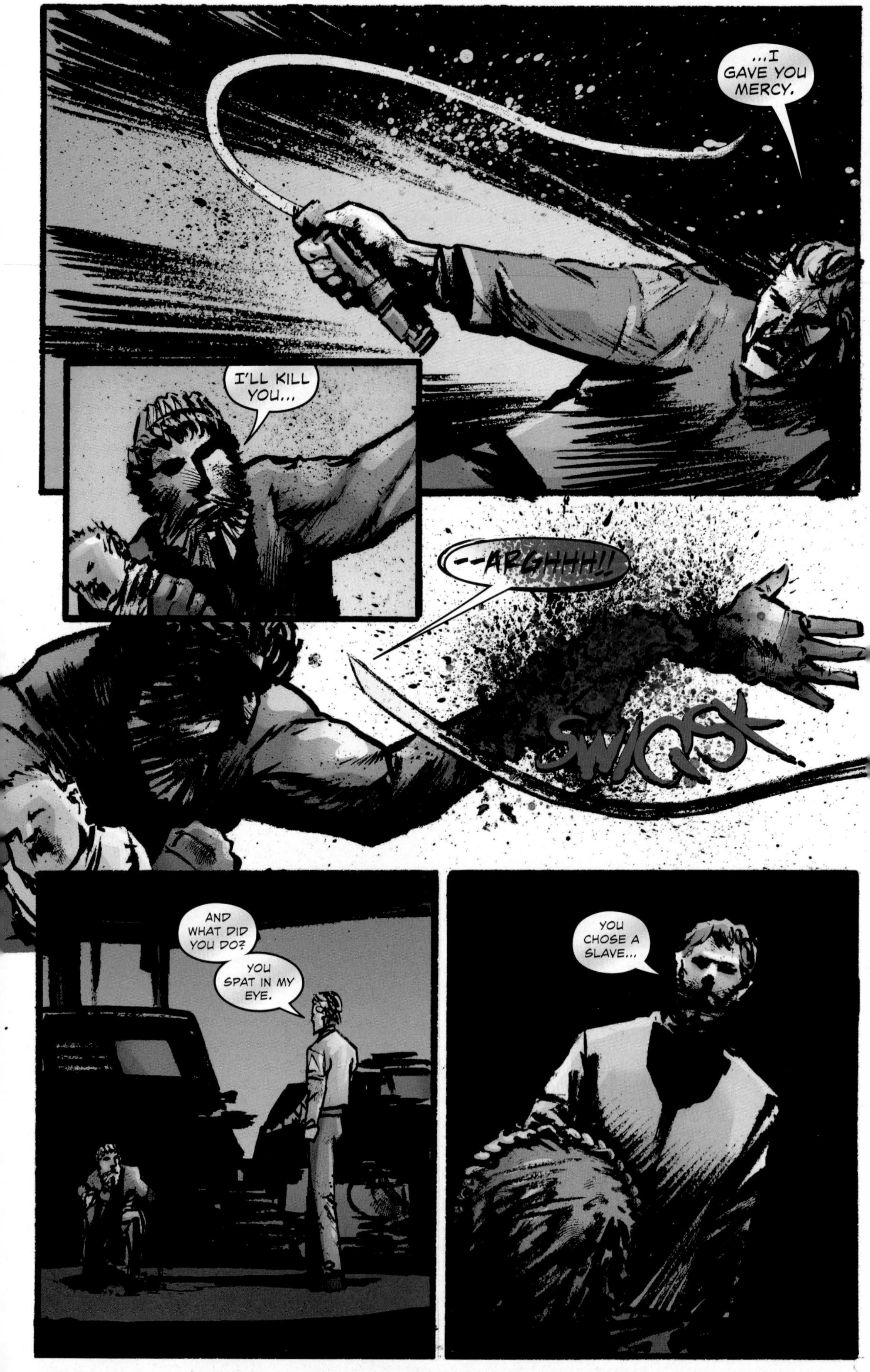
...I GAVE YOU MERCY.
I'LL KILL YOU...
--ARGHHH!!
SWIGSK
AND WHAT DID YOU DO?
YOU SPAT IN MY EYE.
YOU CHOSE A SLAVE...

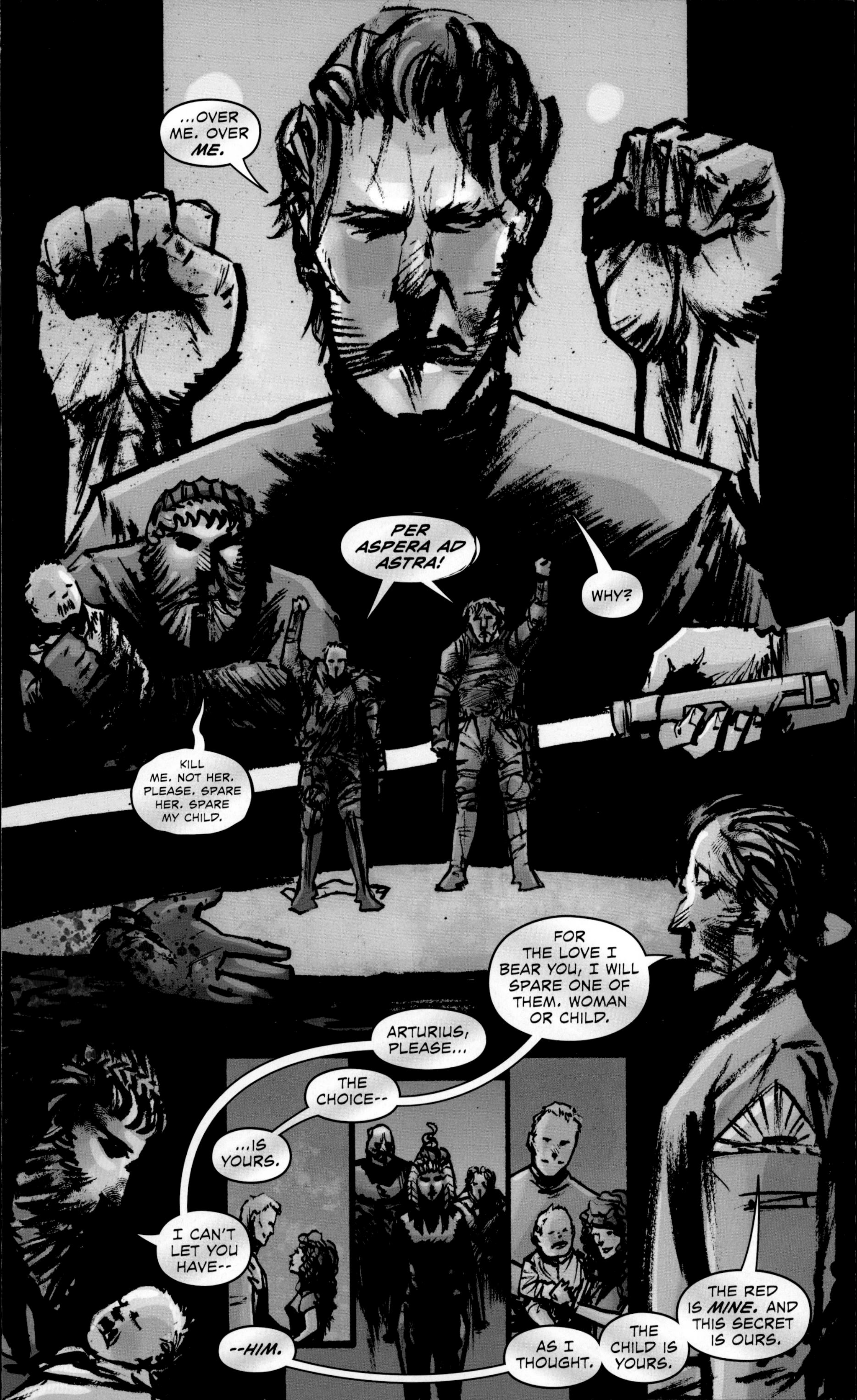

...OVER ME. OVER *ME.*
PER ASPERA AD ASTRA!
WHY?
KILL ME. NOT HER. PLEASE. SPARE HER. SPARE MY CHILD.
FOR THE LOVE I BEAR YOU, I WILL SPARE ONE OF THEM. WOMAN OR CHILD.
ARTURIUS, PLEASE...
THE CHOICE--
...IS YOURS.
I CAN'T LET YOU HAVE--
--HIM.
AS I THOUGHT.
THE CHILD IS YOURS.
THE RED IS *MINE.* AND THIS SECRET IS OURS.

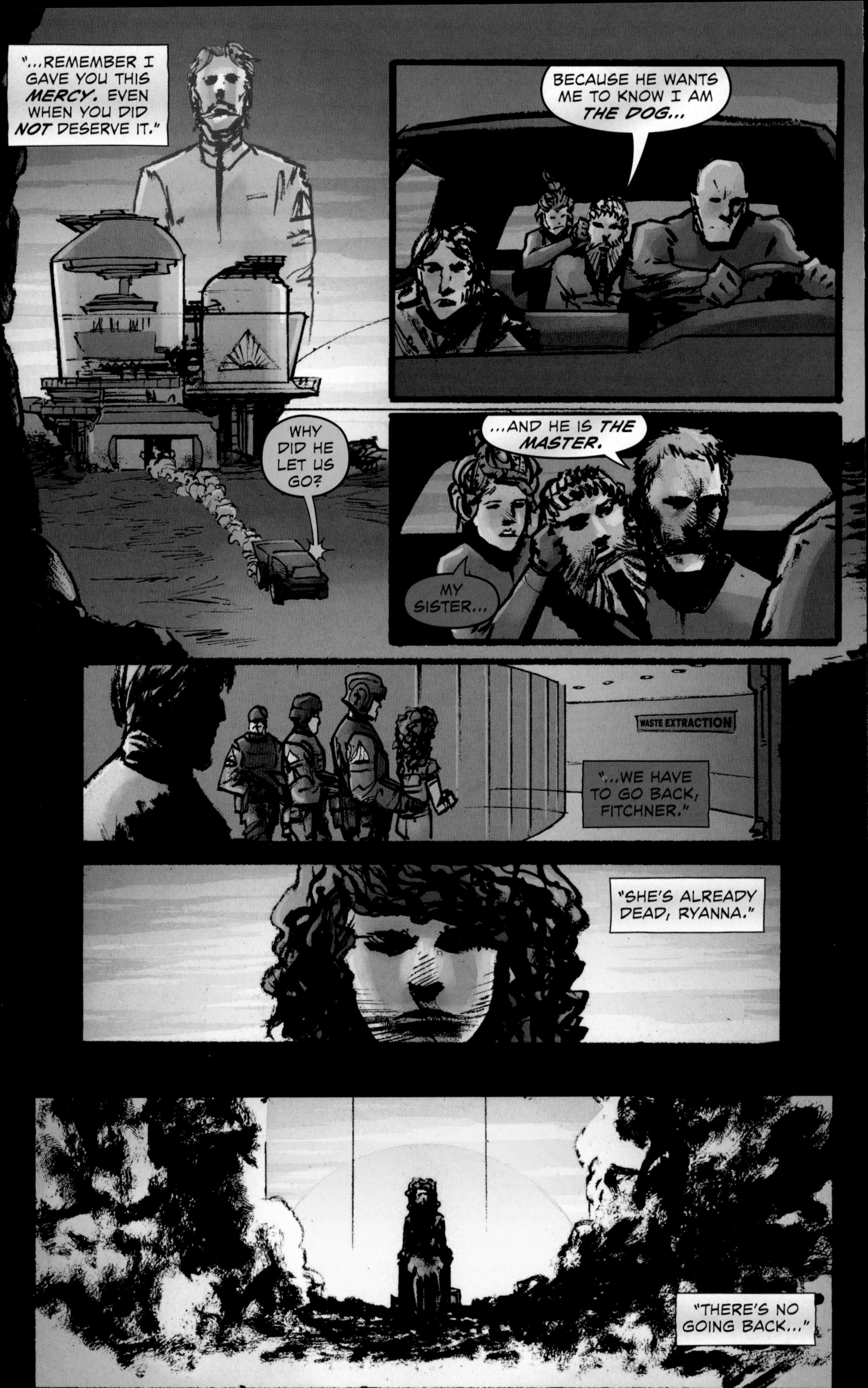
"...REMEMBER I GAVE YOU THIS MERCY. EVEN WHEN YOU DID NOT DESERVE IT."
WHY DID HE LET US GO?
BECAUSE HE WANTS ME TO KNOW I AM THE DOG...
...AND HE IS THE MASTER.
MY SISTER...
WASTE EXTRACTION
"...WE HAVE TO GO BACK, FITCHNER."
"SHE'S ALREADY DEAD, RYANNA."
"THERE'S NO GOING BACK..."

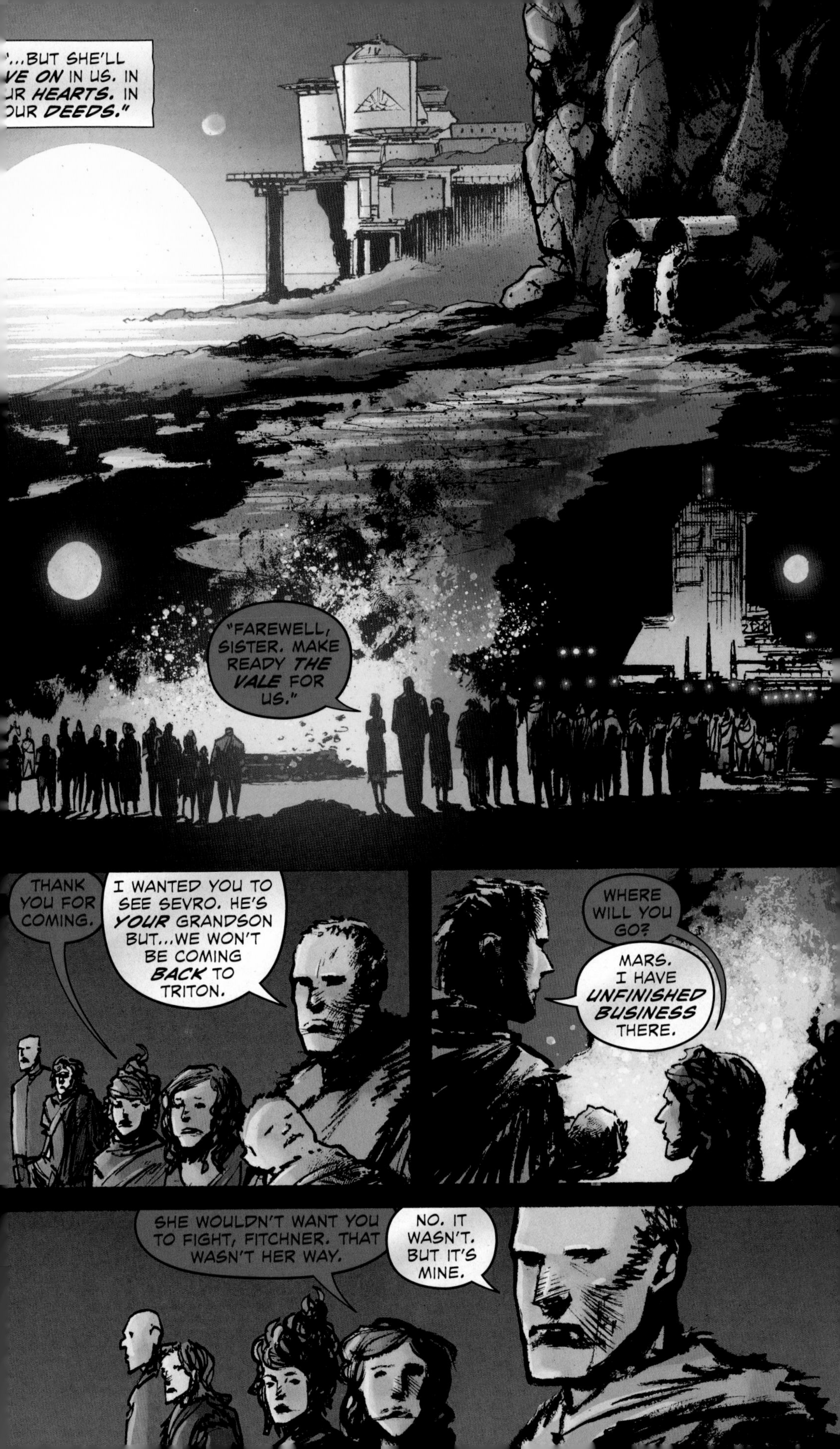
"...BUT SHE'LL VE ON IN US. IN UR HEARTS. IN OUR DEEDS."
"FAREWELL, SISTER. MAKE READY THE VALE FOR US."
THANK YOU FOR COMING.
I WANTED YOU TO SEE SEVRO. HE'S YOUR GRANDSON BUT...WE WON'T BE COMING BACK TO TRITON.
WHERE WILL YOU GO?
MARS. I HAVE UNFINISHED BUSINESS THERE.
SHE WOULDN'T WANT YOU TO FIGHT, FITCHNER. THAT WASN'T HER WAY.
NO. IT WASN'T. BUT IT'S MINE.

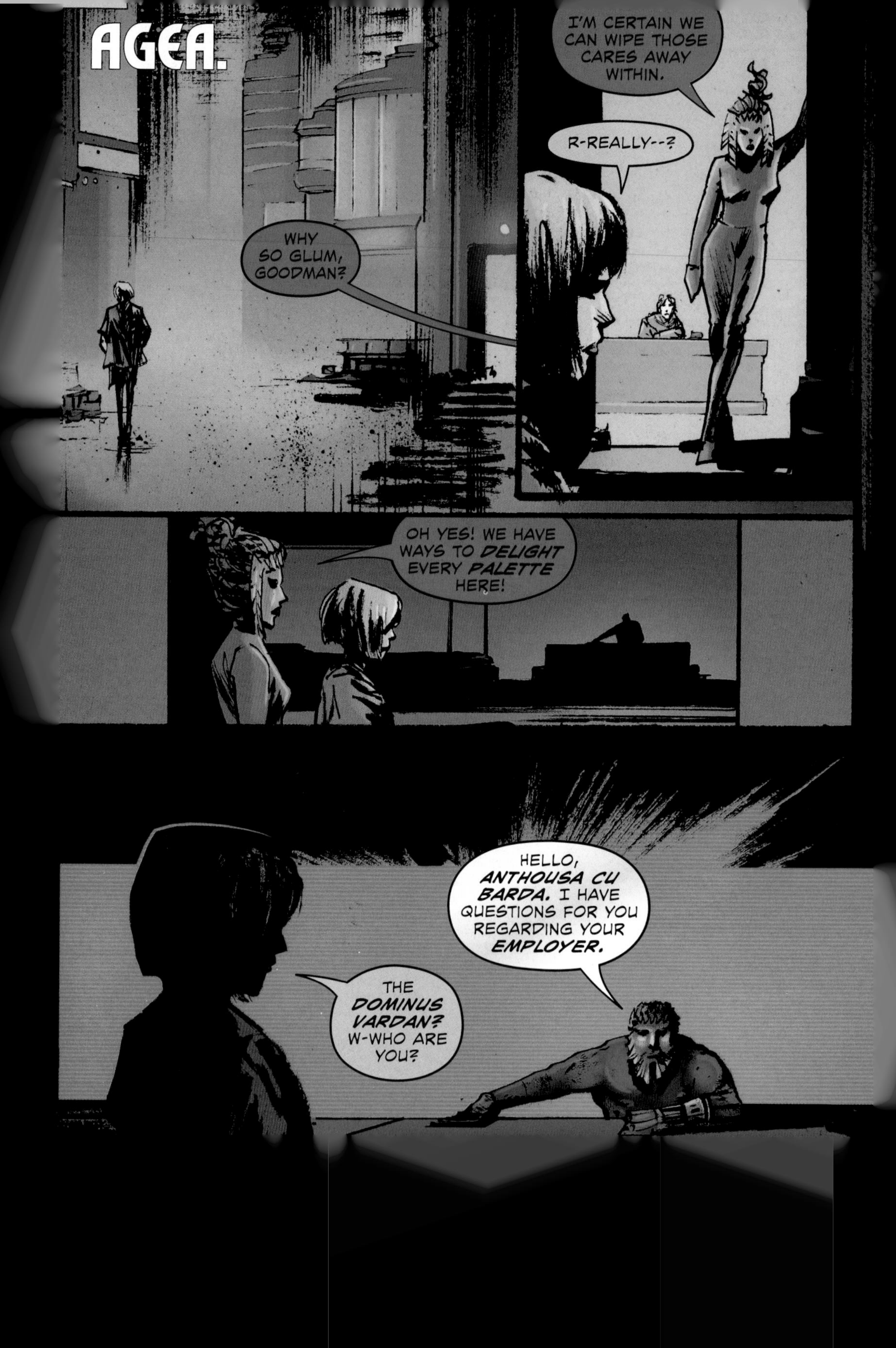
AGEA.
I'M CERTAIN WE CAN WIPE THOSE CARES AWAY WITHIN.
R-REALLY--?
WHY SO GLUM, GOODMAN?
OH YES! WE HAVE WAYS TO *DELIGHT* EVERY *PALETTE* HERE!
HELLO, ***ANTHOUSA CU BARDA.*** I HAVE QUESTIONS FOR YOU REGARDING YOUR ***EMPLOYER.***
THE *DOMINUS VARDAN?* W-WHO ARE YOU?

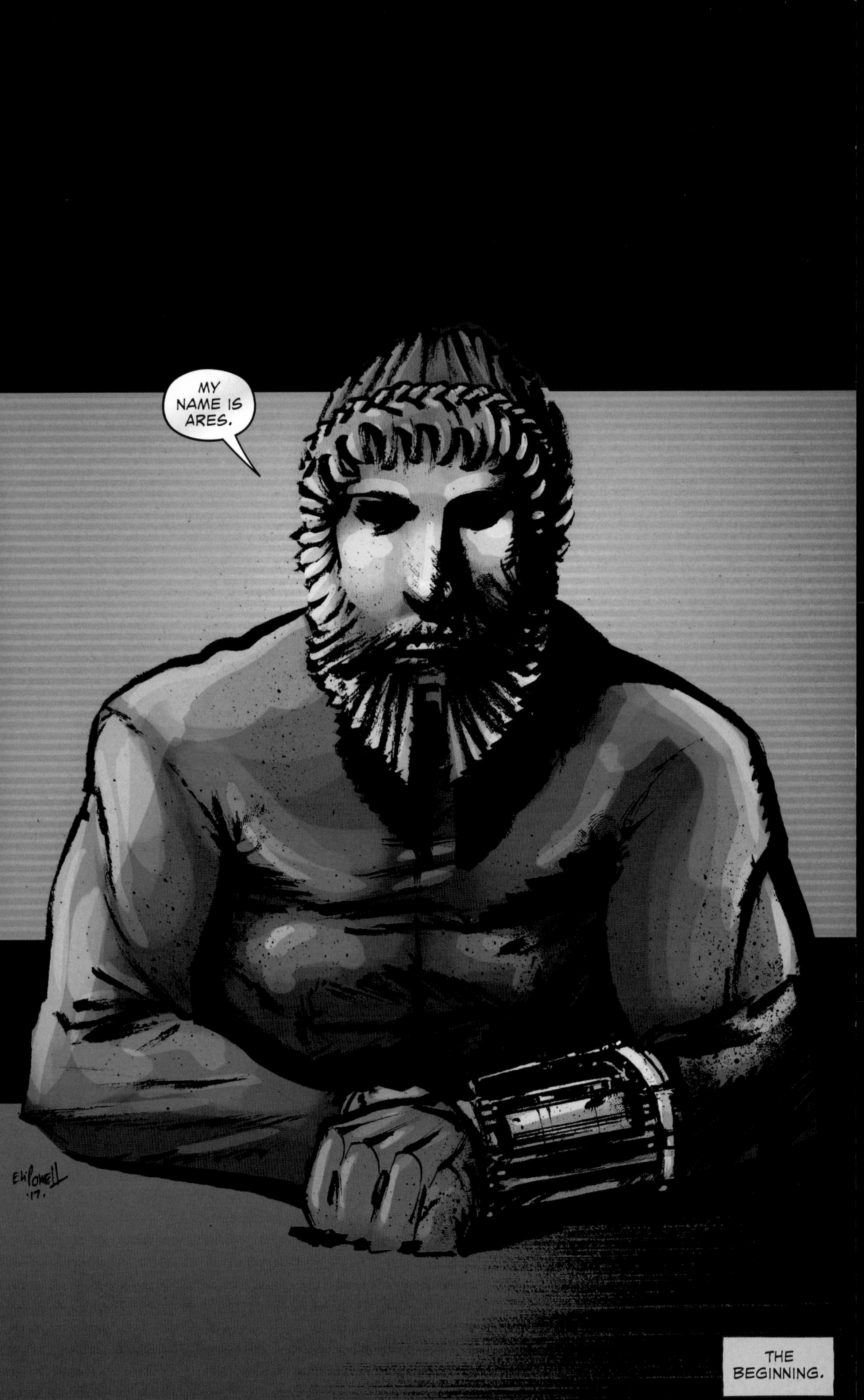
MY NAME IS ARES.
THE BEGINNING.

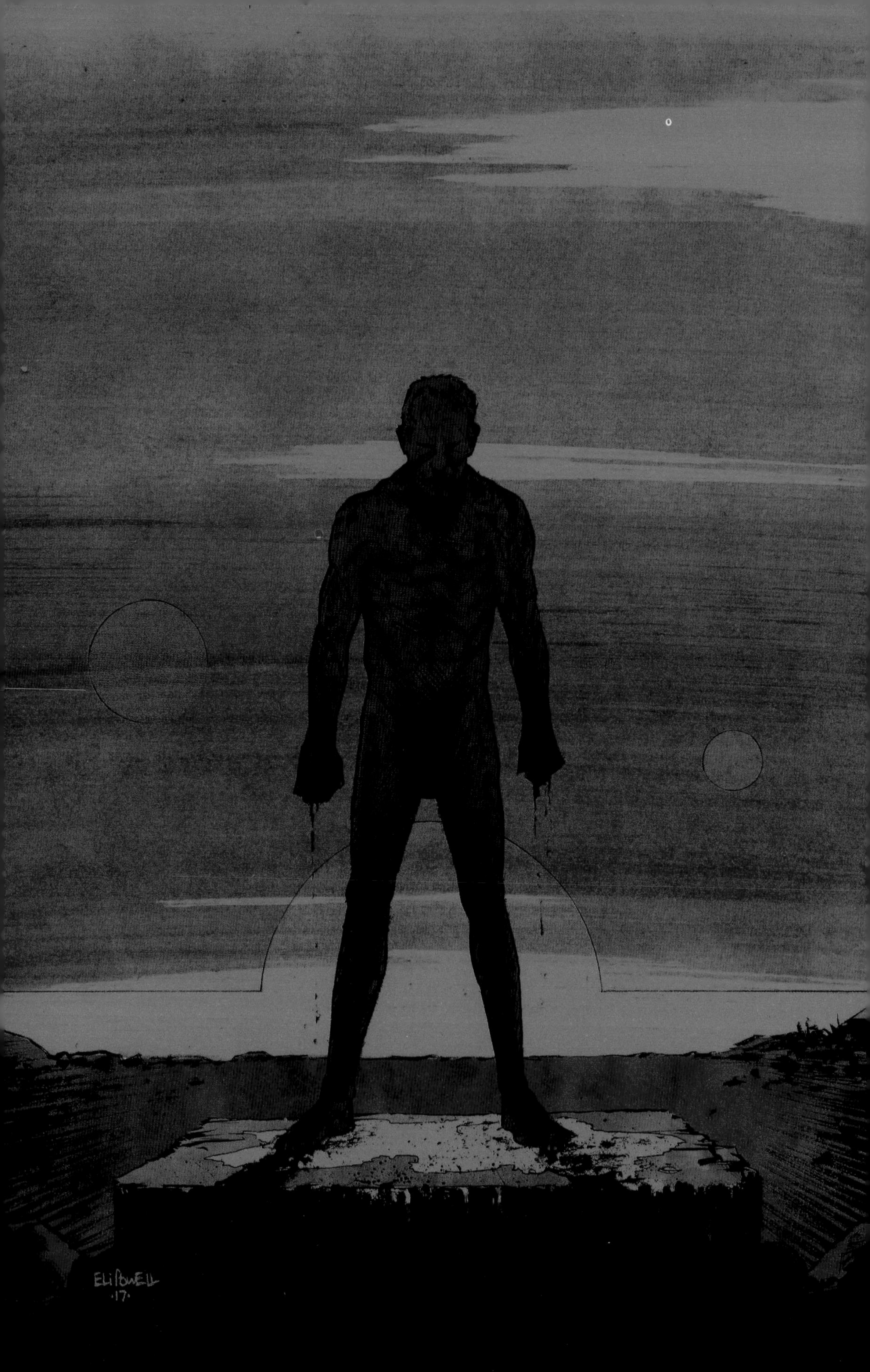
ELI POWELL
·17·

ISSUE ONE | COVER ART BY ELI POWELL

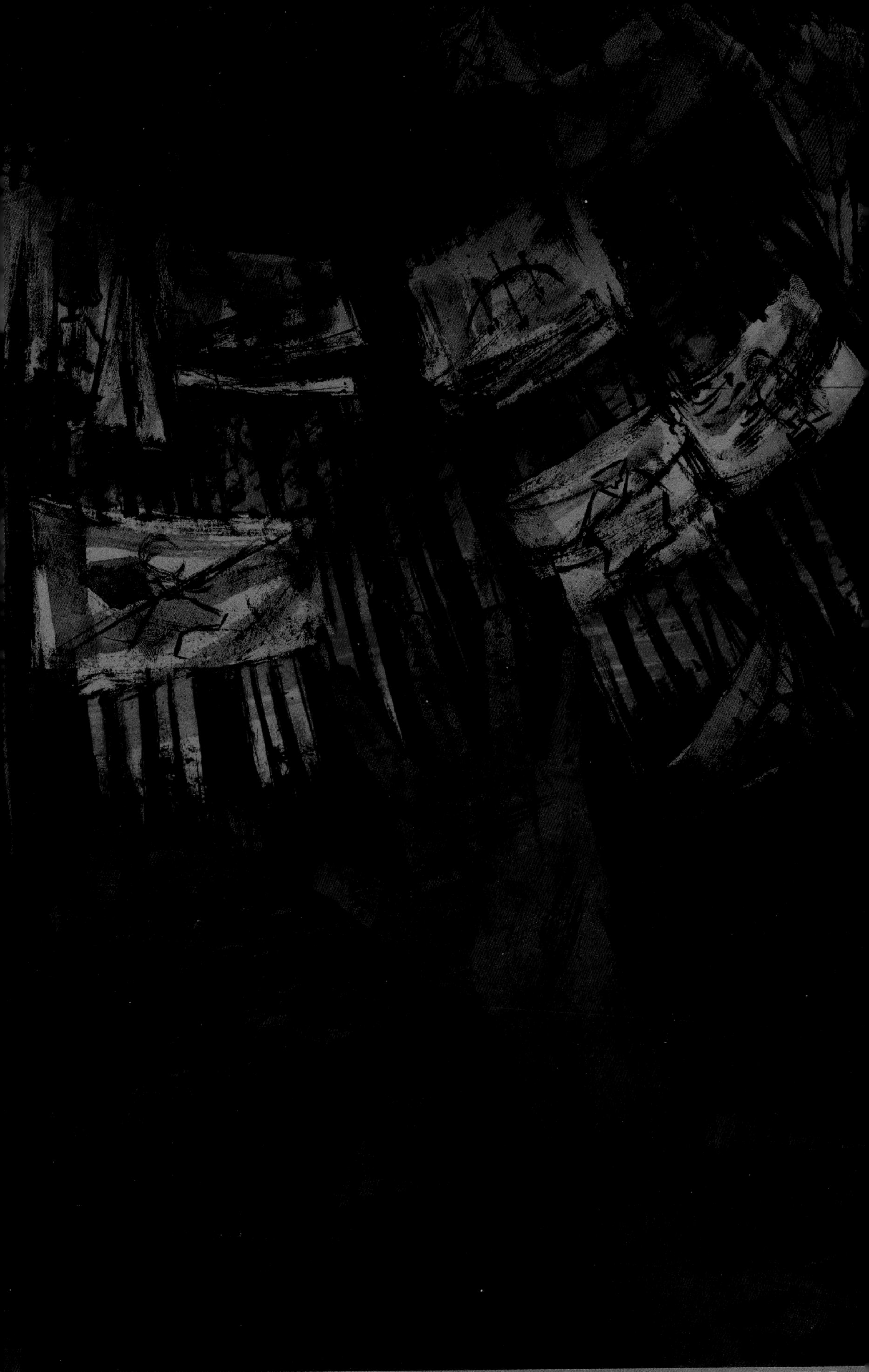

ISSUE TWO | COVER ART BY ELI POWELL

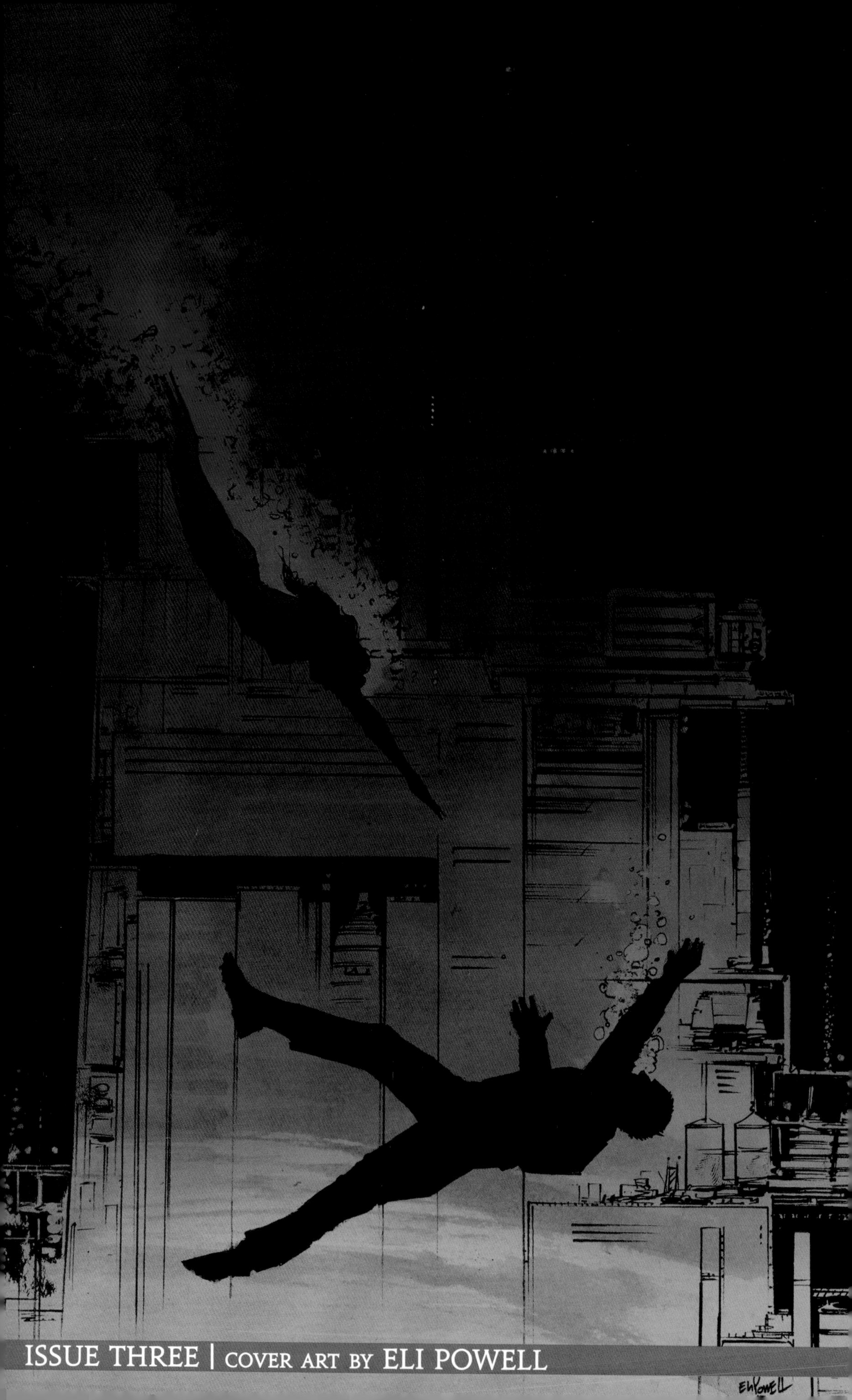
ELI POWELL

ISSUE THREE | COVER ART BY ELI POWELL

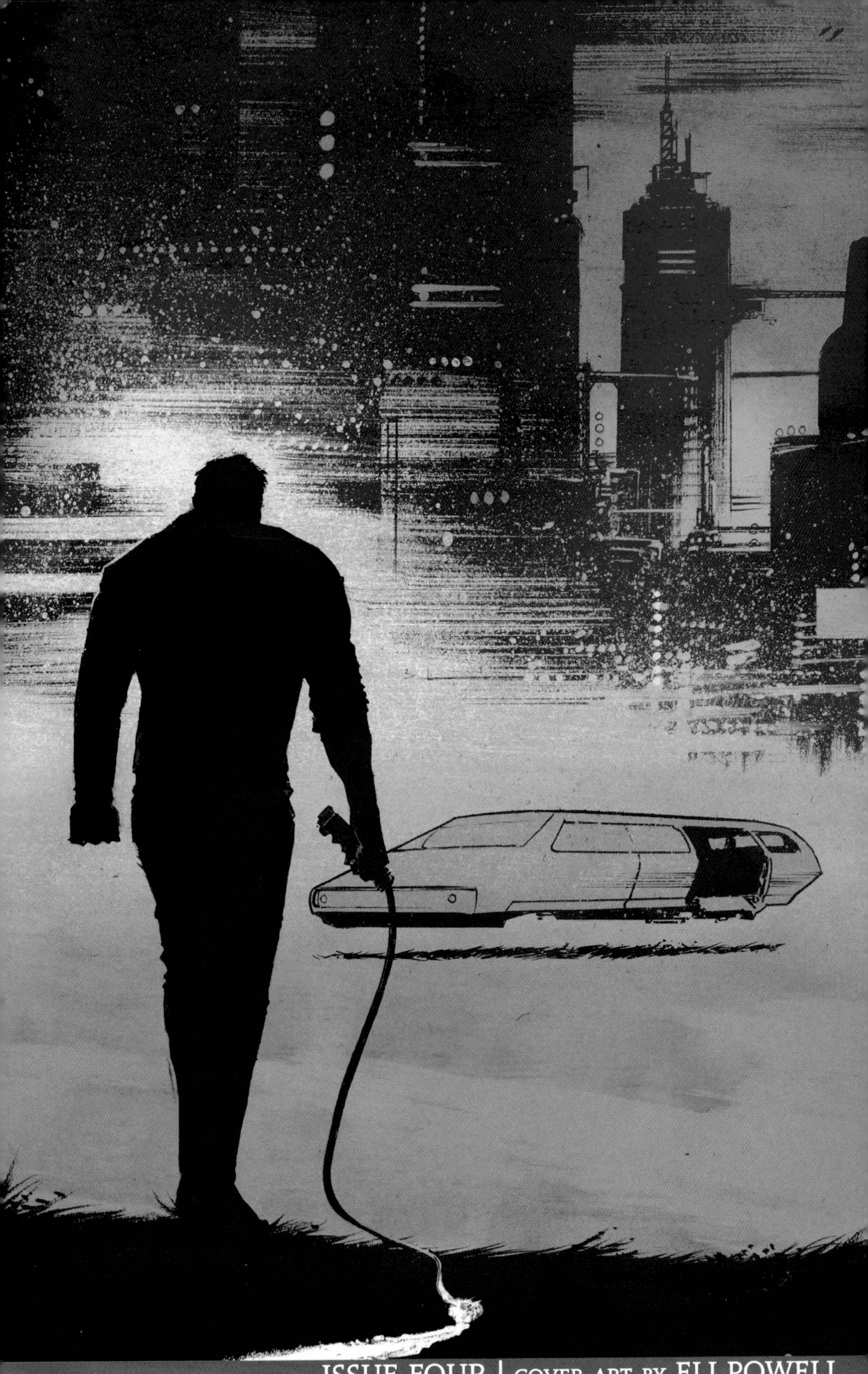
ISSUE FOUR | COVER ART BY ELI POWELL

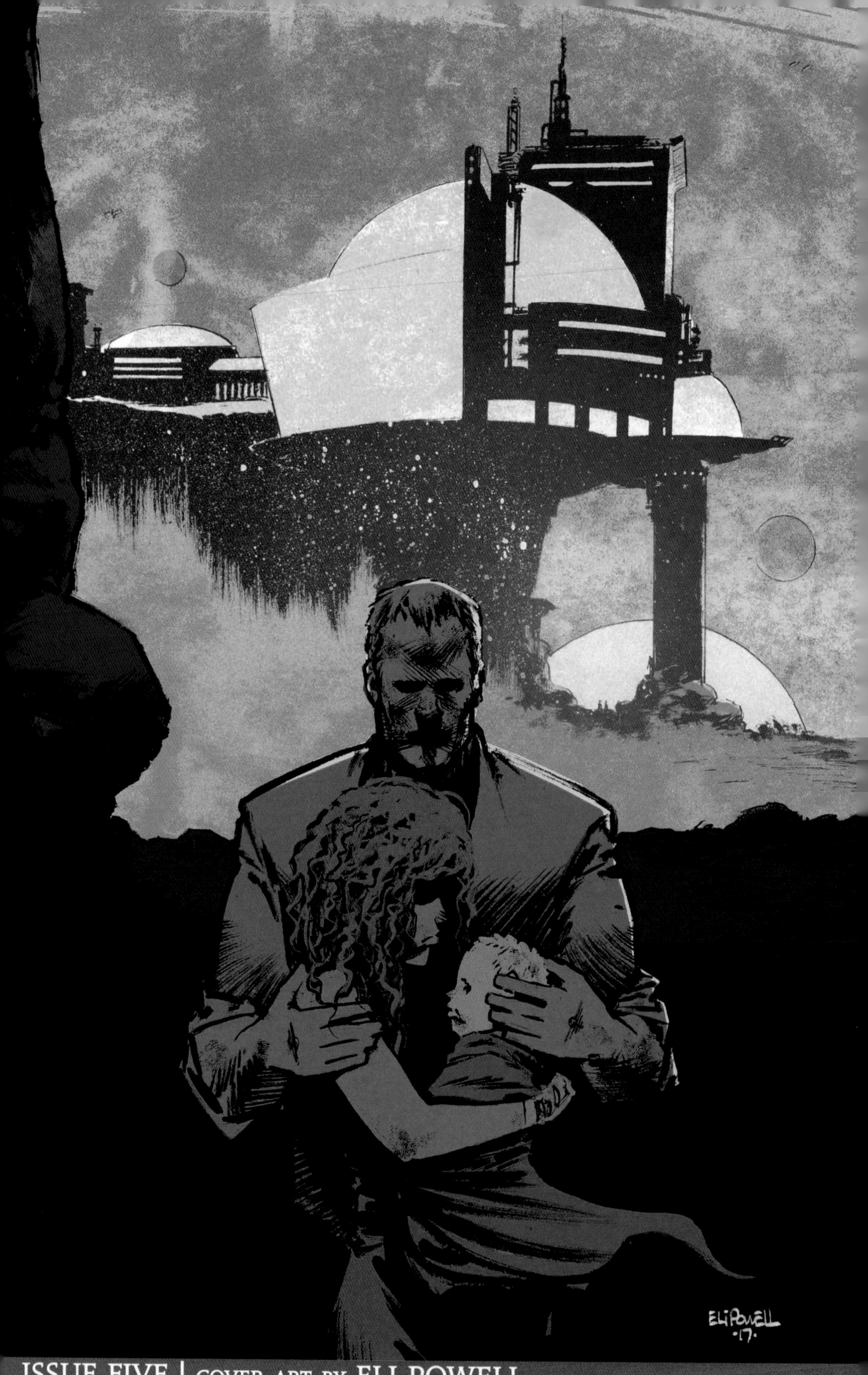
ELI POWELL
·17·

ISSUE FIVE | COVER ART BY ELI POWELL

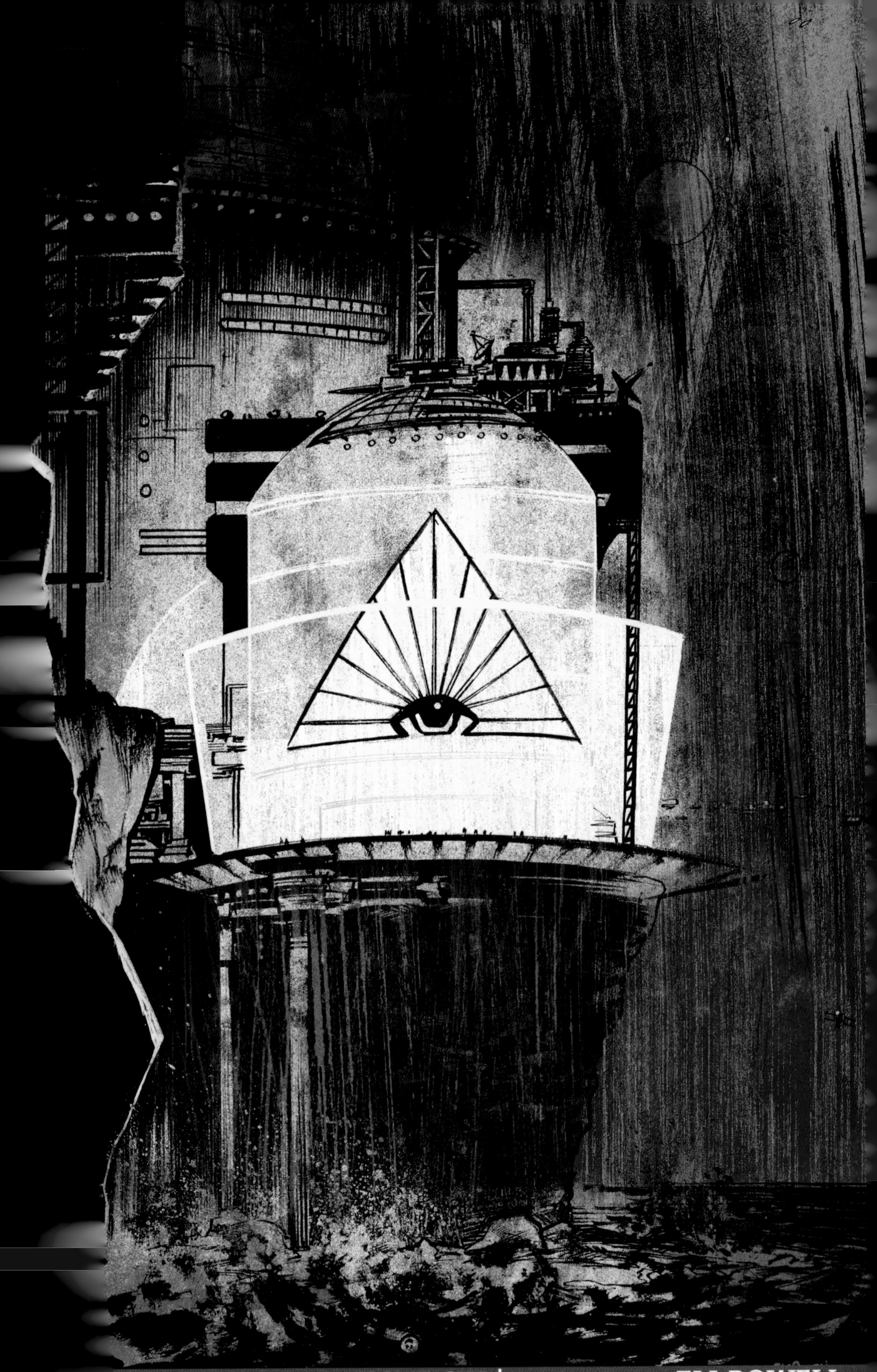

ISSUE SIX | COVER ART BY ELI POWELL

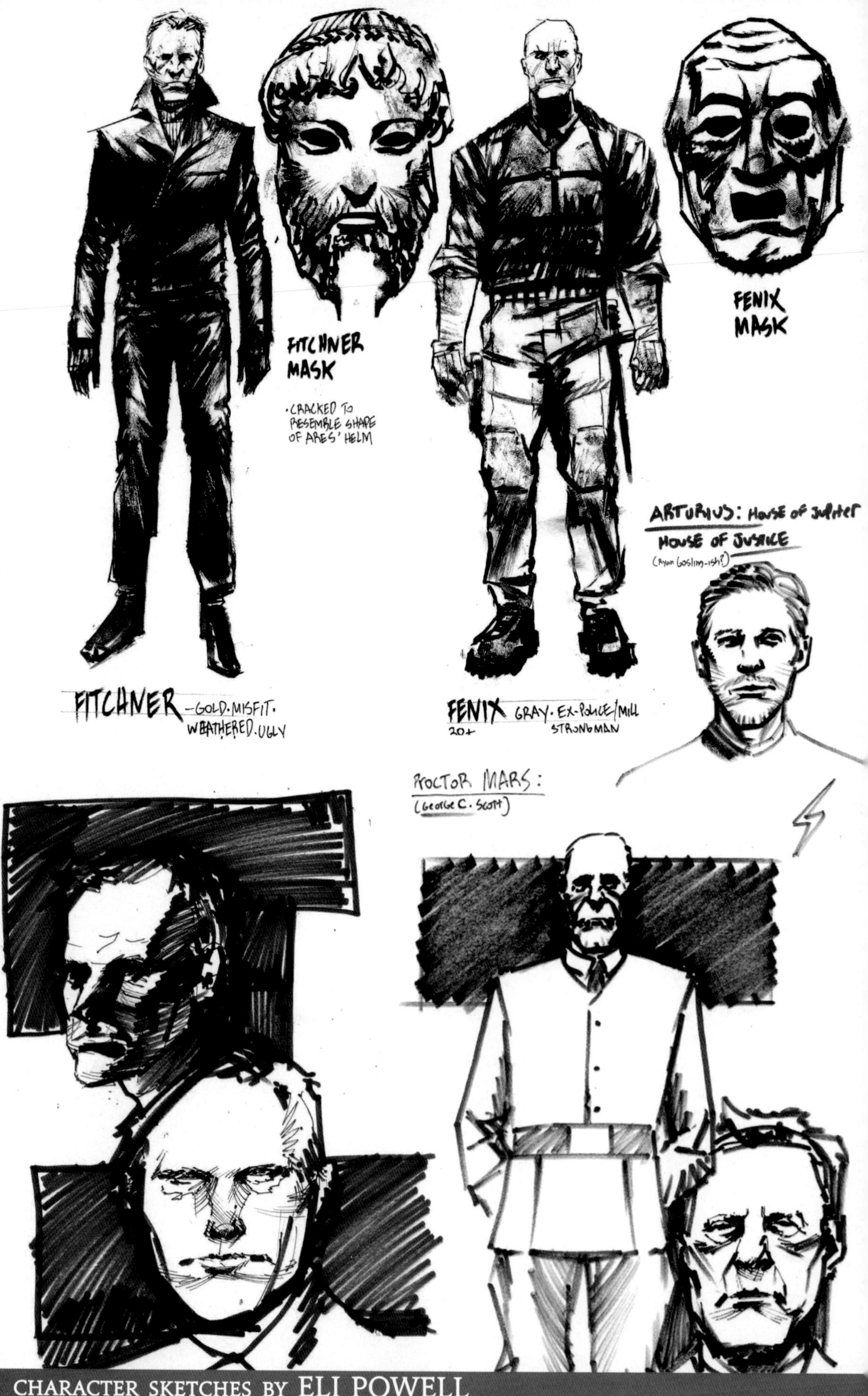
FITCHNER MASK
·CRACKED TO RESEMBLE SHAPE OF ARES' HELM
FENIX MASK
ARTURIUS: House of Jupiter
HOUSE OF JUSTICE
(Ryan Gosling-ish?)
FITCHNER—GOLD·MISFIT· WEATHERED·UGLY
FENIX GRAY·EX-POLICE/MILL STRONGMAN
20+
PROCTOR MARS:
(George C. Scott)

CHARACTER SKETCHES BY ELI POWELL

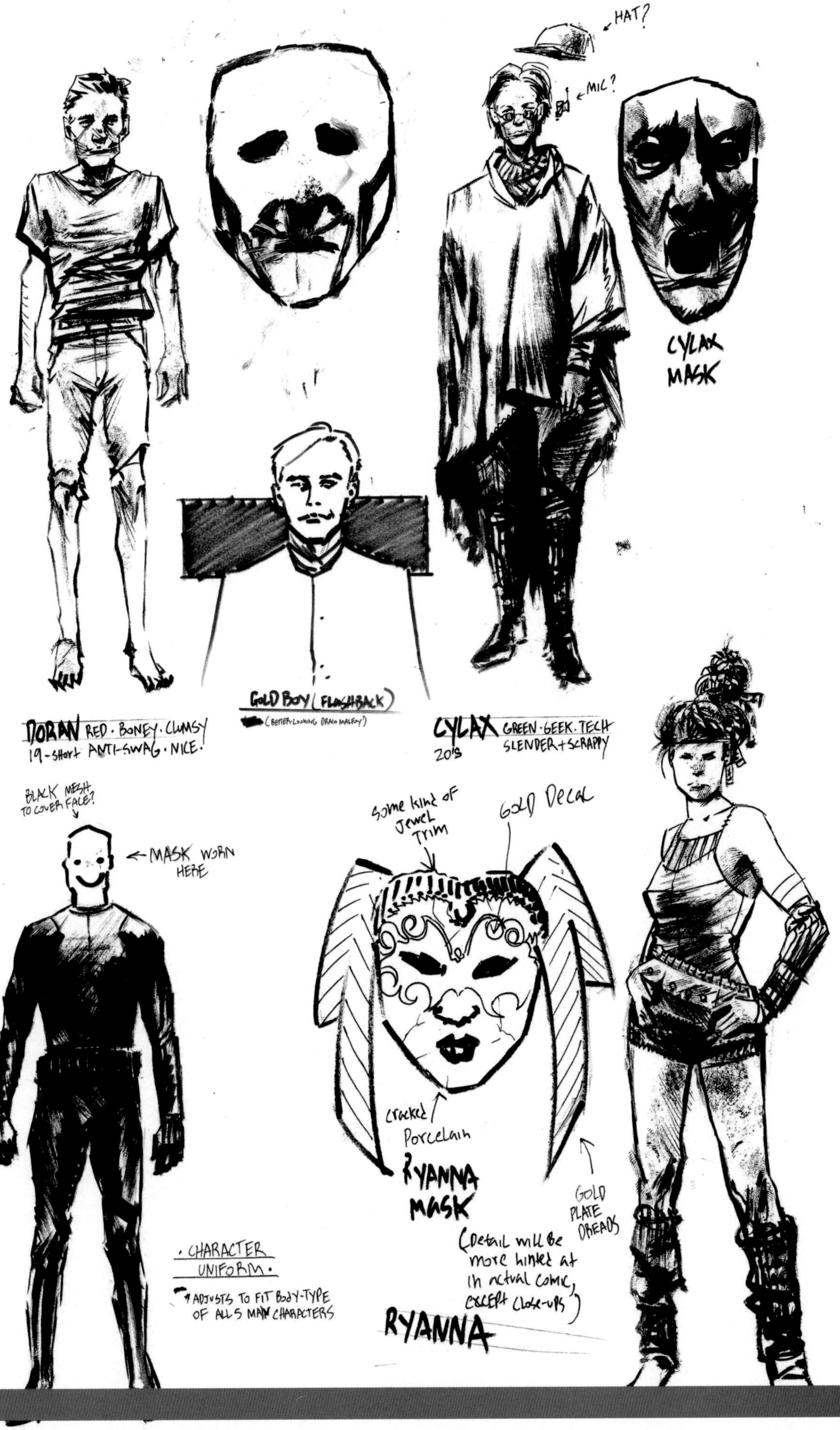
HAT?
MIC?
CYLAX MASK
GOLD BOY (FLASHBACK)
(BETTER-LOOKING DRACO MALFOY)
DORAN RED · BONEY · CLUMSY
19 - short ANTI-SWAG · NICE!
CYLAX GREEN · GEEK · TECH
20's SLENDER + SCRAPPY
BLACK MESH TO COVER FACE?
← MASK WORN HERE
Some kind of Jewel Trim
GOLD Decal
Cracked Porcelain
RYANNA MASK
GOLD PLATE DREADS
(Detail will be more limited at in actual comic, except close-ups)
RYANNA
· CHARACTER UNIFORM ·
* ADJUSTS TO FIT BODY-TYPE OF ALL 5 MAIN CHARACTERS

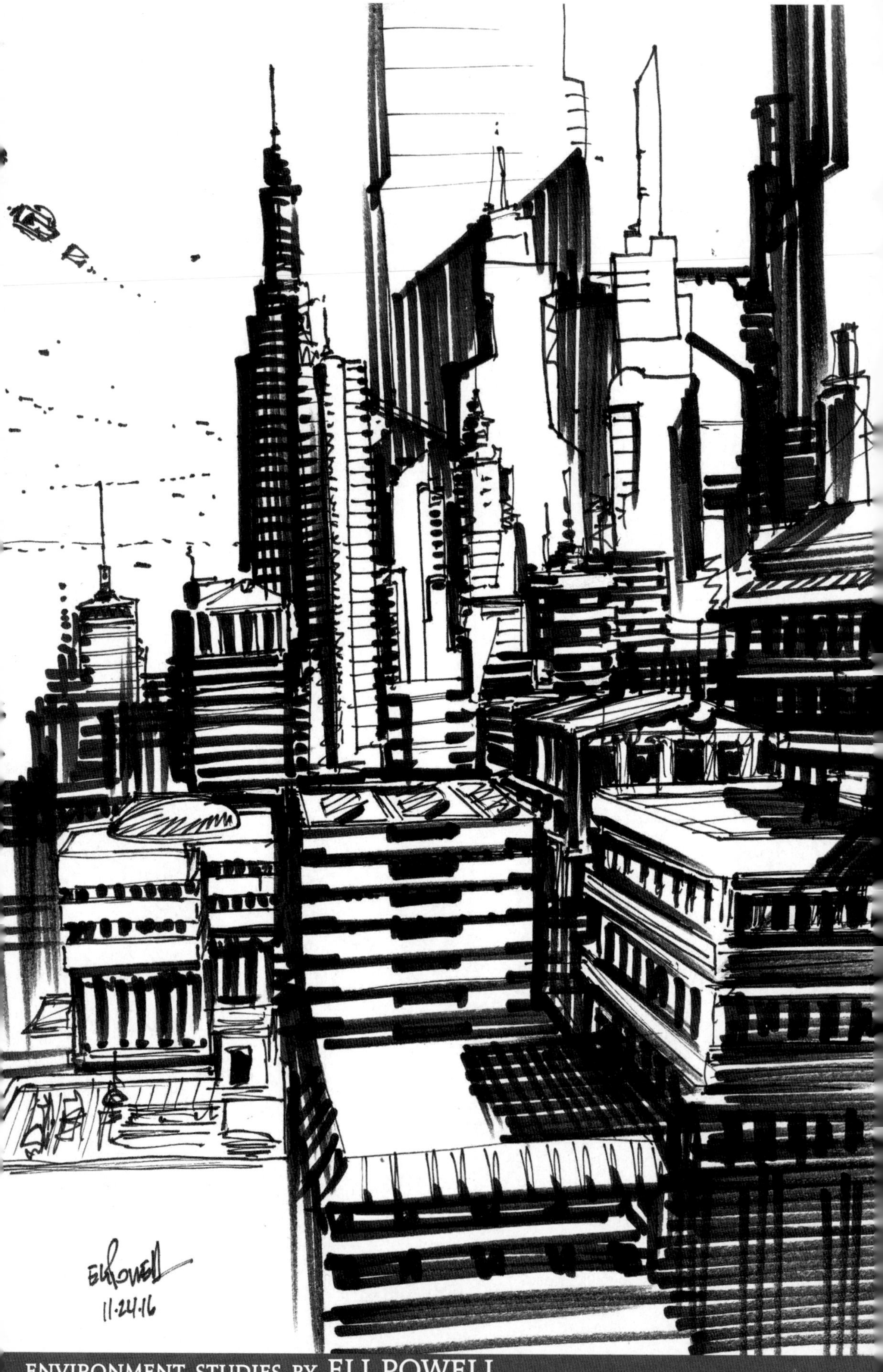
ELI POWELL
11·24·16

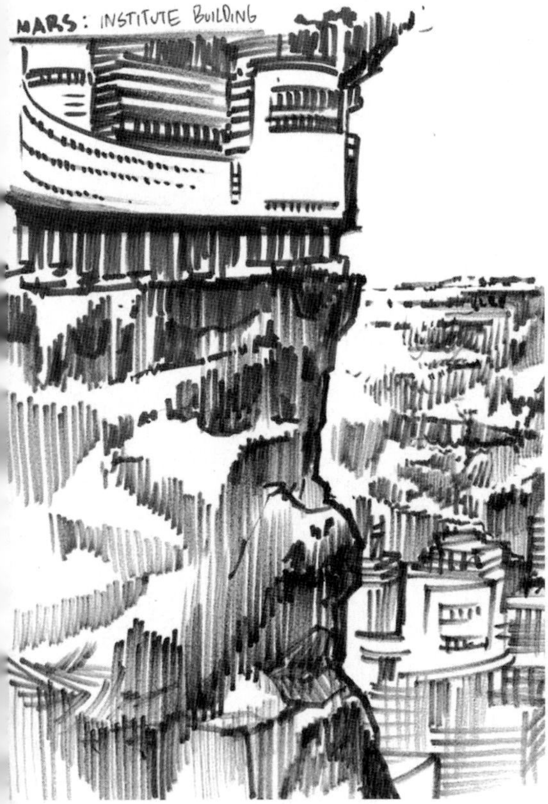
MARS: INSTITUTE BUILDING

HOUSE MARS (HOUSE OF RAGE)

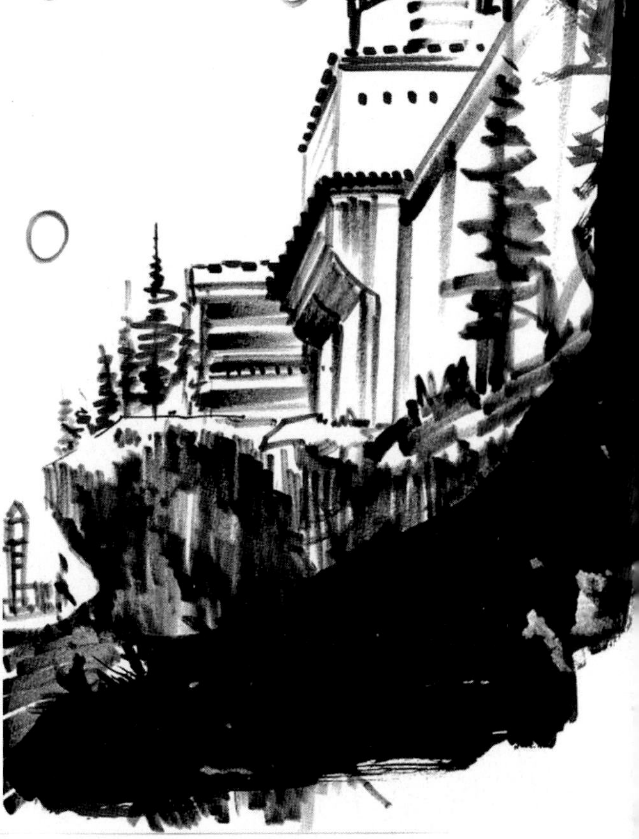

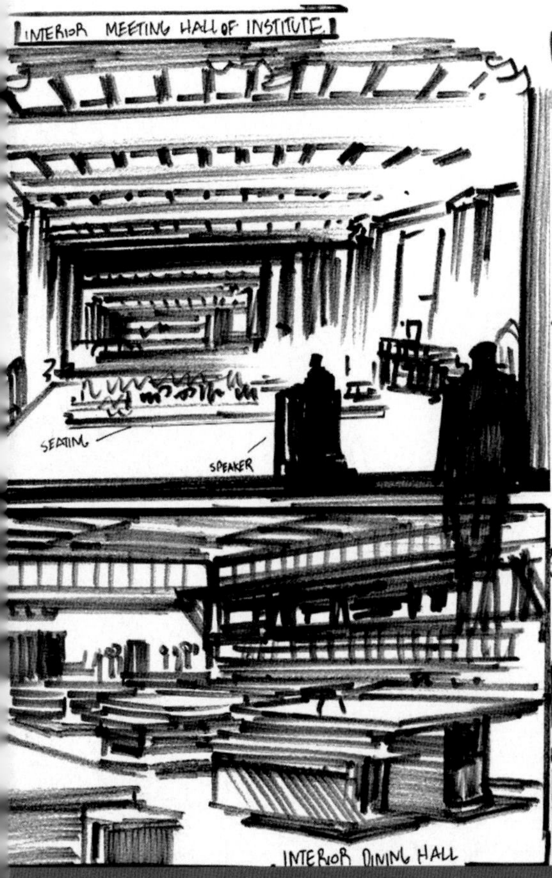
INTERIOR MEETING HALL OF INSTITUTE
SEATING
SPEAKER
INTERIOR DINING HALL

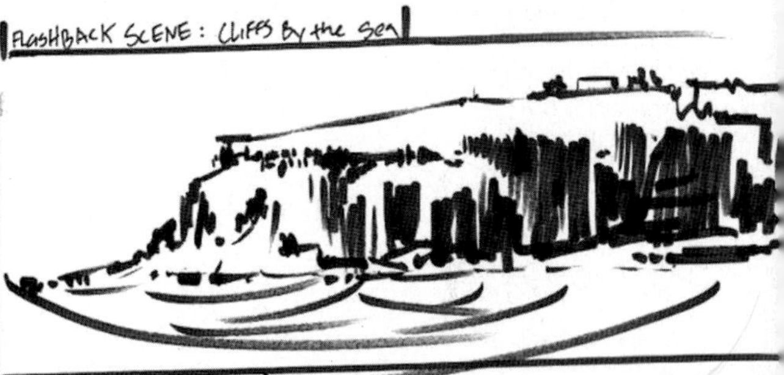
FLASHBACK SCENE: CLIFFS BY the Sea

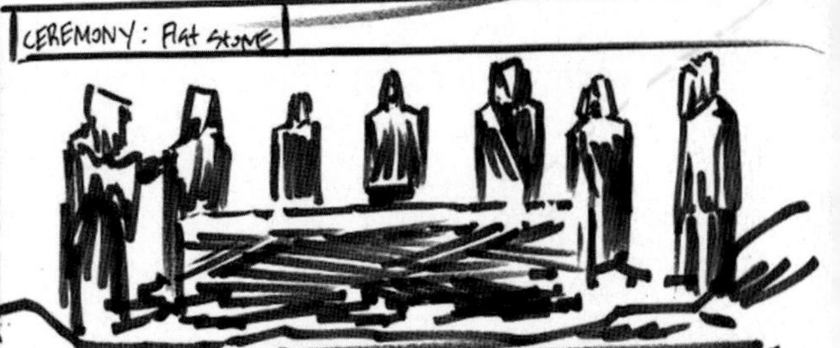
CEREMONY: Flat stone

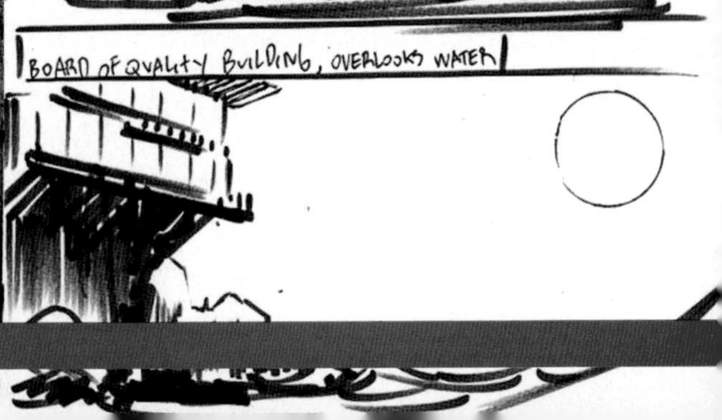
BOARD OF QUALITY BUILDING, OVERLOOKS WATER